NATURAL THEOLOGY:

OR,

EVIDENCES

OF THE EXISTENCE AND ATTRIBUTES OF THE DEITY
COLLECTED FROM THE APPEARANCES
OF NATURE,

BY

WILLIAM PALEY, D. D.

ILLUSTRATED BY

THE PLATES, AND BY A SELECTION FROM THE NOTES

OF

JAMES PAXTON.

WITH

ADDITIONAL NOTES, ORIGINAL AND SELECTED, FOR THIS EDITION.
AND A VOCABULARY OF SCIENTIFIC TERMS.

BY JOHN WARE M D.

NEW YORK:

SHELDON & COMPANY,

No. 8 MURRAY STREET.

PUBLISHERS' NOTICE.

SEVERAL years since the publishers of this valuable and very popular work engaged the services of Dr. John Ware, of this city, to prepare an improved edition, by the addition of forty elegant pages of the illustrations of Paxton, with references to the same in the text; extensive notes, original and selected; a vocabulary of scientific terms, etc.; with a view of adapting it more perfectly to the wants of our colleges and schools, so as thereby to increase its circulation and usefulness.

The sale, with these additions and improvements, has been gradually on the increase, until it has become very generally introduced into our best schools and colleges throughout the country; and having passed through some forty or more editions, the publishers found the plates, by constant use, very much worn, and in some cases imperfect. They have consequently procured an entirely new and beautiful set of illustrations, which, with other improvements, render the work all that can be desired. and in view of which they anticipate a wider and still more extensive sale of the work.

BOSTON, January, 1854.

PREFACE

TO THE

REVISED AMERICAN EDITION.

THE present edition of the Natural Theology of Dr. Paley was under aken with the view of making this admirable work more extensively useful than it could ever be under the form in which it has been usually circulated. A great proportion of those who have read it must have sensi bly felt the disadvantage under which they labor in comprehending the descriptions; and of course the arguments of the author, from the want of a knowledge of the subjects to which they relate. No man could so well supply the want of this knowledge, by clearness of statement and description, as Dr. Paley; and it is probable that few other writers would have made a book so intelligible, which relates to subjects remote from common observation, without the aid of plates and illustrations. Still it must be imperfectly comprehended in many important parts, except by those acquainted with the sciences from which his illustrations are drawn. Enough it is true may be understood by all, to carry them along with the argument, and produce a general conviction of its truth. But the conceptions even of professional readers would be much more clear, definite, and satisfactory, were the description aided by visible representations.

It was the original design of the publishers to have merely attached the plates and references of Paxton, which have been published in England and in this country in a separate volume, to the text of Dr. Paley. It was, however, suggested to them that the value of their edition might be increased by the addition of Notes, and they had made arrangements for this purpose and were going on with the work, when Mr. Paxton's edition of the Natural Theology fell into their hands, containing, beside the plates, a considerable number of Notes. From these Notes a selection has been made of such as seemed most valuable and interesting. A number of Notes have also been made up of quotations from the excellent treatise of Mr. Charles Bell on Animal Mechanics, published in the Library of Useful Knowledge ; a tract which cannot be too highly recommended to the perusal of those who take pleasure in studying the indications of a wise and benevolent Providence in the works of creation.

A few additional Notes have also been subjoined, which have not been before published.

It seems to be supposed by some, that the progress made in science since the writing of this work must have furnished ample materials for valuable additions to it. It will readily appear, however, upon reflection that this is not likely to be the case, and that no particular advantage to the *argument* is to be expected from bringing it down, as it is often expressed, to the present state of science. The object of the work is, not to teach science in its connexion with Natural Theology, a plan entirely different, and one upon which distinct works may, and have been written, but to gather materials from the knowledge communicated by science, wherewith to construct an argument for the existence and attributes of God. The excellence of such a work, then, will not consist in the number of illustrations, or in the copiousness and completeness of the materials, but in the judgment with which they are selected, and the aptness with which they are made to bear upon the question at issue.

So far, therefore, as the *argument* is concerned, no additional strength will be given to it by new discoveries in science. As Dr. Paley has himself admitted, a single case thoroughly made out, proves all that can be proved, and, generally speaking, the most familiar instances which can be selected and made intelligible are the best for this purpose, and will have the greatest influence upon men's minds. All the knowledge, therefore, which is necessary for the completeness and strength of the argument was possessed long ago.

Still there is an advantage in selecting and arguing from a variety of examples, arising out of the different constitutions of men's minds, or their different habits of thinking and reasoning. Some are more affected by examples of one kind, and some by those of another. In this way much more might be done in the way of illustrating and enforcing the argument, and holding it up in every possible light, than has been attempted in the present edition. The principal object here had in view, has been to make such additions, as with the help of the engraved views, would bring the argument, as stated by the author, clearly within reach of all readers.

To give a correct edition, various English and American copies have been consulted, in which variations have been found; but those readings have been adopted, which appeared best to comport with that familiarity, and originality of expression, which gives its principal charm, and its great force and clearness to Dr Paley's style.

                                    J W

TO THE

RIGHT HONORABLE AND RIGHT REVEREND

SHUTE BARRINGTON, LL. L.

LORD BISHOP OF DURHAM.

MY LORD,

THE following work was undertaken at your Lordship's recommendation; and amongst other motives, for the purpose of making the most acceptable return I could make for a great and important benefit conferred upon me.

It may be unnecessary, yet not perhaps, quite impertinent, to state to your Lordship and to the reader, the several inducements that have led me once more to the press. The favor of my first and ever honored patron had put me in possession of so liberal a provision in the church, as abundantly to satisfy my wants, and much to exceed my pretensions. Your Lordship's munificence, in conjunction with that of some other excellent Prelates, who regarded my services with the partiality with which your Lordship was pleased to consider them, hath since placed me in ecclesiastical situations, more than adequate to every object of reasonable ambition. In the meantime, a weak, and, of late, a painful state of health, deprived me of the power of discharging the duties of my station, in a manner at all suitable, either to my sense of those duties, or to my most anxious wishes concerning them. My inability for the public functions of my profession, amongst other consequences, left me much at leisure. That leisure was not to be lost. It was only in my study that I could repair my deficiencies in the church. It was only through the press that I could speak. These circumstances, in particular, entitled your Lordship to call upon me for the only species of exertion of which I was capable, and disposed me, without hesitation, to obey the call in the best manner that I could. In the choice of a subject I had no place left for doubt : in saying which, I do not so much refer, either to the supreme importance of the subject, or to any skepticism concerning it with which the present times are charged, as I do, to its connexion with the subjects treated of in my former publications. The following discussion alone was wanted to make up my works into a system : in which works, such as they are, the public have now before them, the evidences of natural reli

A

gion, the evidences of revealed religion, and an account of the duties that result from both. It is of small importance, that they have been written in an order, the very reverse of that in which they ought to be read. I commend therefore the present volume to your Lordship's protection, not only as, in all probability, my last labor, but as the completion of a consistent and comprehensive design.

Hitherto, my Lord, I have been speaking of myself and not of my Patron. Your Lordship wants not the testimony of a dedication, nor any testimony from me : I consult therefore the impulse of my own mind alone when I declare, that in no respect has my intercourse with your Lordship been more gratifying to me, than in the opportunities, which it has afforded me, of observing your earnest, active, and unwearied solicitude, for the advancement of substantial Christianity: a solicitude, nevertheless, accompanied with that candor of mind, which suffers no subordinate differences of opinion, when there is a coincidence in the main intention and object, to produce an alienation of esteem, or diminution of favor. It is fortunate for a country, and honorable to its government, when qualities and dispositions like these are placed in high and influential stations. Such is the sincere judgment which I have formed of your Lordship's character, and of its public value: my personal obligations I can never forget. Under a due sense of both these considerations, I beg leave to subscribe myself, with great respect and gratitude,

My Lord,
Your Lordship's faithful
And most devoted servant.

WILLIAM PALEY

MY LORD,

To your suggestion the world is indebted for the existence of Dr. Paley's valuable work on Natural Theology. The universal and permanent esteem in which it has been held in this country, and its favorable reception in France, even after the desolating influence of the Revolution, have abundantly approved your Lordship's selection both of the subject and of the person to whom you intrusted it.

In looking round, then, for a patron for these ILLUSTRATIONS, it was natural to have recourse to him who was the original suggestor of the work which it is their object to explain. Nor was I disappointed in my wish; your Lordship not only condescending to approve of the design, but to encourage me in its prosecution, by your very liberal support. For this distinguished honor you will believe me deeply sensible; and if I may indulge the hope that my humble efforts will increase the utility of so eminent a writer, I shall consider it the highest gratification.

I am, my LORD,
With great veneration,
Your Lordship's most obliged,
And obedient servant,

JAMES PAXTON

CONTENTS

NATURAL THEOLOGY

CHAPTER I.

STATE OF THE ARGUMENT

In crossing a heath, suppose I pitched my foot against a stone, and were asked how the stone came to be there; I might possibly answer, that for anything I knew to the contrary, it had lain there forever: nor would it perhaps be very easy to show the absurdity of this answer. But suppose I had found a *watch* upon the ground, and it should be inquired how the watch happened to be in that place; I should hardly think of the answer which I had before given, that, for anything I knew, the watch might have always been there. Yet why should not this answer serve for the watch as well as for the stone? Why is it not as admissible in the second case, as in the first? For this reason, and for no other, viz. that, when we come to inspect the watch, we perceive (what we could not discover in the stone) that its several parts are framed and put together for a purpose, *e. g.* that they are so formed and adjusted as to produce motion, and that motion so regulated as to point out the hour of the day; that if the different parts had been differently shaped from what they are, of a different size from what they are, or placed after any other manner, or in any other order, than that in which they are placed, either no motion at all would have been carried on in the machine, or none which would have answered the use that is now served by it. To reckon up a few of the plainest of these parts, and of their offices, all tending to one result: [See Plate I.]—We see a cylindrical box containing a coiled elastic spring, which, by its endeavor to relax itself, turns round the box. We next observe a flexible chain (artificially wrought for the sake of flexure) communicating the action of the spring from the box to the fusee. We then

A*

find a series of wheels, the teeth of which catch in, and apply to each other, conducting the motion from the fusee to the balance, and from the balance to the pointer; and at the same time, by the size and shape of those wheels, so regulating that motion, as to terminate in causing an index by an equable and measured progression, to pass over a given space in a given time. We take notice that the wheels are made of brass in order to keep them from rust; the springs of steel, no other metal being so elastic; that over the face of the watch there is placed a glass, a material employed in no other part of the work; but in the room of which, if there had been any other than a transparent substance, the hour could not be seen without opening the case. This mechanism being observed (it requires indeed an examination of the instrument, and perhaps some previous knowledge of the subject, to perceive and understand it; but being once, as we have said, observed and understood,) the inference, we think, is inevitable; that the watch must have had a maker; that there must have existed, at sometime, and at some place or other, an artificer or artificers, who formed it for the purpose which we find it actually to answer; who comprehended its construction, and designed its use.

I. Nor would it, I apprehend, weaken the conclusion, that we had never seen a watch made: that we had never known an artist capable of making one; that we were altogether incapable of executing such a piece of workmanship ourselves, or of understanding in what manner it was performed; all this being no more than what is true of some exquisite remains of ancient art, of some lost arts, and, to the generality of mankind, of the more curious productions of modern manufacture. Does one man in a million know how oval frames are turned? Ignorance of this kind exalts our opinion of the unseen and unknown artist's skill, if he be unseen and unknown, but raises no doubt in our minds of the existence and agency of such an artist, at some former time, and in some place or other. Nor can I perceive that it varies at all the inference, whether the question arise concerning a human agent, or concerning an agent of a different species, or an agent possessing, in some respects, a different nature.

II. Neither, secondly, would it invalidate our conclusion, that the watch sometimes went wrong, or that it seldom went exactly right. The purpose of the machinery, the design and the designer, might be evident, and in the case supposed would be evident, in whatever way we accounted for the irregularity of the movement, or whether we could account for it or not. It is not necessary that a machine be perfect, in order to show with what design it was made: still less necessary, where the only question is, whether it were made with any design at all.

III. Nor, thirdly, would it bring any uncertainty into the argument, if there were a few parts of the watch, concerning which we could not discover, or had not yet discovered, in what manner they conduced to the general effect; or even some parts, concerning which we could not ascertain whether they conduced to that effect in any manner whatever. For, as to the first branch of the case; if by the loss, or disorder, or decay of the parts in question, the movement of the watch were found in fact to be stopped, or disturbed, or retarded, no doubt would remain in our minds as to the utility or intention of these parts, although we should be unable to investigate the manner according to which, or the connexion by which, the ultimate effect depended upon their action or assistance; and the more complex is the machine, the more likely is this obscurity to arise. Then, as to the second thing supposed, namely, that there were parts which might be spared, without prejudice to the movement of the watch, and that we had proved this by experiment—these superfluous parts, even if we were completely assured that they were such, would not vacate the reasoning which we had instituted concerning other parts. The indication of contrivance remained, with respect to them, nearly as it was before.

IV. Nor, fourthly, would any man in his senses think the existence of the watch, with its various machinery, accounted for, by being told that it was one out of possible combinations of material forms; that whatever he had found in the place where he found the watch, must have contained some internal configuration or other; and that this configuration might be the structure now exhibited, viz. of the works of a watch, as well as a different structure.

V. Nor, fifthly, would it yield his inquiry more satisfaction to be answered, that there existed in things a principle of order, which had disposed the parts of the watch into their present form and situation. He never knew a watch made by the principle of order; nor can he even form to himself an idea of what is meant by a principle of order distinct from the intelligence of the watchmaker.

VI. Sixthly, he would be surprised to hear that the mechanism of the watch was no proof of contrivance, only a motive to induce the mind to think so.

VII. And not less surprised to be informed, that the watch in his hand was nothing more than the result of the laws of *metallic* nature. It is a perversion of language to assign any law as the efficient, operative cause of anything A law presupposes an agent; for it is only the mode according to which an agent proceeds: it implies a power; for it is the order, according to which that power acts Without this agent, without this power, which are both distinct from itself, the *law* does nothing; is nothing. The expression, "the law of metallic nature," may sound strange and harsh to a philosophic ear; but it seems quite as justifiable as some others which are more familiar to him, such as "the law of vegetable nature," "the law of animal nature," or indeed as "the law of nature" in general, when assigned as the cause of phenomena, in exclusion of agency and power; or when it is substituted into the place of these.

VIII. Neither, lastly, would our observer be driven out of his conclusion, or from his confidence in its truth, by being told that he knew nothing at all about the matter. He knows enough for his argument. He knows the utility of the end: he knows the subserviency and adaptation of the means to the end. These points being known, his ignorance of other points, his doubts concerning other points, affect not the certainty of his reasoning. The consciousness of knowing little need not beget a distrust of that which he does know.

CHAPTER II.

STATE OF THE ARGUMENT CONTINUED.

Suppose, in the next place, that the person who found the watch, should, after sometime, discover, that in addition to all the properties which he had hitherto observed in it, it possessed the unexpected property of producing, in the course of its movement, another watch like itself, (the thing is conceivable;) that it contained within it a mechanism, a system of parts, a mould for instance, or a complex adjustment of lathes, files, and other tools, evidently and separately calculated for this purpose; let us inquire, what effect ought such a discovery to have upon his forme conclusion.

I. The first effect would be to increase his admiration of the contrivance, and his conviction of the consummate skill of the contriver. Whether he regarded the object of the contrivance, the distinct apparatus, the intricate, yet in many parts intelligible mechanism, by which it was carried on, he would perceive, in this new observation, nothing but an additional reason for doing what he had already done,—for referring the construction of the watch to design, and to supreme art. If that construction *without* this property, or, which is the same thing, before this property had been noticed, proved intention and art to have been employed about it, still more strong would the proof appear, when he came to the knowledge of this farther property, the crown and perfection of all the rest.

II. He would reflect, that though the watch before him were, *in some sense*, the maker of the watch which was fabricated in the course of its movements, yet it was in a very different sense from that in which a carpenter, for instance, is the maker of a chair; the author of its contrivance, the cause of the relation of its parts to their use. With respect to these, the first watch was no cause at all to the second: in no such sense as this was it the author of the constitution and order, either of the parts which the new watch contained, or of the parts by the aid and instrumentality of which it was produced. We might possibly say, but with great latitude of expression, that a stream of water ground corn; but no latitude of expression would allow us to say, no stretch of conjecture could lead us to think, that the stream of water built the mill, though it were too ancient for us to know who the builder was. What the stream of water does in the affair, is neither more nor less than this; by the application of an unintelligent impulse to a mechanism previously arranged, arranged independently of it, and arranged by intelligence, an effect is produced, viz. the corn is ground. But the effect results from the arrangement. The force of the stream cannot be said to be the cause or author of the effect, still less of the arrangement. Understanding and plan in the formation of the mill were not the less necessary, for any share which the water has in grinding the corn; yet is this share the same as that which the watch would have contributed to the production of the new watch, upon the supposition assumed in the last section. Therefore,

III. Though it be now no longer probable, that the individual watch which our observer had found was made immediately by the hand of an artificer, yet doth not this alteration in any-wise affect the inference, that an artificer had been originally employed and concerned in the production. The argument from design remains as it was. Marks of design and contrivance are no more accounted for now than they were before. In the same thing, we may ask for the cause of different properties. We may ask for the cause of the color of a body, of its hardness, of its heat; and these causes may be all different. We are now asking for the cause of that subserviency to a use, that relation to an end, which we have remarked in the watch before us. No answer is given to this question by telling us that a preceding watch produced it. There cannot be design without a designer; contrivance, without a contriver; order, without choice; arrangement, without anything capable of arranging; subserviency and relation to a purpose, without that which could intend a purpose; means suitable to an end, and executing their office in accomplishing that end, without the end ever having been contemplated, or the means accommodated to it. Arrangement, disposition of parts, subserviency of means to an end, relation of instruments to a use, imply the presence of intelligence and mind. No one, therefore, can rationally believe, that the insensible, inanimate watch, from which the watch before us issued, was the proper cause of the mechanism we so much admire in it;—could be truly said to have constructed the instrument, disposed its parts, assigned their office, determined their order, action, and mutual dependency, combined their several motions into one result, and that also a result connected with the utilities of other beings. All these properties, therefore, are as much unaccounted for as they were before.

IV. Nor is anything gained by running the difficulty farther back, i. e. by supposing the watch before us to have been produced from another watch, that from a former, and so on indefinitely. Our going back ever so far brings us no nearer to the least degree of satisfaction upon the subject. Contrivance is still unaccounted for. We still want a contriver. A designing mind is neither supplied by this supposition, nor dispensed with. If the difficulty were diminished the farther we went back, by going back indefinitely we might exhaust it. And this is the only case to which this sort of reasoning applies. Where there is a tendency, or, as we increase the number of terms, a continual approach towards a limit, there, by supposing the number of terms to be what is called infinite, we may conceive the limit to be attained: but where there is no such tendency, or approach, nothing is effected by lengthening the series. There is no difference, as to the point in question, (whatever there may be as to many points,) between one series and another; between a series which is finite, and a series which is infinite. A chain, composed of an infinite number of links, can no more support itself, than a chain composed of a finite number of links. And of this we are assured, (though we never *can* have tried the experiment, because, by increasing the number of links, from ten, for instance, to a hundred, from a hundred to a thousand, &c. we make not the smallest approach, we observe not the smallest tendency, towards self-support. There is no difference in this respect (yet there may be a great difference in several respects) between a chain of a greater or less length, between one chain and another, between one that is finite and one that is infinite This very much resembles the case before us. The machine which we are inspecting demonstrates, by its construction, contrivance and design. Contrivance must have had a contriver; design, a designer; whether the machine immediately proceeded from another machine or not. That circumstance alters not the case. That other machine may, in like manner, have proceeded from a former machine: nor does that alter the case; contrivance must have had a contriver. That former one from one preceding it: no alteration still; a contriver is still necessary. No tendency is perceived, no approach towards a diminution of this necessity. It is the same with any and every succession of these machines; a succession of ten, of a hundred, of a thousand; with one series as with another; a series which is finite, as with a series which is infinite. In whatever other respects they may differ, in this they do not. In all, equally, contrivance and design are unaccounted for.

The question is not simply, How came the first watch into existence? which question, it may be pretended, is done away by supposing the series of watches thus produced from one another to have been infinite, and consequently to have had no such *first*, for which it was necessary to provide a cause. This, perhaps, would have been nearly the state of the question, if nothing had been before us but an unorganized, unmechanized substance, without mark or indication of contrivance. It might be difficult to show that such substance could not have existed from eternity, either in succession (if it were possible, which I think it is not, for unorganized bodies to spring from one another, or by individual perpetuity. But that is not the question now. To suppose it to be so, is to suppose that it made no difference whether we had found a watch or a stone. As it is, the metaphysics of that question have no place, for, in the watch which we are examining, are seen contrivance, design; an end, a purpose; means for the end, adaptation to the purpose. And the question which irresistibly presses upon our thoughts, is, whence this contrivance and design? The thing required is the intending mind, the adapting hand, the intelligence by which that hand was directed. This question, this demand, is not shaken off, by increasing a number or succession of substances, destitute of these properties; nor the more, by increasing that number to infinity. If it be said, that, upon the supposition of one watch being produced from another in the course of that other's movements, and by means of the mechanism within it, we have a cause for the watch in my hand, viz. the watch from which it proceeded: I deny, that for the design, the contrivance, the suitableness of means to an end, the adaptation of instruments to a use, (all which we discover in a watch,) we have any cause whatever. It is in vain, therefore, to assign a series of such causes, or to allege that a series may be carried back to infinity; for I do not admit that we have yet any cause at all of the phenomena, still less any series of causes either finite or infinite. Here is contrivance, but no contriver: proofs of design, but no designer.

V. Our observer would farther also reflect, that the maker of the watch before him, was, in truth and reality, the maker of every watch produced from it; there being no difference (except that the latter manifests a more exquisite skill) between the making of another watch with his own hands, by the mediation of files, lathes, chisels, &c. and the disposing, fixing, and inserting of these instruments, or of others equivalent to them, in the body of the watch already made, in such a manner as to form a new watch in the course of the movements which he had given to the old one. It is only working by one set of tools instead of another.

The conclusion which the *first* examination of the watch, of its works, construction, and movement, suggested, was, that it must have had, for the cause and author of that construction, an artificer, who understood its mechanism, and designed its use. This conclusion is invincible. A *second* examination presents us with a new discovery. The watch is found, in the course of its movement, to produce another watch, similar to itself: and not only so, but we perceive in it a system or organization, separately calculated for that purpose. What effect would this discovery have or ought it to have, upon our former inference? What, as hath already been said, but to increase, beyond measure, our admiration of the skill which had been employed in the formation of such a machine! Or shall it, instead of this all at once turn us round to an opposite conclusion, viz that no art or skill whatever has been concerned in the business, although all other evidences of art and skill remain as they were, and this last and supreme piece of art be now added to the rest? Can this be maintained without absurdity? Yet this is atheism.

CHAPTER III.

APPLICATION OF THE ARGUMENT.

THIS is atheism: for every indication of contrivance, every manifestation of design, which existed in the watch, exists in the works of nature; with the difference, on the side of nature, of being greater and more, and that in a degree which exceeds all computation. I mean, that the contrivances of nature surpass the contrivances of art, in the complexity, subtilty, and curiosity of the mechanism; and still more, if possible, do they go beyond them in number and variety: yet, in a multitude of cases, are not less evidently mechanical, not less evidently contrivances, not less evidently accommodated to their end, or suited to their office, than are the most perfect productions of human ingenuity.

I know no better method of introducing so large a subject, than that of comparing a single thing with a single thing; an eye, for example, with a telescope. As far as the examination of the instrument goes, there is precisely the same proof that the eye was made for vision, as there is that the telescope was made for assisting it. They are made upon the same principles; both being adjusted to the laws by which the transmission and refraction of rays of light are regulated. I speak not of the origin of the laws themselves; but such laws being fixed, the construction, in both cases, is adapted to them. For instance; these laws require, in order to produce the same effect, that the rays of light, in passing from water into the eye, should be

refracted by a more convex surface than when it passes
out of air into the eye.   Accordingly we find, that the eye
of a fish, in that part of it called the crystalline lens, is much
rounder than the eye of terrestrial animals. [Plate II. fig. 1.]
What plainer manifestation of design can there be than this
difference?   What could a mathematical instrument-maker
have done more, to show his knowledge of his principle,
his application of that knowledge, his suiting of his means
to his end; I will not say to display the compass or excellence of his skill and art, for in these all comparison is
indecorous, but to testify counsel, choice, consideration,
purpose?

To some it may appear a difference sufficient to destroy
all similitude between the eye and the telescope, that the
one is a perceiving organ, the other an unperceiving instrument.   The fact is, that they are both instruments.   And,
as to the mechanism, at least as to mechanism being employed, and even as to the kind of it, this circumstance varies not the analogy at all.   For, observe what the constitution of the eye is. [Plate II. fig. 2.]   It is necessary, in
order to produce distinct vision, that an image or picture of
the object be formed at the bottom of the eye.   Whence this
necessity arises, or how the picture is connected with the
sensation, or contributes to it, it may be difficult, nay we
will confess, if you please, impossible for us to search out.
But the present question is not concerned in the inquiry.   It
may be true, that, in this, and in other instances, we trace
mechanical contrivance a certain way; and that then we
come to something which is not mechanical, or which is in-
scrutable.   But this affects not the certainty of our investigation, as far as we have gone.   The difference between
an animal and an automatic statue, consists in this,—that,
in the animal, we trace the mechanism to a certain point,
and then we are stopped; either the mechanism becoming
too subtile for our discernment, or something else beside
the known laws of mechanism taking place: whereas, in
the automaton, for the comparatively few motions of which
it is capable, we trace the mechanism throughout.   But,
up to the limit, the reasoning is as clear and certain in the
one case as in the other.   In the example before us, it is a
matter of certainty, because it is a matter which experience
and observation demonstrate, that the formation of an image at the bottom of the eye is necessary to perfect vision
The image itself can be shown.   Whatever affects the distinctness of the image, affects the distinctness of the vision.
The formation then of such an image being necessary (no

matter how) to the sense of sight, and to the exercise of that sense, the apparatus by which it is formed is constructed and put together, not only with infinitely more art, but upon the selfsame principles of art, as in the telescope or the camera obscura. The perception arising from the image may be laid out of the question; for the production of the image, these are instruments of the same kind. The end is the same; the means are the same. The purpose in both is alike, the contrivance for accomplishing that purpose is in both alike.* The lenses of the telescope, [Plate II. fig. 3, 4.] and the humours of the eye, bear a complete resemblance to one another, in their figure, their position, and in their power over the rays of light, viz. in bringing each pencil to a point at the right distance from the lens; namely, in the eye, at the exact place where the membrane is spread to receive it. How is it possible, under circumstances of such close affinity, and under the operation of equal evidence, to exclude contrivance from the one, yet to acknowledge the proof of contrivance having been employed, as the plainest and clearest of all propositions, in the other?

The resemblance between the two cases is still more accurate, and obtains in more points than we have yet represented, or than we are, on the first view of the subject, aware of. In dioptric telescopes there is an imperfection of this nature. Pencils of light, in passing through glass lenses, are separated into different colors, thereby tinging the object, especially the edges of it, as if it were viewed through a prism. To correct this inconvenience had been long a desideratum in the art. At last it came into the mind of a sagacious optician, to inquire how this matter was managed in the eye; in which there was exactly the same difficulty to contend with as in the telescope. His observation taught him, that, in the eye, the evil was cured by combining lenses composed of different substances, i. e. of substances which possessed different refracting powers. Our artist borrowed thence his hint, and produced a correction of the defect by imitating, in glasses

---

* The comparison with the lens of the telescope is not perfectly exact for the crystalline lens is a substance composed of concentric layers, of unequal density, the hardness of which increases from the surface to the centre; and hence possesses a more refractive power than any artificial lens. Mr. Ramsden supposes that this texture tends to correct the aberration occasioned by the spherical form of the cornea, and the focus of each oblique pencil of rays falls accurately on the concave surface of the retina — *Paxton*

made from different materials, the effects of the different humours through which the rays of light pass before they reach the bottom of the eye. Could this be in the eye without purpose, which suggested to the optician the only effectual means of attaining that purpose? *

But farther; there are other points, not so much perhaps of strict resemblance between the two, as of superiority of the eye over the telescope, which being found in the laws that regulate both, may furnish topics of fair and just comparison. Two things were wanted, to the eye, which were not wanted (at least in the same degree) to the telescope: and these were the adaptation of the organ, first to different degrees of light; and, secondly, to the vast diversity of distance at which objects are viewed by the naked eye, viz. from a few inches to as many miles. These difficulties present not themselves to the maker of the telescope. He wants all the light he can get; and he never directs his instrument to objects near at hand. In the eye, both these cases were to be provided for; and for the purpose of providing for them a subtile and appropriate mechanism is introduced:—

* " It does not appear that the hint of this discovery was taken by Mr. Dollond from the structure of the eye, as supposed by our author, but was obtained in a different manner. This circumstance does not however lessen the force of the reasoning. The principle thus applied in the construction of achromatic telescopes, has been since carried still farther, and in its new application, illustrates more strongly, if possible, the point so well insisted on by Dr. Paley, namely, the resemblance between the eye and our optical instruments. In the best achromatic telescopes, composed of the different kinds of glass, according to the discovery of Mr. Dollond, white or luminous objects are not shown *perfectly* free from color, their edges being tinged on one side with a claret colored, and on the other with a greenish fringe. This remaining imperfection has been got rid of by the combination of *solid* and *fluid* lenses in the object and eye-glasses of telescopes. For this beautiful discovery science is indebted to Dr. Blair of Edinburgh, who found that by placing a concave lens of muriatic acid with a metallic solution, between two convex lenses of glass, a combined lens was formed which refracted rays with perfect regularity and equality. A lens like this has been used with great advantage. The most important point is, however, to consider this improvement in its application to the argument, and it will be seen how much nearer this construction brings the telescope to the eye. In Dollond's telescope there is a combination of *solid* lenses of different substances.—In Blair's, a combination of *fluid* and solid; which is exactly the case in the human eye. The only difference is, that in the eye there is a solid lens between two fluid ones; and in the telescope a fluid between two solid. The combination is closely similar, and the final cause in both, probably the same, namely, to correct the unequal refraction of light, (see *Edinburgh Journal of Science,* No. VIII., p. 212, and *Library of Useful Knowledge,* Nos. I. and II.)   ED.

1. In order to exclude excess of light, when it is excessive, and to render objects visible under obscurer degrees of it, when no more can be had, the hole or aperture in the eye, through which the light enters, is so formed, as to contract or dilate itself for the purpose of admitting a greater or less number of rays at the same time. The chamber of the eye is a camera obscura,* which, when the light is too small, can enlarge its opening; when too strong, can again contract it; and that without any other assistance than that of its own exquisite machinery. It is farther also, in the human subject, to be observed, that this hole in the eye, which we call the pupil, under all its different dimensions, retains its exact circular shape. This is a structure extremely artificial. Let an artist only try to execute the same; he will find that his threads and strings must be disposed with great consideration and contrivance to make a circle, which shall continually change its diameter, yet preserve its form. This is done in the eye by an application of fibres, *i. e.* of strings, similar, in their position and action, to what an artist would and must employ, if he had the same piece of workmanship to perform. [Plate II. Fig. 5 & 6.]†

* As the rays of light flowing from all the points of an object through the *pupil* of the eye, by the refraction of the lens and humours of the eye, form an exact representation at the bottom of the eye on the retina; so the camera obscura, by means of a lens refracting the rays, exhibits a picture of the scene before it on the opposite wall.—*Paxton.*

† Some eminent anatomists have doubted the muscularity of the iris, and have given very different explanations of its motions, attributing the contraction and dilatation either to the varied impulse of the blood in its vessels, or to its own vita propria. The enlightened physiologist Magendie affirms, that the latest researches upon the anatomy of the iris proves its muscular structure, and that it is composed of two layers of fibres, the external, Plate II. (Fig. 5.) *radiated*, which dilate the pupil, the other (Fig. 6.) *circular*, which contract the pupil. The external circular fibres appear to be supported by a species of ring, which each of the radiated fibres contribute to form, and in which they slide during the alternate contractions and relaxations of the pupil.—*Paxton.*

There is a curious circumstance in the way in which light produces the contraction of the opening of the iris, which strengthens very much the argument derived from design manifested in its structure and adaptation to its purpose. The object of the iris, it is to be observed, has reference to the quantity of light to be admitted upon the retina or expansion of the optic nerve. It is the state of the retina then which regulates the motions of the iris, and it is the action of the light on the retina which causes those motions and not its action upon the iris itself. This has been shown by a very delicate experiment. If a ray of light be accurately thrown in such a direction, that it shall fall upon the circle of the iris itself, and not pass through its aperture, no contraction of the aperture takes place; but if it

II. The second difficulty which has been stated, was the suiting of the same organ to the perception of objects tha. lie near at hand, within a few inches, we will suppose, of the eye, and of objects which are placed at a considerable distance from it, that, for example, of as many furlongs; (I speak in both cases of the distance at which distinct vision can be exercised.) Now this, according to the principles of optics, that is, according to the laws by which the transmission of light is regulated, (and these laws are fixed,) could not be done without the organ itself undergoing an alteration and receiving an adjustment, that might correspond with the exigency of the case, that is to say, with the different inclination to one another under which the rays of light reached it. Rays issuing from points placed at a small distance from the eye, and which consequently must enter the eye in a spreading or diverging order, cannot, by the same optical instrument in the same state, be brought to a point, *i. e.* be made to form an image, in the same place with rays proceeding from objects situated at a much greater distance, and which rays arrive at the eye in directions nearly (and physically speaking) parallel. It requires a rounder lens to do it. The point of concourse behind the lens must fall critically upon the retina, or the vision is confused;* yet other things remaining the same, this point, by the immutable properties of light, is carried farther back when the rays proceed from a near object than when they are sent from one that is remote. A person who was using an optical instrument, would manage this matter by changing, as the occasion required, his lens or his telescopes; or by adjusting the distance of his glasses with his hand or his screw: but how is it to be managed in the eye? What the alteration was, or in what part of the eye it took place, or by what means it was effected, (for if the known

be so thrown as to pass through the aperture, and fall upon the retina without touching the iris at all, still a contraction of the iris immediately takes place. So that light upon the iris alone occasions no contraction, although it is the part which really contracts when the same light falls upon a distant part. The design here is too obvious to need being enlarged upon. How could the iris acquire the power of contracting when light falls on another membrane, for the protection of that membrane? although it does not contract when the light falls upon itself alone?—[*Ed.*

* The focus of the refracted rays must fall exactly on the retina, so that the point of vision may be neither produced beyond it, nor shortened so as not to reach it. The latter defect exists in short-sighted persons, from too great convexity of the cornea or lens. The former is the defect of long-sighted persons, in whom there is an opposite conformation of those parts.- *Paxton.*

s which govern the refraction of light be maintained, some alteration in the state of the organ there must be,) had long formed a subject of inquiry and conjecture. The change, though sufficient for the purpose, is so minute as to elude ordinary observation. Some very late discoveries, deduced from a laborious and most accurate inspection of the structure and operation of the organ, seem at length to have ascertained the mechanical alteration which the parts of the eye undergo. It is found, that by the action of certain muscles [Pl. II. fig. 7.] called the straight muscles, and which action is the most advantageous that could be imagined for the purpose,—it is found, I say, that whenever the eye is directed to a near object, three changes are produced in it at the same time, all severally contributing to the adjustment required. The cornea, or outermost coat of the eye, is rendered more round and prominent; the crystalline lens underneath is pushed forwards; and the axis of vision, as the depth of the eye is called, is elongated These changes in the eye vary its power over the rays of light in such a manner and degree as to produce exactly the effect which is wanted, viz. the formation of an image *upon the retina*, whether the rays come to the eye in a state of divergency, which is the case when the object is near to the eye, or come parallel to one another, which is the case when the object is placed at a distance. Can anything be more decisive of contrivance than this is? The most secret laws of optics must have been known to the author of a structure endowed with such a capacity of change. It is as though an optician, when he had a nearer object to view, should *rectify* his instrument by putting in another glass, at the same time drawing out also his tube to a different length.

Observe a new-born child first lifting up its eyelids What does the opening of the curtain discover? The anterior part of two pellucid globes, which, when they come to be examined, are found to be constructed upon strict optical principles; the selfsame principles upon which we ourselves construct optical instruments. We find them perfect for the purpose of forming an image by refraction; composed of parts executing different offices; one part having fulfilled its office upon the pencil of light, delivering it over to the action of another part; that to a third, and so onward; the progressive action depending for its success upon the nicest and minutest adjustment of the parts concerned; yet these parts so in fact adjusted as to

produce, not by a simple action or effect, but by a combination of actions and effects, the result which is ultimately
wanted.   And forasmuch as this organ would have to operate under different circumstances, with strong degrees of
light and with weak degrees, upon near objects, and upon
remote ones, and these differences demanded, according to
the laws by which the transmission of light is regulated, a
corresponding diversity of structure; that the aperture,
for example, through which the light passes, should be
larger or less; the lenses rounder or flatter, or that their
distance from the tablet, upon which the picture is delineated, should be shortened or lengthened: this, I say, being
the case, and the difficulty to which the eye was to be
adapted, we find its several parts capable of being occasionally changed, and a most artificial apparatus provided
to produce that change.   This is far beyond the common
regulator of a watch, which requires the touch of a foreign
hand to set it; but it is not altogether unlike Harrison's contrivance for making a watch regulate itself, by inserting
within it a machinery, which, by the artful use of the different expansion of metals, preserves the equability of the
motion under all the various temperatures of heat and cold
in which the instrument may happen to be placed.   The
ingenuity of this last contrivance has been justly praised.
Shall, therefore, a structure which differs from it, chiefly by
surpassing it, be accounted no contrivance at all? or, if it
be a contrivance, that it is without a contriver?

But this, though much, is not the whole: by different
species of animals the faculty we are describing is possessed, in degrees suited to the different range of vision which
their mode of life, and of procuring their food, requires.
Birds, for instance, in general, procure their food by means
of their beak; and, the distance between the eye and the
point of the beak being small, it becomes necessary that
they should have the power of seeing very near objects
distinctly.   On the other hand, from being often elevated
much above the ground, living in air, and moving through
it with great velocity, they require, for their safety, as well
as for assisting them in descrying their prey, a power
of seeing at a great distance; a power, of which, in birds
of rapine, surprising examples are given.   The fact accordingly is, that two peculiarities are found in the eyes
of birds, both tending to *facilitate* the change upon which
the adjustment of the eye to different distances depends.
The one is a bony, yet, in most species, a flexible rim or

hoop,* [Plate III. fig. 1, 2.] surrounding the broadest part of the eye; which, confining the action of the muscles to that part, increases the effect of their lateral pressure upon the orb, by which pressure its axis is elongated for the purpose of looking at very near objects. The other is an additional muscle, called the marsupium, [Plate III. fig. 3, 4, 6.] to draw, upon occasion, the crystalline lens *back*, and to fit the same eye for the viewing of very distant objects By these means, the eyes of birds can pass from one extreme to another of their scale of adjustment, with more ease and readiness than the eyes of other animals.

The eyes of *fishes* also, compared with those of terrestrial animals, exhibit certain distinctions of structure adapted to their state and element. We have already observed upon the figure of the crystalline compensating by its roundness the density of the medium through which their light passes. To which we have to add, that the eyes of fish, in their natural and indolent state, appear to be adjusted to near objects, in this respect differing from the human eye, as well as those of quadrupeds and birds. The ordinary shape of the fish's eye being in a much higher degree convex than that of land animals, a corresponding difference attends its muscular conformation, viz. that it is throughout calculated for *flattening* the eye.

The *iris* also in the eyes of fish does not admit of contraction. This is a great difference, of which the probable reason is, that the diminished light in water is never too strong for the retina.

In the *eel*, [Plate III. fig. 5.] which has to work its head

* *The flexible rim, or hoop*, consists of bony plates, which in all birds occupy the front of the sclerotic; lying close together and overlapping each other. These bony plates in general form a slightly convex ring, Fig. 1, but in the *accipitres* they form a concave ring, as in Fig. 2, the bony rim of a hawk. It is a principle in optics, that the rays of light, passing through a lens, will be refracted to a point or focus beyond the lens, and this focus will be less distant in proportion as the lens approaches to a sphere in shape. This principle is very naturally applied to the explanation of the use of this apparatus. These scales partly lying over each other, so as to allow of motion, will, on the contraction of the straight muscles inserted into and covering them, move over each other, and diminish the circle of the sclerotica; and thus the cornea, which is immediately within the circle made by these scales, must be pressed forwards and rendered more convex, from the focus of the eye becoming altered, by its axis being elongated. This consequent convexity of the cornea renders small objects near the animal very distinct. Without this structure a bird would be continually liable to dash itself against trees when flying in a thick forest, and would be unable to see the minute objects on which it sometimes feeds.—*Paxton.*

through sand and gravel, the roughest and harshest substances, there is placed before the eye, and at some distance from it, a transparent, horny, convex case or covering, which, without obstructing the sight, defends the organ To such an animal, could anything be more wanted,
or more useful?

Thus, in comparing the eyes of different kinds of animals, we see, in their resemblances and distinctions, one
general plan laid down, and that plan varied with the varying exigencies to which it is to be applied.

There is one property, however, common, I believe, to
all eyes, at least to all which have been examined,* namely,
that the optic nerve enters the bottom of the eye, not in the
centre or middle, but a little on one side; not in the point
where the axis of the eye meets the retina, but between
that point and the nose. The difference which this makes
is, that no part of an object is unperceived by both eyes at
the same time.

In considering vision as achieved by the means of an
image formed at the bottom of the eye, we can never reflect without wonder upon the smallness, yet correctness,
of the picture, the subtilty of the touch, the fineness of the
lines. A landscape of five or six square leagues is brought
into a space of half an inch diameter; yet the multitude of
objects which it contains, are all preserved; are all discrim-
inated in their magnitudes, positions, figures, colors. The
prospect from Hampstead-hill is compressed into the compass of a sixpence, yet circumstantially represented. A
stage-coach, travelling at its ordinary speed for half an
hour, passes, in the eye, only over one-twelfth of an inch,
yet is this change of place in the image distinctly perceived throughout its whole progress; for it is only by
means of that perception that the motion of the coach itself is made sensible to the eye. If anything can abate
our admiration of the smallness of the visual tablet compared with the extent of vision, it is a reflection, which the
view of nature leads us, every hour, to make, viz. that in
he hands of the Creator, great and little are nothing.

Sturmius held, that the examination of the eye was
a cure for atheism. Besides that conformity to optical
principles which its internal constitution displays, and
which alone amounts to a manifestation of intelligence nav
ing been exerted in the structure; besides this, which forms

* The eye of the seal or sea-calf, I understand, is an exception.— Mem
Acad Paris, 1701, p. 123.

no doubt, the leading character of the organ, there is to be seen, in everything belonging to it and about it, an extraordinary degree of care, and anxiety for its preservation, due, if we may so speak, to its value and its tenderness. It is lodged in a strong, deep, bony socket, composed by the junction of seven different bones,* hollowed out at their *edges.* In some few species, as that of the coatimondi,† the orbit is not bony throughout; but whenever this is the case, the upper, which is the deficient part, is supplied by a cartilaginous ligament; a substitution which shows the same care. Within this socket it is embedded in fat, of all animal substances the best adapted both to its repose and motion. It is sheltered by the eyebrows; an arch of hair, which, like a thatched penthouse, prevents the sweat and moisture of the forehead from running down into it.

But it is still better protected by its *lid.* Of the superficial parts of the animal frame, I know none which, in its office and structure, is more deserving of attention than the eyelid. It defends the eye; it wipes it; it closes it in sleep.‡ Are there, in any work of art whatever, purposes more evident than those which this organ fulfils? or an apparatus for executing those purposes more intelligible, more appropriate, or more mechanical? If it be overlooked by the observer of nature, it can only be because it is obvious and familiar. This is a tendency to be guarded against. We pass by the plainest instances, whilst we are exploring those which are rare and curious; by which conduct of the understanding, we sometimes neglect the strongest observations, being taken up with others, which, though more recondite and scientific, are, as solid arguments, entitled to much less consideration.

In order to keep the eye moist and clean, (which qualities are necessary to its brightness and its use,) a wash is constantly supplied by a secretion for the purpose; and the superfluous brine is conveyed to the nose through a perforation in the bone as large as a goose-quill. [Plate IV. fig. 1.] When once the fluid has entered the nose, it spreads itself upon the inside of the nostril, and is evaporated by the current of warm air, which, in the course of respiration, is con-

* Heister, sect 89.   † Mem. of the R. Ac. Paris, p. 117.

‡ The muscles which accomplish these actions are seen in TAB. XIV. Fig. 1, 2. The eyelids also moderate the force of a too brilliant light, and exclude, by a partial closure, that excess of it which would offend the eye. The eyelashes have a similar office, that of regulating the quantity of light: and it is believed, that they protect the eye from the small particles of dust that float in the air. — *Paxton.*

tinually passing over it.   Can any pipe or outlet for carry
ing off the waste liquor from a dye-house or a distillery, be
more mechanical than this is?   It is easily perceived, that
the eye must want moisture: but could the want of the eye
generate the gland which produces the tear, or bore the hole
by which it is discharged,—a hole through a bone?

It is observable, that this provision is not found in fish;
the element in which they live supplying a constant lotion
to the eye.

It were, however, injustice to dismiss the eye as a piece
of mechanism, without noticing that most exquisite of all
contrivances, the *niclitating membrane*, which is found in
the eyes of birds and of many quadrupeds. [Plate IV. fig.
2.]   Its use is to sweep the eye, which it does in an instant; to spread over it the lachrymal humour; to defend
it also from sudden injuries: yet not totally, when drawn
upon the pupil, to shut out the light.   The commodious
ness with which it lies folded up in the inner corner of
the eye, ready for use and action, and the quickness with
which it executes its purpose, are properties known and
obvious to every observer: but what is equally admirable,
though not quite so obvious, is the combination of two
different kinds of substance, muscular and elastic, and of
two different kinds of action, by which the motion of this
membrane is performed.   It is not, as in ordinary cases,
by the action of two antagonist muscles, one pulling forward and the other backward, that a reciprocal change is
effected; but it is thus: The membrane itself is an elastic
substance, capable of being drawn out by force like a piece
of elastic gum, and by its own elasticity returning, when
the force is removed, to its former position.   Such being
its nature, in order to fit it up for its office, it is connected
by a tendon or thread with a muscle in the back part of
the eye: this tendon or thread, though strong, is so fine
as not to obstruct the sight, even when it passes across it;
and the muscle itself, being placed in the *back* part of the
eye, [Plate IV. fig. 3, 4, and 5,] derives from its situation
the advantage, not only of being secure, but of being out
of the way; which it would hardly have been in any position that could be assigned to it in the anterior part of the
orb, where its function lies.   When the muscle behind the
eye contracts, the membrane, by means of the communicating thread, is instantly drawn over the fore-part of it.
When the muscular contraction (which is a positive, and,
most probably, a voluntary effort,) ceases to be exerted
the elasticity alone of the membrane brings it back again

'o its position.* Does not this, if anything can lo it, bespeak an artist, master of his work, acquainted with his
materials? " Of a thousand other things," say the French
academicians, " we perceive not the contrivance, because
we understand them only by the effects, of which we know
not the causes: but we here treat of a machine, all the
parts whereof are visible; and which need only to be
looked upon to discover the reasons of its motion and action."†

In the configuration of the muscle which, though placed
behind the eye, draws the nictitating membrane over the
eye, there is, what the authors just now quoted, deserved-
ly call a marvellous mechanism. I suppose this structure
to be found in other animals; but, in the memoirs from
which this account is taken, it is anatomically demonstrated only in the cassowary. The muscle is *passed through
a loop formed by another muscle;* and is there inflected,
as if it were round a pulley. This is a peculiarity; and
observe the advantage of it. A single muscle with a
straight tendon, which is the common muscular form, would
have been sufficient, if it had had power to draw far
enough. But the contraction, necessary to draw the membrane over the whole eye, required a longer muscle than
could lie straight at the bottom of the eye. Therefore,
in order to have a greater length in a less compass, the
cord of the main muscle makes an angle. This, so far,
answers the end; but, still farther, it makes an angle,
not round a fixed pivot, but round a loop formed by another
muscle; which second muscle, whenever it contracts, o
course twitches the first muscle at the point of inflection
and thereby assists the action designed by both.

One question may possibly have dwelt in the reader's
mind during the perusal of these observations, namely, Why
should not the Deity have given to the animal the faculty
of vision *at once?* Why this circuitous perception; the
ministry of so many means; an element provided for the
purpose; reflected from opaque substances, refracted
through transparent ones; and both according to precise
laws; then, a complex organ, an intricate and artificial apparatus, in order, by the operation of this element, and in
conformity with the restrictions of these laws, to produce an
image upon a membrane communicating with the brain?

*Phil. Tran. 1796.
† Memoirs for a Natural History of Animals y the Royal Academy
of Sciences at Paris, dono into English by order of the Royal Society
1701, p. 249.

Wherefore all this? Why make the difficulty in order to surmount it? If to perceive objects by some other mode than that of touch, or objects which lay out of the reach of that sense, were the thing purposed, could not a simple volition of the Creator have communicated the capacity? Why resort to contrivance, where power is omnipotent? Contrivance, by its very definition and nature, is the refuge of imperfection. To have recourse to expedients, implies difficulty. impediment, restraint, defect of power. This question belongs to the other senses, as well as to sights; to the general functions of animal life, as nutrition, secretion, respiration; to the economy of vegetables; and indeed to almost all the operations of nature. The question, therefore, is of very wide extent; and amongst other answers which may be given to it, beside reasons of which probably we are ignorant, one answer is this· It is only by the display of contrivance, that the existence, the agency, the wisdom of the Deity, *could* be testified to his rational creatures. This is the scale by which we ascend to all the knowledge of our Creator which we possess, so far as it depends upon the phenomena, or the works of nature. Take away this, and you take away from us every subject of observation, and ground of reasoning; I mean as our rational faculties are formed at present. Whatever is done God could have done without the intervention of instruments or means: but it is in the construction of instruments, in the choice and adaptation of means, that a creative intelligence is seen. It is this which constitutes the order and beauty of the universe. God, therefore, has been pleased to prescribe limits to his own power, and to work his ends within those limits. The general laws of matter have perhaps the nature of these limits; its inertia, its reaction; the laws which govern the communication of motion, the refraction and reflection of light, the constitution of fluids non-elastic and elastic, the transmission of sound through the latter; the laws of magnetism, of electricity; and probably others, yet undiscovered. These are general laws; and when a particular purpose is to be effected, it is not by making a new law, nor by the suspension of the old ones, nor by making them wind, and bend, and yield to the occasion; (for nature with great steadiness adheres to and supports them;) but it is, as we have seen n the eye, by the interposition of an apparatus, correspond-ing with these laws, and suited to the exigency which results from them, that the purpose is at length attained. As we have said therefore. God prescrib limits to his power

that he may let in the exercise, and thereby exhibit demon-
strations of his wisdom.   For then, *i. e.* such laws and lim-
itations being laid down, it is as though one Being should
have fixed certain rules; and, if we may so speak, provided certain materials; and, afterwards, have committed to
another Being out of these materials, and in subordination
to these rules, the task of drawing forth a creation: a supposition which evidently leaves room, and induces indeed a
necessity for contrivance.   Nay, there may be many such
agents, and many ranks of these.   We do not advance this
as a doctrine either of philosophy or of religion; but we say
that the subject may safely be represented under this
view, because the Deity, acting himself by general laws,
will have the same consequences upon our reasoning,
as if he had prescribed these laws to another.   It has been
said, that the problem of creation was, "attraction and
matter being given, to make a world out of them:" and,
as above explained, this statement perhaps does not convey
a false idea.

———

We have made choice of the eye as an instance upon
which to rest the argument of this chapter.   Some single
example was to be proposed; and the eye offered itself under the advantage of admitting of a strict comparison with
optical instruments.   The ear, it is probable, is no less
artificially and mechanically adapted to its office than the
eye.   But we know less about it: we do not so well understand the action, the use, or the mutual dependency of
its internal parts.   Its general form, however, both external
and internal, is sufficient to show that it is an instrument
adapted to the reception of *sound*; that is to say, already
knowing that sound consists in pulses of the air, we perceive, in the structure of the ear, a suitableness to receive impressions from this species of action, and to propagate these
impressions to the brain.   For of what does this structure
consist? [Pl. V. fig. 1.] An external ear, (the concha,) calculated, like an ear-trumpet, to catch and collect the pulses of
which we have spoken; in large quadrupeds, turning to
the sound, and possessing a configuration, as well as motion, evidently fitted for the office: of a tube which leads
into the head, lying at the root of this outward ear, the
folds and sinuses thereof tending and conducting the air
towards it: of a thin membrane, like the pelt of a drum,
stretched across this passage upon a bony rim: of a chain
of moveable, and infinitely curious bones, forming a com-

munication. and the only communication that can be observed, between the membrane last mentioned and the interior channels and recesses of the skull: of cavites, similar in shape and form to wind instruments of music, being spiral or portions of circles: of the eustachian tube, like the hole in a drum, to let the air pass freely into and out of the barrel of the ear, as the covering membrane vibrates, or as the temperature may be altered: the whole labyrinth hewn out of a rock; that is, wrought into the substance of the hardest bone of the body. This assemblage of connected parts constitutes together an apparatus, plainly enough relative to the transmission of sound, or of the impulses received from sound, and only to be lamented in not being better understood.

The communication within, formed by the small bones of the ear, is, to look upon, more like what we are accustomed to call machinery, than anything I am acquainted with in animal bodies. [Pl. V. fig. 2.] It seems evidently designed to continue towards the sensorium, the tremulous motions which are excited in the membrane of the tympanum, or what is better known by the name of the " drum of the ear." The compages of bones consists of four, which are so disposed, and so hinge upon one another, as that if the membrane, the drum of the ear, vibrate, all the four are put in motion together; and, by the result of their action, work the base of that which is the last in the series, upon an aperture which it closes, and upon which it plays, and which aperture opens into the tortuous canals that lead to the brain. This last bone of the four is called the *stapes*. The office of the drum of the ear is to spread out an extended surface, capable of receiving the impressions of sound, and of being put by them into a state of vibration. The office of the stapes is to repeat these vibrations. It is a repeating frigate, stationed more within the line. From which account of its action may be understood, how the sensation of sound will be excited by anything which communicates a vibratory motion to the stapes, though not, as in all ordinary cases, through the intervention of the membrana tympani. This is done by solid bodies applied to the bones of the skull, as by a metal bar held at one end between the teeth, and touching at the other end a tremulous body. It likewise appears to be done, in a considerable degree, by the air itself, even when this membrane, the drum of the ear, is greatly damaged. Either in the natural or preternatural state of the organ, the use of the chain of bones is to propagate the impulse in a di rection towards the brain, and to propagate it with the advantage of a lever; which advantage consists in increasing the force and strength of the vibration, and at the same time diminishing the space through which it oscillates; both of which changes may augment or facilitate the still deeper action of the auditory nerves.

The benefit of the eustachian tube to the organ, may be made out upon known pneumatic principles. Behind the drum of the ear is a second cavity, or barrel, called the tympanum. The eustachian tube is a slender pipe, but sufficient for the passage of air, leading from this cavity into the back part of the mouth. Now, it would not have done to have had a vacuum in this cavity; for, in that case, the pressure of the atmosphere from without would have burst the membrane which covered it. Nor would it have done to have filled the cavity with lymph or any other secretion; which would necessarily have obstructed, both the vibration of the membrane and the play of the small bones. Nor, lastly, would it have done to have occupied the space with confined air, because the expansion of that air by heat, or its contraction by cold, would have distended or relaxed the covering membrane, in a degree inconsistent with the purpose which it was assigned to execute. The only remaining expedient, and that for which the eustachian tube serves, is to open to this cavity a communication with the external air. In one word; it exactly answers the purpose of the hole in a drum.

The membrana tympani itself, likewise, deserves all the examination which can be made of it. It is not found in the ears of fish; which furnishes an additional proof of what indeed is indicated by everything about it, that it is appropriated to the action of air, or of an elastic medium. It bears an obvious resemblance to the pelt or head of a drum, from which it takes its name. It resembles also a drum-head in this principal property, that its use depends upon its tension. *Tension* is the state essential to it. Now we know that, in a drum, the pelt is carried over a hoop, and braced, as occasion requires, by the means of strings attached to its circumference. In the membrane of the ear, the same purpose is provided for, more simply, but not less mechanically, nor less successfully, by a different expedient, viz. by the end of a bone (the handle of the malleus) pressing upon its centre. It is only in very large animals that the texture of this membrane can be discerned. In the Philosophical Transactions for the year 1800, (vol i.) Sir Everard Home has given some curious observa tions upon the ear, and the drum of the ear of an *elephant* [Pl v. fig 4.] He discovered in it what he cal s a radiated muscle, that is, straight muscular fibres, passing along the membrane from the circumference to the centre; from the bony rim which surrounds it towards the handle of the malleus to which the central part is attached. This mus cle he supposes to be designed to bring the membrane into unison with different sounds: but then he also discovered, that this muscle itself cannot act, unless the membrane be drawn to a stretch, and kept in a due state of tightness, by what m iy be called a foreign force, viz. the action of the muscles of the malleus. Our author, supposing his ex- planation of the use of the parts to be just, is well founded in the reflection which he makes upon it: "that this mode of adapting the ear to different sounds, is one of the most beautiful applications of muscles in the body; *the mechan- ism is so simple, and the variety of effects so great.*" *

In another volume of the transactions above referred to, and of the same year, two most curious cases are related, of persons who retained the sense of hearing, not in a perfect, but in a very considerable degree, notwithstanding he almost total loss of the membrane we have been de- scribing In one of these cases, the use here assigned to

---

* As the ear of man and fish has been described, it may not be im- proper in this place to state, that the other classes of animals are no less admirably provided with an ear, adapted to their peculiar habits and economy.

In amphibious animals the organ of hearing has an intermediate struc- ture; in some species of this class, the ear resembling fish, in others it more resembles the formation of terrestrial animals.

There is an important addition to this organ in birds: viz. a cochlea ard proper tympanum.

In quadrupeds we find a more complicated organization; to collect the vibrations of sound, they have an external ear, and all those parts, though of a different figure, which belong to the human ear.

The capacity for enjoyment of music is mental, but all the curious varieties of sound, which are the source of this enjoyment, are communi- cated by the mechanical provisions of the ear. We are astonished at the varieties of sensation; the ear is capable of perceiving four or five hundred variations of tone in sound.

"Hence we may conceive a prodigious variety in the same tone, arising from irregularities of it occasioned by constitution, figure, situation or manner of striking the sonorous body; from the constitution of the elastic medium, or its being disturbed by other motions; and from the constitution of the ear itself, upon which the impression is made. A flute, a violin, a hautboy, a French horn, n ay all sound the same tone, and be easily distinguishable. Nay, if twenty human v)ices sound the same note, and with equal strength, there will be some difference." Reid's Enquiry, page 98.—*Paxton.*

.hat membrane, of modifying the impressions of sound by change of tension, was attempted to be supplied by strai ing the muscles of the outward ear. "The external ear, ' we are told, "had acquired a distinct motion upward and backward, which was observable whenever the patient istened to anything which he did not distinctly hear; when he was addressed in a whisper, the ear was seen im mediately to move; when the tone of voice was louder, it then remained altogether motionless."

It appears probable, from both these cases, that a collate ral, if not principal, use of the membrane, is to cover and protect the barrel of the ear which lies behind it. Both the patients suffered from cold: one, "a great increase of deafness from catching cold;" the other, "very considerable pain from exposure to a stream of cold air." Bad effects therefore followed from this cavity being left open to the external air; yet, had the Author of nature shut it up by any other cover, than what was capable, by its texture, of receiving vibrations from sound, and, by its connexion with the interior parts, of transmitting those vibrations to the brain, the use of the organ, so far as we can judge must have been entirely obstructed.

CHAPTER IV.

OF THE SUCCESSION OF PLANTS AND ANIMALS.

THE *generation* of the animal no more accounts for the contrivance of the eye or ear, than, upon the supposition stated in a preceding chapter, the production of a watch by the motion and mechanism of a former watch, would account for the skill and intention evidenced in the watch so produced; than it would account for the disposition of the wheels, the catching of their teeth, the relation of the several parts of the works to one another, and to their common end; for the suitableness of their forms and places to their offices, for their connexion, their operation, and the useful result of that operation. I do insist most strenu ously upon the correctness of this comparison; that it holds as to every mode of specific propagation; and that whatever was true of the watch, under the hypothesis above mentioned, is true of plants and animals.

I. To begin with the fructification of plants. Can it be doubted but that the seed contains a particular organiza tion? Whether a latent plantule with the means of temporary n .trition, or whatever else it be, it encloses an organization suited to the germination of a new plant. Has the plant which produced the seed anything more to d with that organization, than the watch would have had to do with the structure of the watch which was produced in the course of its mechanical movement? I mean, Has it anything at all to do with the *contrivance?* The maker and contriver of one watch, when he inserted within it a mechanism suited to the production of another watch, was, in truth, the maker and contriver of that other watch. All the properties of the new watch were to be referred to his agency: the design manifested in it, to his intention: the art, to him as the artist: the collocation of each part to his placing: the action, effect, and use, to his counsel, intelligence, and workmanship. In producing it by the intervention of a former watch, he was only working by one set of tools instead of another. So it is with the plant and the seed produced by it. Can any distinction be assigned between the two cases; between the producing watch, and the producing plant; both passive, unconscious substances; both, by the organization which was given to them, producing their like, without understanding or design; both, that is, instruments?

II. From plants we may proceed to oviparous animals, from seeds to eggs. Now, I say, that the bird has the same concern in the formation of the egg which she lays, as the plant has in that of the seed which it drops; and no other, nor greater. The internal constitution of the egg is as much a secret to the hen, as if the hen were inanimate. Her will cannot alter it, or change a single feather of the chick. She can neither foresee nor determine o. which sex her brood shall be, or how many of either; yet the thing produced shall be, from the first, very different in its make, according to the sex which it bears. So far, therefore, from adapting the means, she is not beforehand apprized of the effect. If there be concealed within that smooth shell a provision and a preparation for the production and nourishment of a new animal, they are not of her providing or preparing: if there be contrivance, it is none of hers. Although, therefore, there be the difference of life and perceptivity between the animal and the plant, it is a difference which enters not into the account. It is a foreign circumstance. It is a difference of properties not employed. The animal function and the vegetable function are alike destitute of any design which can operate upon

.he form of the thing produced. The plant has no de·
sign in producing the seed, no comprehension of the na·
ture or use of what it produces; the bird with respect to its
egg, is not above the plant with respect to its seed. Neither the one nor the other bears that sort of relation to what
proceeds from them, which a joiner does to the chair which
he makes. Now a cause, which bears *this* relation to the
effect, is what we want, in order to account for the suitableness of means to an. end, the fitness and fitting of one
thing to another, and this cause the parent plant or ani·
mal does not supply.

It is farther observable concerning the propagation of
plants and animals, that the apparatus employed exhibits
no resemblance to the thing produced; in this respect
holding an analogy with instruments and tools of art. The
filaments, antheræ, and stigmata of flowers, bear no more
resemblance to the young plant, or even to the seed, which
is formed by their intervention, than a chisel or a plane
does to a table or chair. What then are the filaments,
antheræ, and stigmata of plants, but instruments strictly
so called? *

III. We may advance from animals which bring forth
eggs, to animals which bring forth their young alive: and
of this latter class, from the lowest to the highest; from
irrational to rational life, from brutes to the human species;

* Nearly akin to the reproduction of plants and animals by generation,
is the reproduction of parts of animal bodies which have been destroyed,
and the reparation of those which have been injured. To say nothing of
the reproduction of limbs in crustaceous animals, the wonderful but well
attested fact, of the formation of a new eye in an animal of the lizard kind,
in the place of one which had been cut out of the socket, is one which no
atheistical theory can approach, in the way of explanation. In the process by which a new eye is formed, the apparatus, instruments and
materials, employed, bear no resemblance to the organ to be formed. The
small capillary vessels of the root of the eye, construct a new eye, out of
the blood which circulates in them. To use a mode of expression like
that of our author—the vessels which thus construct a new eye, bear no
more resemblance to it, than a chisel or a plane, to a table or a chair; and
the blood out of which it is made, no more resemblance to it when made,
than the metallic ores when taken out of the mine, to a complete and
perfectly constructed watch. In this case, we find a contrivance existing in a whole race of animals, for the accomplishment of a purpose
which it is not called upon to accomplish in one instance out of a thousand.
If the reader will examine the several atheistical modes of evading the force
of the arguments for the existence of God, referred to in the next
chapter, as well as in various other parts of this volume, he will find that
they signally fail in their application to this case. ...*Ed*

without perceiving, as we proceed, any alteration whatever in the terms of the comparison. The rational animal does not produce its offspring with more certainty or success than the irrational animal; a man than a quadruped, a quadruped than a bird; nor (for we may follow the gradation through its whole scale) a bird than a plant; nor a plant than a watch, a piece of dead mechanism, would do, upon the supposition which has already so often been repeated. Rationality therefore has nothing to do in the business. If an account must be given of the contrivance which we observe; if it be demanded, whence arose either the contrivance by which the young animal is produced, or the contrivance manifested in the young animal itself, it is not from the reason of the parent that any such account can be drawn. He is the cause of his offspring in the same sense as that in which a gardener is the cause of the tulip which grows upon his parterre, and in no other. We admire the flower; we examine the plant; we perceive the conduciveness of many of its parts to their end and office; we observe a provision for its nourishment, growth, protection, and fecundity; but we never think of the gardener in all this. We attribute nothing of this to his agency; yet it may still be true, that without the gardener we should not have had the tulip: just so it is with the succession of animals even of the highest order. For the contrivance discovered in the structure of the thing produced, we want a contriver. The parent is not that contriver. His consciousness decides that question. He is in total ignorance why that which is produced took its present form rather than any other. It is for him only to be astonished by the effect. We can no more look therefore to the intelligence of the parent animal for what we are in search of, a cause of relation, and of subserviency of parts to their use, which relation and subserviency we see in the procreated body, than we can refer the internal conformation of an acorn to the intelligence of the oak from which it dropped, or the structure of the watch to the intelligence of the watch which produced it; there being no difference, as far as argument is concerned, between an intelligence which is not exerted, and a intelligence which does not exist.

CHAPTER V.

APPLICATION OF THE ARGUMENT CONTINUED.

EVERY observation which was made in our first chapter, concerning the watch, may be repeated with strict propriety concerning the eye; concerning animals; concerning plants; concerning, indeed, all the organized parts of
the works of nature.   As,

I. When we are inquiring simply after the *existence* of
an intelligent Creator, imperfection, inaccuracy, liability
to disorder, occasional irregularities, may subsist in a considerable degree, without inducing any doubt into the
question: just as a watch may frequently go wrong, seldom
perhaps exactly right, may be faulty in some parts, defective in some, without the smallest ground of suspicion from
thence arising that it was not a watch; not made; or not
made for the purpose ascribed to it.   When faults are
pointed out, and when a question is started concerning the
skill of the artist, or the dexterity with which the work is
executed, then, indeed, in order to defend these qualities
from accusation, we must be able, either to expose some
intractableness and imperfection in the materials, or point
out some invincible difficulty in the execution, into which
imperfection and difficulty the matter of complaint may be
resolved; or if we cannot do this, we must adduce such
specimens of consummate art and contrivance, proceeding
from the same hand, as may convince the inquirer of the
existence, in the case before him, of impediments like those
which we have mentioned, although, what from the nature
of the case is very likely to happen, they be unknown and
unperceived by him.   This we must do in order to vindi-
cate the artist's skill, or, at least, the perfection of it; as
we must also judge of his intention, and of the provision
employed in fulfilling that intention, not from an instance
in which they fail, but from the great plurality of instances
in which they succeed.   But, after all, these are different
questions from the question of the artist's existence; or,
which is the same, whether the thing before us be a work of
art or not: and the question ought always to be kept separate in the mind.   So likewise it is in the works of nature
Irregularities and imperfections are of little or no weight
in the consideration, when that consideration relates simply to the existence of a Creator.   When the argument re

spect; his attributes, they are of weight; but are then to
be taken in conjunction (the attention is not to rest upon
them, but they are to be taken in conjunction) with the
unexceptionable evidences which we possess, of skill,
power, and benevolence, displayed in other instances:
which evidences may, in strength, number, and variety, be
such, and may so overpower apparent blemishes, as to induce us, upon the most reasonable ground, to believe, that
these last ought to be referred to some cause, though we
be ignorant of it, other than defect of knowledge or of benevolence in the author.

II. There may be also parts of plants and animals, as
there were supposed to be of the watch, of which, in some
instances, the operation, in others, the use, is unknown
These form different causes; for the operation may be unknown, yet the use be certain.   Thus it is with the lungs of
animals. It does not, I think, appear, that we are acquainted
with the action of the air upon the blood, or in what manner that action is communicated by the lungs; yet we find
that a very short suspension of their office destroys the
life of the animal.   In this case, therefore, we may be said
to know the use, nay we experience the necessity, of the
organ, though we be ignorant of its operation.   Nearly the
same thing may be observed of what is called the lymphatic system.   We suffer grievous inconveniences from its disorder, without being informed of the office which it sustains in the economy of our bodies.   There may possibly
also be some few examples of the second class, in which
not only the operation is unknown, but in which experiments may seem to prove that the part is not necessary;
or may leave a doubt, how far it is even useful to the plant
or animal in which it is found.   This is said to be the case
with the spleen; which has been extracted from dogs, without any sensible injury to their vital function.   Instances
of the former kind, namely, in which we cannot explain
the operation, may be numerous; for they will be so in
proportion to our ignorance.   They will be more or fewe
to different persons, and in different stages of science
Every improvement of knowledge diminishes their number
There is hardly, perhaps, a year passes that does not, in
the works of nature, bring some operation, or some mode
of operation, to light, which was before undiscovered,—probably unsuspected.   Instances of the second kind, namely,
where the part appears to be totally useless, I believe to be
extremely rare; compared with the number of those of
which the use is evident they are beneath any assignable

proportion; and, perhaps, have never be,n submitted to a trial and examination sufficiently accurate, long enough continued, or often enough repeated. No accounts which I have seen are satisfactory. The mutilated animal may live and grow fat, (as was the case of the dog deprived of its spleen,) yet may be defective in some other of its functions; which, whether they can all, or in what degree of vigor and perfection, be performed, or how long preserved, without the extirpated organ, does not seem to be ascertained by experiment. But to this case, even were it fully made out, may be applied the consideration which we suggested concerning the watch, viz. that these superfluous parts do not negative the reasoning which we instituted concerning those parts which are useful, and of which we know the use. The indication of contrivance, with respect to them, remains as it was before.

III. One atheistic way of replying to our observations upon the works of nature, and to the proofs of a Deity which we think that we perceive in them, is to tell us, that all which we see must necessarily have had some form, and that it might as well be its present form as any other. Let us now apply this answer to the eye, as we did before to the watch. Something or other must have occupied that place in the animal's head; must have filled up, we will say, that socket: we will say also, that it must have been of that sort of substance which we call animal substance, as flesh, bone, membrane, cartilage, &c. But that it should have been an *eye*, knowing as we do, what an eye comprehends,—viz. that it should have consisted, first, of a series of transparent lenses (very different, by the by, even in their substance, from the opaque materials of which the rest of the body is, in general at least, composed; and with which the whole of its surface, this single portion of it excepted, is covered:) secondly, of a black cloth or canvass (the only membrane of the body which is black) spread at behind these lenses, so as to receive the image formed y pencils of light transmitted through them; and placed at the precise geometrical distance at which, and at which alone, a distinct image could be formed, namely, at the concourse of the refracted rays: thirdly, of a large nerve communicating between this membrane and the brain; without which, the action of light upon the membrane, however modified by the organ, would be lost to the purposes of sensation:—that this fortunate conformation of parts should have been the lot, not of one individual out of many thousand individuals, like the great prize in a lottery, or like some singularity in nature, but the happy chance of a whole species; nor of one species out of many thousand species, with which we are acquainted, but of by far the greatest number of all that exist; and that under varieties, not casual or capricious, but bearing marks of being suited to their respective exigencies:—that all this should have taken place, merely because something must have occupied those points in every animal's fore-head,—or, that all this should be thought to be accounted for, by the short answer, "that whatever was there, must have had some form or other," is too absurd to be made more so by any augmentation. We are not contented with this answer; we find no satisfaction in it, by way of accounting for appearances of organization far short of those of the eye, such as we observe in fossil shells, petri-fied bones, or other substances which bear the vestiges of animal or vegetable recrements, but which, either in re-spect of utility, or of the situation in which they are dis-covered, may seem accidental enough. It is no way of accounting even for these things, to say that the stone, for instance, which is shown to us, (supposing the question to be concerning a petrification,) must have contained some internal conformation or other. Nor does it mend the an-swer to add, with respect to the singularity of the confor-mation, that, after the event, it is no longer to be comput-ed what the chances were against it. This is always to be computed, when the question is, whether a useful or imi-tative conformation be the produce of chance, or not: I de-sire no greater certainty in reasoning, than that by which chance is excluded from the present disposition of the nat-ural world. Universal experience is against it. What does chance ever do for us? In the human body, for in-stance, chance, *i. e.* the operation of causes without design, may produce a wen, a wart, a mole, a pimple, but never ar eye. Amongst inanimate substances, a clod, a pebble, a liquid drop might be; but never was a watch, a telescope, an organized body of any kind, answering a valuable pur-pose by a complicated mechanism, the effect of chance In no assignable instance hath such a thing existed without intention somewhere.

IV. There is another answer, which has the same ef-fect as the resolving of things into chance; which answer would persuade us to believe, that the eye, the animal to which it belongs, every other animal, every plant, indeed every organized body which we see, are only so many out of the possible varieties and combinations of being, which the lapse of infinite ages has brought into existence; **that** the present world is the relic of that variety; millions of other bodily forms and other species having perished, being by the defect of their constitutions incapable of preservation, or of continuance by generation. Now there is no foundation whatever for this conjecture in anything which we observe in the works of nature; no such experiments are going on at present; no such energy operates, as that which is here supposed, and which should be constantly pushing into existence new varieties of beings: Nor are there any appearances to support an opinion, that every possible combination of vegetable or animal structure has formerly been tried. Multitudes of conformations, both of vegetables and animals, may be conceived capable of existence and succession, which yet do not exist. Perhaps almost as many forms of plants might have been found in the fields, as figures of plants can be delineated upon paper. A countless variety of animals might have existed, which do not exist. Upon the supposition here stated, we should see unicorns and mermaids, sylphs and centaurs, the fancies of painters, and the fables of poets, realized by examples. Or, if it be alleged that these may transgress the limits of possible life and propagation, we might, at least, have nations of human beings without nails upon their fingers, with more or fewer fingers and toes than ten; some with one eye, others with one ear, with one nostril, or without the sense of smelling at all. All these, and a thousand other imaginable varieties, might live and propagate. We may modify any one species many different ways, all consistent with life, and with the actions necessary to preservation, although affording different degrees of conveniency and enjoyment to the animal. And if we carry these modifications through the different species which are known to subsist, their number would be incalculable. No reason can be given why, if these deperdits ever existed, **they** have now disappeared. Yet, if all possible existences **have** been tried, they must have formed part of the catalogue.

But, moreover, the division of organized substances **into** animals and vegetables, and the distribution and sub-distribution of each into genera and species, which distribution is not an arbitrary act of the mind, but founded in the order which prevails in external nature, appear to me to contradict the supposition of the present world being the remains of an indefinite variety of existences; of a variety which rejects all plan. The hypothesis teaches, that every possible variety of being hath, at one time or other, found its way into existence, (by what cause or in what manner is not said,) and that those which were badly formed, perished; but how or why those which survived should be cast, as we see that plants and animals are cast, into regular classes, the hypothesis does not explain; or rather, the hypothesis is inconsistent with this phenomenon.

The hypothesis, indeed, is hardly deserving of the consideration which we have given to it. What should we think of a man who, because we had never ourselves seen watches, telescopes, stocking mills, steam engines, &c made, knew not how they were made, or could prove by testimony when they were made, or by whom,—would have us believe that these machines, instead of deriving their curious structures from the thought and design of their inventors and contrivers, in truth derive them from no other origin than this, viz. that a mass of metals and other materials having run when melted into all possible figures, and combined themselves in all possible forms and shapes, and proportions, these things which we see, are what were left from the accident, as best worth preserving; and, as such, are become the remaining stock of a magazine, which, at one time or other, has, by this means, contained every mechanism, useful and useless, convenient and inconvenient, into which such like materials could be thrown? I cannot distinguish the hypothesis as applied to the works of nature, from this solution, which no one would accept, as applied to a collection of machines.

V. To the marks of contrivance discoverable in animal bodies, and to the argument deduced from them, in proof of design, and of a designing Creator, this turn is sometimes attempted to be given, viz. that the parts were not intended for the use, but that the use arose out of the parts. This distinction is intelligible. A cabinet maker rubs his mahogany with fish skin; yet it would be too much to assert that the skin of the dogfish was made rough and granulated on purpose for the polishing of wood, and the use of cabinet-makers. Therefore the distinction is intelligible. But I think that there is very little place for it in the works of nature. When roundly and generally affirmed of them, as it hath sometimes been, it amounts to such another stretch of assertion, as it would be to say, that all the implements of the cabinet-maker's workshop, as well as the fish skin, were substances accidentally configurated, which he had picked up, and converted to his use; that his adzes, saws, planes and gimlets, were not made, as we suppose, to hew cun, smooth, shape out, or bore wood with; but that, these things being made, no matter with what design, or whether with any, the cabinet-maker perceives that they were applicable to his purpose, and turned them to account.

But, again. So far as this solution is attempted to be applied to those parts of animals, the action of which does not depend upon the will of the animal, it is fraught with still more evident absurdity. Is it possible to believe that the eye was formed without any regard to vision; that it was the animal itself which found out, that, though formed with no such intention, it would serve to see with; and that the use of the eye, as an organ of sight, resulted from this discovery, and the animal's application of it? The same question may be asked of the ear; the same of all the senses. None of the senses fundamentally depend upon the election of the animal; consequently, neither upon his sagacity, nor his experience. It is the impression which objects make upon them, that constitutes their use. Under that impression, he is passive. He may bring objects to the sense, or within its reach; he may select these objects: but over the impression itself he has no power, or very little; and that properly is the sense.

Secondly, There are many parts of animal bodies which seem to depend upon the will of the animal in a greater degree than the senses do, and yet, with respect to which, this solution is equally unsatisfactory. If we apply the solution to the human body, for instance, it forms itself into questions, upon which no reasonable mind can doubt; such as, whether the teeth were made expressly for the mastication of food, the feet for walking, the hands for holding; or whether, these things being as they are, being in fact in the animal's possession, his own ingenuity taught him that they were convertible to these purposes, though no such purposes were contemplated in their formation.

All that there is of the appearance of reason in this way of considering the subject is, that, in some cases, the organization seems to determine the habits of the animal, and its choice, to a particular mode of life; which, in a certain sense, may be called "the use arising out of he part." Now to all the instances, in which there is any place for this suggestion, it may be replied, that the organization determines the animal to habits beneficial and salutary to itself; and that this effect would not be seen so regularly to follow, if the several organizations did not bear a concerted and contrived relation to the substance by which the animal was surrounded. They would, otherwise, be capacities without objects; powers without employment. The web foot determines, you say, the duck to swim: but what would that avail, if there were no water to swim in? The strong hooked bill, and sharp talons, of one species of bird, determine it to prey upon animals, the soft straight bill, and weak claws, of another species, determine it to pick up seeds: but neither determination could take effect in providing for the sustenance of the birds, if animal bodies and vegetable seeds did not lie within their reach. The peculiar conformation of the bill, and tongue, and claws of the woodpecker, [Pl. XXVII. fig. 1, 2, 3] determines that bird to search for his food amongst the insects lodged behind the bark, or in the wood, of decayed trees: but what would this profit him, if there were no trees, no decayed trees, no insects lodged under their bark, or in their trunk? The proboscis with which the bee is furnished, determines him to seek for honey: but what would that signify, if flowers supplied none? Faculties thrown down upon animals at random, and without reference to the objects amidst which they are placed, would not produce to them the services and benefits which we see; and if there be that reference, then there is intention.

Lastly, the solution fails entirely when applied to plants The parts of plants answer their uses, without any concur rence from the will or choice of the plant.

VI. Others have chosen to refer everything to a *princi ple of order* in nature. A principle of order is the word· but what is meant by a principle of order, as differen from an intelligent Creator, has not been explained eithei by definition or example; and, without such explanation, it should seem to be a mere substitution of words for reasons, names for causes. Order itself is only the adaptation of means to an end: a principle of order, therefore, can only signify the mind and intention which so adapts them. Or, were it capable of being explained in any other sense, is there any experience, any analogy to sustain it? Was a watch ever produced by a principle of order? and why might not a watch be so produced as well as an eye?

Furthermore, a principle of order, acting blindly and without choice, is negatived by the observation, that order is not universal; which it would be, if it issued from a constant and necessary principle; nor indiscriminate, which it would be, if it issued from an unintelligent principle. Where order is wanted, there we find it; where order is not wanted, i. e. where if it prevailed, it would be useless, there we do not find it.   In the structure of the eye, (for we adhere to our example,) in the figure and position of its several parts, the most exact order is maintained.   In the forms of rock and mountains in the lines which bound the coasts of continents and islands, in the shape of bays and promontories, no order whatever is perceived, because it would have been superfluous.   No useful purpose would have arisen from moulding rocks and mountains into regular solids, bounding the channel of the ocean by geometrical curves, or from the map of the world resembling a table of diagrams in Euclid's Elements, or Simpson's Conic Sections.

VII. Lastly, the confidence which we place in our observations upon the works of nature, in the marks which we discover of contrivance, choice, and design, and in our reasoning upon the proofs afforded us, ought not to be shaken, as it is sometimes attempted to be done, by bringing forward to our view our own ignorance, or rather the general imperfection of our knowledge of nature.   Nor, in many cases, ought this consideration to affect us, even when it respects some parts of the subject immediately under our notice.   True fortitude of understanding consists in not suffering what we know to be disturbed by what we do not know.   If we perceive a useful end, and means adapted to that end, we perceive enough for our conclusion If these things be clear, no matter what is obscure.   The argument is finished.   For instance; if the utility of vision to the animal which enjoys it, and the adaptation of the *eye* to this office, be evident and certain, (and I can mention nothing which is more so,) ought it to prejudice the inference which we draw from these premises, that we cannot explain the use of the spleen?   Nay, more; if there be parts of the eye, *viz.* the cornea, the crystalline, the retina, in their substance, figure, and position, manifestly suited to the formation of an image by the refraction of rays of light, at least, as manifestly as the glasses and tubes of a dioptric telescope are suited to that purpose; it concerns not the proof which these afford of design, and of a designer, that there may perhaps be other parts, certain muscles, for instance, or nerves in the same eye, of the agency or effect of which we can give no account; any more than we should be inclined to doubt, or ought to doubt, about the construction of a telescope, *viz.* for what purpose it was constructed, or whether it were constructed at all, because there belonged to it certain screws and pins, the use or action of which we did not comprehend.   I take it to be a general way of infusing doubts and scruples into the mind to recur to its own ignorance, its own imbecility: to tell us that upon these subjects we know little; that little imperfectly; or rather, that we know nothing properly about the matter. These suggestions so fall in with our consciousnesses, as sometimes to produce a general distrust of our faculties and our conclusions. But this is an unfounded jealousy. The uncertainty of one thing, does not necessarily affect the certainty of another thing. Our ignorance of many points need not suspend our assurance of a few Before we yield, in any particular instance, to the skepticism which this sort of insinuation would induce, we ought accurately to ascertain, whether our ignorance or doubt concern those precise points upon which our conclusion rests. Other points are nothing. Our ignorance of other points may be of no consequence to these, though they be points, in various respects, of great importance. A just reasoner removes from his consideration, not only what he knows, but what he does not know, touching matters not strictly connected with his argument, *i. e.* not forming the very steps of his deduction; beyond these, his knowledge and his ignorance are alike relative.

CHAPTER VI.

THE ARGUMENT CUMULATIVE.

WERE there no example in the world of contrivance except that of the *eye*, it would be alone sufficient to support the conclusion which we draw from it, as to the necessity of an intelligent Creator. It could never be got rid of, because it could not be accounted for by any other supposition, which did not contradict all the principles we possess of knowledge: the principles, according to which things do, as often as they can be brought to the test of experience, turn out to be true or false. Its coats and humours constructed as the lenses of a telescope are constructed, for the refraction of rays of light to a point, which forms the proper office of the organ: the provision in its muscles for turning its pupil to the object, similar to that which is given to the telescope by screws, and upon which power of direction in the eye, the exercise of its office as an optical instrument depends; the farther provision for its defence, for its constant lubricity and moisture, which we see in its socket and its lids, in its gland for the secretion

of the matter of tears, its outlet or communication with the
nose for carry ng off the liquid after the eye is washed with
it; these provisions compose altogether an apparatus, a
system of parts, a preparation of means, so manifest in their
design, so exquisite in their contrivance, so successful in
their issue, so precious, and so infinitely beneficial in their
use, as, in my opinion, to bear down all doubt that can be
raised upon the subject.   And what I wish, un ler the title
of the present chapter, to observe is, that if other parts
of nature were inaccessible to our inquiries, or even if
other parts of nature presented nothing to our examination
out disorder and confusion, the validity of this example
would remain the same.   If there were but one watch in
the world, it would not be less certain that it had a maker
If we had never in our lives seen any but one single kind
of hydraulic machine, yet, if of that one kind we understood
the mechanism and use, we should be as perfectly assured
that it proceeded from the hand, and thought, and skill of
a workman, as if we visited a museum of the arts, and saw
collected there twenty different kinds of machines for
drawing water, or a thousand different kinds for other
purposes.   Of this point, each machine is a proof, inde
pendently of all the rest.   So it is with the evidences of a
divine agency.   The proof is not a conclusion which lies
at the end of a chain of reasoning, of which chain each
instance of contrivance is only a link, and of which, if one
link fail, the whole falls; but it is an argument separately
supplied by every separate example.   An error in stating
an example affects only that example.   The argument is
cumulative, in the fullest sense of that term.   The eye
proves it without the ear; the ear without the eye.   The
proof in each example is complete; for when the design of
the part, and the conduciveness of its structure to that design is shown, the mind may set itself at rest; no future
consideration can detract anything from the force of the
example

CHAPTER VII

THE MECHANICAI AND IMMECHANICAL PARTS AND FUNC-
TIONS OF ANIMALS AND VEGETABLES

It is not that every part of an animal or vegetable has
not proceeded from a contriving mind; or that every part
is not constructed with a view to its proper end and pur-

pose, according to the laws belonging to and governing the substance or the action made use of in that part, or that each part is not so constructed as to effectuate its purpose whilst it operates according to these laws; but it is because these laws themselves are not in all cases equally understood; or, what amounts to nearly the same thing, are not equally exemplified in more simple processes, and more simple machines; that we lay down the distinction, here proposed, between the mechanical parts and other parts of animals and vegetables.

For instance; the principle of muscular motion, viz. upon what cause the swelling of the belly of the muscle and consequent contraction of its tendons, either by an act of the will, or by involuntary irritation, depends, is wholly unknown to us. The substance employed, whether it be fluid, gaseous, elastic, electrical, or none of these, or nothing resembling these, is also unknown to us: of course, the laws belonging to that substance, and which regulate its action, are unknown to us. We see nothing similar to this contraction in any machine which we can make, or any process which we can execute. So far (it is confessed) we are in ignorance, but no farther. This power and principle, from whatever cause it proceeds, being assumed, the collocation of the fibres to receive the principle, the disposition of the muscles for the use and application of the power, is mechanical; and is as intelligible as the adjustment of the wires and strings by which a puppet is moved. We see, therefore, as far as respects the subject before us, what is not mechanical in the animal frame, and what is. The nervous influence (for we are often obliged to give names to things which we know little about)—I say the nervous influence, by which the belly, or middle, of the muscle is swelled, is not mechanical. The utility of the effect we perceive; the means, or the preparation of means, by which it is produced, we do not. But obscurity as to the origin of muscular motion brings no doubtfulness into our observations upon the sequel of the process: Which observations relate, 1st, to the constitution of the muscle; in consequence of which constitution, the swelling of the belly or middle part is necessarily and mechanically followed by a retraction of the tendons: 2dly, to the number and variety of the muscles, and the corresponding number and variety of useful powers—which they supply to the animal; which is astonishingly great: 3dly, to the judicious, (if we may be permitted to use that term, in speaking of the author or of the works of nature,) to the wise and well-contrived disposition of each muscle for its specific purpose; for moving the joint this way, and that way, and the other way; for pulling and drawing the part to which it is attached, in a determinate and particular direction; which is a mechanical operation, exemplified in a multitude of instances. To mention only one: The tendon of the trochlear muscle of the eye, to the end that it may draw in the line required, is passed through a cartilaginous ring, at which it is reverted, exact y in the same manner as a rope in a ship is carried over a block or round a stay, in order to make it pull in the direction which is wanted. [Pl. V. fig. 1.] All this, as we have said, is mechanical; and is accessible to inspection, as capable of being ascertained, as the mechanism of the automaton in the Strand. Suppose the automaton to be put in motion by a magnet, (which is probable,) it will supply us with a comparison very apt for our present *purpose. Of the magnetic effluvium, we know perhaps as little as we do of the nervous fluid. But, magnetic attraction being assumed, (it signifies nothing from what cause it proceeds,) we can trace, or there can be pointed out to us, with perfect clearness and certainty, the mechanism, viz. the steel bars, the wheels, the joints, the wires, by which the motion so much admired is communicated to the fingers of the im age: and to make any obscurity, or difficulty, or controversy in the doctrine of magnetism, an objection to our knowledge or our certainty concerning the contrivance, or the marks of contrivance, displayed in the automaton, would be exactly the same thing, as it is to make our ignorance (which we acknowledge) of the cause of nervous agency, or even of the substance and structure of the nerves themselves, a ground of question or suspicion as to the reasoning which we institute concerning the mechanical part of our frame. That an animal is a machine, is a proposition neither correctly true nor wholly false. The distinction which we have been discussing will serve to show how far the comparison, which this expression implies, holds; and wherein it fails. And whether the distinction be thought of importance or not, it is certainly of importance to remember, that there is neither truth nor justice in endeavouring to bring a cloud over our understandings, or a distrust into our reasonings upon this subject, by suggesting that we know nothing of voluntary motion, of irritability, of the principle of life, or sensation, of animal heat, upon all which the animal functions depend; for, our ignorance of these parts of the animal frame concerns not at all our knowledge of the mechanical parts of the same frame. I contend, therefore, that there is mechanism in animals; that this mechanism is as properly such, as it is in machines made by art; that this mechanism is intelligible and certain; that it is not the less so, because it often begins or terminates with something which is not mechanical: that whenever it is intelligible and certain, it demonstrates intention and contrivance, as well in the works of nature as in those of art; and that it is the best demonstration which either can afford.

But whilst I contend for these propositions, I do not exclude myself from asserting, that there may be, and that there are, other cases, in which, although we cannot exhibit mechanism, or prove indeed that mechanism is employed, we want not sufficient evidence to conduct us to the same conclusion.

There is what may be called the *chemical* part of our frame; of which, by reason of the imperfection of our chemistry, we can attain to no distinct knowledge; I mean, not to a knowledge, either in degree or kind, similar to that which we possess of the mechanical part of our frame. It does not, therefore, afford the same species of argument as that which mechanism affords; and yet it may afford an argument in a high degree satisfactory. The *gastric juice*, or the liquor which digests the food in the stomachs of animals, is of this class. Of all menstrua, it is the most active, the most universal. In the human stomach, for instance, consider what a variety of strange substances, and how widely different from one another, it, in a few hours, reduces to a uniform pulp, milk, or mucilage. It seizes upon everything, it dissolves the texture of almost everything that comes in its way. The flesh of perhaps all animals; the seeds and fruits of the greatest number of plants; the roots, and stalks, and leaves of many, hard and tough as they are, yield to its powerful pervasion. The change wrought by it is different from any chemical solution which we can produce, or with which we are acquainted, in this respect as well as many others, that, in our chemistry, particular menstrua act only upon particular substances. Consider, moreover, that this fluid, stronger in its operation than a caustic alkali or mineral acid, than red precipitate, or aqua-fortis itself, is nevertheless as mild, and bland, and inoffensive to the touch or taste, as saliva or gum-water, which it much resembles. Consider, I say, these several properties of the digestive organ, and of the juice with which it is supplied, or rather with which it is made to supply itself, and you will confess it to be entitled to a name, which it has sometimes received, that of "the chemical wonder of animal nature."

Still we are ignorant of the composition of this fluid, and of the mode of its action: by which is meant. that we are not capable, as we are in the mechanical part of our frame. of collating it with the operations of art. And this I call the imperfection of our chemistry; for should the time ever arrive, which is not perhaps to be despaired of, when we can compound ingredients, so as to form a solvent which will act in the manner in which the gastric juice acts, we may be able to ascertain the chemical principles upon which its efficacy depends, as well as from what part, and by what concoction, in the human body, these principles are generated and derived.

In the meantime, ought that, which is in truth the defect of our chemistry, to hinder us from acquiescing in the inference, which a production of nature, by its place, its properties, its action, its surprising efficacy, its invaluable use, authorises us to draw in respect of a creative design?

Another most subtile and curious function of animal bodies is *secretion*. This function is semi-chemical and semi-mechanical; exceedingly important and diversified in its effects, but obscure in its process and in its apparatus. The importance of the secretory organs is but too well attested by the diseases, which an excessive, a deficient, or a vitiated secretion is almost sure of producing. A single secretion being wrong, is enough to make life miserable, or sometimes to destroy it. Nor is the variety less than the importance. From one and the same blood (I speak of the human body) about twenty different fluids are separated; in their sensible properties, in taste, smell, color, and consistency, the most unlike one another that is possible; thick, thin, salt, bitter, sweet: and, if from our own we pass to other species of animals, we find amongst their secretions not only the most various, but the most opposite properties; the most nutritious aliment, the deadliest poison; the sweetest perfumes, the most fetid odors. Of these the greater part, as the gastric juice, the saliva, the bile, the slippery mucilage which lubricates the joints, the tears which moisten the eye, the wax which defends the ear, are, after they are secreted, made use of in the animal economy; are evidently subservient, and are actually contributing to the utilites of the animal itself. Other fluids seem to be separated only to be rejected. That this also is necessary (though why it was originally necessary we cannot tell) is shown by the consequence of the separation being long suspended; which consequence is disease and death. Akin to secretion, if not the same thing, is assimilation, by which one and the same blood is converted into bone, muscular flesh, nerves, membranes, tendons; things as different as the wood and iron, canvass and cordage, of which a ship with its furniture is composed. We have no operation of art wherewith exactly to compare all this, for no other reason perhaps than that all operations of art are exceeded by it. No chemical election, no chemical analysis or resolution of a substance into its constituent parts, no mechanical sifting or divison, that we are acquainted with, in perfection or variety, come up to animal secretion. Nevertheless, the apparatus and process are obscure; not to say absolutely concealed from our inquiries. In a few, and only a few instances, we can discern a little of the constitution of a gland. In the kidneys of large animals, we can trace the emulgent artery dividing itself into an infinite number of branches; their extremities everywhere communicating with little round bodies, in the substance of which bodies the secret of the machinery seems to reside, for there the change is made. We can discern pipes laid from these round bodies towards the pelvis, which is a basin within the solid of the kidney. (Pl. VI. fig. 2.) We can discern these pipes joining and collecting together into larger pipes; and when so collected, ending in innumerable papillæ, through which the secreted fluid is continually oozing into its receptacle. This is all we know of the mechanism of a gland, even in the case in which it seems most capable of being investigated. Yet to pronounce that we know nothing of animal secretion, or nothing satisfactorily, and with that concise remark to dismiss the article from our argument, would be to dispose of the subject very hastily and very irrationally. For the purpose which we want, that of evincing intention, we know a great deal. And what we know is this. We see the blood carried by a pipe, conduit, or duct, *to* the gland. We see an organized apparatus, be its construction or action what it may, which we call that gland. We see the blood, or part of the blood, after it has passed through and undergone the action of the gland, coming *from* it by an emulgent vein or artery, *i. e.* by another pipe or conduit. And we see also at the same time a new and specific fluid issuing from the same gland by its excretory duct, *i. e.* by a third pipe or conduit; which new fluid is in some cases discharged out of the body, in more cases retained within it, and there executing some important and intelligent office. Now supposing, or admitting, that we know nothing of the proper internal constitution of a gland, or of the mode of its acting upon the blood; then our situation is precisely like that of an unmechanical look-er-on, who stands by a stocking-loom, a corn-mill, a card-ng-machine, or a threshing-machine, at work, the fabric and mechanism of which, as well as all that passes within, is hidden from his sight by the outside case; or, if seen, would be too complicated for his uninformed, uninstructed understanding to comprehend. And what is that situation? This spectator, ignorant as he is, sees at one end a mate rial enter the machine, as unground grain the mill, raw cot-ton the carding-machine, sheaves of unthreshed corn the threshing-machine; and, when he casts his eye to the other end of the apparatus, he sees the material issuing from it in a new state; and, what is more, in a state manifestly adapted to future uses; the grain in meal fit for the making of bread, the wool in rovings ready for spinning into threads, the sheaf in corn dressed for the mill. Is it ne-cessary that this man, in order to be convinced that design, that intention, that contrivance has been employed about the machine, should be allowed to pull it to pieces; should be enabled to examine the parts separately; explore their action upon one another, or their operation, whether simul-taneous or successive, upon the material which is presented to them? He may long to do this, to gratify his curiosity; he may desire to do it to improve his theoretic know-ledge; or he may have a more substantial reason for re-questing it, if he happen, instead of a common visiter, to be a mill wright by profession, or a person sometimes call-ed in to repair such-like machines when out of order; but, for the purpose of ascertaining the existence of counsel and design in the formation of the machine, he wants no such intromission or privity. What he sees is sufficient. The effect upon the material, the change produced in it, he utility of that change for future applications, abundantly estify, be the concealed part of the machine or of its con-struction what it may, the hand and agency of a contriver.

If any confirmation were wanting to the evidence which the animal secretions afford of design, it may be derived, as has been already hinted, from their variety, and from their appropriation to their place and use. They all come from the same blood: they are all drawn off by glands: yet the produce is very different, and the difference exactly adapted to the work which is to be done, or the end to be answered. No account can be given of this, without resorting to appointment. Why, for instance, is the saliva which is diffused over the seat of taste, insipid, whilst so many others of the secretions, the urine, the tears, and the sweat, are salt? Why does the gland within the ear separate a viscid substance, which defends that passage; the gland in the upper angle of the eye, a thin brine, which washes the ball? Why is the synovia of the joints mucilaginous; the bile bitter, stimulating, and soapy? Why does the juice which flows into the stomach, contain powers, which make that organ the great laboratory, as it is by its situation the recipient, of the materials of future nutrition? These are all fair questions; and no answer can be given to them, but what calls in intelligence and intention.

My object in the present chapter has been to teach three things: first, that it is a mistake to suppose that, in reasoning from the appearances of nature, the imperfection of our knowledge proportionably affects the certainty of our conclusion; for in many cases it does not affect it at all: secondly, that the different parts of the animal frame may be classed and distributed, according to the degree of exactness with which we can compare them with works of art: thirdly, that the *mechanical* parts of our frame, or those in which this comparison is most complete, although constituting, probably, the coarsest portions of nature's workmanship, are the most proper to be alleged as proofs and specimens of design.

CHAPTER VIII.

OF MECHANICAL ARRANGEMENT IN THE HUMAN FRAME

WE proceed, therefore, to propose certain examples taken out of this class: making choice of such as, amongst those which have come to our knowledge, appear to be the most striking, and the best understood; but obliged, perhaps, to postpone both these recommendations to a third; that of the example being capable of explanation without plates, or figures, or technical language.

OF THE BONES.

I challenge any man to produce, in the joints and pivots of the most complicated or the most flexible machine hat was ever contrived, a construction more artifi cial, or more evidently artificial, than that which is seen in the vertebræ of the *human neck*. [Pl. VII. fig. 1.] Two things were to be done. The head was to have the power of bending forward and backward, as in the act of nodding, stooping, looking upward or downward; and, at the same time, of turning itself round upon the body to a certain extent, the quadrant we will say, or rather, perhaps, a hundred and twenty degrees of a circle. For these two purposes, two distinct contrivances are employed: [Pl. VII. fig. 2, 3, 4.] First, the head rests immediately upon the uppermost of the vertebræ, and is united to it by a *hinge-joint*; upon which joint the head plays freely forward and backward, as far either way as is necessary, or as the ligaments allow; which was the first thing required.—But then the rotatory motion is unprovided for. Therefore, secondly, to make the head capable of this, a farther mechanism is introduced; not between the head and the uppermost bone of the neck, where the hinge is, but between that bone, and the bone next underneath it. It is a mechanism resembling a *tenon and mortice*. This second, or uppermost bone but one, has what anatomists call a process, viz. a projection, somewhat similar, in size and shape, to a tooth; which tooth, entering a corresponding hole or socket in the bone above it, forms a pivot or axle, upon which that upper bone, together with the head which it supports, turns freely in a circle; and as far in the circle as the attached muscles permit the head to turn. Thus are both motions perfect, without interfering with each other. When we nod the head, we use the hinge-joint, which lies between the head and the first bone of the neck When we turn the head round, we use the tenon and mortice, which runs between the first bone of the neck and the second. We see the same contrivance, and the same principle, employed in the frame or mounting of a telescope. It is occasionally requisite, that the object-end of the instrument be moved up and down, as well as horizontally, or equatorially. For the vertical motion, there is a hinge, upon which the telescope plays; for the horizontal or equatorial motion, an axis upon which the telescope and the hinge turn round together. And this is exactly the mechanism which is applied to the motion of the head. nor will any one here doubt of the existence of counsel and design, except it be by that debility of mind, which can trust to its own reasonings in nothing.

We may add, that it was on another account also, expedient, that the motion of the head backward and for-

ward should be performed upon the upper surface of the
first vertebræ: for, if the first vertebræ itself had bent forward, it would have brought the spinal marrow, at the very
beginning of its course, upon the point of the tooth.

II. Another mechanical contrivance, not unlike the last
in its object, but different and original in its means, is seen
in what anatomists call the *fore-arm;* that is, in the arm
from the elbow to the wrist. [Pl. VIII fig. 1, 2.] Here,
for the perfect use of the limb, two motions are wanted; a
motion at the elbow backward and forward, which is called
a reciprocal motion; and a rotatory motion, by which the
palm of the hand, as occasion requires, may be turned upward. How is this managed? The fore-arm, it is well
known, consists of two bones lying alongside each other,
but touching only towards the ends. One, and only one of
these bones, is joined to the cubit, or upper part of the arm,
at the elbow; the other alone, to the hand at the wrist.
The first by means, at the elbow, of a hinge-joint. (which
allows only of motion in the same plane,) swings backward
and forward, carrying along with it the other bone, and
the whole fore-arm. In the meantime, as often as there is
occasion to turn the palm upward, that other bone, to
which the hand is attached, rolls upon the first, by the
help of a groove or hollow near each end of one bone,
to which is fitted a corresponding prominence in the other
If both bones had been joined to the cubit, or upper arm,
at the elbow, or both to the hand at the wrist, the
thing could not have been done. The first was to be at
liberty at one end, and the second at the other: by which
means the two actions may be performed together. The
great bone, which carries the fore-arm, may be swinging
upon its hinge at the elbow, at the very time that the les
ser bone, which carries the hand, may be turning round it
in the grooves. The management also of these grooves,
or rather of the tubercles and grooves, is very observable
The two bones are called the *radius* and the *ulna.* Above,
i. e. towards the elbow, a tubercle of the radius plays into
a socket of the ulna; whilst below, i. e. towards the wrist,
the radius finds the socket, and the ulna the tubercle. A
single bone in the fore-arm, with a ball and socket joint at
the elbow, which admits of motion in all directions, might,
in some degree, have answered the purpose of both moving
the arm and turning the hand. But how much better it is
accomplished by the present mechanism, any person may
convince himself, who puts the ease and quickness, with
which he can shake his hand at the wrist circularly, (mov

ing likewise, if he pleases, his arm at the elbow at the same time,) in competition with the comparatively slow and laborious motion with which his arm can be made to turn round at the shoulder, by the aid of a ball and socket joint.

III. The *spine*, or back bone, is a chain of joints of very wonderful construction. [Pl. IX. fig. 1, 2.] Various, difficult, and almost inconsistent offices were to be executed by the same instrument. It was to be firm, yet flexible. (now I know no chain made by art, which is both these, for by firmness I mean, not only strength, but stability:) *firm*, to support the erect position of the body: *flexible*, to allow of the bending of the trunk in all degrees of curvature. It was farther also (which is another, and quite a distinct purpose from the rest) to become a pipe or conduit for the safe conveyance from the brain, of the most important fluid* of the animal frame, that, namely, upon which all voluntary motion depends, the spinal marrow; a substance not only of the first necessity to action, if not to life, but of a nature so delicate and tender, so susceptible, and so impatient of injury, as that any unusual pressure upon it, or any considerable obstruction of its course, is followed by paralysis or death. Now the spine was not only to furnish the main trunk for the passage of the medullary substance from the brain, but to give out, in the course of its progress, small pipes therefrom, which, being afterwards indefinitely subdivided, might, under the name of nerves, distribute this exquisite supply to every part of the body. The same spine was also to serve another use not less wanted than the preceding, viz. to afford a fulcrum, stay, or basis, (or, more properly speaking, a series of these) for the insertion of the muscles which are spread over the trunk of the body; in which trunk there are not, as in the limbs, cylindrical bones, to which they can be fastened and, likewise, which is a similar use, to furnish a support for the ends of the ribs to rest upon

Bespeak of a workman a piece of mechanism which shall comprise all these purposes, and let him set about to contrive it; let him try his skill upon it; let him feel the

---

* It seems proper to remark here, that the form of expression made use of in this case implies what is not strictly true. The spinal marrow, or more properly the spinal nerve, is not a fluid but a solid cord extending from the brain down through the canal of the spine, from which branches are distributed to all parts of the body. Dr. Paley in this instance probably had in view the animal spirits, a subtile fluid, which was formerly believed to be seated in the brain, and carried through the nerves to the different parts.—*Ed.*

difficulty of accomplishing the task, before he be told how the same thing is effected in the animal frame.   Nothing will enable him to judge so well of the wisdom which has been employed; nothing will dispose him to think of it so truly.   First, for the firmness, yet flexibility, of the spine, 't is composed of a great number of bones (in the human subject, of twenty-four) joined to one another, and compacted by broad bases.   The breadth of the bases upon which the parts severally rest, and the closeness of the junction, give to the chain its firmness and stability; the number of parts, and consequent frequency of joints, its flexibility. Which flexibility, we may also observe, varies in different parts of the chain: is least in the back, where strength more than flexure, is wanted; greater in the loins, which it was necessary should be more supple than the back, and greatest of all in the neck, for the free motion of the head.   Then, secondly, in order to afford a passage for the descent of the medullary substance, each of these bones is bored through the middle in such a manner, as that, when put together, the hole in one bone falls into a line, and corresponds with the holes in the two bones contiguous to it.   By which means the perforated pieces, when joined, form an entire, close, uninterrupted channel; at least, whilst the spine is upright, and at rest.   But, as a settled posture is inconsistent with its use, a great difficulty still remained, which was to prevent the vertebræ shifting upon one another, so as to break the line of the canal as often as the body moves or twists; or the joints gaping externally, whenever the body is bent forward, and the spine thereupon made to take the form of a bow.   These dangers, which are mechanical, are mechanically provided against.   The vertebræ, by means of their processes and projections, and of the articulations which some of these form with one another at their extremities, are so locked in and confined, as to maintain, in what are called the bodies or broad surfaces of the bones, the relative position nearly unaltered; and to throw the change and the pressure, produced by flexion, almost entirely upon the intervening cartilages, the springiness and yielding nature of whose substance admits of all the motion which is necessary to be performed upon them, without any chasm being produced by a separation of the parts.   I say, of all the motion which is necessary; for although we bend our backs to every degree almost of inclination, the motion of each vertebra is very small: such is the advantage we receive from the chain being composed of so many links, the spine of so many bones

Had it consisted of three or four bones only, in bending the body the spinal marrow must have been bruised at every angle. The reader need not be told, that these intervening cartilages are gristles; and he may see them in perfection in a loin of veal. Their form also favors the same intention. They are thicker before than behind; so that, when we stoop forward, the compressible substance of the cartilage, yielding in its thicker and anterior part to the force which squeezes it, brings the surfaces of the adjoining vertebræ nearer to the being parallel with one another than they were before, instead of increasing the inclination of their planes, which must have occasioned a fissure or opening between them. Thirdly, for the medullary canal giving out in its course, and in a convenient order, a supply of nerves to different parts of the body, notches are made in the upper and lower edge of every vertebra, two on each edge, equi-distant on each side from the middle line of the back. When the vertebræ are put together, these notches, exactly fitting, form small holes, through which the nerves, at each articulation, issue out in pairs, in order to send their branches to every part of the body, and with an equal bounty to both sides of the body. The fourth purpose assigned to the same instrument is the insertion of the bases of the muscles, and the support of the ends of the ribs; and for this fourth purpose, especially the former part of it, a figure, specifically suited to the design, and unnecessary for the other purposes, is given to the constituent bones. Whilst they are plain, and round, and smooth, towards the front, where any roughness or projection might have wounded the adjacent viscera, they run out behind, and on each side, into long processes, to which processes the muscles necessary to the motions of the trunk are fixed; and fixed with such art, that, whilst the vertebræ supply a basis for the muscles, the muscles help to keep these bones in their position, or by their tendons to tie them together.

That most important, however, and general property, viz the strength of the compages, and the security against luxation, was to be still more specially consulted: for where so many joints were concerned, and where, in every one, derangement would have been fatal, it became a subject of studious precaution. For this purpose, the vertebræ are articulated, that is, the moveable joints between them are formed by means of those projections of their substance, which we have mentioned under the name of processes; and these so lock in with, and overwrap one another.

o secure the body of the vertebræ, not only from accident ally slipping, but even from being pushed out of its place by any violence short of that which would break the bone. I have often remarked and admired this structure in the chine of a hare. In this, as in many instances, a plain observer of the animal economy may spare himself the disgust of being present at human dissections, and yet learn enough for his information and satisfaction, by even examining the bones of the animals which come upon his table. Let him take, for example, into his hands, a piece of the clean-picked bone of a hare's back; consisting, we will suppose, of three vertebræ. He will find the middle bone of the three so implicated by means of its projections or processes, with the bone on each side of it, that no pressure which he can use, will force it out of its place between them. It will give way neither forward, nor backward, nor on either side. In whichever direction he pushes, he perceives, in the form, or junction, or overlapping of the bones, an impediment opposed to his attempt; a check and guard against dislocation. In one part of the spine, he will find a still farther fortifying expedient, in the mode according to which the ribs are annexed to the spine. Each rib rests upon two vertebræ. That is the thing to be remarked, and any one may remark it in carving a neck of mutton. The manner of it is this: the end of the rib is divided by a middle ridge into two surfaces; which surfaces are joined to the bodies of two contiguous vertebræ, the ridge applying itself to the intervening cartilage. Now this is the very contrivance which is employed in the famous iron bridge at my door at Bishop-Wearmouth; and for the same purpose of stability; viz. the cheeks of the bars, which pass between the arches, ride across the joints, by which the pieces composing each arch are united. Each cross-bar rests upon two of these pieces at their place of junction; and by that position resists, at least in one direction, any tendency in either piece to slip out of its place. Thus perfectly, by one means or the other, is the danger of slipping laterally, or of being drawn aside out of the *line* of the back, provided against: and to withstand the bones being pulled asunder longitudinally, or in the direction of that line, a strong membrane runs from one end of the chain to the other, sufficient to resist any force which is ever likely to act in the direction of the back, or parallel to it, and consequently to secure the whole combination in their places. The general result is, that not only the motions of the human body necessary for the ordinary offices of life are performed with safety, but that it is an accident hard-ly ever heard of, that even the gesticulations of a harlequin distort his spine.

Upon the whole, and as a guide to those who may be inclined to carry the consideration of this subject farther, there are three views under which the spine ought to be regarded, and in all which it cannot fail to excite our admiration. These views relate to its articulations, its ligaments, and its perforation, and to the corresponding advantages which the body derives from it, for action, for strength, and for that which is essential to every part, a secure communication with the brain.*

* It will be useful to append to the remarks of Dr. Paley upon the mechanism of the spine and of other parts of the body, some observations by a very eminent anatomist and surgeon now living, who has lately considered the subject of Animal Mechanism in its connexion with Natural Theology, and has presented some striking and original views. These observations have been published as one of the treatises of the Society for the Diffusion of Useful Knowledge, which forms the ninth number of the series. These extracts will be the more instructive as giving views of a professional observer in confirmation of those of our author; and they will also serve as additional illustrations of the same great truths which he has endeavoured to enforce.—*Ed.*

"The spinal column, as it is called, serves three purposes: it is the great bond of union between all the parts of the skeleton; it forms a tube for the lodgement of the spinal marrow, a part of the nervous system as important to life as the brain itself; and lastly, it is a column to sustain the head.

We now see the importance of the spine, and we shall next explain how the various offices are provided for.

If the protection of the spinal marrow had been the only object of this structure, it is natural to infer that it would have been a strong and unyielding tube of bone; but, as it must yield to the inflexion of the body, it cannot be constituted in so strict an analogy with the skull. It must, therefore, bend; but it must have no abrupt or considerable bending at one part; for the spinal marrow within would in this way suffer.

By this consideration we perceive why there are twenty-four bones in the spine, each bending a little; each articulated or making a joint with its fellow; all yielding in a slight degree, and, consequently, permitting in the whole spine that flexibility necessary to the motions of the body. It is next to be observed that, whilst the spine by this provision moves in every direction, it gains a property which it belongs more to our present purpose to understand. The bones of the spine are called vertebræ; at each interstice between these bones, there is a peculiar gristly substance, which is squeezed out from between the bones, and, therefore, permits them to approach and play a little in the motions of the body. This gristly substance is enclosed in an elastic binding, or membrane of great strength, which passes from the edge or border of one vertebra, to the border of the one next it. When a weight is upon the body, the soft gristle is pressed out, and the membrane yields: the moment the weight is remov-

The structure of the spine is not in general different in different animals.   In the serpent tribe, however, it is con-

ed, the membranes recoil by their elasticity, the gristle is pressed into its place, and the bones resume their position.

We can readily understand how great the influence of these twenty four joinings must be in giving elasticity to the whole column ; and how much this must tend to the protection of the brain.   Were it not for this interposition of elastic material, every motion of the body would produce a jar to the delicate texture of the brain, and we should suffer almost as much in alighting on our feet, as in falling on our head.   It is, as we have already remarked, necessary to interpose thin plates of lead or slate between the different pieces of a column to prevent the edges (technically called arrises) of the cylinders from coming in contact, as they would, in that case, chip or split off.

But there is another very curious provision for the protection of the brain; we mean the curved form of the spine.   If a steel spring, perfectly straight, be pressed between the hands from its extremities, it will resist, notwithstanding its elasticity, and when it does give way, it will be with a jerk.

Such would be the effect on the spine if it stood upright, one bone perpendicular to another; for then the weight would bear equally; the spine would yield neither to one side nor to the other; and, consequently, there would be a resistance from the pressure on all sides being balanced. We, therefore, see the great advantage resulting from the human spine being in the form of an italic *f*.   It is prepared to yield in the direction of its curves; the pressure is of necessity more upon one side of the column than on the other; and its elasticity is immediately in operation without a jerk.   It yields, recoils, and so forms the most perfect spring; admirably calculated to carry the head without jar, or injury of any kind.

The most unhappy illustration of all this is the condition of old age The tables of the skull are then consolidated, and the spine is rigid: if an old man should fall with his head upon the carpet, the blow, which would be of no consequence to the elastic frame of a child, may to him prove fatal; and the rigidity of the spine makes every step which he takes, vibrate to the interior of the head, and jar on the brain.

We have hinted at a comparison between the attachment of the spine to the pelvis and the insertion of the mast of a ship into the hull.   The mast goes directly through the decks without touching them, and the heel of the mast goes into the step, which is formed of large solid pieces of oak timber laid across the keelson.   The keelson is an inner keel resting upon the floor-timbers of the ship and directly over the proper keel. These are contrivances for enlarging the base on which the mast rests as a column; for as, in proportion to the height and weight of a column, its base must be enlarged, or it would sink into the earth; so, if the mast were to bear upon a point, it would break through the bottom of the ship.

The mast is supported upright by the shrouds and stays.   The shrouds secure it against the lateral or rolling motion, and the stays and backstays against the pitching of the ship.   These form what is termed the standing rigging.

The mast does not bear upon the deck or on the beams of the ship; indeed there is a space covered with canvass between the deck and the mast

siderably varied; but with a strict reference to the conveniency of the animal. [Pl. IX. fig. 3, 4, 5] For, whereas in

We often hear of a new ship going to sea to stretch her rigging; that
is, to permit the shrouds and stays to be stretched by the motion of the
ship, after which they are again braced tight; for if she were overtaken
by a storm before this operation, and when the stays and shrouds were
relaxed, the mast would lean against the upper deck, by which it would
be sprung or carried away. Indeed, the greater proportion of masts that
are lost are lost in this manner. There are no boats which keep the sea
in such storms as those which navigate the gulf of Finland. Their masts
are not attached at all to the hull of the ship, but simply rest upon the
step.

Although the spine has not a strict resemblance to the mast, the con
trivances of the ship-builder, however different from the provisions of nature, show what object is to be attained; and when we are thus made
aware of what is necessary to the security of a column on a moveable
base, we are prepared to appreciate the superior provisions of nature for
giving security to the human spine.

The human spine rests on what is called the *pelvis*, or basin;—a circle
of bones, of which the haunches are the extreme lateral parts; and the sacrum (which is the keystone of the arch) may be felt at the lower part
of the back. To this central bone of the arch of the pelvis the spine is
connected; and, taking the similitude of the mast, the sacrum is as the
step on which the base of the pillar, like the heel of the mast, is socket-
ed or morticed. The spine is tied to the lateral parts of the pelvis by
powerful ligaments, which may be compared to the shrouds. They secure the lower part of the spine against the shock of lateral motion or
rolling; but, instead of the stays to limit the play of the spine forwards
and backwards in pitching, or to adjust the rake of the mast, there is a
very beautiful contrivance in the lower part of the column.

The spine forms here a semicircle which has this effect; that whether
by the exertion of the lower extremities, the spine is to be carried forward
upon the pelvis, or whether the body stops suddenly in running, the jar
which would necessarily take place at the lower part of the spine, if it
stood upright like a mast, is distributed over several of the bones of the
spine; and, therefore, the chance of injury at any particular part is diminished.

For example, the sacrum, or centre bone of the pelvis, being carried
forward, as when one is about to run, the force is communicated to the
lowest bone of the spine. But, then, the surfaces of these bones stand
with a very slight degree of obliquity to the line of motion; the shock
communicated from the lower to the second bone of the vertebræ is still in
a direction very nearly perpendicular to its surface of contact. The same
takes place in the communication of force from the second to the third,
and from the third to the fourth; so that before the shock of the horizontal
motion acts upon the perpendicular spine, it is distributed over four bones
of that column, instead of the whole force being concentrated upon the
joining of any two.

If the column stood upright, it would be jarred at the lowest point of
contact with its base. But by forming a semicircle, the motion would
produce a jar on the very lowest part of the column, and which is distributed over a considerable portion of the column; and in point of fact, this
part of the spine never gives way. Indeed, we should be inclined to of-

quadrupeds tne number of vertebræ is from thirty o forty
in the serpent it is nearly one hundred and fifty whereas in men and quadrupeds the surfaces of the bones are
flat, and these flat surfaces laid one against the other, and
bound tight by sinews; in the serpent the bones play one
within another like a ball and socket,* so that they have
a free motion upon one another in every direction; that is
to say, in men and quadrupeds, firmness is more consulted;
in serpents, pliancy.   Yet even pliancy is not obtained at
the expense of safety.   The backbone of a serpent, for
coherence and flexibility, is one of the most curious pieces
of animal mechanism with which we are acquainted.   The
chain of a watch, (I mean the chain which passes between
the spring-barrel and the fusee,) which aims at the same
properties, is but a bungling piece of workmanship in comparison with that of which we speak.†

IV.   The reciprocal enlargement and contraction of the
chest to allow for the play of the lungs, depends upon a
simple yet beautiful mechanical contrivance, referrible to
the structure of the bones which enclose it.   [Pl. X. fig. 1]
The ribs are articulated to the backbone, or rather to its side

for this model to the consideration of nautical men, as fruitful in hints
for improving naval architecture.

Every one who has seen a ship pitching in a heavy sea, must have
asked himself why the masts are not upright, or rather, why the fore mast
stands upright, whilst the main and mizzen masts stand oblique to the deck
or, as the phrase is, rake aft or towards the stern of the ship.

The main and mizzen masts incline backwards, because the strain is
greatest in the forward pitch of the vessel; for the mast having received
an impulse forwards, it is suddenly checked as the head of the ship rises;
but the mast being set with an inclination backwards, the motion falls
more in a perpendicular line from the head to the heel.   This advantage
is lost in the upright position of the foremast, but it is sacrificed to a superior advantage gained in working the ship; the sails upon this mast act
more powerfully in swaying the vessel round, and the perpendicular position causes the ship to tack or stay better; but the perpendicular position,
as we have seen, causes the strain in pitching to come at right angles to
the mast, and is, therefore, more apt to spring.

These considerations give an interest to the fact, that the human spine,
from its utmost convexity near its base, inclines backwards.''—*Bell's
Treatise on Animal Mechanics.*

* Der. Phys. Theol. p. 396.

† In fish, which have more elastic, but less flexible bodies, the structure
of the spine differs.   The end of each vertebra is a cup containing a viscid
fluid, which keeps the bones from approaching nearer to each other than
he mean state of the elasticity of the lateral ligaments ; the fluid is in-
compressible, therefore forms a ball round which the bony cups move ;
the ball having no cohesion, the centre of motion is always adapted t ne
change which the joint undergoes without producing friction.--*Pa: n*

projections *obliquely:* * that is, in their natural position, they
bend or slope from the place of articulation downwards
But the basis upon which they rest at this end being fixed
the consequence of the obliquity, or the inclination downwards, is, that when they come to move, whatever pulls
the ribs upwards, necessarily, at the same time, draws
them out; and that, whilst the ribs are brought to a right
angle with the spine behind, the sternum, or part of the
chest to which they are attached in front, is thrust forward.
The simple action, therefore, of the elevating muscles does
the business; whereas, if the ribs had been articulated with
the bodies of the vertebræ at right angles, the cavity of the
thorax could never have been farther enlarged by a change
of their position. If each rib had been a rigid bone, articulated at both ends to fixed bases, the whole chest had
been immoveable. Keill has observed, that the breastbone
in an easy inspiration, is thrust out one-tenth of an inch
and he calculates that this, added to what is gained to the
space within the chest by the flattening or descent of the
diaphragm, leaves room for forty-two cubic inches of air to
enter at every drawing-in of the breath. When there is a
necessity for a deeper and more laborious inspiration, the
enlargement of the capacity of the chest may be so increased by effort, as that the lungs may be distended with seventy
or a hundred such cubic inches. † The thorax, says Schel-
hammer, forms a kind of bellows, such as never have been,
nor probably will be, made by any artificer.‡

* For the mode of articulation of the ribs with the vertebræ, see Plate
IX. Fig. 1 and 2.

† Anat. p. 229.

‡ The thorax, or chest, is composed of bones and cartilages, so disposed as to sustain and protect the most vital parts, the heart and lungs,
and to turn and twist with perfect facility in every motion of the body;
and to be in incessant motion in the act of respiration, without a moment's
interval during a whole life. In anatomical description, the thorax is
formed of the vertebral column, or spine, on the back part, the ribs on
either side, and the breastbone, or sternum, on the fore part. But the
thing most to be admired is the manner in which these bones are united,
and especially the manner in which the ribs are joined to the breastbone,
by the interposition of cartilages, or gristle, of a substance softer than
bone, and more elastic and yielding. By this quality they are fitted for
protecting the chest against the effects of violence, and even for sustaining
life after the muscular power of respiration has become too feeble to continue without this support.

the ribs were complete circles, formed of bone, and extending from
the spine to the breastbone, life would be endangered by any accidental
fracture; and even the rubs and jolts to which the human frame is continually exposed, would be too much for their delicate and brittle texture

V   The *patella*, or kneepan is a curious little bone, in its form and office, unlike any other bone of the body. [Pl. X. fig. 2, 3.]   It is circular: the size of a crown piece; pretty thick; a little convex on both sides, and covered with a smooth cartilage.   It lies upon the front of the knee: and the powerful tendons, by which the leg is brought forward, pass into it, (or rather it makes a part of their continuation,) from their origin in the thigh to their insertion in

But these evils are avoided by the interposition of the elastic cartilage. On their fore part the ribs are eked out, and joined to the breastbone by means of cartilages, of a form corresponding to that of the ribs, being, as it were, a completion of the arch of the rib, by a substance more adapted to yield in every shock or motion of the body.   The elasticity of this portion subdues those shocks which would occasion the breaking of the ribs.   We lean forward, or to one side, and the ribs accommodate themselves, not by a change of form in the bones, but by the bending or elasticity of the cartilages.   A severe blow upon the ribs does not break them, because their extremities recoil and yield to the violence.   It is only in youth, however, when the human frame is in perfection, that this pliancy and elasticity have full effect.   When old age approaches, the cartilages of the ribs become bony.   They attach themselves firmly to the breastbone, and the extremities of the ribs are fixed, as if the whole arch were formed of bone unyielding and inelastic.   Then every violent blow upon the side is attended with fracture of the rib, an accident seldom occurring in childhood, or in youth.

But there is a purpose still more important to be accomplished by means of the elastic structure of the ribs, as partly formed of cartilage. This is in the action of breathing, or respiration; especially in the more highly-raised respiration which is necessary in great exertions of bodily strength, and in violent exercise.   There are two acts of breathing—*expiration*, or the sending forth of the breath ; and *inspiration*, or the drawing in of the breath.   When the chest is at rest, it is neither in a state of expiration nor in that of inspiration ; it is in an intermediate condition between these two acts.   And the muscular effort by which either inspiration or expiration is produced, is an act in opposition to the elastic property of the ribs.   The property of the ribs is to preserve the breast in the intermediate state between expiration and inspiration.   The muscles of respiration are excited alternately, to dilate or to contract the cavity of the chest, and, in doing so, to raise or to depress the ribs.   Hence it is, that both in inspiration and in expiration the elasticity of the ribs is called into play; and, were it within our province, it would be easy to show, that the dead power of the cartilages of the ribs preserve life by respiration, after the vital muscular power would, without such assistance, be too weak to continue life.

It will at once be understood, from what has now been explained, how, in age, violent exercise or exertion, is under restraint, in so far as it depends on respiration.   The elasticity of the cartilages is gone, the circle of the ribs is now unyielding, and will not allow that high breathing, that sudden and great dilating and contracting of the cavity of the chest, which is required for circulating the blood through the lungs, and relieving the heart amidst the more tumultuous flowing of the blood which exercise and exertion produce.—*Bell's Treatise on Animal Mechanics.*

the tibia. It protects both the tendon and the joint from any injury which either might suffer by the rubbing of one against the other, or by the pressure of unequal surfaces. It also gives to the tendons a very considerable mechanical advantage, by altering the line of their direction, and by advancing it farther out from the centre of motion; and this upon the principles of the resolution of force, upon which principles all machinery is founded. These are its uses. But what is most observable in it is, that it appears to be supplemental, as it were, to the frame; added, as it snould almost seem, afterward; not quite necessary, but very convenient. It is separate from the other bones; that is, it is not connected with any other bones by the common mode of union. It is soft, or hardly formed, in infancy; and produced by an ossification, of the inception or progress of which no account can be given from the structure or exercise of the part.

VI. The *shoulder-blade* is, in some material respects, a very singular bone: appearing to be made so expressly for its own purpose, and so independently of every other reason. [Pl. X. fig. 4.] In such quadrupeds as have no collar-bones, which are by far the greater number, the shoulder-blade has no bony communication with the trunk, either by a joint, or process, or in any other way. It does not grow to, or out of, any other bone of the trunk. It does not apply to any other bone of the trunk; (I know not whether this be true of any second bone in the body, except perhaps the os hyoïdes.) [Pl. X. fig. 5.] In strictness, it forms no part of the skeleton. It is bedded in the flesh; attached only to the muscles. It is no other than a foundation bone for the arm, laid in separate, as it were, and distinct, from the general ossification. The lower limbs connect themselves at the hip with bones which form a part of the skeleton; but this connexion, in the upper limbs, being wanted, a basis, whereupon the arm might be articulated, was to be supplied by a detached ossification for the purpose.

I. The above are a few examples of bones made remarkable by their configuration: but to almost all the bones belong *joints*; and in these, still more clearly than in the form or shape of the bones themselves, are seen both contrivance and contriving wisdom. Every joint is a curiosity, and is also strictly mechanical. There is the hinge-joint, and the mortice and tenon joint; each as manifestly such, and as accurately defined, as any which can be produced out of a cabinet-maker's sho·; and one

E*

or the other prevails, as either is adapted to the motion which is wanted: e. g. a mortice and tenon, or ball and socket joint, is not required at the knee, the leg standing in need only of a motion backward and forward in the same plane, for which a hinge-joint is sufficient; a mortice and tenon, o ball and socket joint, is wanted at the hip, that not only the progressive step may be provided for, but the interval between the limbs may be enlarged or contracted at pleasure.   Now, observe, what would have been the inconveniency, i. e. both the superfluity and the defect of articulation, if the case had been inverted: if the ball and socket joint had been at the knee, and the hinge-joint at the hip.   The thighs must have been kept constantly together, and the legs have been loose and straddling.   There would have been no use, that we know of, in being able to turn the calves of the legs before; and there would have been great confinement by restraining the motion of the thighs to one plane.   The disadvantage would not have been less, if the joints at the hip and the knee had been both of the same sort; both balls and sockets, or both hinges: yet why, independently of utility, and of a Creator who consulted that utility, should the same bone (the thigh-bone) be rounded at one end, and channelled at the other?

The *hinge-joint* is not formed by a bolt passing through the two parts of the hinge, and thus keeping them in their places; but by a different expedient.   A strong, tough, parchment-like membrane, rising from the receiving bones, and inserted all round the received bones a little below their heads, encloses the joint on every side.   This membrane ties, confines, and holds the ends of the bones together; keeping the corresponding parts of the joint, i. e. the relative convexities and concavities, in close application o each other.*

For the *ball and socket joint*, beside the membrane already described, there is in one important joint, as an additional security, a short, strong, yet flexible ligament, inserted by one end into the head of the ball, by the other

* This membrane is the *capsular*, or *bursal ligament*, common to every movable joint.   It certainly connects the bones together, but does not possess much strength: its chief use is to produce and preserve the synovia in the part where it is required.   The security and strength of the hinge-joint depends on certain ligaments called lateral ligaments, and the tendons of those muscles which pass over it.   In the particular instance of the knee, from its being the largest joint in the body, there is as we shall presently find, an additional contrivance to prevent dislocation
Paxton.

into the bottom of the cup; which ligament keeps the two parts of the joint so firmly in their place, that none of the motions which the limb naturally performs, none of the jerks and twists to which it is ordinarily liable, nothing less indeed than the utmost and the most unnatural violence, can pull them asunder   [Pl. XI. fig. 1.]   It is hardly imaginable, how great a force is necessary, even to stretch, still more to break, this ligament; yet so flexible is it, as to oppose no impediment to the suppleness of the joint * By its situation also, it is inaccessible to injury from sharp edges. As it cannot be ruptured, (such is its strength,) so it cannot be cut, except by an accident which would sever the limb. If I had been permitted to frame a proof of contrivance, such as might satisfy the most distrustful inquirer, I know not whether I could have chosen an example of mechanism more unequivocal, or more free from objection, than this ligament. Nothing can be more mechanical; nothing, however subservient to the safety, less capable of being generated by the action of the joint I would particularly solicit the reader's attention to this provision, as it is found in the head of the *thigh-bone*; to its strength, its structure, and its use. It is an instance upon which I lay my hand. One single fact, weighed by a mind in earnest, leaves oftentimes the deepest impression. For the purpose of addressing different understandings and different apprehensions—for the purpose of sentiment, for the purpose of exciting admiration of the Creator's works, we diversify our views, we multiply examples; but for the purpose of strict argument, one clear instance is sufficient; and not only sufficient, but capable, perhaps, of generating a firmer assurance than what can arise from a divided attention.

The *ginglymus*, or hinge-joint, does not, it is manifest, admit of a ligament of the same kind with that of the ball and socket joint, but it is always fortified by the species of ligament of which it does admit. The strong, firm, investing membrane, above described, accompanies it in every part; and in particular joints, this membrane, which is properly a ligament, is considerably stronger on the sides than either before or behind, in order that the convexities may play true in their concavities, and not be subject to slip sideways, which is the chief danger; for the muscular

* This ligament is also common to all quadrupeds, even in the more large and unwieldy, as the Hippopotamus and Rhinoceros—it is wanting in the elephant only, whose limbs, ill qualified for active increments, de not seem to require this security to the joint.—*Paxton*.

tendons generally restrain the parts from going farther than they ought to go in the plane of their motion. In the *knee*, which is a joint of this form, and of great importance, there are superadded to the common provisions for the stability of the joint, two strong ligaments which cross each other; and cross each other in such a manner, as to secure the joint from being displaced in any assignable direction. [Pl. XI. fig. 2.] "I think," says Cheselden, "that the knee cannot be completely dislocated without breaking the *cross* ligaments."* We can hardly help comparing this with the binding up of a fracture, where the fillet is almost always strapped across, for the sake of giving firmness and strength to the bandage.

Another no less important joint, and that also of the ginglymus sort, is the *ankle*; yet, though important, (in order, perhaps, to preserve the symmetry and lightness of the limb,) small, and, on that account, more liable to injury. [Pl. XI fig 4.] Now this joint is strengthened, *i. e.* is defended from dislocation, by two remarkable processes or prolongations of the bones of the leg: which processes form the protuberances that we call the inner and outer ankle. It is part of each bone going down lower than the other part, and thereby overlapping the joint: so that, if the joint be in danger of slipping outward, it is curbed by the inner projection, *i. e.* that of the tibia; if inward, by the outer projection, *i. e.* that of the fibula. Between both, it is locked in its position. I know no account that can be given of this structure, except its utility. Why should the tibia terminate, at its lower extremity, with a double end, and the fibula the same, but to barricade the joint on both sides by a continuation of part of the thickest of the bone over it? †

* Ches. Anat. ed. 7th, p. 45.

† The most obvious proof of contrivance is the junction of the foot to the bones of the leg at the ankle-joint. The two bones of the leg, called the *tibia* and the *fibula*, receive the great articulating bone of the foot (the *astragalus*) between them. And the extremities of these bones of the leg project so as to form the outer and inner ankle. Now, when we step forward, and whilst the foot is raised, it rolls easily upon the ends of these bones, so that the toe may be directed according to the inequalities of the ground we are to tread upon; but when the foot is planted, and the body is carried forward perpendicularly over the foot, the joint of the leg and foot becomes fixed, and we have a steady base to rest upon. We next observe, that, in walking, the heel first touches the ground. If the bones of the leg were perpendicular over the part which first touches the ground, we should come down with a sudden jolt, instead of which a descends end in a semicircle, the centre of which is the point of the heel And when the toes have come to the ground we are far from losing the

The joint at the *shoulder* compared with the joint at the hip, though both ball and socket joints, discovers a difference in their form and proportions, well suited to the different offices which the limbs have to execute. The cup or socket at the shoulder is much shallower and flatter than it is at the hip, and is also in part formed of cartilage set round the rim of the cup. The socket, into which the head of the thigh-bone is inserted, is deeper, and made of more solid materials.* This agrees with the duties as-

advantages of the structure of the foot, since we stand upon an e'astic arch, the hinder extremity of which is the heel, and the anterior the balls of the toes. A finely formed foot should be high in the instep. The walk of opera dancers is neither natural nor beautiful; but the surprising exercises which they perform give to the joints of the foot a freedom of motion almost like that of the hand. We have seen the dancers, in their morning exercises, stand for twenty minutes on the extremities of their toes, after which the effort is to bend the inner ankle down to the floor, in preparation for the Bolero step. By such unnatural postures and exercises the foot is made unfit for walking, as may be observed in any of the retired dancers and old *figurantes*. By standing so much upon the toes, the human foot is converted to something more resembling that of a quadruped, where the heel never reaches the ground, and where the paw is nothing more than the phalanges of the toes.

This arch of the foot, from the heel to the toe, has the astragalus, resembling the keystone of an arch; but, instead of being fixed, as in masonry, it plays freely between two bones, and from these two bones, a strong elastic ligament is extended, on which the bone rests, sinking or rising as the weight of the body bears upon it, or is taken off, and this it is enabled to do by the action of the ligament which runs under it.

This is the same elastic ligament which runs extensively along the back of the horse's hind leg and foot, and gives the fine spring to it, but which s sometimes ruptured by the exertion of the animal in a leap, producing irrecoverable lameness.

Having understood that the arch of the foot is perfect from the heel to the toe, we have next to observe, that there is an arch from side to side for when a transverse section is made of the bones of the foot, the exposed surface presents a perfect arch of wedges, regularly formed like the stones of an arch in masonry. If we look down upon the bones of the foot, we shall see that they form a complete circle horizontally, leaving a space in their centre. These bones thus form three different arches--forward; across; and horizontally: they are wedged together, and bound by ligaments, and this is what we alluded to when we said that the foundations of the Eddystone were not laid on a better principle; but our admiration is more excited in observing, that the bones of the foot are not only wedged together, like the courses of stone for resistance, but that solidity is combined with elasticity and lightness.

Notwithstanding the mobility of the foot in some positions, yet when the weight of the body bears directly over it, it becomes immovable, and the bones of the leg must be fractured before the foot yields.

Bell's Treatise on Animal Mechanics.

* The socket for the head of the thigh bone is indeed deeper than that at the shoulder, but the " materials " which form the concavities are ina

signed to each part The arm is an instrument of motion principally, if not solely. Accordingly the shallowness of the socket at the shoulder, and yieldingness of the cartilaginous substance with which its edge is set round, and which in fact composes a considerable part of its concavity, are excellently adapted for the allowance of a free motion and a wide range; both which the arm wants. Whereas, the lower limb, forming a part of the column of the body; having to support the body, as well as to be the means of its locomotion; firmness was to be consulted, as well as action. With a capacity for motion, in all directions indeed, as at the shoulder, but not in any direction to the same extent as in the arm, was to be united stability, or resistance to dislocation. Hence the deeper excavation of the socket; and the presence of a less proportion of cartilage upon the edge.

The suppleness and pliability of the joints we every moment experience; and the *firmness* of animal articulation, the property we have hitherto been considering, may be judged of from this single observation, that, at any given moment of time, there are millions of animal joints in complete repair and use, for one that is dislocated; and this, notwithstanding the contortions and wrenches to which the limbs of animals are continually subject.

II. The *joints*, or rather the ends of the bones which form them, display also, in their configuration, another use. The nerves, blood-vessels, and tendons, which are necessary to the life, or for the motion of the limbs, must, it is evident, in their way from the trunk of the body to the place of their destination, travel over the movable joints; and it is no less evident, that, in this part of their course, they will have, from sudden motions, and from abrupt changes of curvature, to encounter the danger of compression, attrition, or laceration. To guard fibres so tender against consequences so injurious, their path is in those parts protected with peculiar care; and that by a provision in the figure of the bones themselves. The nerves which supply the *fore-arm*, especially the inferior cubital nerves, are at the elbow conducted, by a kind of covered way, between the condyles, or rather under the inner extuberances of the bone, which composes the upper part of the arm.'

same; both are solid bone covered by cartilage, and both have a rim of a strong fibro-cartilaginous texture, not only for the purpose of rendering the socket deeper, but for preventing fractures of the rim in robust exercises, to which, were it bony, it would be very liable—*Paxton*
Clas. An o 255, ed. 7th

At the *knee*, the extremity of the thigh-bone is divided by a sinus or cleft into two heads or protuberances: and these heads on the back part stand out beyond the cylinder of the bone. Through the hollow, which lies between the hind parts of these two heads, that is to say, under the ham, between the hamstrings, and within the concave recess of the bone formed by the extuberances on each side; in a word, along a defile, between rocks, pass the great vessels and nerves which go to the leg.* Who led these vessels by a road so defended and so secured? In the joint at the *shoulder*, in the edge of the cup which receives the head of the bone, is a *notch* which is joined or covered at the top with a ligament. Through this hole, thus guarded, the blood-vessels steal to their destination in the arm, instead of mounting over the edge of the concavity.†

III. In all joints, the ends of the bones, which work against each other, are tipped with *gristle*. In the ball and socket joint, the cup is lined, and the ball capped with it. The smooth surface, the elastic and unfriable nature of cartilage, render it of all substances the most proper for the place and purpose. I should, therefore, have pointed this out amongst the foremost of the provisions which have been made in the joints for the facilitating of their action, had it not been alleged, that cartilage in truth is only nascent or imperfect bone; and that the bone in these places is kept soft and imperfect, in consequence of a more complete and rigid ossification being prevented from taking place by the continual motion and rubbing of the surfaces; which being so, what we represent as a designed advantage, is an unavoidable effect. I am far from being convinced that this is a true account of the fact, or that, if it were so, it answers the argument. To me, the surmounting of the ends of the bones with gristle, looks more like a plating with a different metal, than like the same metal kept in a different state by the action to which it is exposed At all events, we have a great particular benefit, though arising from a general constitution: but this last not being quite what my argument requires, lest I should seem by applying the instance to overrate its value, I have thought it fair to state the question which attends it.

IV. In some joints, very particularly in the knees, there are loose cartilages or gristles between the bones, and within the joint, so that the ends of the bones, instead of working upon one another, work upon the intermediate cartilages. [Pl. XI. fig. 3.] Cheselden has observed‡ that the

* Ches. An. p. 35.　† Ib. 30.　‡ Ib. p. 13.

contrivance of a loose ring is practised by mechanics, where the friction of the joints of any of their machines is great, as between the parts of crooked-hinges of large gates, or under the head of the male screw of large vices. The cartilages of which we speak, have very much of the form of these rings. The comparison moreover shows the reason why we find them in the knees rather than in other joints. It is an expedient, we have seen, which a mechanic resorts to, only when some strong and heavy work is to be done. So here the thigh bone has to achieve its motion at the knee, with the whole weight of the body pressing upon it, and often, as in rising from our seat, with the whole weight of the body to lift. It should seem also, from Cheselden's account, that the slipping and sliding of the loose cartilages, though it be probably a small and obscure change, humored the motion of the end of the thigh-bone, under the particular configuration which was necessary to be given to it for the commodious action of the tendons; (and which configuration requires what he calls a variable socket, that is, a concavity, the lines of which assume a different curvature in different inclinations of the bones.)

V. We have now done with the configuration: but there is also in the joints, and that common to them all, another exquisite provision, manifestly adapted to their use, and concerning which there can, I think, be no dispute, namely, the regular supply of a *mucilage*, more emollient and slippery than oil itself, which is constantly softening and lubricating the parts that rub upon each other, and thereby diminishing the effect of attrition in the highest possible degree.* For the continual secretion of this important liniment, and for the feeding of the cavities of the joint with it, glands are fixed near each joint; the excretory ducts of which glands dripping with their balsamic contents, hang loose like fringes within the cavity of the joints. A late improvement in what are called friction wheels, which consists of a mechanism so ordered, as to be regularly dropping oil into a box, which encloses the axis, the nave, and certain balls upon which the nave revolves, may be said, in some sort, to represent the contrivance in the animal joint; with this superiority, however, on the

* This mucilage is termed *synovia* ; vulgarly called joint oil, but it has no property of oil. It is very viscid, and at the same time smooth and slippery to the touch; and therefore better adapted than any oil to lubricate the interior of the joints and prevent ill effects from friction.
Paxton

part of the joint, viz. that here, the oil is not only dropped, but *made.**

In considering the joints, there is nothing, perhaps, which ought to move our gratitude more than the reflection, *how well they wear.* A limb shall swing upon its hinge, or play in its socket, many hundred times in an hour, for sixty years together, without diminution of its agility: which is a long time for anything to last; for anything so much worked and exercised as the joints are. This durability I should attribute, in part, to the provision which is made for the preventing of wear and tear, first by the polish of the cartilaginous surfaces, secondly, by the healing lubrication of the mucilage; and, in part, to that astonishing property of animal constitutions, assimilation; by which, in every portion of the body, let it consist of what it will, substance is restored, and waste repaired.†

* A joint then consists of the union of two bones, of such a form as to permit the necessary motion; but they are not in contact; each articulating surface is covered with cartilage, to prevent the jar which would result from the contact of the bones. This cartilage is elastic, and the celebrated Dr. Hunter discovered that the elasticity was in consequence of a number of filaments closely compacted, and extending from the surface of the bone, so that each filament is perpendicular to the pressure made upon it. The surface of the articulating cartilage is perfectly smooth, and is lubricated by a fluid called *synovia,* sygnifying a mucilage, a viscous or thick liquor. This is vulgarly called *joint oil,* but it has no property of oil, although it is better calculated than any oil to lubricate the interior of the joint.

When inflammation comes upon a joint, this fluid is not supplied, and the joint is stiff, and the surfaces creak upon one another like a hinge without oil. A delicate membrane extends from bone to bone, confining this lubricating fluid, and forming the boundary of what is termed the cavity of the joint, although, in fact, there is no unoccupied space. External to this capsule of the joint, there are strong ligaments going from point to point of the bones, and so ordered as to bind them together without preventing their proper motions. From this description of a single joint, we can easily conceive what a spring or elasticity is given to the foot, where thirty-six bones are joined together.—*Bell's Treatise on Animal Mechanics.*

† If the ingenious author's mind had been professionally called to contemplate this subject, he would have found another explanation. There is no resemblance between the provisions against the wear and tear of machinery and those for the preservation of a living part. As the structure of the parts is originally perfected by the action of the vessels, the function or operation of the part is made the stimulus to those vessels. The cuticle on the hands wears away like a glove; but the pressure stimulates the living surface to force successive layers of skin under that which is wearing, or, as the anatomists call it, desquamating; by which they mean, that the cuticle does not change at once, but comes off in *squamæ,* or scales. The teeth are subject to pressure in chewing or masticating, and they would, by this action, have been driven deeper in the jaw, and

Movable joints, I think, compose the curiosity of bones but their union, even where no motion is intended or wanted, carries marks of mechanism and of mechanical wisdom. The teeth, especially the front teeth, are one bone fixed in another, like a peg driven into a board. The sutures of the skull are like the edges of two saws clapped together, in such a manner as that the teeth of one enter the intervals of the other.* We have sometimes one bone lapping over another, and planed down at the edges; sometimes also the thin lamella of one bone received into a narrow furrow of another. In all which varieties, we seem to discover the same design, viz. firmness of juncture, without clumsiness in the seam.

CHAPTER IX.

OF THE MUSCLES.

MUSCLES, with their tendons, are the instruments by which animal motion is performed. It will be our business

rendered useless, had there not been a provision against this mechanical effect. This provision is a disposition to grow, or rather to shoot out of their sockets; and this disposition to project, balances the pressure which they sustain: and when one tooth is lost, its opposite rises, and is in danger of being lost also, for want of that very opposition.—*Bell's Treatise on Animal Mechanics.*

* Most of the bones of the skull are composed of two plates or *tablets*, with an intermediate spongy, vascular substance; the outer tablet is *fibrous*, having the edges curiously indented and united by a *dove-tailed* sure; the inner from its brittleness is called *vitreous*, and therefore merely joined together in a straight line; this mode of union is not accidental—not the result of chance, but design. The author of the treatise on "Animal Mechanics" gives the following admirable illustration of the structure:—

"Suppose a carpenter employed upon his own material—he would join a box with regular indentations by dove-tailing, because he knows that the material on which he works, from its softness and toughness, admits of such adjustment of its edges. The processes of bone shoot into the opposite cavities with an exact resemblance to the fox-tail wedge of the carpenter.

"But if a workman in glass or marble were to join these materials, he would smooth the edges and unite them by cement; for if he could succeed in indenting the line of union, he knows that his material would chip off on the slightest vibration.

"Now apply this principle to the skull, the outer table, which resembles wood, is indented and dove-tailed; the inner glassy table has its edges simply laid in contact."—*Paxton.*

r) p .nt out instances in which, and properties with respect to which, the disposition of these muscles is as strictly mechanical, as that of the wires and strings of a puppet.*

I. We may observe, what I believe is universal, an exact relation between the joint and the muscles which move it. Whatever motion the joint, by its mechanical construction, is capable of performing, that motion, the annexed muscles, by their position, are capable of producing. For example; if there be, as at the knee and elbow, a hinge-joint, capable of motion only in the same plane, the leaders, as they are called, i. e. the muscular tendons, are placed in directions parallel to the bone, so as, by the contraction or relaxation of the muscles to which they belong to produce that motion and no other. If these joints were capable of a freer motion, there are no muscles to produce it. Whereas at the shoulder and the hip, where the ball and socket joint allows by its construction of a rotatory or sweeping motion, tendons are placed in such a position, and pull in such a direction, as to produce the motion of which the joint admits. For instance, the sartorius or tailor's muscle, rising from the spine, running diagonally across the thigh, and taking hold of the inside of the main bone of the leg, a little below the knee, enables us, by its contraction, to throw one leg and thigh over the other; giving effect, at the same time, to the ball and socket joint at the hip, and the hinge-joint at the knee. [Pl. XII. fig. 1.]

There is, as we have seen, a specific mechanism in the bones, for the rotatory motions of the head and hands; there is, also, in the oblique direction of the muscles belonging to them, a specific provision for the putting of this mechanism of the bones into action. [Pl. XII. fig. 2.] And mark the consent of uses. The oblique muscles would have been inefficient without that particular articulation; that particular articulation would have been lost, without the oblique muscles. It may be proper, however, to observe with respect to the *head*, although I think it does not vary the case, that its oblique motions and inclinations are often motions in a *diagonal*, produced by the joint action of mus-

* Muscles are the *fleshy* parts of the body which surround the bones, having a fibrous texture; a muscle being composed of a number of *muscular faciculi*, which are composed of fibres still smaller; these result from fibres of a less volume, until by successive division we arrive at very small fibres no longer divisible. These muscular fibres are longer o shorter according to the muscles to which they belong; and every fibre is fixed by its two extremities to *tendon* or *aponeurosis*, which are the " wires and strings which conduct the muscular power when they contract.—*Paxton.*

cles lying in straight direction. But whether the pull be single or combined, the articulation is always such, as .o be
capable of obeying the action of the muscles. The oblique
muscles attached to the head, are likewise so disposed, as
to be capable of the steadying the globe, as well as of mov-
,ng it. The head of a new-born infant is often obliged to
oe filleted up. After death, the head drops and rolls in
every direction. So that it is by the equilibre of the muscles, by the aid of a considerable and equipollent muscular
force in constant exertion, that the head maintains its erect
posture. The muscles here supply what would otherwise
be a great defect in the articulation; for the joint in the
neck, although admirably adapted to the motion of the head,
is insufficient for its support. It is not only by the means of
a most curious structure of the bones that a man turns his
head, but by virtue of an adjusted muscular power, that he
even holds it up.

As another example of what we are illustrating, viz. con
formity of use between the bones and the muscles, it has
been observed of the different vertebræ, that their processes are exactly proportioned to the quantity of motion which
the other bones allow of, and which the respective muscles
are capable of producing.

II. A muscle acts only by contraction. Its force is exerted in no other way. When the exertion ceases, it relax-
es itself, that is, it returns by relaxation to its former state;
but without energy. This is the nature of the muscular
fibre: and being so, it is evident that the reciprocal *ener-*
getic motion of the limbs, by which we mean motion *with*
force in opposite directions, can only be produced by the
instrumentality of opposite or antagonist muscles; of flexors
and extensors answering to each other. For instance, the
biceps and brachiæus *internus* muscles, placed in the front
part of the upper arm, by their contraction bend the elbow;
and with such degree of force, as the case requires, or the
strength admits of. [Pl. XIII. fig. 1.] The relaxation of
these muscles, after the effort, would merely let the fore-
arm drop down. For the *back stroke*, therefore, and that
the arm may not only bend at the elbow, but also extend and
straighten itself, with force, other muscles, the longus and
brevis brachiæus *externus*, and the anconæus, placed on
the hinder part of .he arms, by their contractile twitch fetch
back the fore-arm into a straight line with the cubit, with
no less force than that with which it was bent out of it
The same thing obtains in all the limbs, and in every mov
able part of the body. A finger is not bent and straigl ter

ed, without the contraction of two muscles taking place. It is evident, therefore, that the animal functions require that particular disposition of the muscles which we describe by the name of antagonist muscles. And they are accordingly so disposed. Every muscle is provided with an adversary. They act, like two sawyers in a pit by an opposite pull; and nothing surely can more strongly indicate design and attention to an end, than their being thus stationed; than this collocation. The nature of the muscular fibre being what it is, the purposes of the animal could be answered by no other. And not only the capacity for motion, but the aspect and symmetry of the body, is preserved by the muscles being marshalled according to this order, *e. g.* the mouth is *holden* in the middle of the face, and its angles kept in a state of exact correspondency, by several muscles drawing against, and balancing each other. [See Pl. XI. fig. 3.] In a hemiplegia, when the muscles on one side are weakened, the muscles on the other side draw the mouth awry.

III Another property of the muscles, which could only be the result of care, is, their being almost universally so disposed, as not to obstruct or interfere with one another's action. I know but one instance in which this impediment is perceived. We cannot easily swallow whilst we gape. This, I understand, is owing to the muscles employed in the act of deglutition, being so implicated with the muscles of the lower jaw, that, whilst these last are contracted, the former cannot act with freedom. The obstruction is, in this instance, attended with little inconveniency; but it shows what the effect is where it does exist; and what loss of faculty there would be if it were more frequent. Now, when we reflect upon the number of muscles, not fewer than four hundred and forty-six in the human body, known and named,* how contiguous they lie to each other, in layers, as it were, over one another, crossing one another, sometimes embedded in one another; sometimes perforating one another; an arrangement, which leaves to each its liberty, and its full play, must necessarily require meditation and counsel

IV. The following is oftentimes the case with the muscles. Their action is wanted, where their situation would be inconvenient. In which case, the body of the muscle is placed in some commodious position at a distance, and made to communicate with the point of action, by slender

* Keill's Anat. p. 295, edit. 3. There are, however, five hundred and twenty-seven muscles described by more modern anatomists.
Paston.

G*

strings or wires. If the muscles which move the fingers had been placed in the palm or back of the hand, they would have swelled that part to an awkward and clumsy thickness. The beauty, the proportions of the part would have been destroyed. They are, therefore, disposed in the arm, and even up to the elbow; and act by long tendons strapped down at the wrist, and passing under the ligaments to the fingers, and to the joints of the fingers, which they are severally to move. [Pl. XIII. fig. 1, 2.] In like manner, the muscles which move the toes, and many of the joints of the foot, how gracefully are they disposed in the calf of the leg, instead of forming an unwieldy tumefaction in the foot itself The observation may be repeated of the muscle which draws the nictitating membrane over the eye. Its office is in the front of the eye; but its body is lodged in the back part of the globe, where it lies safe, [Pl. IV. fig 2, 3,] and where it encumbers nothing.*

V. The great mechanical variety in the figure of the muscles may be thus stated. It appears to be a fixed law, that the contraction of a muscle shall be towards its centre Therefore, the subject for mechanism on each occasion is, so to modify the figure, and adjust the position of the muscle, as to produce the motion required, agreeably with this law. This can only be done by giving to different muscles a diversity of configuration, suited to their several offices, and to their situation with respect to the work which they have to perform. On which account we find them under a multiplicity of forms and attitudes; sometimes with double, sometimes with treble tendons, sometimes with none: sometimes one tendon to several muscles, at other times one muscle to several tendons. The shape of the organ is susceptible of an incalculable variety, whilst the original property of the muscle, the law and line of its contraction, remains the same, and is simple. Herein the muscular system may be said to bear a perfect resemblance to our works of art. An artist does not alter the native

* The convenience and beauty of the tendons seem only an ulterior object, their necessity and utility principally claim our attention. The force which a muscle possesses is as the number of the muscular fibres, but a limited number of fibres only can be fixed to any certain point of bone destined to be moved, therefore the contrivance is, to attach them to a cord, called a sinew or tendon, which can be conveniently conducted and fixed to the bone. If we are desirous of moving a heavy weight, we tie a strong cord to it, that a greater number of men may apply their strength. Thus a similar effect is produced—the muscular fibres are the moving powers, the tendons are the cords attached to the point to be moved.- -*Paxton.*

quality of his materials, or their laws of action. He takes these as he finds them. His skill and ingenuity are employed in turning them, such as they are, to his account, by giving to the parts of his machine a form and relation, in which these unalterable properties may operate to the production of the effects intended.

VI. The ejaculations can never too often be repeated. — How many things must go right for us to be an hour at ease! how many more, to be vigorous and active! Yet vigor and activity are, in a vast plurality of instances, preserved in human bodies, notwithstanding that they depend upon so great a number of instruments of motion, and notwithstanding that the defect or disorder sometimes of a very small instrument, of a single pair, for instance, out of the four hundred and forty-six muscles which are employed, may be attended with grievous inconveniency. There is piety and good sense in the following observation taken out of the *Religious Philosopher:* "With much compassion," says this writer, "as well as astonishment at the goodness of our loving Creator, have I considered the sad state of a certain gentleman, who, as to the rest, was in pretty good health, but only wanted the use of these *two little muscles* that serve to lift up the eyelids, [Pl. XIV. fig. 1, 2,] and so had almost lost the use of his sight, being forced, as long as this defect lasted, to shove up his eyelids every moment with his own hands!" In general we may remark, how little those who enjoy the perfect use of their organs, know the comprehensiveness of the blessing, the variety of their obligation. They perceive a result, but they think little of the multitude of concurrences and rectitudes which go to form it.

Besides these observations, which belong to the muscular organ as such, we may notice some advantages of structure, which are more conspicuous in muscles of a certain class or description than in others. Thus:

I. The variety, quickness, and precision, of which muscular motion is capable, are seen, I think, in no part so remarkable as in the *tongue.* It is worth any man's while to watch the agility of his tongue; the wonderful promptitude with which it executes changes of position, and the perfect exactness. Each syllable of articulated sound requires for its utterance a specific action of the tongue and of the parts adjacent to it. The disposition and configuration of the mouth, appertaining to every letter and word, is not only peculiar, but, if nicely and accurately attended to, perceptible to the sight, insomuch, that curious persons have availed themselves of this circumstance to teach the deaf to speak, and to understand what is said by others In the same person, and after his habit of speaking is formed, one, and only one, position of the parts, vill produce a given articulate sound correctly. How instantaneously are these positions assumed and dismissed! how numerous are the permutations, how various, yet how infallible! Arbitrary and antic variety is not the thing we admire; but variety obeying a rule, conducing to an effect, and commensurate with exigencies infinitely diversified. I believe also that the anatomy of the tongue corresponds with these observations upon its activity. The muscles of the tongue are so numerous and so implicated with one another, that they cannot be traced by the nicest dissection; nevertheless (which is a great perfection of the organ,) neither the number, nor the complexity. nor what might seem to be the entanglement of its fibres, in anywise impede its motion, or render the determination or success of its efforts uncertain.

I here entreat the reader's permission to step a little out of my way, to consider *the parts of the mouth*, in some of their other properties. It has been said, and that by an eminent physiologist, that, whenever nature attempts to work two or more purposes by one instrument, she does both or all imperfectly. Is this true of the tongue, regarded as an instrument of speech, and of taste; or regarded as an instrument of speech, of taste and of deglutition? So much otherwise, that many persons, that is to say, nine hundred and ninety-nine persons out of a thousand, by the instrumentality of this one organ, talk, and taste, and swallow, very well. In fact, the constant warmth and moisture of the tongue, the thinness of the skin, the papillæ upon its surface, qualify this organ for its office of tasting, as much as its inextricable multiplicity of fibres do for the rapid movements which are necessary to speech. Animals which feed upon grass, have their tongues covered with a perforated skin, so as to admit the dissolved food to the papil.æ underneath, which, in the meantime, remain defended from the rough action of the unbruised spiculæ.*

---

* *Papillæ* are small bodies situated on the surface and sides of the tongue; they are furnished by the extreme filaments of the gustatory nerve, through which medium we acquire the sense of tasting. In her oivorous animals the papillæ are sharp pointed and directed backwards ﹘ assist in laying hold of the grass. In the cat kind there is a horny or prickly set covering the tongue, rendering it rough, and enabling it to

There are brought together within the cavity of the mouth more distinct uses, and parts executing more distinct offices, than I think can be found lying so near to one another, or within the same compass, in any other portion of the body: viz. teeth of different shape,* first for cutting; secondly for grinding: muscles, most artificially disposed for carrying on the compound motion of the lower jaw, half lateral and half vertical, by which the mill is worked: fountains of saliva, springing up in different parts of the cavity for the moistening of the food, whilst the mastication is going on: glands,† to feed the fountains; a muscular constriction of a very peculiar kind in the back part of the cavity, for the guiding of the prepared aliment into its passage towards the stomach, and in many cases for carrying it along that passage; for, although we may imagine this to be done simply by the weight of the food itself, it in truth is not so, even in the upright posture of the human neck; and most evidently is not the case with quadrupeds, with a horse for instance, in which, when pasturing, the food is thrust upward by muscular strength, instead of descending of its own accord.

In the meantime, and within the same cavity, is going on another business, altogether different from what is here described, that of respiration and speech. In addition therefore, to all that has been mentioned, we have a passage opened, from this cavity to the lungs, for the admission of air, exclusively of every other substance; we have muscles, some in the larynx, and without number in the tongue, for the purpose of modulating that air in its passage, with a variety, a compass, and precision, of which no other musical instrument is capable. And, lastly, which in my opinion crowns the whole as a piece of machinery, we have a specific contrivance for dividing the pneumatic part from

take firmer hold of the prey. Birds also have a similar contrivance. In fish the tongue is covered by a number of teeth, serving the same purpose.
Paxton.

* In each jaw there are *four incisores*, or cutting teeth, *two canine* which may be ranked with the former, only more pointed; four small *molar*, and six large molar or grinding teeth. And as the teeth of animals indicate the food on which they are destined to subsist, so from analogy we may infer that man is called to use either animal or vegetable aliments, or both, *i. e.* keeps a mean between graminivorous and carnivorous animals, in the structure and complication of his digestive apparatus, without deserving on that account to be called omnivorous: for it is known, that, a great number of the substances upon which animals feed are of no use in the support of man.—*Paxton.*

† The principal of these are the *parotids*, see Plate XX.

the mechanical, and for preventing one set of actions in
terfering with the other. Where various functions are
united, the difficulty is to guard against the inconveniences of a too great complexity. In no apparatus put
together by art, and for the purposes of art, do I know such
multifarious uses so aptly combined, as in the natural organization of the human mouth; or, where the structure,
compared with the uses, is so simple. The mouth, with all
these intentions to serve, is a single cavity; is one machine,
with its parts neither crowded nor confused, and each un-
embarrassed by the rest: each at least at liberty in a degree sufficient for the end to be attained. If we cannot
eat and sing at the same moment, we can eat one moment,
and sing the next: the respiration proceeding freely all the
while.

There is one case, however, of this double office, and
that of the *earliest* necessity, which the mouth alone could
not perform; and that is, carrying on together the two actions of sucking and breathing. Another route, therefore,
is opened for the air, namely, through the nose, which lets
the breath pass backward and forward, whilst the lips, in the
act of sucking, are necessarily shut close upon the body
from which the nutriment is drawn. This is a circumstance which always appeared to me worthy of notice.
The nose would have been necessary, although it had not
been the organ of smelling. The making it the seat of a
sense, was superadding a new use to a part already wanted;
was taking a wise advantage of an antecedent and a con-
stitutional necessity.

But to return to that which is the proper subject of the
present section—the celerity and precision of muscular motion. These qualities may be particularly observed in the
execution of many pieces of instrumental *music*, in which
the changes produced by the hand of the musician are exceedingly rapid; are exactly measured, even when most
minute; and display, on the part of the muscles, an obedience of action, alike wonderful for its quickness and its
correctness.

Or let a person only observe his own hand whilst he is
writing; the number of muscles which are brought to
bear upon the pen: how the joint and adjusted operation
of several tendons is concerned in every stroke, yet that
five hundred such strokes are drawn in a minute. Not a
letter can be turned without more than one, or two, or three
tendinous retractions, definite, both as to the choice of

the tendon, and as to the space through which the retraction moves; yet how currently does the work proceed
and when we look at it, how faithful have the muscles
been to their duty, how true to the order which endeavour
or habit hath inculcated! For let it be remembered, that
whilst a man's hand-writing is the same, an exactitude of
order is preserved, whether he write well or ill These
two instances, of music and writing, show not only the
quickness and precision of muscular action, but the do
cility.

II.   Regarding the particular configuration of muscles
sphincter or circular muscles appear to me admirable pieces
of mechanism. [Pl. XIV. fig. 3.] It is the muscular power most happily applied; the same quality of the muscular
substance, but under a new modification.   The circular
disposition of the fibres is strictly mechanical; but, though
the most mechanical, is not the only thing in sphincters
which deserves our notice.   The regulated degree of contractile force with which they are endowed, sufficient for
retention, yet vincible when requisite; together with their
ordinary state of actual contraction, by means of which
their dependence upon the will is not constant, but occasional, gives to them a constitution, of which the conveniency
is inestimable.   This their semi-voluntary character, is exactly such as suits with the wants and functions of the animal.

III.   We may also, upon the subject of muscles, observe,
that many of our most important actions are achieved by
the combined help of different muscles.   Frequently, a
diagonal motion is produced by the retraction of tendons
pulling in the direction of the sides of the parallelogram.
This is the case, as hath been already noticed, with some
of the oblique nutations of the head.   Sometimes the number of co-operating muscles is very great.   Dr. Nieuentyt,
in the Leipsic Transactions, reckons up a hundred muscles
that are employed every time we breathe; yet we take in,
or let out, our breath, without reflecting what a work is
thereby performed; what an apparatus is laid in, of instruments for the service, and how many such contribute their
assistance to the effect!   Breathing with ease, is a blessing
of every moment; yet, of all others, it is that which we
possess with the least consciousness.   A man in an asthma
is the only man who knows how to estimate it.

IV.   Sir Everard Home has observed,* that the most
important and the most delicate actions are performed in the

* Phil. Trans. part 1 1800. p 8

body by the smallest muscles; and he mentions, as his examples, the muscles which have been discovered in the iris of the eye, and the drum of the ear. The tenuity of these muscles is astonishing. They are microscopic hairs, must be magnified to be visible; yet they are real, effective muscles; and not only such, but the grandest and most precious of our faculties, sight and hearing, depend upon their health and action.

V. The muscles act in the limbs with what is called a mechanical disadvantage. The muscle at the shoulder, [Pl. XIII. fig. 1. f.] by which the arm is raised, is fixed nearly in the same manner as the load is fixed upon a steelyard, within a few decimals, we will say, of an inch, from the centre upon which the steelyard turns. In this situation, we find that a very heavy draught is no more than sufficient to countervail the force of a small lead plummet, placed upon the long arm of the steelyard, at the distance of perhaps fifteen or twenty inches from the centre, and on the other side of it. And this is the disadvantage which is meant. And an absolute disadvantage, no doubt, would be, if the object were to spare the force of muscular contraction. But observe how conducive is this constitution to animal conveniency. Mechanism has always in view one or other of these two purposes; either to move a great weight slowly, and through a small space; or to move a light weight rapidly, through a considerable sweep. For the former of these purposes, a different species of lever, and a different collocation of the muscles, might be better than the present; but for the second, the present structure is the true one. Now so it happens, that the second, and not the first, is that which the occasions of animal life principally call for. In what concerns the human body, it is of much more consequence to any man to be able to carry his hand to his head with due expedition, than it would be to have the power of raising from the ground a heavier load (of two or three more hundred weight, we will suppose,) than he can lift at present. This last is a faculty, which on some extraordinary occasions he may desire to possess, but the other is what he wants, and uses every hour and minute. In like manner, a husbandman, or a gardener, will do more execution, by being able to carry his scythe, his rake, or his flail, with a sufficient despatch through a sufficient space, than if, with greater strength, his motions were proportionably more confined and slow. It is the same with a mechanic in the use of his tools. It is the same also with other animals in the use of their limbs. In general, the vivacity of their motions would be ill exchanged for greater force under a clumsier structure.

We have offered our observations upon the structure of muscles in general; we have also noticed certain species of muscles; but there are also *single* muscles, which bear marks of mechanical contrivance, appropriate as well as particular. Out of many instances of this kind, we select the following:—

I. Of muscular actions, even of those which are well understood, some of the most curious are incapable of popular explanation; at least, without the aid of plates and figures.* This is in a great measure the case, with a very familiar, but, at the same time, a very complicated motion—that of the *lower jaw*; and with the muscular structure by which it is produced One of the muscles concerned may, however, be described in such a manner, as to be, I think, sufficiently comprehended for our present purpose. The problem is to pull the lower jaw *down*. The obvious method should seem to be, to place a straight muscle, viz. to fix a string from the chin to the breast, the contraction of which would open the mouth, and produce the motion required at once. But it is evident that the form and liberty of the neck forbid a muscle being laid in such a position; and that, consistently with the preservation of this form, the motion, which we want, must be effectuated by some muscular mechanism disposed farther back in the jaw. The mechanism adopted is as follows: [Pl. XV. fig. 1, 2.] A certain muscle called the *digastric*, rises on the side of the face, considerably *above* the insertion of the lower jaw, and comes down, being converted in its progress into a round tendon. Now, it is evident, that the tendon, whilst it pursues a direction *descending* towards the jaw, must, by its contraction, pull the jaw up, instead of down. What then was to be done? This, we find is done: The descending tendon, when it is got low enough, is passed through a loop, or ring, or pulley, in the os hyoïdes, and then made to ascend: and, having thus changed its line of direction, is inserted into the inner part of the chin: by which device, viz. the turn at the loop, the action of the muscle (which in all muscles is contraction) that before would have pulled the jaw up, now as necessarily draws it down. "The mouth," says Heister, "is opened by means of this trochlea in a most wonderful and elegant manner."

II. What contrivance can be more mechanical than

* The want of the aid of plates and figures, which the author here expresses, is now supplied in this Boston edition.

the following, viz. a slit in one tendon to let another ten
don pass through it?   This structure is found in the ten
dons which move the toes and fingers.   The long tendon
as it is called, in the foot, which bends the first joint of the
toe, passes *through* the short tendon which bends the second joint; which course allows to the sinew more liberty,
and a more commodious action than it would otherwise
have been capable of exerting.* [Pl. XVI. fig. 1, 2.] Thero
is nothing, I believe, in a silk or cotton mill, in the belts,
or straps, or ropes, by which motion is communicated fiom
one part of the machine to another, that is more artificial,
or more evidently so, than this *perforation*.

III.   The next circumstance which I shall mention, under this head of muscular arrangement, is so decisive a
mark of intention, that it always appeared to me, to super-
sede, in some measure, the necessity of seeking for any
other observation upon the subject; and that circumstance
is, the tendons, which pass from the leg to the foot, being
bound down by a ligament at the ankle. [Pl. XVI. fig. 3.]
The foot is placed at a considerable angle with the leg
It is manifest, therefore, that flexible strings, passing along
the interior of the angle, if left to themselves, would, when
stretched, start from it.   The obvious preventive is to tie
them down.   And this is done in fact.   Across the instep,
or rather just above it, the anatomist finds a strong ligament *under* which the tendons pass to the foot.   The ef
fect of the ligament as a bandage, can be made evident to
the senses; for if it be cut, the tendons start up.   The
simplicity, yet the clearness of this contrivance, its exact
resemblance to established resources of art, place it amongst
the most indubitable manifestations of design with which
we are acquainted.

There is also a farther use to be made of the present
example, and that is, as it precisely contradicts the opinion, that the parts of animals may have been all formed
by what is called appetency, *i. e.* endeavour, perpetuated,
and imperceptibly working its effect, through an incalcu-
able series of generations.   We have here no endeavour.
but the reverse of it; a constant reniteney and reluctance
The endeavour is all the other way.   The pressure of the
ligament constrains the tendons; the tendons react upon
the pressure of the ligament.   It is impossible that the ligament should ever have been generated by the exercise of
the tendon, or in the course of that exercise, forasmuch as

* Ches. Anat. p. 94, 119

the force of the tendon perpendicularly resists the fibre which confines it, and is constantly endeavouring, not to form, but to rupture and displace, the threads of which the ligament is composed.

Keill has reckoned up, in the human body, four hundred and forty-six muscles, [See note, p. 77,] dissectible and describable; and hath assigned a use to every one of the number. This cannot be all imagination.

Bishop Wilkins hath observed from Galen, that there are, at least, ten several qualifications to be attended to in each particular muscle; viz. its proper figure; its just magnitude; its fulcrum; its point of action, supposing the figure to be fixed; its collocation, with respect to its two ends, the upper and the lower; the place; the position of the whole muscle; the introduction into it of nerves, arteries, and veins. How are things, including so many adjustments, to be made, or, when made, how are they to be put together, without intelligence?

I have sometimes wondered, why we are not struck with mechanism in animal bodies, as readily and as strongly as we are struck with it, at first sight, in a watch or a mill. One reason of the difference may be, that animal bodies are, in a great measure, made up of soft, flabby substances, such as muscles and membranes; whereas we have been accustomed to trace mechanism in sharp lines, in the configuration of hard materials, in the moulding, chiseling, and filing into shapes, such articles as metals or wood. There is something, therefore, of habit in the case; but it is sufficiently evident, that there can be no proper reason for any distinction of the sort. Mechanism may be displayed in one kind of substance, as well as in the other.

Although the few instances we have selected, even as they stand in our description, are nothing short perhaps of logical proofs of design, yet it must not be forgotten, that, in every part of anatomy, description is a poor substitute for inspection. It is well said by an able anatomist,* and said in reference to the very part of the subject which we have been treating of:—"Imperfecta hæc musculorum descriptio, non minùs arida est legentibus quàm inspectantibus fuerit jucunda eorundem præparatio Elegantiss·ma enim mechanicês artificia, creberrimè in illis obvia verbis nonnisi obscurè exprimuntu·: carnium

* Sterno in Blas. Anat. Animal. p. 2. c 4.

autem ductu, tendinum colore, insertionum proportione
et trochlearium distributione, oculis exposita, omnen su-
perant admiralionem."

The following remarks upon the structure of the tendons, from the Animal Mechanics already quoted, will form an instructive addition to he fore-
going chapter, to the subject of which they bear a near relation.—*Ea*

Of the Cordage of the Tendons.

Where nature has provided a perfect system of columns and
levers, and pullies, we may anticipate that the cords by which the
force of the muscles is concentrated on the movable bones, must
ne constructed with as curious a provision for their offices.   In
this surmise we shall not be disappointed.

To understand what is necessary to the strength of a rope or a
cable, we must learn what has been the object of the improvements and patents in this manufacture. The first process in rope-
making, is hatchelling the hemp: that is, combing out the short
fibres, and placing the long ones parallel to one another. The
second is, spinning the hemp into yarns. And here the principle
must be attended to, which goes through the whole process in
forming a cable; which is that the fibres of the hemp shall
bear an equal strain: and the difficulty may be easily conceived,
since the twisting must derange the parallel position of the fibres.
Each fibre, as it is twisted, ties the other fibres together, so as to
form a continued line, and it bears, at the same time, a certain portion of the strain, and so each fibre alternately. The third step of
the process is making the yarns. Warping the yarns, is stretching
them to a certain length; and for the same reason, that so much
attention has been paid to the arrangement of the fibres for the
yarns, the same care is taken in the management of the yarns for
the strands. The fourth step of the process is to form the strands
into ropes. The difficulty of the art has been to make them bear
alike, especially in great cables, and this has been the object of patent machinery. The *hardening*, by twisting, is also an essential
part of the process of rope-making: for without this, it would be
little better than extended parallel fibres of hemp. In this twisting, first of the yarns, and then of the strands, those which are on
the outer surface must be more stretched than those near the centre; consequently, when there is a strain upon the rope, the outer
fibres will break first, and the others in succession. It is to avoid
this, that each yarn and each strand, as it is twisted or hardened,
shall be itself revolving, so that when drawn into the cable, the
whole component parts may, as nearly as possible, resist the strain
in an equal degree; but the process is not perfect, and this we
must conclude from observing how different the construction of a
tendon is from that of a rope. A tendon consists of a strong cord,
apparently fibrous; but which, by the art of the anatomist, may
be separated into lesser cords, and these, by maceration, can be

shown to consist of cellular membrane, the common tissue that gives firmness to all the textures of the animal body. The pecu liarity here results merely from its remarkable condensation. But the cords of which the larger tendons consists, do not lie paralle to each other, nor are they simply twisted like the strands of a rope; they are, on the contrary, plaited or interwoven together.

If the strong tendon of the heel, or Achilles tendon, be taken as an example, on first inspection, it appears to consist of parallel fibres, but by maceration, these fibres are found to be a web of twisted cellular texture. If you take your handkerchief, and, slightly twisting it, draw it out like a rope, it will seem to consist of parallel cords; such is, in fact, so far the structure of a tendon. But, as we have stated, there is something more admirable than this, for the tendon consists of subdivisions, which are like the strands of a rope; but instead of being twisted simply as by the process of hardening, they are plaited or interwoven in a way that could not be imitated in cordage by the turning of a wheel. Here then is the difference—by the twisting of a rope, the strands cannot resist the strain equally, whilst we see that this is provided for in the tendon by the regular interweaving of the yarn, if we may so express it, so that every fibre deviates from the parallel line in the same degree, and, consequently, receives the same strain when the tendon is pulled. If we seek for examples illustrative of this structure of the tendons, we must turn to the subject of ship-rig ging, and see there how the seaman contrives, by undoing the strands and yarns of a rope, and twisting them anew, to make his splicing stronger than the original cordage. A sailor opens the ends of two ropes, and places the strand of one opposite and be- tween the strand of another, and so interlaces them. And this ex- plains why a hawser-rope, a sort of small cable, is spun of *three* strands; for as they are necessary for many operations in the rigging of a ship, they must be formed in a way that admits of being cut and spliced, for the separation of three strands, at least, is necessa- ry for knotting, splicing, whipping, mailing, &c., which are a few of the many curious contrivances for joining the ends of ropes, and for strengthening them by filling up the interstices to preserve them from being cut or frayed. As these methods of splicing and plaiting in the subdivisions of the rope make an intertexture strong er than the original rope, it is an additional demonstration, if any were wanted, to show the perfection of the cordage of an animal machine, since the tendons are so interwoven; and until the yarns of one strand be separated and interwoven with the yarns of another strand, and this done with regular exchange, the most ap- proved patent ropes must be inferior to the corresponding part of the animal machinery.

A piece of cord of a new patent has been shown to us, which is said to be many times stronger than any other cord of the same diameter. It is so far upon the principle here stated, that the strands are plaited instead of being twisted; but the tendon has still its superiority, for the lesser yarns of each strand in it are in- terwoven with those of other strands. It however, gratifies us o see, that the principle we draw from the animal body is here con-

H*

firmed. It may be asked, do not the tendons of the human body someti es break? They do; but in circumstances which only add to the interest of the subject. By the exercise of the tendons (and their exercise is the act of being pulled upon by the mus cles, or having a strain made on them,) they become firmer and stronger; but in the failure of muscular activity, they become less capable of resisting the tug made upon them, and if, after a long confinement, a man has some powerful excitement to muscular exertion, then the tendon breaks. An old gentleman, whose habits have been long staid and sedentary, and who is very guarded in his walk, is upon an annual festival tempted to join the young people in a dance; then he breaks his tendo Achilles. Or a sick person, long confined to bed, is, on rising, subject to a rupture or hernia, because the tendinous expansions guarding against protrusion of the internal parts, have become weak from disuse.

Such circumstances remind us that we are speaking of a living body, and that, in estimating the properties of the machinery, we ought not to forget the influence of life, and that the natural exercise of the parts, whether they be active or passive, is the stimulus to the circulation through them, and to their growth and perfection.

CHAPTER X.

OF THE VESSELS OF ANIMAL BODIES.

THE circulation of the *blood*, through the bodies of men and quadrupeds, and the apparatus by which it is carried on, compose a system, and testify a contrivance, perhaps the best understood of any part of the animal frame. The lymphatic vessels or the nervous system, may be more subtile and intricate; nay, it is possible that in their structure they may be even more artificial than the sanguiferous; but we do not know so much about them.

The utility of the circulation of the blood I assume as an acknowledged point. One grand purpose is plainly answered by it; the distributing to every part, every extremity, every nook and corner of the body, the nourishment which is received into it by one aperture. What en ters at the mouth finds its way to the fingers' ends. A more difficult mechanical problem could hardly, I think, be proposed, than to discover a method of constantly repairing the waste, and of supplying an accession of substance to every part of a complicated machine, at the same time. This system presents itself under two views: first, the disposition of the blood-vessels, *i. e.* the laying of the pipes and secondly, the construction of the engine at the centre viz. the heart, for driving the blood through them.

I. The disposition of the blood-vessels, as far as regards the supply of the body, is like that of the water pipes in a city, viz. large and main trunks branching off by smaller pipes (and these again by still narrower tubes) in every direction, and towards every part in which the fluid, which they convey, can be wanted. So far the water pipes, which serve a town, may represent the vessels which carry the blood from the heart. But there is another thing necessary to the blood, which is not wanted for the water; and that is, the carrying of it back again to its source. For this office, a reversed system of vessels is prepared, which, uniting at their extremities with the extremities of the first system, collects the divided and subdivided stream-lets, first by capillary ramifications into larger branches; secondly, by these branches into trunks; and thus returns the blood (almost exactly inverting the order in which it went out) to the fountain whence its motion proceeded. All which is evident mechanism.

The body, therefore, contains two systems of blood-vessels, arteries and veins. Between the constitution of the systems there are also two differences, suited to the functions which the systems have to execute. The blood, in going out, passing always from wider into narrower tubes; and, in coming back, from narrower into wider; it is evident, that the impulse and pressure upon the sides of the blood-vessel, will be much greater in one case than the other. Accordingly, the arteries which carry out the blood, are formed with much tougher and stronger coats, than the veins which bring it back. That is one difference: the other is still more artificial, or, if I may so speak, indicates, still more clearly, the care and anxiety of the artificer Forasmuch as in the arteries, by reason of the great force with which the blood is urged along them, a wound or rupture would be more dangerous than in the veins; these vessels are defended from injury, not only by their texture, but by their situation; and by every advantage of situation which can be given to them. They are buried in sinuses, or they creep along grooves, made for them in the bones; for instance, the under edge of the ribs is sloped and furrowed solely for the passage of these vessels. Sometimes they proceed in channels, protected by stout parapets on each side; which last description is remarkable in the bones of the fingers these being hollowed out. on the under side, like a scoop, and with such a concavity that the finger may be cut across to the bone, without hurting the artery which runs along it.   At other times, the arteries pass in canals wrought in the substance, and in the very middle of the substance of the bone; this takes place in the lower jaw; and is found where there would, otherwise, be danger of compression by sudden curvature.   All this care is wonderful, yet not more than what the importance of the case required.   To those who venture their lives in a ship, it has been often said, that there is only an inch board between them and death; but in the body itself, especially in the arterial system, there is, in many parts, only a membrane, a skin, a thread.   For which reason, this system lies deep under the integuments; whereas the veins, in which the mischief that ensues from injuring the coats is much less, lie in general above the arteries; come nearer to the surface; are more exposed.

It may be farther observed concerning the two systems taken together, that though the arterial, with its trunks and branches and small twigs, may be imagined to issue or proceed, in other words, to *grow* from the heart, like a plant from its root, or the fibres of a leaf from its foot-stalk, (which however, were it so, would be only to resolve one mechanism into another,) yet the venal, the returning system, can never be formed in this manner.   The arteries might go on shooting out from their extremities, *i. e.* lengthening and subdividing indefinitely; but an inverted system, continually uniting its streams, instead of dividing, and thus carrying back what the other system carried out, could not be referred to the same process.

II.   The next thing to be considered is the engine which works this machinery, viz. the *heart*.   [Pl. XVII. fig. 1.] For our purpose it is unnecessary to ascertain the principle upon which the heart acts.   Whether it be irritation excited by the contact of the blood, by the influx of the nervous fluid, or whatever else be the cause of its motion, it is something which is capable of producing, in a living muscular fibre, reciprocal contraction and relaxation.   This is the power we have to work with; and the inquiry is, how this power is applied in the instance before us.   There is provided, in the central part of the body, a hollow muscle, invested with spiral fibres, running in both directions, the layers intersecting one another; in some animals, however, appearing to be semicircular rather than spiral.   By the contraction of these fibres, the sides of the muscular cavities are necessarily squeezed together, so as to force out from them any fluid wnich they may at that time contain: by the relaxation of the same fibres, the cavities are in their turn dilated, and, of course, prepared to admit every fluid which may be poured into them.   Into these cavities are inserted the great trunks, both of the arteries which carry out the blood, and of the veins which bring it back.   This is a general account of the apparatus: and the simplest idea of its action is, that, by each contraction, a portion of blood is forced by a syringe into the arteries; and, at each dilatation, an equal portion is received from the veins.   This produces, at each pulse, a motion, and change in the mass of blood, to the amount of what the cavity contains, which, in a full-grown human heart, I understand, is about an ounce, or two table-spoons full.   How quickly these changes succeed one another, and by this succession how sufficient they are to support a stream or circulation throughout the system, may be understood by the following computation, abridged from Keill's Anatomy, p. 117. ed. 3: " Each ventricle will at least contain one ounce of blood.   The heart contracts four thousand times in one hour; from which it follows, that there pass through the heart, every hour, four thousand ounces, or three hundred and fifty pounds of blood.   Now the whole mass of blood is said to be about twenty-five pounds; so that a quantity of blood, equal to the whole mass of blood, passes through the heart fourteen times in one hour; which is about once every four minutes."   Consider what an affair this is, when we come to very large animals.   The aorta of a whale is larger in the bore than the main pipe of the water-works at London bridge; and the water roaring in its passage through that pipe is inferior in impetus and velocity, to the blood gushing from the whale's heart.   Hear Ir. Hunter's account of the dissection of a whale:—" The aorta measured a foot diameter.   Ten or fifteen gallons of blood are thrown out of the heart at a stroke with an immense velocity, through a tube of a foot diameter.   The whole idea fills the mind with wonder."*

The account which we have here stated, of the injection of blood into the arteries by the contraction, and of the corresponding reception of it from the veins by the dilatation of the cavities of the heart, and of the circulation being thereby maintained through the blood-vessels of the body, is true, but imperfect.   The heart performs this office, but it is in conjunction with another of equal curios

* Dr Hunter's account of the dissection of a whale   Phil. Trans

94

ty and importance.   It was necessary that the blood should
be successively brought into contact, or contiguity, or prox
imity, with the *air*.   I do not know that the chemical reason, upon which this necessity is founded, has been yet
sufficiently explored.   It seems to be made to appear, that
the atmosphere which we breathe is a mixture of two kinds
of air; one pure and vital, the other, for the purposes of
life, effete, foul, and noxious: that when we have drawn
in our breath, the blood in the lungs imbibes from the air,
thus brought into contiguity with it, a portion of its pure in-
gredient, and, at the same time, gives out the effete or
corrupt air which it contained, and which is carried away,
along with the halitus, every time we respire.   At least,
by comparing the air which is breathed from the lungs
with the air which enters the lungs, it is found to have
lost some of its pure part, and to have brought away with
it an addition of its impure part.   Whether these experiments
satisfy the question, as to the need which the blood stands
in of being visited by continual accesses of air, is not for
us to inquire into, nor material to our argument: it is sufficient to know, that in the constitution of most animals,
such a necessity exists, and that the air, by some means or
other, *must* be introduced into a near communication with
the blood.   The lungs of animals are constructed for this
purpose.   They consist of blood-vessels and air-vessels, lying close to each other; and wherever there is a branch
of the trachea or windpipe, there is a branch accompanying
it of the vein and artery, and the air-vessel is always in the
middle between the blood-vessels.*   The internal surface
of these vessels, upon which the application of the air to
the blood depends, would, if collected and expanded, be,
in a man, equal to a superficies of fifteen feet square.   Now,
in order to give the blood in its course the benefit of this
organization, (and this is the part of the subject with which
we are chiefly concerned,) the following operation takes
place.   As soon as the blood is received by the heart
from the veins of the body, and *before* that is sent out
again into its arteries, it is carried by the force of the
contraction of the heart, and by means of a separate and
supplementary artery, to the lungs, and made to enter
the vessels of the lungs; from which, after it has undergone the action, whatever it be, of that viscus, it is
brought back by a large vein once more to the heart, in
order, when thus concocted and prepared to be thence

* Keill's Anat. 121

distributed anew into he system. This assigns to the heart a double office. The pulmonary circulation is a system within a system and one action of the heart is the origin of both.

For this complicated function, four cavities become necessary; and four are accordingly provided: two, called ventricles, which *send out* the blood, viz. one into the lungs, in the first instance; the other into the mass, after it has returned from the lungs: two others also, called auricles, which *receive* the blood from the veins; viz. one, as it comes immediately from the body; the other, as the same blood comes a second time after its circulation through the lungs. So that there are two receiving cavities, and two forcing cavities. The structure of the heart has reference to the lungs; for without the lungs, one of each would have been sufficient. The translation of the blood in the heart itself is after this manner. The receiving cavities respectively communicate with the forcing cavities, and, by their contraction, unload the received blood into them. The forcing cavities, when it is their turn to contract, compel the same blood into the mouths of the arteries.

The account here given will not convey to a reader, ignorant of anatomy, anything like an accurate notion of the form, action, or use of the parts, (nor can any short and popular account do this;) but it is abundantly sufficient to testify contrivance; and although imperfect, being true as far as it goes, may be relied upon for the only purpose for which we offer it, the purpose of this conclusion.

"The wisdom of the Creator," saith Hamburgher, "is in nothing seen more gloriously than in the heart." And how well doth it execute its office! An anatomist, who understood the structure of the heart, might say beforehand that it would play; but he would expect, I think, from the complexity of its mechanism, and the delicacy of many of its parts, that it should always be liable to derangement, or that it would soon work itself out. Yet shall this wonderful machine go, night and day, for eighty years together, at the rate of a hundred thousand strokes every twenty-four hours, having, at every stroke, a great resistance to overcome; and shall continue this action for this length of time, without disorder and without weariness.

But farther: from the account which has been given of the mechanism of the heart, it is evident that it must require the interposition of *valves;* that the success indeed of its action must depend upon these; for when any one of its cavities contracts, the necessary tendency of the force will be to drive the enclosed blood, not only into the mouth of the artery where it ought to go, but also back again into the mouth of the vein from which it flowed. In like manner, when by the relaxation of the fibres the same cavity is dilated, the blood would not only run into it from the vein, which was the course intended, but back from the artery, through which it ought to be moving forward. The way of preventing a reflux of the fluid, in both these cases, is to fix valves, which, like flood-gates, may open a way to the stream in one direction, and shut up the passage against it in another. [Pl. XVII. fig. 2, 3, 4.] The heart, constituted as it is, can no more work without valves than a pump can. When the piston descends in a pump, if it were not for the stoppage by the valve beneath, the motion would only thrust down the water which it had before drawn up A similar consequence would frustrate the action of the heart. Valves, therefore, properly disposed, *i. e.* properly with respect to the course of the blood which it is necessary to promote, are essential to the contrivance. *And valves so disposed, are accordingly provided.* A valve is placed in the communication between each auricle and its ventricle, lest when the ventricle contracts, part of the blood should get back again into the auricle, instead of the whole entering, as it ought to do, the mouth of the artery. A valve is also fixed at the mouth of each of the great arteries which take the blood from the heart; leaving the passage free, so long as the blood holds its proper course forward; closing it, whenever the blood, in consequence of the relaxation of the ventricle, would attempt to flow back. There is some variety in the construction of these valves, though all the valves of the body act nearly upon the same principle, and are destined to the same use. In general they consist of a thin membrane, lying close to the side of the vessel, and consequently allowing an open passage whilst the stream runs one way, but thrust out from the side by the fluid getting behind it, and opposing the passage of the blood, when it would flow the other way.* Where more than one membrane is employed, the different membranes only compose

* The veins and absorbent vessels present in their cavities folds of a parabolic form, called *valves*, like the semilunar valve; the one edge adheres to the sides of the vein, the other is loose; the first is farthest from the heart, the other nearer. The number of valves is greatest where the blood flows contrary to the force of its own weight See Fig. 7.

Paxton

one valve   Their joint action fulfils the office of a valve, for instance; over the entrance of the right auricle of the heart into the right ventricle, three of these skins or membranes are fixed, of a triangular figure, the bases of the triangles fastened to the flesh; the sides and summits loose; but, though loose, connected by threads of a determinate length, with certain small fleshy prominences adjoining. The effect of this construction is, that, when the ventricle contracts, the blood endeavouring to escape in all directions, and amongst other directions pressing upwards, gets *between* these membranes and the sides of the heart; and thereby forces them up into such a position, as that, together, they constitute, when raised, a hollow cone, (the strings, before spoken of, hindering them from proceeding or separating farther;) which cone, entirely occupying the passage, prevents the return of the blood into the auricle A shorter account of the matter may be this: So long as the blood proceeds in its proper course, the membranes which compose the valve are pressed close to the side of the vessel, and occasion no impediment to the circulation: when the blood would regurgitate, they are raised from the side of the vessel, and, meeting in the middle of its cavity, shut up the channel.   Can any one doubt of contrivance here or is it possible to shut our eyes against the proof of it?

This valve, also, is not more curious in its structure, than it is important in its office.   Upon the play of the valve, even upon the proportioned length of the strings or fibres which check the ascent of the membranes, depends, as it should seem, nothing less than the life itself of the animal.   We may here likewise repeat, what we before observed concerning some of the ligaments of the body, that they could not be formed by any action of the parts themselves.   There are cases in which, although good uses appear to arise from the shape or configuration of a part, yet that shape or configuration itself may seem to be produced by the action of the part, or by the action or pressure of adjoining parts.   Thus the bend, and the internal smooth concavity of the ribs, may be attributed to the equal pressure of the soft bowels; the particular shape of some bones and joints, to the traction of the annexed muscles, or to the position of contiguous muscles.   But valves could not be so formed.   Action and pressure are all against them. The blood, in its proper course, has no tendency to produce such things; and, in its improper or reflected current, has a tendency to prevent their production.   Whilst we see, therefore the se and necessity of this machinery, we can look to no other account of its origin or formation than the intending mind of a Creator. Nor can we without admiration reflect, that such thin membranes, such weak and tender instruments, as these valves are, should be able to hold out for seventy or eighty years.

Here also we cannot consider but with gratitude, how happy it is that our vital motions are *involuntary*. We should have enough to do, if we had to keep our hearts beating, and our stomachs at work. Did these things depend, we will not say upon our effort, but upon our bidding, our care, or our attention, they would leave us leisure for nothing else. We must have been continually upon the watch, and continually in fear; nor would this constitution have allowed of sleep.

It might perhaps be expected, that an organ so precious, of such central and primary importance as the heart is, should be defended by *a case*. The fact is, that a membranous purse or bag, made of strong, tough materials, is provided for it; holding the heart within its cavity; sitting loosely and easily about it; guarding its substance, without confining its motion; and containing likewise a spoonful or two of water, just sufficient to keep the surface of the heart in a state of suppleness and moisture. How should such a loose covering be generated by the action of the heart? Does not the enclosing of it in a sack, answering no other purpose but that enclosure, show the care that has been taken of its preservation?

One use of the circulation of the blood probably (amongst other uses) is, to distribute nourishment to the different parts of the body. How minute and multiplied the ramifications of the blood-vessels, for that purpose, are; and how thickly spread, over at least the superfices of the body, is proved by the single observation, that we cannot prick the point of a pin into the flesh, without drawing blood, *i. e.* without finding a blood-vessel. Nor, internally, is their diffusion less universal. Blood-vessels run along the surface of membranes, pervade the substance of muscles, penetrate the bones. Even into every tooth, we trace, through a small hole in the root, an artery to feed the bone, as well as a vein to bring back the spare blood from it; both which, with the addition of an accompanying nerve, form a thread only a little thicker than a horse-hair.

Wherefore, when the nourishment taken in at the mouth has once reached, and mixed itself with the blood, every part of the body is in the way of being supplied with it. And this introduces another grand topic, namely, the man ter in which the aliment gets into the *blood;* which is a subject distinct from the preceding, and brings us to the consideration of another entire system of vessels.

II. For this necessary part of the animal economy, an apparatus is provided, in a great measure capable of being what anatomists call demonstrated, that is, shown in the dead body;—and a line or course of conveyance, which we can pursue by our examinations.

First, The food descends by a wide passage into the intestines, undergoing two great preparations on its way; one, in the mouth by mastication and moisture—(can it be doubted with what design the teeth were placed in the road to the stomach, or that there was choice in fixing them in this situation?) The other, by digestion in the stomach itself. Of this last surprising dissolution I say nothing, because it is chemistry, and I am endeavouring to display mechanism. The figure and position of the stomach (I speak all along with a reference to the human organ) are calculated for detaining the food long enough for the action of its digestive juice. [Pl. XVIII. fig. 1.] It has the shape of the pouch of a bagpipe; lies across the body; and the pylorus, or passage by which the food leaves it, is somewhat higher in the body than the cardia, or orifice by which it enters; so that it is by the contraction of the muscular coat of the stomach, that the contents, after having undergone the application of the gastric menstruum, are gradually pressed out. In dogs and cats, this action of the coats of the stomach has been displayed to the eye. It is a slow and gentle undulation, propagated from one orifice of the stomach to the other. For the same reason that I omitted, for the present, offering any observation upon the digestive fluid, I shall say nothing concerning the bile or the pancreatic juice, farther than to observe upon the mechanism, viz. that from the glands in which these secretions are elaborated, pipes are laid into the first of the intestines, through which pipes the product of each gland flows into that bowel, [Pl. XVIII. fig. 2,] and is there mixed with the aliment, as soon almost as it passes the stomach; adding also as a remark, how grievously this same bile offends the stomach itself, yet cherishes the vessel that lies next to it.

Secondly, We have now the aliment in the intestines converted into pulp; and, though lately consisting of ten different viands, reduced to nearly a uniform substance, and to a state fitted for yielding its essence, which is called chyle, but which is milk, or more nearly resembling milk than any other liquor with which it can be compared. For the straining off this fluid from the digested aliment in the course of its long progress through the body, myriads of capillary tubes, *i. e.* pipes as small as hairs, open their orifices into the cavity of every part of the intestines. [Pl XIX.] These tubes, which are so fine and slender as not to be visible unless when distended with chyle, soon unite into larger branches. The pipes, formed by this union, terminate in glands, from which other pipes of a still larger diameter arising, carry the chyle from all parts, into a common reservoir or *receptacle*. This receptacle is a bag large enough to hold about a table-spoon full; and from this vessel a duct or main pipe proceeds, climbing up the back part of the chest, and afterwards creeping along the gullet till it reach the neck. Here it meets the river: here it discharges itself into a large vein, which soon conveys the chyle, now flowing along with the old blood, to the heart. This whole route can be exhibited to the eye; nothing is left to be supplied by imagination or conjecture. Now, beside the subserviency of this whole structure, to a manifest and necessary purpose, we may remark two or three separate particulars in it, which show, not only the contrivance, but the perfection of it. We may remark, first, the length of the intestines, which, in the human subject, is six times that of the body. Simply for a passage, these voluminous bowels, this prolixity of gut, seems in nowise necessary; but, in order to allow time and space for the successive extraction of the chyle from the digested aliment, namely that the chyle which escapes the lacteals of one part of the guts, may be taken up by those of some other part, the length of the canal is of evident use and conduciveness. Secondly, we must also remark their peristaltic motion; which is made up of contractions, following one another like waves upon the surface of a fluid, and not unlike what we observe in the body of an earth-worm crawling along the ground; and which is effected by the joint action of longitudinal and of spiral, or rather perhaps of a great number of separate semicircular fibres. This curious action pushes forward the grosser part of the aliment at the same time that the more subtile parts, which we call chyle, are, by a series of gentle compressions, squeezed into the narrow orifices of the lacteal vessels. Thirdly, it was necessary that these tubes, which we denominate lacteals, or their mouths at least, should be as narrow as possible, in order to deny admission into the blood to any particle which is of size enough to make a lodge-

ment afterwards in the small arteries, and thereby to obstruct the circulation: and it was also necessary that this
extreme tenuity should be compensated by multitude; for,
a large quantity of chyle (in ordinary constitutions, not
less, it has been computed, than two or three quarts in a
day) is, by some means or other, to be passed through
them. Accordingly, we find the number of the lacteals
exceeding all powers of computation; and their pipes so
fine and slender, as not to be visible, unless filled, to the nak
ed eye; and their orifices, which open into the intestines,
so small, as not to be discernible even by the best microscope. Fourthly, the main pipe, which carries the chyle
from the reservoir to the blood, viz. the thoracic duct, being fixed in an almost upright position, and wanting that
advantage of propulsion which the arteries possess, is furnished with a succession of valves to check the ascending
fluid, when once it has passed them, from falling back.
These valves look upward, so as to leave the ascent free,
but to prevent the return of the chyle, if, for want of sufficient force to push it on, its weight should at any time
cause it to descend. Fifthly, the chyle enters the blood
in an odd place, but perhaps the most commodious place
possible, viz. at a large vein near the neck, so situated with
respect to the circulation, as speedily to bring the mixture
to the heart. And this seems to be a circumstance of
great moment; for had the chyle entered the blood at an
artery, or at a distant vein, the fluid, composed of the old
and new materials, must have performed a considerable
part of the circulation, before it received that churning in
the lungs, which is probably, necessary for the intimate
and perfect union of the old blood with the recent chyle.
Who could have dreamed of a communication between the
cavity of the intestines and the left great vein near the
neck? Who could have suspected that this communication
should be the medium through which all nourishment is
derived to the body? or this the place, where, by a side
inlet, the important junction is formed between the blood
and the material which feeds it?

II. We postponed the consideration of *digestion*, lest it
should interrupt us in tracing the course of the food to the
blood; but, in treating of the alimentary system, so p.in-
cipal a part of the process cannot be omitted.

Of the gastric juice, the immediate agent by which that
change which food undergoes in our stomachs is effected
we shall take our account, from the numerous, careful, and
varied experiments of the Abbé Spallanzani.

I*

1. It is not a simple diluent, but a real solvent A quarter of an ounce of beef had scarcely touched the stomach of a crow, when the solution began.

2. It has not the nature of saliva; it has not the nature of bile; but is distinct from both. By experiments out of the body it appears, that neither of these secretions acts upon the alimentary substances, in the same manner as the gastric juice acts.

3 Digestion is not *putrefaction;* for, the digesting fluid resists putrefaction most pertinaciously; nay, not only checks its farther progress, but restores putrid substances

4. It is not a *fermentative* process; for the solution begins at the surface, and proceeds towards the centre, contrary to the order in which fermentation acts and spreads.

5. It is not the *digestion of heat,* for, the cold maw of a cod or sturgeon will dissolve the shells of crabs or lobsters, harder than the sides of the stomach which contains them.

In a word, animal digestion carries about it the marks of being a power and a process completely *sui generis;* distinct from every other; at least from every chemical process with which we are acquainted.   And the most wonderful thing about it is its appropriation; its subserviency to the particular economy of each animal.   The gastric juice of an owl, falcon, or kite, will not touch grain; no, not even to finish the macerated and half-digested pulse which is left in the crops of the sparrows that the bird devours. In poultry, the trituration of the gizzard, and the gastric juice, conspire in the work of digestion.   The gastric juice will not dissolve the grain whilst it is whole.   Entire grains of barley, enclosed in tubes or spherules, are not affected by it.   But if the same grain be by any means broken or ground, the gastric juice immediately lays hold of it.   Here then is wanted, and here we find, a combination of mechanism and chemistry.   For the preparatory grinding, the gizzard lends its mill.   And, as all mill-work should be strong, its structure is so, beyond that of any other muscle belonging to the animal.   The internal coat also, or lining of the gizzard, is, for the same purpose, hard and cartilaginous. But, forasmuch as this is not the sort of animal substance suited for the reception of glands, or for secretion, the gastric juice in this family, is not supplied, as in membranous stomachs, by the stomach itself, but by the gullet, in which the feeding glands are placed, and from which it trickles down into the stomach.

In sheep, the gastric fluid has no effect in digesting plants, *unless they have been previously masticated.* It only produces a slight maceration; nearly such as common water would produce, in a degree of heat somewhat exceeding the medium temperature of the atmosphere. But provided that the plant has been reduced to pieces by chewing, the gastric juice then proceeds with it, first by softening its substance; next, by destroying its natural consistency; and, lastly, by dissolving it so completely, as not even to spare the toughest and most stringy parts, such as the nerves of the leaves.

So far our accurate and indefatigable Abbé.—Dr. Stevens of Edinburgh, in 1777, found, by experiments tried with perforated balls, that the gastric juice of the sheep and the ox speedily dissolved vegetables, but made no impression upon beef, mutton, and other animal bodies. Dr. Hunter discovered a property of this fluid, of a most curious kind; viz. that in the stomachs of animals which feed upon flesh, irresistibly as this fluid acts upon animal substances, it is only upon the *dead* substance, that it operates at all. The *living* fibre suffers no injury from lying in contact with it. Worms and insects are found alive in the stomachs of such animals. The coats of the human stomach, in a healthy state, are insensible to its presence: yet, in cases of sudden death, (wherein the gastric juice, not having been weakened by disease, retains its activity,) it has been known to eat a hole through the bowel which contains it.* How nice is this discrimination of action, yet how necessary?

But to return to our hydraulics.

III. The gall-bladder is a very remarkable contrivance. It is the reservoir of a canal. [Pl. XVIII. fig. 1, 2.] It does not form the channel itself, *i. e.* the direct communication between the liver and the intestine which is by another passage, viz. the ductus hepaticus, continued under the name of the ductus communis; but it lies adjacent to this channel, joining it by a duct of its own, the ductus cysticus; by which structure it is enabled, as occasion may require, to add its contents to, and increase the flow of bile into the duodenum. And the position of the gall-bladder is such as to apply this structure to the best advantage. In its natural situation, it touches the exterior surface of the stomach, and consequently is compressed by the distension of that vessel: the effect of which compression

* Phil. Trans. vol. lxii. p. 447.

is, to force out fro n the bag, and send into the duodenum
an extraordinary quantity of bile, to meet the extraordinary
demand which the repletion of the stomach by food is about
to occasion.* Cheselden describes† the gall-bladder as
seated against the duodenum, and thereby liable to have its
fluid pressed out, by the passage of the aliment through that
cavity; which likewise will have the effect of causing it to
be received into the intestine, at a right time, and in a due
proportion.

There may be other purposes answered by this contrivance; and it is probable that there are. The contents of
the gall-bladder are not exactly of the same kind as what
passes from the liver through the direct passage.‡ It is
possible that the gall may be changed, and for some purposes meliorated, by keeping.

The entrance of the gall-duct into the duodenum, furnishes another observation. Whenever either smaller tubes
are inserted into larger tubes, or tubes into vessels and
cavities, such receiving tubes, vessels, or cavities, being
subject to muscular constriction, we always find a contrivance to prevent *regurgitation*. In some cases, valves
are used; in other cases, amongst which is that now before us, a different expedient is resorted to; which may
be thus described: The gall-duct enters the duodenum
obliquely: after it has pierced the first coat, it runs near
two fingers' breadth *between* the coats, before it opens into
the cavity of the intestine.§ The same contrivance is used
in another part, where there is exactly the same occasion
for it, viz. in the insertion of the ureters in the bladder.
These enter the bladder near its neck, running obliquely for
the space of an inch between its coats.|| It is, in both
cases, sufficiently evident, that this structure has a necessary mechanical tendency to resist regurgitation; for,
whatever force acts in such a direction as to urge the fluid
back into the orifices of the tubes, must, at the same time,
stretch the coats of the vessels, and thereby compress that
part of the tube, which is included between them.

IV. Amongst the *vessels* of the human body, the pipe
which conveys the saliva from the place where it is made,
to the place where it is wanted, deserves to be reckoned
amongst the most intelligible pieces of mechanism with
which we are acquainted. [Pl. XX. fig. 1, 2.] The saliva,
we all know, is used in the mouth; but much of it is

* Keill's Anat. p. 64.   † Anat p. 164
‡ Keill's from Malpighius p. 62   § Keill's Anat. p 62.
|| Ches Anat. p 250.

manufactured on the outside of the cheek, by the parotid gland, which lies between the ear and the angle of the lower jaw. In order to carry the secretion to its destination, there is laid from the gland, on the outside, a pipe about the thickness of a wheat straw, and about three fingers' breadth in length; which, after riding over the masseter musc'e, bores for itself a hole through the very middle of the cheek; enters by that hole, which is a complete perforation of the buccinator muscle, into the mouth; and there discharges its fluid very copiously.

V. Another exquisite structure, differing indeed from the four preceding instances in that it does not relate to the conveyance of fluids, but still belonging, like these, to the class of pipes, or conduits of the body, is seen in the *larynx*. [Pl. XXI. fig. 1, 2.] We all know that there go down the throat two pipes, one leading to the stomach, the other to the lungs; the one being the passage for the food, the other for the breath and voice: we know also that both these passages open into the bottom of the mouth; the gullet, necessarily, for the conveyance of the food; and the windpipe, for speech, and the modulation of sound, not much less so; therefore the difficulty was, the passages being so contiguous, to prevent the food, especially the liquids, which we swallow into the stomach, from entering the windpipe, *i. e.* the road to the lungs; the consequence of which error, when it does happen, is perceived by the convulsive throes that are instantly produced. This business, which is very nice, is managed in this manner. The gullet (the passage for food) opens into the mouth like the cone or upper part of a funnel, the capacity of which forms indeed the bottom of the mouth. Into the side of this funnel, at the part which lies the lowest, enters the windpipe, by a chink or slit, with a lid or flap, like a little tongue, accurately fitted to the orifice. The solids or liquids which we swallow, pass over this lid or flap, as they descend by the funnel into the gullet Both the weight of the food, and he action of the musc.es concerned in swallowing, contribute to keep the lid close down upon the aperture, whilst anything is passing; whereas, by means of its natural cartilaginous spring, it raises itself a little as soon as the food is passed, thereby allowing a free inlet and outlet for the respiration of air by the lungs. And we may here remark the almost complete success of the expedient, viz. how seldom it fails of its purpose, compared with the number of instances in which it fulfils it. Reflect how frequently we swallow how constantly we breathe. In a city feast, for example, what deglutition, what anhelation! yet does this little cartilage, he epiglottis, so effectually interpose its office, so securely guard the entrance of the windpipe, that whilst morsel after morsel, draught after draught, are coursing one another over it, an accident of a crumb or a drop slipping into this passage, (which nevertheless must be opened for the breath every second of time,) excites in the whole company, not only alarm by its danger, but surprise by its novelty. Not two guests are choked in a century.*

There is no room for pretending that the action of the parts may have gradually formed the epiglottis: I do not mean in the same individual, but in a succession of generations. Not only the action of the parts has no such tendency, but the animal could not live, nor consequently the parts act, either without it, or with it in a half-formed state. The species was not to wait for the gradual formation or expansion of a part which was, from the first, necessary to the life of the individual.

Not only is the larynx curious, but the whole windpipe possesses a structure adapted to its peculiar office. It is made up (as any one may perceive by putting his fingers to his throat) of stout cartilaginous ringlets placed at small and equal distances from one another. Now this is not the case with any other of the numerous conduits of the body. The use of these cartilages is to keep the passage for the air *constantly* open; which they do mechanically. A pipe with soft membranous coats, liable to collapse and close when empty, would not have answered here; although this be the general vascular structure, and a structure which serves very well for those tubes which are kept in a state of perpetual distension by the fluid they enclose, or which afford a passage to solid and protruding substances.

Nevertheless (which is another particularity well worthy

---

* The same general structure of these parts is found in all other animals of the same class with mankind, but there is a singular variation from it in the elephant, by which, if possible, the influence of a deriving intelligence is more wonderfully exemplified than in the ordinary structure. It is well known that this animal drinks by sucking up the liquid into its trunk, and then after thrusting the end of it into its mouth, blowing the liquid into its throat. In this case, the act of blowing through the trunk and swallowing, must be both going on at the same instant, and not in successive instants as in man. The liquid must be passing down the throat, while the epiglottis is open and the air issuing. In order to provide against interfe ence, a channel is provided on each side of the epiglottis, along which e drink passes quietly on, without running into the windpipe. --*Ed.*

of notice) these rings are not complete, that is. are not car
tilaginous and stiff all round; but their hinder part, which
is contiguous to the gullet, is membranous and soft, easily
yielding to the distensions of that organ occasioned by the
descent of solid food. The same rings are also bevelled off
at the upper and lower edges, the better to close upon one
another, when the trachea is compressed or shortened

The constitution of the trachea may suggest likewise an
other reflection. The membrane which lines its inside. is
perhaps, the most sensible irritable membrane of the body
It rejects the touch of a crumb of bread, or a drop of water,
with a spasm which convulses the whole frame; yet, left to
itself, and its proper office, the intromission of air alone
nothing can be so quiet. It does not even make itself felt
a man does not know that he has a trachea. This capaci
ty of perceiving with such acuteness, this impatience or
offence, yet perfect rest and ease when let alone; are properties, one would have thought, not likely to reside in the
same subject. It is to the junction, however, of these almost inconsistent qualities, in this, as well as in some other
delicate parts of the body, that we owe our safety and our
comfort;—our safety to their sensibility, our comfort to
their repose.

The larynx, or rather the whole windpipe taken together,
(for the larynx is only the upper part of the windpipe,) besides its other uses, is also a musical instrument, that is to
say, it is *mechanism* expressly adapted to the modulation of
sound; for it has been found upon trial, that, by relaxing
or tightening the tendinous bands at the extremity of the
windpipe, and blowing in at the other end, all the cries
and notes might be produced of which the living animal
was capable. It can be sounded, just as a pipe or flute is
sounded. Birds, says Bonnet, have at the lower end of
the windpipe, a conformation like the reed of a hautboy,
for the modulation of their notes. A tuneful bird is a ven·
triloquist. The seat of the song is in the breast. [Pl
XXI. fig. 3.]

The use of the lungs in the system has been said to be
obscure: one use however is plain, though, in some sense,
external to the system, and that is, the formation, in conjunction with the larynx, of voice and speech. They are, to
animal utterance, what the bellows are to the organ.

For the sake of method, we have considered animal bodies under three divisions: their bones, their muscles, and
their vessels, and we have stated our observations upon

.hese parts separately.   But this is to diminish the strength
of the argument.   The wisdom of the Creator is seen, not
'n their separate but their collective action; in their mutual subserviency and dependence; in their contributing *together* to one effect, and one use.   It has been said, that a
man cannot lift his hand to his head, without finding enough
to convince him of the existence of a God.   And it is well
said; for he has only to reflect, familiar as this action is,
and simple as it seems to be, how many things are requisite
for the performing of it: how many things which we understand, to say nothing of many more, probably, which we
do not; viz. first, a long, hard, strong cylinder, in order to
give to the arm its firmness and tension; but which, being
rigid, and in its substance inflexible, can only turn upon
joints: secondly, therefore, joints for this purpose, one at
the shoulder to raise the arm, another at the elbow to bend
it; these joints continually fed with a soft mucilage to make
the parts slip easily upon one another, and holden together
by strong braces, to keep them in their position: then, thirdly, strings and wires, *i. e.* muscles and tendons, artificially
inserted for the purpose of drawing the bones in the directions in which the joints allow them to move.   Hitherto we
seem to understand the mechanism pretty well; and, under
standing this, we possess enough for our conclusion: nevertheless, we have hitherto only a machine standing still; a
dead organization—an apparatus.   To put the system in a
state of activity, to set it at work, a farther provision is necessary, viz. a communication with the brain by means of
nerves.   We know the existence of this communication,
because we can see the communicating threads, and can
trace them to the brain: its necessity we also know, because if the thread be cut, if the communication be intercepted, the muscle becomes paralytic: but beyond this we
know little, the organization being too minute and subtile
for our inspection.
   To what has been enumerated, as officiating in the single
act of a man's raising his hand to his head, must be added
likewise, all that is necessary, and all that contributes to the
growth, nourishment, and sustentation of the limb, the repair of its waste, the preservation of its health: such as the
circulation of the blood through every part of it; its lymphatics, exhalants, absorbents; its excretions and integuments.   All these share in the result; join in the effect; and
how all these, or any of them, come together without a designing, disposing intelligence, it is impossible to conceive

CHAPTER XI.

OF THE ANIMAL STRUCTURE REGARDED AS A MASS.

CONTEMPLATING *an animal body* in its collective capacity, we cannot forget to notice, what a number of instruments are brought together, and often within how small a compass. It is a cluster of contrivances. In a Canary bird, for instance, and in the single ounce of matter which composes its body, (but which seems to be all employed,) we have instruments for eating, for digesting, for nourishment, for breathing, for generation, for running, for flying, for seeing, for hearing, for smelling, each appropriate,—each entirely different from all the rest.

The human, or indeed the animal frame, considered as a mass or assemblage, exhibits in its composition three properties, which have long struck my mind as indubitable evidences, not only of design, but of a great deal of attention and accuracy in prosecuting the design.

I. The first is, the exact correspondency of the two sides of the same animal; the right hand answering to the left, leg to leg, eye to eye, one side of the countenance to the other; and with a precision, to imitate which in any tolerable degree, forms one of the difficulties of statuary, and requires, on the part of the artist, a constant attention to this property of his work, distinct from every other.

It is the most difficult thing that can be to get a wig made even; yet how seldom is the *face* awry! And what care is taken that it should not be so, the anatomy of its bones demonstrates. The upper part of the face is composed of thirteen bones, six on each side, answering each to each, and the thirteenth, without a fellow, in the middle: the lower part of the face is in like manner composed of six bones, three on each side respectively corresponding, and the lower jaw in the centre. In building an arch, could more be done in order to make the curve *true, i. e.* the parts equi-distant from the middle, alike in figure and position?

The exact resemblance of the *eyes*, considering how compounded this organ is in its structure, how various and how delicate are the shades of color with which its iris is tinged; how differently, as to effect upon appearance, the eye may be mounted in its socket, and how differently in different heads eyes actually are set,—is a property of an

K

imal bodies much to be admired. Of ten thousand eyes, I do not know that it would be possible to match one, except with its own fellow; or to distribute them into suitable pairs by any other selection than that which obtains.

This regularity of the animal structure is rendered more remarkable by the three following considerations:—First, the limbs, *separately* taken, have not this correlation of parts; but the contrary of it. A knife drawn down the chine, cuts the human body into two parts, externally equal and alike; you cannot draw a straight line which will divide a hand, a foot, the leg, the thigh, the cheek, the eye, the ear, into two parts equal and alike. Those parts which are placed upon the middle or partition line of the body, or which traverse that line, as the nose, the tongue, the lips, may be so divided, or, more properly speaking, are double organs; but other parts cannot. This shows that the correspondency which we have been describing, does not arise by any necessity in the nature of the subject: for, if necessary, it would be universal; whereas it is observed only in the system or assemblage: it is not true of the separate parts; that is to say, it is found where it conduces to beauty or utility; it is not found where it would subsist at the expense of both. The two wings of a bird always correspond: the two sides of a feather frequently do not. In centipedes, millepedes, and that whole tribe of insects, no two legs on the same side are alike; yet there is the most exact parity between the legs opposite to one another.

2. The next circumstance to be remarked is, that whilst the cavities of the body are so configurated, as *externally* to exhibit the most exact correspondency of the opposite sides, the contents of these cavities have no such correspondency. A line drawn down the middle of the breast, divides the thorax into two sides exactly similar; yet these two sides enclose very different contents. The heart lies on the left side; a lobe of the lungs on the right; balancing each other neither in size nor shape. The same thing holds of the abdomen. The liver lies on the right side,* without any similar viscus opposed to it on the left. The spleen indeed is situated over against the liver; but agreeing with the liver neither in bulk nor form. There is no equipollency between these. The stomach is a vessel both irregular in its shape, and oblique in its position. The foldings and doublings of the intestines do not present a parity

---

* The principal lobe of the liver is on the right, but a smaller is extended in to the left side. See PLATE XXII.

ot sides.   Yet that symmetry which depends upon the correlation o. the sides, is externally preserved throughout the whole trunk; and is the more remarkable in the lower parts of it, as the integuments are soft; and the shape, consequently, is not, as the thorax is by its ribs, reduced by natural stays.   It is evident, therefore, that the external proportion does not arise from any equality in the shape or pressure of the internal contents.   What is it indeed but a co. rection of inequalities? an adjustment, by mutual compensation, of anomalous forms into a regular congeries? the effect, in a word, of artful, and, if we might be permitted so to speak, of studied collocation?

3. Similar also to this, is the third observation; that an internal inequality in the feeding vessels is so managed, as to produce no inequality in parts which were intended to correspond.   The right arm answers accurately to the left, both in size and shape; but the arterial branches, which supply the two arms, do not go off from their trunk, in a pair, in the same manner, at the same place, or at the same angle.   Under which want of similitude, it is very difficult to conceive how the same quantity of blood should be pushed through each artery: yet the result i right; the two limbs, which are nourished by them, perceive no difference of supply, no effects of excess or deficiency.

Concerning the difference of manner, in which the subclavian and carotid arteries, upon the different sides of the body, separate themselves from the aörta, Cheselden seems to have thought, that the advantage which the left gain by going off at a much more acute angle than the right, is made up to the right by their going off together in one branch.*   It is very possible that this may be the compensating contrivance: and if it be so, how curious, how hydrostatical?

II.   Another perfection of the animal mass is *package* [Pl. XXII. fig. 1.]   I know nothing which is so surprising Examine the contents of the trunk of any large animal Take notice how soft, how tender, how intricate they are how constantly in action, how necessary to life!   Reflect upon the danger of any injury to their substance, any derangement of their position, any obstruction to their office. Observe the heart pumping at the centre, at the rate of eighty strokes in a minute: one set of pipes carrying the stream away from it, another set bringing, in its course, the

* Ches. Anat. p. 184. ed 7.

fluid back to it again; the lungs performing their elaborate office, viz. distending and contracting their many thousand vesicles, by a reciprocation which cannot cease for a minute; the stomach exercising its powerful chemistry; the bowels silently propelling the changed aliment; collecting from it, as it proceeds, and transmitting to the blood an incessant supply of prepared and assimilated nourishment; that blood pursuing its course; the liver, the kidneys, the pancreas, the parotid, with many other known and distinguishable glands, drawing off from it, all the while, their proper secretions. These several operations, together with others more subtile but less capable of being investigated, are going on within us, at one and the same time. Think of this; and then observe how the body itself, the case which holds this machinery, is rolled, and jolted, and tossed about, the mechanism remaining unhurt, and with very ittle molestation, even of its nicest motions. Observe a rope dancer, a tumbler, or a monkey: the sudden inversions and contortions which the internal parts sustain by the postures into which their bodies are thrown; or rather observe the shocks which these parts, even in ordinary subjects, sometimes receive from falls and bruises, or by abrupt jerks and twists, without sensible, or with soon-recovered damage. Observe this, and then reflect how firmly every part must be secured, how carefully surrounded, how well tied down and packed together.

This property of animal bodies has never, I think, been considered under a distinct head, or so fully as it deserves. I may be allowed, therefore, in order to verify my observation concerning it, to set forth a short anatomical detail, though it oblige me to use more technical language than I should wish to introduce into a work of this kind.

1. The *heart* (such care is taken of the centre of life) is placed between the soft lobes of the lungs; *tied* to the mediastinum and to the pericardium; which pericardium is not only itself an exceedingly strong membrane, but *adheres* firmly to the duplicature of the mediastinum, and, by its point, to the middle tendon of the diaphragm. The heart is also *sustained* in its place by the great blood-vessels which issue from it *

2. The *lungs* are *tied* to the sternum by the mediastinum, before; to the vertebræ by the pleura, behind. It seems indeed to be the very use of the mediastinum (which is a membrane that goes straight through the middle of the

* Keill's Anat. p. 107. ed. 8.

thorax, from the breast to the back) to keep the contents of the thorax in their places; in particular to hinder one lobe of the lungs from incommoding another, or the parts of the lungs from pressing upon each other when we lie on one side.*

3. The *liver* is fastened in the body by two ligaments, the first, wh'ch is large and strong, comes from the covering of the diaphragm, and penetrates the substance of the liver; the second is the umbilical vein, which, after birth, degenerates into a ligament. The first, which is the principal, fixes the liver in its situation, whilst the body holds an erect posture; the second prevents it from pressing upon the diaphragm when we lie down; and both together *sling* or suspend the liver when we lie upon our backs, so that it may not compress or obstruct the ascending vena cava,† to which belongs the important office of returning the blood from the body to the heart.

4. The *bladder* is tied to the naval by the urachus, transformed into a ligament: thus, what was a passage for the urine to the fœtus, becomes, after birth, a support or stay to the bladder. The peritonæum also keeps the viscera from confounding themselves with, or pressing irregularly upon, the bladder: for the kidneys and bladder are contained in a distinct duplicature of that membrane, being thereby partitioned off from the other contents of the abdomen.

5. The *kidneys* are lodged in a bed of fat.

6. The *pancreas*, or sweetbread, is strongly tied to the peritonæum, which is the great wrapping sheet, that encloses all the bowels contained in the lower belly.‡

7. The *spleen* also is confined to its place by an adhesion to the peritonæum and diaphragm, and by a connexion with the omentum.§ It is possible, in my opinion, that the spleen may be merely a *stuffing*, a soft cushion to fill up a vacancy or hollow, which, unless occupied, would leave the package loose and unsteady: for, supposing that it answers no other purpose than this, it must be vascular, and admit of a circulation through it, in order to be kep alive, or be a part of a living body.

8. The *omentum*, epiploön, or caul, is an apron uck ed up, or doubling upon itself, at its lowest part. The upper edge is tied to the bottom of the stomach, to the spleen as hath already been observed, and to part of the duodenum. The reflected edge also, after forming the doubling

* Keill's Anat. p. 119. ed. 3. ‖ Ches. Anat. p. 162.
† Keill's Anat. p. 57. § Ches. Anat. p. 167

K

comes up behind the front flap and is tied to the colon and adjoining viscera.*

9. The septa of the brain probably prevent one part of that organ from pressing with too great a weight upon another part. The processes of the dura mater divide the cavity of the skull, like so many inner partition walls, and thereby confine each hemisphere and lobe of the brain to the chamber which is assigned to it, without its being liable to rest upon, or incommode the neighbouring parts. The great art and caution of packing is to prevent one thing hurting another. This, in the head, the chest, and the abdomen, of an animal body, is, amongst other methods, provided for by membranous partitions and wrappings, which keep the parts separate.

The above may serve as a short account of the manner in which the principal viscera are sustained in their places. But of the provisions for this purpose, by far, in my opinion, the most curious, and where also such a provision was most wanted, is in the *guts*. It is pretty evident, that a long narrow tube (in man, about five times the length of the body) laid from side to side in folds upon one another, winding in oblique and circuitous directions, composed also of a soft and yielding substance, must, without some extraordinary precaution for its safety, be continually displaced by the various, sudden, and abrupt motions of the body which contains it. I should expect that, if not bruised or wounded by every fall, or leap, or twist, it would be entangled, or be involved with itself, or, at the least, slipped and shaken out of the order in which it is disposed, and which order is necessary to be preserved for the carrying on of the important functions, which it has to execute in the animal economy. Let us see, therefore, how a danger so serious, and yet so natural to the length, narrowness, and tubular form of the part, is provided against. The expedient is admirable, and it is this; the intestinal canal, throughout its whole progress, is knit to the edge of a broad fat membrane called the *mesentery*. [Pl. XXII. fig. 2.] It forms the margin of this mesentery, being stitched and fastened to it like the edging of a ruffle: being four times as long as the mesentery itself, it is what a sempstress would call, 'puckered or gathered on" to it. This is the nature of the connexion of the gut with the mesentery; and being thus joined to, or rather made a part of the mesentery, it is folded and wrapped up together with it. Now the mesentery, having a considerable dimension in breadth, being in

* Ches Anat. p. 149.

its substance, withal, both thick and suety s capable of a close and safe folding, in comparison of what the intestinal tube would admit of, if it had remained loose. The mesentery, likewise, not only keeps the intestinal canal in its proper place and position, under all the turns and windings of its course, but sustains the numberless small vessels, the arteries, the veins, the lympheducts, and, above all, the lacteals, which lead from or to almost every point of its coats and cavity. This membrane, which appears to be the great support and security of the alimentary apparatus, is itself strongly tied to the first three vertebræ of the loins.*

III. A third general property of animal forms is *beauty* I do not mean relative beauty, or that of one individual above another of the same species, or of one species compared with another species; but I mean generally, the provision which is made in the body of almost every animal, to adapt its appearance to the perception of the animals with which it converses. In our own species, for example, only consider what the parts and materials are, of which the fairest body is composed; and no farther observation will be necessary to show, how well these things are wrapped up, so as to form a mass, which shall be capable of symmetry in its proportion, and of beauty in its aspect; how the bones are covered, the bowels concealed, the roughnesses of the muscles smoothed and softened; and how over the whole is drawn an integument, which converts the disgusting materials of a dissecting-room into an object of attraction to the sight, or one upon which it rests, at least, with ease and satisfaction. Much of this effect is to be attributed to the intervention of the cellular or adipose membrane, which lies immediately under the skin; is a kind of lining to it; is moist, soft, slippery, and compressible; everywhere filling up the interstices of the muscles, and forming thereby the roundness and flowing line, as well as the evenness and polish of the whole surface.

All which seems to be a strong indication of design, and of a design studiously directed to this purpose. And it being once allowed, that such a purpose existed with respect to *any* of the productions of nature, we may refer, with a considerable degree of probability, other particulars to the same intention; such as the tints of flowers, the plumage of birds, the furs of beasts, the bright scales of fishes, the painted wings of butterflies and beetles, the rich colors and spotted lustre of many tribes of insects

* Keill's Anat. p. 45.

There are parts also of animals ornamental, and the properties by which they are so, not subservient, that we know of, to any other purpose. The *irides* of most animals are very beautiful, without conducing at all, by their beauty, to the perfection of vision; and nature could in no part have employed her pencil to so much advantage, because no part presents itself so conspicuously to the observer, or communicates so great an effect to the whole aspect.

In plants, especially in the flowers of plants, the principle of beauty holds a still more considerable place in their composition; is still more confessed than in animals. Why, for one instance out of a thousand, does the corolla of the tulip, when advanced to its size and maturity, change its color? The purposes, so far as we can see, of vegetable nutrition, might have been carried on as well by its continuing green. Or, if this could not be, consistently with the progress of vegetable life, why break into such a variety of colors? This is no proper effect of age, or of declension in the ascent of the sap; for that, like the autumnal tints, would have produced one color on one leaf, with marks of fading and withering. It seems a lame account to call it, as it has been called, a disease of the plant. Is it not more probable, that this property, which is independent, as it should seem, of the wants and utilities of the plant, was calculated for beauty, intended for display?

A ground, I know, of objection, has been taken against the whole topic of argument, namely, that there is no such thing as beauty at all; in other words, that whatever is useful and familiar, comes of course to be thought beautiful; and that things appear to be so, only by their alliance with these qualities. Our idea of beauty is capable of being so modified by habit, by fashion, by the experience of advantage or pleasure, and by associations arising out of that experience, that a question has been made, whether it be not altogether generated by these causes, or would have any proper existence without them. It seems, however, a carrying of the conclusion too far, to deny the existence of the principle, viz. a native capacity of perceiving beauty, on account of the influence, or of varieties proceeding from that influence, to which it is subject, seeing that principles the most acknowledged are liable to be affected in the same manner. I should rather argue thus: the question respects objects of sight. Now every other sense hath its distinction of agreeable and disagreeable. Some tastes

offend the palate, others gratify it.   In brutes and insects,
this distinction is stronger and more regular than in man
Every horse, ox, sheep, swine, when at liberty to choose,
and when in a natural state, that is, when not vitiated by
habits forced upon it, eats and rejects the same plants
Many insects which feed upon particular plants, will rather
die than change their appropriate leaf.   All this looks like
a determination in the sense itself to particular tastes.   In
like manner, smells affect the nose with sensations pleasurable or disgusting. Some sounds, or compositions of sound,
delight the ear; others torture it.   Habit can do much in
all these cases, (and it is well for us that it can; for it is
this power which reconciles us to many necessities,) but has
the distinction, in the meantime, of agreeable and disagreeable, no foundation in the sense itself?   What is true
of the other senses, is most probably true of the eye, (the
analogy is irresistible,) viz. that there belongs to it an original constitution, fitted to receive pleasure from some impressions, and pain from others.

I do not however know, that the argument which al-
leges beauty as a final cause, rests upon this concession.
We possess a sense of beauty, however we come by it.   It
in fact exists.   Things are not indifferent to this sense;
all objects do not suit it; many, which we see, are agreeable to it; many others disagreeable.   It is certainly not
the effect of habit upon the particular object, because the
most agreeable objects are often the most rare; many,
which are very common, continue to be offensive.   If they
be made supportable by habit, it is all which habit can do;
they never become agreeable.   If this sense, therefore, be
acquired, it is a result; the produce of numerous and complicated actions of external objects upon the senses, and of
the mind upon its sensations.   With this *result*, there
must be a certain congruity to enable any particular object
to please: and that congruity, we contend, is consulted in
the *aspect* which is given to animal and vegetable bodies.

IV.   The skin and covering of animals is that upon
which their appearance chiefly depends, and it is that part
which, perhaps, in all animals is most decorated, and most
free from impurities.   But were beauty, or agreeableness
of aspect, entirely out of the question, there is another
purpose answered by this integument, and by the collocation of the parts of the body beneath it, which is of
still greater importance; and that purpose is *concealment*.
Were it possible to view through the skin the mechanism
our bodies, the sight would frighte   is out of our wits

' Durst we make a single movement,'' asks a lively French writer, '' or stir a step from the place we were in, if we *saw* our blood circulating, the tendons pulling, the lungs blowing, the humours filtrating, and all the incomprehensible assemblage of fibres, tubes, pumps, valves, currents, pivots, which sustain an existence, at once so frail, and so presumptuo s?''

V. Of animal bodies, considered as masses, there is another property, more curious than it is generally thought to be; which is the faculty of *standing:* and it is more remarkable in two-legged animals than in quadrupeds, and, most of all, as being the tallest, and resting upon the smallest base, in man.* There is more, I think, in the matter than we are aware of. The statue of a man, placed loosely upon its pedestal, would not be secure of standing half an hour. You are obliged to fix its feet to the block by bolts and solder; or the first shake, the first gust of wind, is sure to throw it down. Yet this statue shall express all the mechanical proportions of a living model. It is not, therefore, the mere figure, or merely placing the centre of gravity within the base, that is sufficient. Either the law of gravitation is suspended in favor of living substances, or something more is done for them, in order to enable them to uphold their posture. There is no reason whatever to doubt, but that their parts descend by gravitation in the same manner as those of dead matter. The gift, therefore, appears to me to consist, in a faculty of perpetually shifting the centre of gravity, by a set of obscure, indeed, but of quick-balancing actions, so as to keep the line of direction, which is a line drawn from that centre to the ground, within its prescribed limits. Of these actions it may be observed, first, that they in part constitute what we call strength. The dead body drops down. . The mere adjustment, therefore, of weight and pressure, which may be the same the moment after death as the moment before, does not support the column. In cases also of extreme

Anatomy explains the mode in which the weight of the body is transmitted to the feet; and we have seen that the muscles which prevent the head from falling forward in standing, have their fixed point in the neck; that those which perform the same office with regard to the vertebral column, have theirs in the pelvis; that those which preserve the pelvis in equilibrium are attached to the thighs, or to the bones of the legs; that those which prevent the thighs from falling backward are inserted into the tibia; and lastly, that those that preserve the tibia in their vertical position have their fixed point in the feet; these preserve us firm in a standing position -*Paxton*

weakness, the patient cannot stand upright. Secondly, that these actions are only in a small degree voluntary. A man is seldom conscious of his voluntary powers in keep· ing himself upon his legs. A child learning to walk is the greatest posture-master in the world; but art, if it may be so called, sinks into habit; and he is soon able to poise himself in a great variety of attitudes, without being sen· sible either of caution or effort. But still there must be an aptitude of parts, upon which habit can thus attach; a previous capacity of motions which the animal is thus taught to exercise: and the facility with which this exercise is acquired forms one object of our admiration What parts are principally employed, or in what manner each contributes its office, is, as hath already been confessed, difficult to explain. Perhaps the obscure motion of the bones of the feet may have their share in this effect. They are put in action by every slip or vacillation of the body, and seem to assist in restoring its balance. Certain it is, that this circumstance in the structure of the foot, viz. its being composed of many small bones, applied to, and articulating with one another, by diversely shaped sur· faces, instead of being made of one piece, like the last of a shoe, is very remarkable.* I suppose also, that it would be difficult to stand firmly upon stilts or wooden legs, though their base exactly imitated the figure and dimensions of the sole of the foot. The alternation of the joints, the knee-joint bending backward, the hip-joint forward; the flexibility, in every direction, of the spine, especially in the loins and neck, appear to be of great moment in preserving the equilibrium of the body. With respect to this last circumstance, it is observable, that the vertebræ are so confined by ligaments, as to allow no more slipping upon

* [See Plate XI.] There is no part of the human frame which is more wonderfully constructed than the foot. It has the requisite strength to support the weight of the body, and often an additional burden; flexibil'ty, that it may be adapted to the inequalities of the surface on which we tread; and elasticity, to assist in walking, running, and springing from the ground. This advantage we possess from the number of joints, the arch of the foot being composed of twenty-six bones. These bones have a con· siderable play on each other; and as each articulating surface is cover ed with cartilage, the essential property of which is *elasticity*, the jarring is thus prevented which would result from a contact of the bones.

"The first question which naturally arises, is, Why there should be so many bones? The answer is—In order that there may be so many joints; for the structure of a joint not only permits motion but bestows elasticity."—*Paxton*

their bases, than what is just sufficient to break the snock which any violent motion may occasion to the body. A certain degree also of tension of the sinews appears to be essential to an erect posture; for it is by the loss of this, that the dead or paralytic body drops down. The whole is a wonderful result of combined powers, and of very complicated operations. Indeed, that *standing* is not so simple a business as we imagine it to be, is evident from the strange gesticulations of a drunken man, who has lost the government of the centre of gravity.

We have said that this property is the most worthy of observation in the *human* body: but a *bird*, resting upon its perch, or hopping upon a spray, affords no mean specimen of the same faculty. A chicken runs off as soon as it is hatched from the egg; yet a chicken, considered geometrically, and with relation to its centre of gravity, its line of direction, and its equilibrium, is a very irregular solid. Is this gift, therefore, or instruction? May it not be said to be with great attention, that nature hath balanced the body upon its pivots?

I observe also in the same *bird* a piece of useful mechanism of this kind. In the trussing of a fowl, upon bending the legs and thighs up towards the body, the cook finds that the claws close of their own accord. Now let it be remembered, that this is the position of the limbs, in which the bird rests upon its perch. And in this position it sleeps in safety; for the claws do their office in keeping hold of the support, not by any exertion of voluntary power, which sleep might suspend, but by the traction of the tendons in consequence of the attitude which the legs and thighs take by the bird sitting down, and to which the mere weight of the body gives the force that is necessary.

VI. Regarding the human body as a mass; regarding the general conformations which obtain in it; regarding also particular parts in respect to those conformations; we shall be led to observe what I call "interrupted analogies." The following are examples of what I mean by these terms, and I do not know how such critical deviations can, by any possible hypothesis, be accounted for without design.

1. All the bones of the body are covered with a *periosteum*, except the teeth; where it ceases, and an enamel of ivory, which saws and files will hardly touch, comes into its place. No one can doubt of the use and propriety of his difference; of the "analogy" being thus "interrupted;" of the rule, which belongs to the conformation of the bones piring where it does stop; for, had so exquisitely sensi-

ble a membrane as the periosteum invested the teeth, as it invests every other bone of the body, *their* action, necessary exposure, and irritation, would have subjected the animal to continual pain. General as it is, it was not the sort of integument which suited the teeth. What they stood in need of, was a strong, hard, insensible, defensive coat; and exactly such a covering is given to them, in the ivory enamel which adheres to their surface.

2. The scarf-skin, which clothes all the rest of the body, gives way, at the extremities of the toes and fingers, to *nails*. A man has only to look at his hand, to observe with what nicety and precision, that covering, which extends over every other part, is here superseded by a different substance, and a different texture. Now, if either the rule had been necessary, or the deviation from it accidental, this effect would not be seen. When I speak of the rule being necessary, I mean the formation of the skin upon the surface being produced by a set of causes constituted without design, and acting, as all ignorant causes must act, by a general operation. Were this the case, no account could be given of the operation being suspended at the fingers' ends, or on the back part of the fingers, and not on the fore part. On the other hand, if the deviation were accidental, an error, an anomalism; were it anything else than settled by intention; we should meet with nails upon other parts of the body. They would be scattered over the surface, like warts or pimples.

3. All the great cavities of the body are enclosed by membranes, except the *skull*. Why should not the brain be content with the same covering as that which serves for the other principal organs of the body? The heart, the lungs, the liver, the stomach, the bowels, have all soft integuments, and nothing else. The muscular coats are all soft and membranous. I can see a reason for this distinction in the final cause, but in no other. The importance of the brain to life, (which experience proves to be immediate,) and the extreme tenderness of its substance, make a solid case more necessary for it, than for any other part; and such a case the hardness of the skull supplies. When the smallest portion of this natural casket is lost, how carefully, yet how imperfectly is it replaced by a plate of metal? If an anatomist should say, that this bony protection is not confined to the brain, but is extended along the course of the spine, I answer, that he adds strength to the argument. If he remark, that the chest also is fortified by bones, I reply, that I should have alleged this instance myself, if the ribs

had not appeared subservient to the purpose of motion as well as of defence   What distinguishes the skull from every other cavity is, that the bony covering completely surrounds its contents, and is calculated, not for motion, but solely for defence.   Those hollows, likewise, and inequalities, which we observe in the inside of the skull, and which exactly fit the folds of the brain, answer the important design of keeping the substance of the brain steady, and of guarding it against concussions

---

CHAPTER XII

COMPARATIVE ANATOMY.

WHENEVER we find a general plan pursued, yet with such variations in it as are, in each case required by the particular exigency of the subject to which it is applied, we possess, in such plan and such adaptation, the strongest evidence that can be afforded of intelligence and design; an evidence which most completely excludes every other hypothesis. • If the general plan proceeded from any fixed necessity in the nature of things, how could it accommodate itself to the various wants and uses which it had to serve under different circumstances, and on different occasions? Arkwright's mill was invented for the spinning of cotton. We see it employed for the spinning of wool, flax, and hemp, with such modifications of the original principle, such variety in the same plan, as the texture of those different materials rendered necessary.   Of the machine's being put together with design, if it were possible to doubt, whilst we saw it only under one mode, and in one form, when we came to observe it in its different applications, with such changes of structure, such additions, and supplements, as the special and particular use in each case demanded, we could not refuse any longer our assent to the proposition, "that intelligence, properly and strictly so called, (including under that name, foresight, consideration, reference to utility,) had been employed, as well in the primitive plan, as in the several changes and accommodations which it is made to undergo."

Very much of this reasoning is applicable to what has been called *Comparative Anatomy.*   In their general economy, in the outlines of the plan, in the construction as well as offices of their principal parts, there exists between all large terrestrial animals a close resemblance. In all ife is sustained, and the body nourished by nearly the same apparatus. The heart, the lungs, the stomach, the liver, the kidneys, are much alike in all. The same fluid (for no distinction of blood has been observed) circulates through their vessels, and nearly in the same order. The same cause, therefore, whatever that cause was, has been concerned in the origin, has governed the production of these different animal forms.

When we pass on to smaller animals, or to the inhabitants of a different element, the resemblance becomes more distant and more obscure; but still the plan accompanies it.

And, what we can never enough commend, and which it is our business at present to exemplify, the plan is attended, through all its varieties and deflections, by subserviencies to special occasions and utilities.

I. The *covering* of different animals (though whether I am correct in classing this under their anatomy I do not know) is the first thing which presents itself to our observation; and is, in truth, both for its variety, and its suitableness to their several natures, as much to be admired as any part of their structure. We have bristles, hair, wool, furs, feathers, quills, prickles, scales; yet in this diversity both of material and form, we cannot change one animal's coat for another, without evidently changing it for the worse; taking care however to remark, that these coverings are, in many cases, armor as well as clothing; intended for protection as well as warmth.

The *human* animal is the only one which is naked, and the only one which can clothe itself. This is one of the properties which renders him an animal of all climates, and of all seasons. He can adapt the warmth or lightness of his covering to the temperature of his habitation. Had he been born with a fleece upon his back, although he might have been comforted by its warmth in high latitudes, it would have oppressed him by its weight and heat, as the species spread towards the equator.

What art, however, does for men, nature has, in many instances, done for those animals which are incapable of art. Their clothing, of its own accord, changes with their necessities. This is particularly the case with that large tribe of quadrupeds which are covered with *furs*. Every dealer in hare-skins and rabbit-skins, knows how much the fur is thickened by the approach of winter. It seems to be a part of the same constitution and the same

design, tha wool in hot countries, degenerate, as it is
called, b t n truth (most happily for the animal's ease)
passes into hair; whilst, on the contrary, that hair on the
dogs of the polar regions, is turned into wool, or something very like it. To which may be referred, what natural
ists have remarked, that bears, wolves, foxes, hares, which
do not take the water, have the fur much thicker on the
back than the belly: whereas in the beaver it is the thickest upon the belly; as are the feathers on waterfow
We know the final cause of all this; and we know no
other.

The *covering of birds* cannot escape the most vulgar observation. Its lightness, its smoothness, its warmth;—the
disposition of the feathers all inclined backward, the down
about their stem, the overlapping of their tips, their different configuration in different parts, not to mention the variety of their colors, constitute a vestment for the body,
so beautiful, and so appropriate to the life which the animal
is to lead, as that, I think, we should have had no conception of anything equally perfect, if we had never seen it,
or can now imagine anything more so. Let us suppose
(what is possible only in supposition) a person who had
never seen a bird, to be presented with a plucked pheasant,
and bid to set his wits to work, how to contrive for it a
covering which shall unite the qualities of warmth, levity,
and least resistance to the air, and the highest degree of
each; giving it also as much of beauty and ornament as
he could afford. He is the person to behold the work of
the Deity, in this part of his creation, with the sentiments
which are due to it.

The commendation, which the general aspect of the
feathered world seldom fails of exciting, will be increased
by farther examination. It is one of those cases in which
the philosopher has more to admire than the common observer. Every *feather* is a mechanical wonder. If we
look at the quill, we find properties not easily brought
together,—strength and lightness. I know few things
more remarkable than the strength and lightness of the
very pen with which I am writing. If we cast our eye
to the upper part of the stem, we see a material, made for
the purpose, used in no other class of animals, and in no
other part of birds; tough, light, pliant, elastic. The
pith, also, which feeds the feathers, is, amongst animal
substances, *sui generis:* neither bone, flesh, membrane,
nor tendon.

But the artificial part of a feather is the *beard* or, as it is sometimes, I believe, called, the vane. By the beards are meant, what are fastened on each side of the stem, and what constitute the breadth of the feather; what we usually strip off, from one side or both, when we make a pen. The separate pieces of laminæ, of which the beard is composed, are called threads, sometimes filaments, or rays. Now the first thing which an attentive observer will remark is, how much stronger the beard of the feather shows itself to be, when pressed in a direction perpendicular to its plane, than when rubbed, either up or down, in the line of the stem; and he will soon discover the structure which occasions this difference, viz. that the laminæ, whereof these beards are composed, are flat, and placed with their flat sides towards each other; by which means, whilst they *easily* bend for the approaching of each other, as any one may perceive by drawing his finger ever so lightly upwards, they are much harder to bend out of their plane, which is the direction in which they have to encounter the impulse and pressure of the air, and in which their strength is wanted and put to the trial.

This is one particularity in the structure of a feather; a second is still more extraordinary. Whoever examines a feather, cannot help taking notice, that the threads or laminæ, of which we have been speaking, in their natural state *unite*; that their union is something more than the mere apposition of loose surfaces; that they are not parted asunder without some degree of force; that nevertheless there is no glutinous cohesion between them, that, therefore, by some mechanical means or other, they catch or clasp among themselves, thereby giving to the beard or vane its closeness and compactness of texture. Nor is this all: when two laminæ, which have been separated by accident or force, are brought together again, they immediately *reclasp;* the connexion, whatever it was, is perfectly recovered, and the beard of the feather becomes as smooth and firm as if nothing had happened to it. Draw your finger down the feather, which is against the grain, and you break probably the junction of some of the contiguous threads; draw your finger up the feather, and you restore all things to their former state. This is no common contrivance: and now for the mechanism by which it is effected.* The threads or laminæ above mentioned, are *in-*

* By the aid of the microscope it appears, that the laminæ are not flat, as they appear to the unassisted eye, but are semi-tubular, having on their outward edge a series of bristles, termed in the text fibres, set in pairs opposite one another, which clasp with the bristles of the approximate

L*

terlaced with one another; and the interlacing is perform
ed by means of a vast number of fibres, or teeth, which
the laminæ shoot forth *on each side*, and which hook and
grapple together. A friend of mine counted fifty of these
fibres in one twentieth of an inch. These fibres are crooked; but curved after a different manner: for those which
proceed from the thread on the side towards the extremity
of the feather, are longer, more flexible, and bent down
ward; whereas those which proceed from the side towards
the beginning, or quill-end of the feather, are shorter, firmer, and turn upwards. The process then which takes
place is as follows: When two laminæ are pressed together, so that these long fibres are forced far enough over
the short ones, *their* crooked parts fall into the cavity made
by the crooked parts of the others; just as the latch that is
fastened to a door enters into the cavity of the catch fixed
to the door-post, and there hooking itself, *fastens* the door;
for it is properly in this manner, that one thread of a
feather is fastened to the other.

This admirable structure of the feather, which it is easy
to see with the microscope, succeeds perfectly for the use
to which nature has designed it; which use was, not only
that the laminæ might be united, but that when one thread
or lamina has been separated from another by some external violence, it might be reclasped with sufficient facility
and expedition.*

In the *ostrich*, this apparatus of crotchets and fibres, of
hooks and teeth, is wanting: and we see the consequence
of the want. The filaments hang loose and separate from
one another, forming only a kind of down; which constitution of the feathers, however it may fit them for the flowing honors of a lady's head-dress, may be reckoned an
imperfection in the bird, inasmuch as wings, composed of
these feathers, although they may greatly assist it in running, do not serve for flight.

But under the present division of our subject, our business with feathers is, as they are the *covering* of the bird.
And herein a singular circumstance occurs. In the small
order of birds which winter with us, from a snipe down-

laminæ, and cause that adhesiveness observable between the several
aminæ of the vane.

The bristles are not of the same form on each side of one lamina ; the
ower tier, TAB. XXIII. fig. 6. form a simple and slight curve, while the
upper, fig. 7 terminate with three or four little hooks, which serve to
catch the simple corresponding bristle, fig. 6. of the next lamina.

* The above account is taken from Memoirs for a Natural History of
Animals by the Royal Academy of Paris, published 1701, p. 209.

wards, let the external color of the feathers be what it will, their Creator has universally given them a bed of *black* down next their bodies. Black, we know, is the warmest color; and the purpose here is, to *keep in* the heat, arising from the heart and circulation of the blood. It is farther likewise remarkable, that this is not found in larger birds; for which there is also a reason:—small birds are much more exposed to the cold than large ones; forasmuch as they present, in proportion to their bulk, a much larger surface to the air. If a turkey were divided into a number of wrens, (supposing the shape of the turkey and the wren to be similar,) the surface of all the wrens would exceed the surface of the turkey, in the proportion of the length, breadth, (or, of any homologous line,) of a turkey to that of a wren; which would be, perhaps, a proportion of ten to one. It was necessary, therefore, that small birds should be more warmly clad than large ones: and this seems to be the expedient by which that exigency is provided for.

II. In comparing different animals, I know no part of their structure which exhibits greater variety, or, in that variety, a nicer accommodation to their respective conveniency, than that which is seen in the different formations of their *mouths*. Whether the purpose be the reception of aliment merely, or the catching of prey, the picking up of seeds, the cropping of herbage, the extraction of juices, the suction of liquids, the breaking and grinding of food, the taste of that food, together with the respiration of air, and, in conjunction with it, the utterance of sound; these various offices are assigned to this one part, and, in different species, provided for, as they are wanted, by its different constitution. In the human species, forasmuch as there are hands to convey the food to the mouth, the mouth is flat, and by reason of its flatness, fitted only for *reception;* whereas the projecting jaws, the wide rictus, the pointed teeth of the dog and his affinities, enable them to apply their mouths to *snatch and seize* the objects of their pursuit. The full lips, the rough tongue, the corrugated cartilaginous palate, the broad cutting teeth of the ox, the deer, the horse, and the sheep, qualify this tribe for *browsing* upon their pasture; either gathering large mouthfuls at once, where the grass is long, which is the case with the ox in particular; or biting close, where it is short, which the horse and the sheep are able to do, in a degree that one could hardly expect. The retired under jaw of a swine *works in the ground*, after the protruding snout like a prong or ploughshare, has made its way to the roots upon which it feeds. A conformation so happy was not the gift of chance.

In *birds*, this organ assumes a new character; new both in substance and in form; but in both, wonderfully adapted to the wants and uses of a distinct mode of existence. We have no longer the fleshy lips, the teeth of enamelled bone; but we have, in the place of these two parts, and to perform the office of both, a hard substance (of the same nature with that which composes the nails, claws, and hoofs of quadrupeds) cut out into proper shapes, and mechanically suited to the actions which are wanted. The sharp edge and tempered point of the *sparrow's* bill picks almost every kind of seed from its concealment in the plant; and not only so, but hulls the grain, breaks and shatters the coats of the seed, in order to get at the kernel. The hooked beak of the hawk tribe separates the flesh from the bones of the animals which it feeds upon, almost with the cleanness and precision of a dissector's knife. The butcher-bird transfixes its prey upon the spike of a thorn, whilst it picks its bones. In some birds of this class, we have the *cross* bill, i. e. both the upper and lower bill hooked, and their tips crossing. The *spoon* bill, enables the goose to graze, to collect its food from the bottom of pools, or to seek it amidst the soft or liquid substances with which it is mixed. The *long* tapering bill of the snipe and woodcock, penetrates still deeper into moist earth, which is the bed in which the food of that species is lodged. This is exactly the instrument which the animal wanted. It did not want strength in its bill, which was inconsistent with the slender form of the animal's neck, as well as unnecessary for the kind of aliment upon which it subsists; but it wanted length to reach its object

But the species of bill which belongs to birds that live by *suction*, deserves to be described in its relation to that office. They are what naturalists call serrated or dentated bills; the inside of them, towards the edge, being thickly set with parallel or concentric rows of short, strong, sharp-pointed prickles. These, though they should be called teeth, are not for the purpose of mastication, like the teeth of quadrupeds: nor yet, as in fish, for the seizing and retaining of their prey; but for a quite different use. They form a filter The *duck* by means of them discusses the mud; examining with great accuracy the puddle, the brake, every mixture which is likely to contain her food. The operation is thus carried on:—The liquid or semi-liquid substances, in which the animal has plunged her bill, she draws, by the action of her lungs, through the narrow interstices which lie between these teeth; catching, as the stream passes across her beak, whatever it may happen to bring along with it, that proves agreeable to her choice. and easily dismissing all the rest. Now, suppose the purpose to have been, out of a mass of confused heterogeneous substances, to separate for the use of the animal, or rather to enable the animal to separate for its own, those few particles which suited its taste and digestion; what more artificial, or more commodious instrument of selection, could have been given to it, than this natural filter?* It has been observed, also, (what must enable the bird to choose and distinguish with greater acuteness, as well, probably, as what increases its gratification and its luxury,) that the bills of this species are furnished with large nerves, that they are covered with a skin,—and that the nerves run down to the very extremity. In the curlew, woodcock, and snipe, there are *three pairs* of nerves, equal almost to the optic nerve in thickness, which pass first along the roof of the mouth, and then along the upper chap, down to the point of the bill, long as the bill is. [Pl. XXIII. fig. 1.]

But to return to the train of our observations.—The similitude between the bills of birds and the mouths of quadrupeds, is exactly such as, for the sake of the argument, might be wished for. It is near enough to show the continuation of the same plan; it is remote enough to exclude the supposition of the difference being produced by action or use. A more prominent contour, or a wider gape might be resolved into the effect of continued efforts, on the part of the species, to thrust out the mouth, or open it to the stretch. But by what course of action, or exercise, or endeavour, shall we get rid of the lips, the gums, the teeth; and acquire, in the place of them, pincers of horn? By what habit shall we so completely change, not only the shape of the part, but the substance of which it is composed? The truth is, if we had seen no other than the mouths of quadrupeds, we should have thought no other could have been formed: little could we have supposed, that all the purposes of a mouth furnished with lips, and armed with

* There is a remarkable contrivance of this kind in the genus *balæna*, or proper whale. Numerous parallel plates of the substance called whalebone, over the palatine surface of the uper jaw, and descend vertically into tne mouth; the lower edges are fringed by long fibres, which serve the animal, when taking in the water, to retain the molluscæ, with which the water abounds, and which constitute its food.—*Paxton*

teeth, could be answered by an instrument which had none of these; could be supplied, and that with many additional advantages, by the hardness, and sharpness, and figure of the bills of birds.

Everything about the animal *mouth* is mechanical. The teeth of fish have their points turned backward, like the teeth of a wool or cotton card. The teeth of lobsters work one against another, like the sides of a pair of shears. In many insects, the mouth is converted into a pump or sucker, fitted at the end sometimes with a wimble, sometimes with a forceps; by which double provisions, viz. of the tube and the penetrating form of the point, the insect first bores through the integuments of its prey, and then extracts the juices. And, what is most extraordinary of all, one sort of mouth, as the occasion requires, shall be changed into another sort. The caterpillar could not live without teeth; in several species, the butterfly formed from it could not use them. The old teeth therefore, are cast off with the exuviæ of the grub; a new and totally different apparatus assumes their place in the fly. Amid these novelties of form, we sometimes forget that it is, all the while, the animal's *mouth*; that, whether it be lips, or teeth, or bill, or beak, or shears, or pump, it is the same part diversified: and it is also remarkable, that, under all the varieties of configuration with which we are acquainted, and which are very great, the organs of taste and smelling are situated near each other.

III. To the mouth adjoins the gullet: in this part also, comparative anatomy discovers a difference of structure, adapted to the different necessities of the animal. In brutes, because the posture of their neck conduces little to the passage of the aliment, the fibres of the gullet, which act in this business, run in two close spiral lines, crossing each other: in men these fibres run only a little obliquely from the upper end of the œsophagus to the stomach, into which, by a gentle contraction, they easily transmit the descending morsels; that is to say, for the more laborious deglutition of animals, which thrust their food *up* instead of *down*, and also through a longer passage, a proportionably more powerful apparatus of muscles is provided; more powerful, not merely by the strength of the fibres, which might be attributed to the greater exercise of their force, but in their collocation, which is a determinate circumstance, and must have been original.

IV. The gullet leads to the *intestines;* here, likewise, as before, comparing quadrupeds with man, under a general similitude we meet with appropriate differences. The *valvulæ conniventes*, or, as they are by some called, the semilunar valves, found in the human intestine, are wanting in that of brutes. These are wrinkles or plaits of the innermost coat of the guts, the effect of which is, to retard the progress of the food through the alimentary canal. It is easy to understand how much more necessary such a provision may be to the body of an animal of an erect posture, and in which, consequently, the weight of the food is added to the action of the intestine, than in that of a quadruped, in which the course of the food, from its entrance to its exit, is nearly horizontal: but it is impossible to assign any cause, except the final cause, for this distinction actually taking place.* [Pl. XXIII. fig. 2.] So far as depends upon the action of the part, this structure was more to be expected in a quadruped than in a man. In truth, it must in both have been formed, not by action, but in direct opposition to action, and to pressure; but the opposition which would arise from pressure, is greater in the upright trunk than in any other. That theory therefore is pointedly contradicted by the example before us. The structure is found where its generation, according to the method by which the theorist would have it generated, is the most difficult; but (*observe*) it is found where its effect is most useful.

The different length of the intestines in carnivorous and herbivorous animals, has been noticed on a former occasion. The shortest, I believe, is that of some birds of prey, in which the intestinal canal is little more than a straight passage from the mouth to the vent. The longest is in the deer kind. The intestines of a Canadian stag, four feet high, measured ninety-six feet.† The intestines of a sheep, unravelled, measures thirty times the length of the body The intestines of a wild cat is only three times the length of the body. Universally, where the substance upon which the animal feeds is of slow concoction, or yields its chyle

* It may be questioned, whether these extremely soft rugæ or folds of the villous coat of the intestine can in the least retard the passage of the food through it's canal ; nor does the erect attitude of man require them ; for since there are as many of the convolutions of the intestines ascending as there are descending, the weight of the food can have no influence in the action of the intestine: it is certain, however, that this arrangement of the internal coat, affords *a more extensive surface for the lacteals and secreting vessels ;* and this appears to be the real use of the *valvulæ conniventes.—Paxton.*
† Mem. of Acad. Paris, 1701, p. 170

with more difficulty, there the passage is circuitous and dilatory, that time and space may be allowed for the change and the absorption which are necessary. Where the food is soon dissolved, or already half assimilated, an unnecessary, or perhaps hurtful, detention is avoided, by giving to it a shorter and a readier route.

V   In comparing the *bones* of different animals, we are struck, in the bones of birds, with *a propriety*, which could only proceed from the wisdom of an intelligent and designing Creator. In the bones of an animal which is to fly, the two qualities required are strength and lightness. Wherein, therefore, do the bones of birds (I speak of the cylindrical bones) differ in these respects from the bones of quadrupeds? In three properties; first, their cavities are much larger in proportion to the weight of the bone than in those of quadrupeds; secondly, these cavities are empty; thirdly, the shell is of a firmer texture than the substance of other bones. It is easy to observe these particulars, even in picking the wing or leg of a chicken. Now, the weight being the same, the diameter, it is evident, will be greater in a hollow bone than in a solid one, and with the diameter, as every mathematician can prove, is increased, *cæteris paribus*, the strength of the cylinder, or its resistance to breaking. In a word, a bone of the *same weight* would not have been so strong in any other form; and to have made it heavier, would have incommoded the animal's flight. Yet this form could not be acquired by use, or the bone become hollow and tubular by exercise. What appetency could excavate a bone?

VI.   The *lungs* also of birds, as compared with the lungs of quadrupeds, contain in them a provision, distinguishingly calculated for this same purpose of levitation; namely, a communication (not found in other kinds of animals) between the air-vessels of the lungs and the cavities of the body; so that by the intromission of air from one to the other (at the will, as it should seem, of the animal,) its body can be occasionally puffed out, and its tendency to descend in the air, or its specific gravity, made less. The bodies of birds are blown up from their lungs (which no other animal bodies are,) and thus rendered buoyant.

VII.   All birds are *oviparous*. This likewise carries on the work of gestation with as little increase as possible of the weight of the body. A gravid uterus would have been a troublesome burden to a bird in its flight. The advantage, in this respect, of an oviparous procreation is, that whilst the whole brood are hatched together, the eggs are

extruded singly, and at considerable intervals. Ten, fifteen, or twenty young birds may be produced in one cletch
or covey, yet the parent bird have never been encum-
bered by the load of more than one full-grown egg at one
time.

VIII. A principal topic of comparison between animals,
is in their *instruments of motion.* These come before us
under three divisions; feet, wings, and fins. I desire any
man to say, which of the three is best fitted for its use; or
whether the same consummate art be not conspicuous in
them all. The constitution of the elements in which the
motion is to be performed, is very different. The animal
action must necessarily follow that constitution. The
Creator, therefore, if we might so speak, had to prepare for
different situations, for different difficulties; yet the purpose
is accomplished not less successfully in one case than in the
other; and, as between *wings* and the corresponding limbs
of quadrupeds, it is accomplished without deserting the
general idea. The idea is modified, not deserted. Strip
a wing of its feathers, and it bears no obscure resemblance
to the fore leg of a quadruped. The articulations at the
shoulder and the cubitus are much alike; and, what is a
closer circumstance, in both cases the upper part of the
limb consists of a single bone, the lower part of two.

But, fitted up with its furniture of feathers and quills, it
becomes a wonderful instrument, more artificial than its
first appearance indicates, though that be very striking: at
least, the use which the bird makes of its wings in flying
is more complicated, and more curious, than is generally
known. One thing is certain, that if the flapping of the
wings in flight were no more than the reciprocal motion of
the same surface in opposite directions, either upwards and
downwards, or estimated in any oblique line, the bird
would lose as much by one motion as she gained by another.
The skylark could never ascend by such an action as this;
for, though the stroke upon the air by the underside of her
wing would carry her up, the stroke from the upper side,
when she raised her wing again, would bring her down.
In order, therefore, to account for the advantage which the
bird derives from her wing, it is necessary to suppose that
the surface of the wing, measured upon the same plane, is
contracted whilst the wing is drawn up; and let out to its
full expansion, when it descends upon the air for the purpose of moving the body by the reaction of that element.
Now, the form and structure of the wing, its external convexity, the disposition and particularly the overlapping

M

of its larger feathers, the action of the muscles,* and joints of the pinions, are all adapted to this alternate adjustmen. of its shape and dimensions. Such a twist, for instance, or semirotatory motion, is given to the great feathers of the wing, that they strike the air with their flat side, but rise from the stroke slantwise. The turning of the oar in rowing whilst the rower advances his hand for a new stroke. is a similar operation to that of the feather, and takes its name from the resemblance. I believe that this faculty is not found in the great feathers of the tail. This is the place also for observing, that the pinions are so set upon the body, as to bring down the wings, not vertically, but in a direction obliquely tending towards the tail; which motion, by virtue of the common resolution of forces, does two things at the same time; supports the body in the air and carries it forward.

The *steerage* of a bird in its flight is effected partly by the wing. but in a principal degree by the tail. And herein we meet with a circumstance not a little remarkable. Birds with long legs have short tails, and in their flight place their legs close to their bodies, at the same time stretching them out backwards as far as they can. In this position the legs extend beyond the rump, and become the rudder; supplying that steerage which the tail could not.

From the *wings* of birds, the transition is easy to the *fins* of fish. They are both, to their respective tribes, the instruments of their motion; but in the work which they have to do, there is a considerable difference, founded on this circumstance. Fish, unlike birds, have very nearly the same specific gravity with the element in which they move. In the case of fish, therefore, there is little or no weight to bear up; what is wanted, is only an impulse sufficient to carry the body through a resisting medium, or to maintain the posture, or to support or restore the balance of the body, which is always the most unsteady where there is no weight to sink it. For these offices the fins are as large as necessary, though much smaller than wings,

---

* There are three powerful muscles (the fleshy part of the breast) called pectoral muscles, which, with other smaller on the bones of the wing which are analogous to the arm, press with vigor on the air, the elasticity of which gives support. " And it is remarkable that the general resemblance which the best form of windmill sails bears to the feathers of the wings of birds is striking, and one of those beautiful instances of truly mathematical principles on which the works of creation are con structed."· *Paxton.*

their action mechanical, their position, and the muscles by which they are moved, in the highest degree convenient The following short account of some experiments upon fish, made for the purpose of ascertaining the use of their fins, will be the best confirmation of what we assert. In most fish, beside the great fin, the tail, we find two pair of fins upon the sides, two single fins upon the back, and one upon the belly, or rather between the belly and the tail. The *balancing* use of these organs is proved in this manner. Of the large-headed fish, if you cut off the pectoral fins *i. e.* the pair which lies close behind the gills, the head falls prone to the bottom; if the right pectoral fin only be cut off, the fish leans to that side; if the ventral fin on the same side be cut away, then it loses its equilibrium entirey; if the dorsal and ventral fins be cut off, the fish reels to the right and left. When the fish dies, that is, when the fins cease to play, the belly turns upwards The use of the same parts for *motion* is seen in the following observation upon them when put in action. The pectoral, and particularly the ventral fins, serve to *raise and depress* the fish: when the fish desires to have a *retrograde* motion, a stroke forward with the pectoral fin effectually produces it; if the fish desire to *turn* either way, a single blow with the tail the opposite way, sends it round at once: if the tail strike both ways, the motion produced by the double lash is *progressive*, and enables the fish to dart forwards with an astonishing velocity.* The result is not only in some cases the most rapid, but in all cases the most gertle, pliant, easy animal motion with which we are acquain. ed. However, when the tail is cut off, the fish loses a motion, and gives itself up to where the water impels it The rest of the fins, therefore, so far as respects motion seem to be merely subsidiary to this. In their mechanica. use, the anal fin may be reckoned the keel; the ventral fins, out-riggers; the pectoral muscles, the oars: and if there be any similitude between these parts of a boat and a fish, observe, that it is not the resemblance of imitation, but the likeness which arises from applying similar mechanical means to the same purpose.

We have seen that the *tail* in the fish is the great instrument of motion. Now, in cetaceous or warm-blooded

* Goldsmith's History of Animated Nature, vol. iv. p. 154. The velocity with which fish swim from one part of the globe to another is astonishing; when a ship is sailing at the rate of fourteen miles an hour, the porpoises will pass it with as much ease as when at anchor
Paxton.

fish, which are obliged to rise every two or three minutes to the surface to take breath, the tail, unlike what it is in other fish, is horizontal; its stroke consequently perpendicular to the horizon, which is the right direction for sending the fish to the top, or carrying it down to the bottom.

Regarding animals in their instruments of motion we have only followed the comparison through the first great division of animals into beasts, birds, and fish. If it were our intention to pursue the consideration farther, I should take in that generic distinction amongst birds, the *web-foot* of water-fowl. It is an instance which may be pointed out to a child. The utility of the web to water-fowl, the inutility to land-fowl, are so obvious, that it seems impossible to notice the difference without acknowledging the design. I am at a loss to know, how those who deny the agency of an intelligent Creator, dispose of this example. There is nothing in the action of swimming, as carried on by a bird upon the surface of the water, that should generate a membrane between the toes. As to that membrane, it is an exercise of constant resistance. The only supposition I can think of is, that all birds have been originally water-fowl, and web-footed; that sparrows, hawks, linnets, &c. which frequent the land, have, in process of time, and in the course of many generations, had this part worn away by treading upon hard ground. To such evasive assumptions must atheism always have recourse! and, after all, it confesses that the structure of the feet of birds, in their original form, was critically adapted to their original destination! The web-feet of amphibious quadrupeds, seals, otters, &c. fall under the same observation.

IX. The *five senses* are common to most large animals: nor have we much difference to remark in their constitution; or much, however, which is referable to mechanism.

The superior sagacity of animals which hunt their prey and which, consequently, depend for their livelihood upon their *nose*, is well known in its use; but not at all known in the organization which produces it.

The external *ears* of beasts of prey, of lions, tigers, wolves, have their trumpet part, or concavity, standing forwards, to seize the sounds which are before them, viz. the sounds of the animals which they pursue or watch. The ears of animals of flight are turned backward, to give notice of the approach of their enemy from behind, whence ne may steal upon them unseen. This is a critical distinction: and is mechanical: but it may be suggested, and I think not without probability, that it is the effect of continued habit.

The *eyes* of animals which follow their prey by night as cats, owls, &c. possess a faculty not given to those of other species, namely, of closing the pupil *entirely*. The final cause of which seems to be this:—It was necessary for such animals to be able to descry objects with very small degrees of light. This capacity depended upon the superior sensibility of the retina; that is, upon its being affected by the most feeble impulses. But that tenderness of structure, which rendered the membrane thus exquisitely sensible, rendered it also liable to be offended by the access of stronger degrees of light. The contractile range, therefore, of the pupil is increased in these animals, so as to enable them to close the aperture entirely: which includes the power of diminishing it in every degree; whereby at all times such portions, and only such portions of light are admitted, as may be received without injury to the sense.

There appears to be also in the figure, and in some properties of the pupil of the eye, an appropriate relation to the wants of different animals. In horses, oxen, goats, sheep, the pupil of the eye is elliptical; the transverse axis being horizontal; by which structure, although the eye be placed on the side of the head, the anterior elongation of the pupil catches the forward rays, or those which come from objects immediately in front of the animal's face

—————

CHAPTER XIII.

PECULIAR ORGANIZATIONS.

I BELIEVE that all the instances which I shall collect under this title, might, consistently enough with technical language, have been placed under the head of *Comparative Anatomy*. But there appears to me an impropriety in the use which that term hath obtained: it being, in some sort, absurd to call that a case of Comparative Anatomy, in which there is nothing to "compare;" in which a conformation is found in one animal, which hath nothing proper-

M*

y answering to it in another.*   Of this kind are the exam
ples which I have to propose in the present chapter: and
the reader will see that, though some of them be the strongest, perhaps, he will meet with under any division of our
subject, they must necessarily be of an unconnected and
miscellaneous nature.   To dispose them, however, into
some sort of order, we will notice first, particularities of
structure which belong to quadrupeds, birds, and fish, as
such, or to many of the kinds included in these classes of
animals; and then, such particularities as are confined to
one or two species.

I.   Along each side of the neck of large *quadrupeds*,
runs a stiff, robust ligament, which butchers call the
pax wax.   No person can carve the upper end of a crop of
beef without driving his knife against it.   It is a tough,
strong, tendinous substance, braced from the head to the
middle of the back; its office is to assist in supporting the
weight of the head.   It is a mechanical provision, of which
this is the undisputed use; and it is sufficient, and not
more than sufficient, for the purpose which it has to execute.   The head of an ox or a horse is a heavy weight,
acting at the end of a long lever, (consequently with a great
purchase,) and in a direction nearly perpendicular to the
joints of the supporting neck.   From such a force, so ad-
vantageously applied, the bones of the neck would be
in constant danger of dislocation, if they were not fortified
by this strong tape.   No such organ is found in the human subject, because, from the erect position of the head,
(the pressure of it acting nearly in the direction of the
spine,) the junction of the vertebræ appears to be sufficiently secure without it.   This cautionary expedient, therefore,
is limited to quadrupeds: the care of the Creator is seen
where it is wanted.

* The objection here made to the use of the term, Comparative Anato
my, does not seem well founded.   As commonly employed, it is intended
to designate the anatomy of animals compared with that of men and of
one another.   It is only by comparison that the use of parts can be discovered.   Generally, conformations found in one animal have something
corresponding to them in other animals; but even where this is not the
case, a comparison is not the less necessary to discover the use of the
conformation.   Thus, particularly, in the first instance mentioned by the
author, he points out the function of the pax wax by the very process
which he affirms cannot have place.   It is by comparing the neck of large
quadrupeds in which this provision *is* found, with that of man in which it
is not found, and by comparing the position maintained by man with that
maintained by quadrupeds, that he illustrates the object for which this
provision is made.—*Ed.*

II The *oil* with which *birds* prune their feathers, and he organ which supplies it, is a specific provision for the winged creation. On each side of the rump of birds is observed a small nipple, yielding upon pressure a butter-like substance, which the bird extracts by pinching the pap with its bill. With this oil, or ointment, thus procured, the bird dresses its coat; and repeats the action as often as its own sensations teach it that it is in any part wanted, or as the ex cretion may be sufficient for the expense. The gland, the pap, the nature and quality of the excreted substance, the manner of obtaining it from its lodgment in the body, the application of it when obtained, form, collectively, an evidence of intention which it is not easy to withstand. Noth ing similar to it is found in unfeathered animals. What blind *conatus* of nature should produce it in birds? should not produce it in beasts?

III. The *air-bladder* also of a *fish*, [Pl. XXIII. fig. 3,] affords a plain and direct instance, not only of contrivance, but strictly of that species of contrivance which we denominate mechanical. It is a philosophical apparatus in the body of an animal. The principle of the contrivance is clear; the application of the principle is also clear. The use of the organ to sustain, and, at will, also to elevate the body of the fish in the water, is proved by observing, what has been tried, that, when the bladder is burst, the fish grovels at the bottom; and also, that flounders, soles, skates, which are without the air-bladder, seldom rise in the water, and that, with effort. The manner in which the purpose is attained, and the suitableness of the means to the end, are not difficult to be apprehended. The rising and sinking of a fish in water, so far as it is independent of the stroke of the fins and tail, can only be regulated by the specific gravity of the body. When the bladder contained in the body of the fish, is contracted, which the fish probably possesses a muscular power of doing, the bulk of the fish is contracted along with it; whereby, since the absolute weight remains the same, the specific gravity, which is the sinking force, is increased, and the fish descends; on the contrary, when, in consequence of the relaxation of the muscles, the elasticity of the enclosed and now compressed air restores the dimensions of the bladder, the tendency downwards becomes proportionably less than it was before, or is turned into a contrary tendency. These are known properties of bodies immersed in a fluid. The enamelled figures, or little glass bubbles, in a jar of water, are made to rise and fal by the same artifice. A diving machine might be made to ascend and descend, upon the like princ ple , n. n. c. ly, by introducing into the inside of it an air-vessel, which by its contraction would diminish, and by its distension enlarge, the bulk of the machine itself, and thus render it specifically heavier, or specifically lighter, than the water which surrounds it. Suppose this to be done, and .he artist to solicit a patent for his invention: the inspec'ors of the model, whatever they might think of the use o; value of the contrivance, could, by no possibility, entertain a question in their minds, whether it were a contrivance or not. No reason has ever been assigned—no reason can be assigned, why the conclusion is not as certain in the fish as it is in the machine; why the argument is not as firm in one case as the other.

It would be very worthy of inquiry, if it were possible to discover, by what method an animal, which lives constantly in water, is able to supply a repository of air. The expedient, whatever it be, forms part, and perhaps the most curious part, of the provision * Nothing similar to the air-bladder, is found in land-animals; and a life in the water has no natural tendency to produce a bag of air. Nothing can be farther from an acquired organization than this is.

These examples mark the attention of the Creator to the three great kingdoms of his animal creation, and to their constitution as such.—The example which stands next in point of generality, belonging to a large tribe of animals, or rather to various species of that tribe, is the poisonous tooth of serpents.

I. The *fang of a viper* is a clear and curious example of mechanical contrivance. [Pl. XXIII. fig. 4, 5.] It is a perforated tooth, loose at the root: in its quiet state, lying down flat upon the jaw, but furnished with a muscle, which with a jerk, and by the pluck as it were of a string, suddenly erects it. Under the tooth, close to its root, and communicating with the perforation, lies a small bag containing the venom. When the fang is raised, the closing of the jaw presses its root against the bag underneath, and the

* Much obscurity still exists concerning the exact purpose which the air-bag is intended to perform. But with regard to the manner in which it is supplied with air, there seems no reason to doubt that it is effected by a secretion from the blood. It is an established fact in physiology, that many of the internal surfaces of the body have the power of producing gases in this way. In the air-bag of many fishes a very vascular organ is found which has been called the air-gland; and in some species vessels have been discovered conveying the air from this gland into the cavity o. the bag. Even where this gland does not exist, it is probable that the internal surface of the bag may perform the same office.—*Ed.*

force of this compression sends out the fluid with a considerable impetus through the tube in the middle of the tooth. What more unequivocal, or effectual apparatus could be devised, for the double purpose of at once inflicting the wound and injecting the poison? Yet, though lodged in the mouth, it is so constituted, as, in its inoffensive and quiescent state, not to interfere with the animal's ordinary office of receiving its food. It has been observed also, that none of the harmless serpents, the black snake, the blind worm, &c. have these fangs, but teeth of an equal size; not movable, as this is, but fixed into the jaw.

II. In being the property of several different species, the preceding example is resembled by that which I shall next mention, which is the *bag of the opossum*. [Pl. XXIV. fig. 1, 2, 3.] This is a mechanical contrivance, most properly so called. The simplicity of the expedient renders the contrivance more obvious than many others, and by no means less certain. A false skin under the belly of the animal forms a pouch, into which the young litter are received at their birth; where they have an easy and constant access to the teats; in which they are transported by the dam from place to place; where they are at liberty to run in and out; and where they find a refuge from surprise and danger. It is their cradle, their conveyance, and their asylum. Can the use of this structure be doubted of? Nor is it a mere doubling of the skin; but it is a new organ, furnished with bones and muscles of its own. Two bones are placed before the os pubis, and joined to that bone as their base. These support, and give a fixture to, the muscles, which serve to open the bag. To these muscles there are antagonists, which serve in the same manner to shut it; and this office they perform so exactly, that, in the living animal, the opening can scarcely be discerned, except when the sides are forcibly drawn asunder.* Is there any action in this part of the animal, any process arising from that action, by which these members could be formed? Any account to be given of the formation, except design? †

* Goldsmith's Nat. Hist. vol. iv. p. 244.
† There is a very considerable number of animals possessed of the same structure which is here described as existing in the opossum, to which the attention of naturalists has been more particularly called since the first publication of this work. The animals of this kind are called marsupial, from the pouch or *marsupium* which distinguishes them. This provision also has a relation to circumstances in the reproduction of these animals to which Dr. Paley has not referred. He appears merely to regard it as a place of refuge and deposit for the young; somewhat in the same way as the wings of a hen are for its brood. The fact is that the young of these

III. As a particularity, yet appertaining to more species than one, and also as strictly mechanical; we may notice a circumstance in the structure of the *claws* of certain birds. The middle claw of the heron and cormorant, is toothed and notched like a saw. [Pl. XXV. fig. 1.] These birds are great fishers, and these notches assist them in holding their slippery prey. The use is evident; but the structure such as cannot at all be accounted for by the effort of the animal, or the exercise of the part. Some other fishing birds have these notches in their *bills,* and for the same purpose. The gannet, or Soland goose, has the edges of its bill irregularly jagged, that it may hold its prey the faster. [Pl. XXV. fig. 2.] Nor can the structure in this, more than in the former case, arise from the manner of employing the part. The smooth surfaces, and soft flesh of fish, were less likely to notch the bills of

animals are born prematurely, and in a very imperfect and unformed state; and the pouch of the parent seems properly intended for a residence during the completion of the process of developement. The kangaroo is an instance of this kind. When full grown it is six feet in extreme length, and weighs an hundred and fifty pounds. When born it is only one inch in length, and weighs but twenty grains. The fore legs are scarcely distinguishable, and the hind ones, which in the adult state form half the length of the body, are marked only by slight projections at the parts where they are afterwards to grow. In fact the kangaroo at birth is as imperfectly formed as the young of any other animal would be when but a quarter part of the proper period of its growth within its parent had elapsed.

It is remarkable that it has never yet been ascertained whether these little embryos are conveyed by the parent animal, or whether they find their own way, into the pouch. Having scarce the exercise of any of the senses, and being without limbs, it seems almost impossible they should make their way there by their own exertions. However this may be, they are found in the pouch closely attached, and as it were glued to the nipples, by the mouth or rather by that aperture which afterwards becomes a mouth. Here they remain, never quitting their hold, until a sufficient period has elapsed for their growth to be completed, and they have thus arrived in regard to form and structure upon an equality with other animals at the usual period of birth. When this is accomplished, they undergo, as it were, a second birth, and emerge from the pouch· but return occasionally for the purpose of feeding, and for that of protection from danger.

No marsupial animal was known before the discovery of America, of which the opossum is a native; and this animal was at first almost regarded as a sort of exception to the laws of nature; since the discovery of New Holland, however, and the investigation of its natural history, it has been found that the marsupial animals, so far from forming an exception to the general construction of animals on that continent, constitute the prevailing model. With a very few exceptions, all the native animals of New Holland are of the marsupial tribe.—*Ed.*

birds than the hard bodies upon which many other species feed.

We now come to particularities strictly so called, as being limited to a single species of animal. Of these I shall take one from a quadruped and one from a bird.

I. The *stomach of the camel* is well known to retain large quantities of water, and to retain it unchanged for a considerable length of time. [Pl. XXVI.] This property qualifies it for living in the desert. Let us see, therefore, what is the internal organization, upon which a faculty so rare, and so beneficial, depends. A number of distinct sacks or bags (in a dromedary thirty of these have been counted) are observed to lie between the membranes of the second stomach, and to open into the stomach near the top by small square apertures. Through these orifices, after the stomach is full, the annexed bags are filled from it; and the water so deposited is, in the first place, not liable to pass into the intestines; in the second place, is kept separate from the solid aliment; and, in the third place, is out of the reach of the digestive action of the stomach, or of mixture with the gastric juice. It appears probable, or rather certain, that the animal, by the conformation of its muscles, possesses the power of squeezing back this water from the adjacent bags into the stomach, whenever thirst excites it to put this power in action.

II. The *tongue of the woodpecker*, is one of those singularities, which nature presents us with when a singular purpose is to be answered. [Pl. XXVII. fig. 1 and 2.] It is a particular instrument for a particular use: and what else but design, ever produces such? The woodpecker lives chiefly upon insects, lodged in the bodies of decayed or decaying trees. For the purpose of boring into the wood, it is furnished with a bill, straight, hard, angular, and sharp. When, by means of this piercer, it has reached the cells of the insects, then comes the office of its tongue; which tongue is, first, of such a length that the bird can dart it out three or four inches from the bill,—in this respect differing greatly from every other species of bird; in the second place, it is tipped with a stiff, sharp, bony thorn; and in the third place, (which appears to me the most remarkable property of all,) this tip is dentated on both sides, like the beard of an arrow or the barb of a hook. The description of the part declares its uses. The bird having exposed the retreats of the insects by the assistance of its bill, with a motion inconceivably quick, launches out at them this long tongue, transfixes them upon the barbed needle at the end of it, and thus draws its prey within its mouth If this be not mechanism, what is? Should it be said, that, by continual endeavours to shoot out the tongue to the stretch, the woodpecker species may by degrees have lengthened the organ itself beyond that of other birds, what account can be given of its form, of its tip? How, in particular, did it get its barb, its dentation? These barbs, in my opinion, wherever they occur, are decisive proofs of mechanical contrivance.

III. I shall add one more example, for the sake of its novelty. It is always an agreeable discovery, when, having remarked in an animal an extraordinary structure, we come at length to find out an unexpected use for it. The following narrative, which Goldsmith has taken from Buffon, furnishes an instance of this kind. The babyrouessa, or Indian hog, a species of wild boar, found in the East Indies, has two *bent* teeth, more than half a yard long, growing upwards, and (which is the singularity) from the upper jaw [Pl. XXVII. fig. 4.] These instruments are not wanted for offence; that service being provided for by two tusks issuing from the upper jaw, and resembling those of the common boar; nor does the animal use them for defence They might seem therefore to be both a superfluity and an encumbrance. But observe the event: the animal hitches one of these bent upper teeth upon the branch of a tree, and then suffers its whole body to swing from it. This is its manner of taking repose, and of consulting for its safety. It continues the whole night suspended by its tooth, both easy in its posture, and secure; being out of the reach of animals which hunt it for prey.* †

* Goldsmith's Natural History, vol. iii. p. 195.
† There does not seem to be any sufficient authority for ascribing this use to the tusks of this animal. Indeed one does not readily see how it could in the way described swing itself clear of its enemies, except by first climbing the tree; which is not pretended. The fact is doubted, it is believed, by many naturalists, and the opinion probably was in the first place founded upon mere conjecture. A modern and distinguished traveller has these remarks upon the subject. "Philosophers had long puzzled themselves in conjectures what the design of nature could be, as she does nothing without design, in giving to this animal a pair of large, curved tusks, pointing inwards to the face in such a manner as made it sufficiently clear they could not be used either for attack or defence, for procuring food, or for assisting the mastication of it when procured. At length it occurred, or was discovered, by whom I do not recollect, that the animal is fond of sleeping in a standing posture, and, that having a large, ponderous head, finds a conveniency in hanging it upon the branch of a tree or shrub within the reach of its tusks, which serve on such occasions for hooks This is at least an ingenious discovery, and may be true; but if so the

CHAPTER XIV.

PROSPECTIVE CONTRIVANCES

I CAN hardly imagine to myself a more distinguishing mark, and consequently a more certain proof of design, than *preparation*, i. e. the providing of things beforehand which are not to be used until a considerable time afterwards: for this implies a contemplation of the future, which belongs only to intelligence.

Of these *prospective* contrivances, the bodies of animals furnish various examples.

I. The human teeth afford an instance, not only of prospective contrivance, but of the completion of the contrivance being designedly suspended. [Pl. XXVIII. fig. 1 and 2] They are formed within the gums, and there they stop; the fact being, that their farther advance to maturity would not only be useless to the new-born animal, but extremely in its way; as it is evident that the act of *sucking*, by which it is for sometime to be nourished, will be performed with more ease both to the nurse and to the infant, whilst the inside of the mouth, and edges of the gums, are smooth and soft, than if set with hard pointed bones. By the time they are wanted, the teeth are ready. They have been lodged within the gums for some months past, but detained as it were in their sockets, so long as their farther protrusion would interfere with the office to which the mouth is destined. Na ture, namely, that intelligence which was employed in creation, looked beyond the first year of the infant's life; yet, whilst she was providing for functions which were after that term to become necessary, was careful not to incommode those which preceded them. What renders it more probable that this is the effect of design, is, that the teeth are imperfect, whilst all other parts of the mouth are perfect. The lips are perfect, the tongue is perfect; the

habits of the animal must vary according to local circumstances. The same species, or one so like it that the difference is not distinguishable by any description or drawing that I have seen, is common among the rocks on the deserts of Southern Africa, where, within the distance of a hundred miles, there is neither tree nor shrub, except a few stunted heaths or shrivelled everlastings, thinly scattered over the barren surface In such situations, where I have hunted and taken them, it would certainly be no easy matter for the babyrouessa to find a peg to hang its head upon."—*Barrow's Voyage to Cochin-China.*—ED

N

jaws, the palate, the pharynx, the larynx, are all perfect the teeth alone are not so. This is the fact with respect to the human mouth: the fact also is, that the parts above enumerated are called into use from the beginning; whereas the teeth would be only so many obstacles and annoyances, if they were there. When a contrary order is necessary, a contrary order prevails. In the worm of the beetle, as hatched from the egg, the teeth are the first things which arrive at perfection. The insect begins to gnaw as soon as it escapes from the shell, though its other parts be only gradually advancing to their maturity.

What has been observed of the teeth, is true of the *horns* of animals, and for the same reason. The horn of a calf or a lamb does not bud, or at least does not sprout to any considerable length, until the animal be capable of browsing upon its pasture; because such a substance upon the forehead of the young animal, would very much incommode the teat of the dam in the office of giving suck.

But in the case of the *teeth*, of the human teeth at least the prospective contrivance looks still farther. A succession of crops is provided, and provided from the beginning; a second tier being originally formed beneath the first, which do not come into use till several years afterwards. And this double or suppletory provision meets a difficulty in the mechanism of the mouth, which would have appeared almost insurmountable. The expansion of the jaw (the consequence of the proportionable growth of the animal, and of its skull,) necessarily separates the teeth of the first set, however compactly disposed, to a distance from one another, which would be very inconvenient. In due time, therefore, *i. e.* when the jaw has attained a great part of its dimensions, a new set of teeth springs up (loosening and pushing out the old ones before them,) more exactly fitted to the space which they are to occupy, and rising also in such close ranks, as to allow for any extension of line which the subsequent enlargement of the head may occasion.

II It is not very easy to conceive a more evidently prospective contrivance than that which, in all viviparous animals, is found in the *milk* of the female parent. At the moment the young animal enters the world, there is its maintenance ready for it. The particulars to be remarked in this economy are neither few nor slight. We have, first, the nutritious quality of the fluid, unlike, in this respect every other excretion of the body; and in which nature hitherto remains unimitated, neither cookery nor chemistry having been able to make milk out of grass. we have secondly, the organ for its reception and retention; we have, thirdly, the excretory duct, annexed to it; and we have, lastly, the determination of the milk to the breast, at the particular juncture when it is about to be wanted. We have all these properties in the subject before us; and they are all indications of design. The last circumstance is the strongest of any. If I had been to guess beforehand, I should have conjectured, that at the time when there was an extraordinary demand for nourishment in one part of the system, there would be the least likelihood of a re-dundancy to supply another part. The advanced preg-nancy of the female has no intelligible tendency to fill the breast with milk. The lacteal system is a constant won-der; and it adds to other causes of our admiration, tha. the number of the teats and paps in each species is found to bear a proportion to the number of the young. In the sow, the bitch, the rabbit, the cat, the at, which have numerous litters, the paps are numerous, a id are disposed along the whole length of the belly: in the cow and mare they are few. The most simple account of this, is to re-fer it to a designing Creator.

But, in the argument before us, we are entitled to con-sider not only animal bodies when framed, but the circum-stances under which they are framed: and in this view of the subject, the constitution of many of their parts is most strictly prospective.

III. The eye is of no use at the time when it is formed. It is an optical instrument made in a dungeon; construct-ed for the refraction of light to a focus, and perfect for its purpose, before a ray of light has had access to it; geo metrically adapted to the properties and action of an ele-ment with which it has no communication. It is about indeed to enter into that communication; and this is pre-cisely the thing which evidences intention. It is provid-ing for the *future* in the closest sense which can be given to these terms; for it is providing for a future change, not for the then subsisting condition of the animal, not for any gradual progress or advance in that same condition, but for a new state, the consequence of a great and sudden alteration, which the animal is to undergo at its birth. Is it to be believed that the eye was formed, or, which is the same thing, that the series of causes was fixed by which the eye is formed, without a view to this change; without a prospect of that condition, in which its fabric, of no use at present, is about to be of the greatest; without a con

sideration of the qualities of that element, hitherto ent rely excluded, but with which it was hereafter to hold so intimate a relation? A young man makes a pair of spectacles for himself against he grows old; for which spectacles
he has no want or use whatever at the time he makes them.
Could this be done without knowing and considering
the defect of vision to which advanced age is subject?
Would not the precise suitableness of the instrument to its
purpose, of the remedy to the defect, of the convex lens
to the flattened eye, establish the certainty of the conclusion, that the case, afterwards to arise, had been considered beforehand, speculated upon, provided for? all which
are exclusively the acts of a reasoning mind. The eye
formed in one state, for use only in another state, and in a
different state, affords a proof no less clear of destination to
a future purpose, and a proof proportionably stronger, as
the machinery is more complicated, and the adaptation more
exact.

IV. What has been said of the eye, holds equally true
of the lungs. Composed of air-vessels, where there is no
air; elaborately constructed for the alternate admission and
expulsion of an elastic fluid, where no such fluid exists;
this great organ, with the whole apparatus belonging to it,
lies collapsed in the fœtal thorax, yet in order, and in readiness for action, the first moment that the occasion requires
its service. This is having a machine locked up in store
for a future use; which incontestably proves, that the case
was expected to occur, in which this use might be experienced: but expectation is the proper act of intelligence.
Considering the state in which an animal exists before its
birth, I should look for nothing less in its body than a system of lungs. It is like finding a pair of bellows in the
bottom of the sea; of no sort of use in the situation in
which they are found; formed for an action which was impossible to be exerted; holding no relation or fitness to the
element which surrounds them, but both to another e e-
ment in another place.

As part and parcel of the same plan, ought to be mentioned, in speaking of the lungs, the provisionary contrivances of the *foramen ovale* and *ductus arteriosus*. [Pl.
XXIX.] In the fœtus, pipes are laid for the passage of the
blood through the lungs; but, until the lungs be inflated
by the inspiration of air, that passage is impervious, or in a
great degree obstructed. What then is to be done? What
would an artist, what would a master do upon the occasion?
He would endeavour, most probably, to provide a *temporary*

passage, which might carry on the communication requir-ed, until the other was open. Now this is the thing which is actually done in the heart: instead of the circuitous route through the lungs, which the blood afterwards takes before it gets from one auricle of the heart to the other, a portion of the blood passes immediately from the right auricle to the left, through a hole placed in the partition which sepa-rates these cavities. This hole anatomists call the *fora-men ovale.* There is likewise another cross cut, answering the same purpose, by what is called the *ductus arteriosus,* lying between the pulmonary artery and the aörta. But both expediencs are so st·ictly temporary, that after birth the one passage is closed, and the tube which forms the other shrivelled up into a ligament. If this be not contri ance, what is?

But, forasmuch as the action of the air upon the blood in the lungs appears to be necessary to the perfect concoc-tion of that fluid, *i. e.* to the life and health of the animal, (otherwise the shortest rout might still be the best,) how comes it to pass that the *fœtus* lives, and grows, and thrives, without it? The answer is, that the blood of the fœtus is the mother's; that it has undergone that action in her .1abit; that one pair of lungs serves for both. When the animals are separated, a new necessity arises; and to meet this necessity as soon as it occurs, an organization is pre-pared. It is ready for its purpose; it only waits for the atmosphere; it begins to play the moment the air is admit-ted to it

---

CHAPTER XV.

RELATIONS.

When several different parts contribute to one effect; or, which is the same thing, when an effect is produced by the joint action of different instruments; the fitness of such parts or instruments to one another, for the purpose of producing, by their united action, the effect, is what I call *relation;* and wherever this is observed in the works of nature or of man, it appears to me to carry along with it decisive evidence of understanding, intention, art. In examining, for instance, the several parts of a *watch*, the spring, the barrel, the chain, the fusee, the balance, the wheels of various sizes, forms, and positions, what is it

N*

which would take an observer's attention, as most plainly evincing a construction, directed by thought, deliberation, and contrivance? It is the suitableness of these parts to one another; first, in the succession and order in which they act; and, secondly, with a view to the effect finally produced. Thus, referring the spring to the wheels, he sees in it that which originates and upholds *their* motion; in the chain, that which transmits the motion to the fusee; in he fusee, that which communicates it to the wheels: in the conical figure of the fusee, if he refer back again to the spring, he sees that which corrects the inequality of its force. Referring the wheels to one another, he notices, first, their teeth, which would have been without use or meaning, if there had been only one wheel, or if the wheels had had no connexion between themselves, or common bearing upon some joint effect; secondly, the correspondency of their position, so that the teeth of one wheel catch into the teeth of another; thirdly, the proportion observed in the number of teeth of each wheel, which determines the rate of going. Referring the balance to the rest of the works, he saw, when he came to understand its action, that which rendered their motions equable. Lastly, in looking upon the index and face of the watch, he saw the use and conclusion of the mechanism, viz. marking the succession of minutes and hours; but all depending upon the motions within, all upon the system of intermediate actions between the spring and the pointer. What thus struck his attention in the several parts of the watch, he might probably designate by one general name of "relation;" and observing with respect to all cases whatever, in which the origin and formation of a thing could be ascertained by evidence, that these relations were found in things produced by art and design, and in no other things, he would rightly deem of them as characteristic of such productions.—To apply the reasoning here described to the works of nature.

The animal economy is full; is made up of these *rela tions :—*

I. There are, first, what in one form or other belong to all animals, the parts and powers which successively act upon their *food*. Compare this action with the process of a manufactory. In men and quadrupeds, the aliment is first broken and bruised by mechanical instruments of mastication, viz. sharp spikes or hard knobs, pressing against or rubbing upon one another: thus ground and comminuted, it is carried by a pipe into the stomach, where it waits to undergo a great chemical action, which we call digestion: when digested, it is delivered through an orifice, which opens and shuts as there is occasion, into the first intestine; there, after being mixed with certain proper ingredients, poured through a hole in the side of the vessel, it is farther dissolved; in this state, the milk, chyle, or part which is wanted, and which is suited for animal nourishment, is strained off by the mouths of very small tubes, opening into the cavity of the intestines: thus freed from its grosser parts, the percolated fluid is carried by a long, winding, but traceable course, into the main stream of the old circulation; which conveys it, in its progress, to every part of the body. Now, I say again, compare this with the process of a manufactory; with the making of cider, for example; with the bruising of the apples in the mill, the squeezing of them when so bruised in the press, the fermentation in the vat, the bestowing of the liquor thus fermented in the hogsheads, the drawing off into bottles, the pouring out for use into the glass. Let any one show me any difference between these two cases, as to the point of contrivance. That which is at present under our consideration, the " relation" of the parts successively employed, is not more clear in the last case, than in the first. The aptness of the jaws and teeth to prepare the food for the stomach, is, at least, as manifest, as that of the cider-mill to crush the apples for the press. The concoction of the food in the stomach is as necessary for its future use, as the fermentation of the stum in the vat is to the perfection of the liquor. The disposal of the aliment afterwards; the action and change which it undergoes, the route which it is made to take, in order that, and until that, it arrive at its destination, is more complex indeed and intricate, but, in the midst of complication and intricacy, as evident and certain, as is the apparatus of cocks, pipes, tunnels, for transferring the cider from one vessel to another; of barrels and bottles for preserving it till fit for use, or of cups and glasses for bringing it, when wanted, to the lip of the consumer. The character of the machinery is in both cases this, that one part answers to another part, and every part to the final result.

This parallel, between the alimentary operation and some of the processes of art, might be carried farther into detail Spallanzani has remarked* a circumstantial resemblance between the stomachs of gallinaceous fowls and the struc-

* Diss. I. Sect. liv.

t ire of *corn-mills.*   Whilst the two sides of the gizzard per
form the office of the mill-stones, the craw or crop supplies
the place of the hopper.   When our fowls are abundantly
supplied with meat they soon fill their craw: but it does
not immediately pass thence into the gizzard; it always
enters in very small quantities, in proportion to the progress
of trituration;—in like manner as, in a mill, a receiver is
fixed above the two large stones which serve for grinding
the corn; which receiver, although the corn be put into it
by bushels, allows the grain o dribble only in small quantities, into the central hole in the upper mill-stone.

But we have not done with the alimentary history.   There
subsists a general *relation* between the external organs of
an animal by which it procures its food, and the internal
powers by which it digests it.*   Birds of prey, by their
talons and beaks, are qualified to seize and devour many
species, both of other birds and of quadrupeds.   The constitution of the stomach agrees exactly with the form of the
members.   The gastric juice of a bird of prey, of an owl,

* This subject of the relation of parts, and the correspondence of one
part of the animal structure to all the others which is here briefly spoken
of by our author, has since been made, in the hands of some distinguished
anatomists, of immense importance in a scientific point of view.   The
following extract from *Mr. Bell's Treatise on Animal Mechanics,*
shows how extensively it is capable of being considered, and what interesting results may be drawn from it.—*Ed.*

" What we have to state has been the result of the studies of many
naturalists; but although they have labored, as it were, in their own department of comparative anatomy, they have failed to seize upon it with
the privilege of genius, and to handle it in the masterly manner of Cuvier.

" Suppose a man ignorant of anatomy to pick up a bone in an unex-
plored country, he learns nothing, except that some animal has lived and
died there; but the anatomist can, by that single bone, estimate, not merely the size of the animal, as well as if he saw the print of its foot, but
the form and joints of the skeleton, the structure of its jaws, and teeth,
the nature of its food, and its internal economy.   This, to one ignorant of
the subject, must appear wonderful, but it is after this manner that the
anatomist proceeds; let us suppose that he has taken up that portion of
bone in the limb of the quadruped which corresponds to the human wrist;
and that he finds that the form of the bone does not admit of free motion
in various directions, like the paw of the carnivorous creature.   It is obvious, by the structure of the part, that the limb must have been merely
for supporting the animal, and for progression, and not for seizing prey.
This leads him to the fact that there were no bones resembling those of
the hand and fingers, or those of the claws of the tiger; for the motions
which that conformation of bones permits in the paw, would be useless,
without the rotation of the wrist—he concludes that these bones were
formed in one mass, like the cannon-bone, pastern-bone, and coffin-bones
of the horse's foot.

' The motion limited to flexion and extension of the foot of a hoofed

a falcon, or a kite, acts upon the animal fibre alone; t wili not act upon seeds or grasses at all. On the other hand the conformation of the mouth of the sheep or of the ox is suited for browsing upon herbage. Nothing about these animals is fitted for the pursuit of living prey. Accordingly it has been found by experiments, tried not many years ago, with perforated balls, that the gastric juice of ruminating animals such as the sheep and the ox, speedily dissolves vegetables, but makes no impression upon animal bodies. This accordancy is still more particular. The gastric juice, even of granivorous birds, will not act upon he grain whilst whole and entire. In performing the ex-

animal implies the absence of a collar-bone and a restrained motion in the shoulder-joint; and thus the naturalist, from the specimen in his hand, has got a perfect notion of all the bones of the anterior extremity! The motions of the extremities imply a condition of the spine which unites them. Each bone of the spine will have that form which permits the bounding of the stag, or the galloping of the horse, but it will not have that form of joining which admits the turning or writhing of the spine, as in the leopard or the tiger.

" And now he comes to the head:—the teeth of a carnivorous animal, he says, would be useless to rend prey, unless there were claws to hold it, and a mobility of the extremities like the hand, to grasp it. He con iders, therefore, that the teeth must have been for bruising herbs, ind the back teeth for grinding. The socketing of these teeth in the jaw gives a peculiar form to these bones, and the muscles which move them are also peculiar; in short, he forms a conception of the shape of the skull. From this point he may set out anew, for by the form of the teeth, he ascertains the nature of the stomach, the length of the intestines, and all the peculiarities which mark a vegetable feeder.

" Thus the whole parts of the animal system are so connected with one another, that from one single bone or fragment of bone, be it of the jaw, or of the spine, or of the extremity, a really accurate con eption of the shape, motions, and habits of the animal, may be formed

" It will readily be understood that the same process of reasoning will ascertain, from a small portion of a skeleton, the existence of a carnivo rous animal, or of a fowl, or of a bat, or of a lizard, or of a fish ; and what a conviction is here brought home to us, of the extent of that plan which adapts the members of every creature to its proper office, and yet exhibits a system extending through the whole range of animated beings, whose motions are conducted by the operation of muscles and bones!

" After all, this is but a part of the wonders disclosed through the knowledge of a thing so despised as a fragment of bone. It carries us into another science ; since the knowledge of the skeleton not only teaches us the classification of creatures, now alive, but affords proofs of the former existence of animated beings which are not now to be found on the surface of the earth. We are thus led to an unexpected conclusion from such premises; not merely the existence of an individual animal, or race of animals; but even the changes which the globe itself has un lergone in times before all existing records, and before the creation of uman beings to inhabit the earth, are opened to our contemplation "

periment of digestion with the gastric juice in vessels, the
grain must be crushed and bruised before it be submitted
to the menstruum; that is to say, must undergo by art without the body, the preparatory action which the gizzard exerts upon it within the body; or no digestion will take place.
So strict, in this case, is the relation betweeen the offices
assigned to the digestive organ, between the mechanical
operation, and the chemical process.

II. The relation of the kidneys to the bladder, and of
the ureters to both, *i. e.* of the secreting organ to the vessel receiving the secreted liquor, and the pipe laid from one
to the other, for the purpose of conveying it from one to
the other, is as manifest as it is amongst the different ves
sels employed in a distillery, or in the communications between them. The animal structure in this case being simple, and the parts easily separated, it forms an instance of
correlation which may be presented by dissection to every
eye, or which indeed, without dissection, is capable of be-
ng apprehended by every understanding. This correla
tion of instruments to one another fixes intention somewhere: especially when every other solution is negatived
by the conformation. If the bladder had been merely an
expansion of the ureter, produced by retention of the fluid,
there ought to have been a bladder for each ureter. One
receptacle, fed by two pipes, issuing from different sides of
the body, yet from both conveying the same fluid, is not
to be accounted for by any such supposition as this.

III. Relation of parts to one another accompanies us
throughout the whole animal economy. Can any relation
be more simple, yet more convincing, than this, that the
eyes are so placed as to look in the direction in which the
legs move and the hands work? It might have happened
very differently if it had been left to chance. There were
at least three-quarters of the compass out of four to have
erred in. Any considerable alteration in the position of
the eye, or the figure of the joints, would have disturbed
the line, and destroyed the alliance between the sense and
the limbs.

IV. But relation perhaps is never so striking, as when
it subsists, not between different parts of the same thing,
but between different things. The relation between a
lock and a key is more obvious than it is between different parts of the lock. A bow was designed for an arrow,
and an arrow for a bow: and the design is more evident
for their being separate implements.

Nor do the works of the Deity want this clearest species of relation. The *sexes* are manifestly made for eac'. other They form the grand relation of animated nature universal, organic, mechanical: subsisting like the clear est relations of art, in different individuals; unequivocal, inexplicable without design.

So much so, that were every other proof of contrivance in nature dubious or obscure, this alone would be sufficient. The example is complete. Nothing is wanting to the argument. I see no way whatever of getting over it.

V. The teats of animals, which give suck, bear a relation to the mouth of the suckling progeny; particularly to the lips and tongue. Here also, as before, is a correspondency of parts: which parts subsist in different individuals.

These are *general* relations, or the relations of parts which are found, either in all animals, or in large classes and descriptions of animals. *Particular* relations, or the relations which subsist between the particular configuration of one or more parts of certain species of animals, and the particular configuration of one or more other parts of the same animal, (which is the sort of relation that is perhaps most striking,) are such as the following:

I. In the *swan;* the web foot, the spoon bill, the long neck, the thick down, the graminivorous stomach, bear all a relation to one another, inasmuch as they all concur in one design, that of supplying the occasions of an aquatic fowl, floating upon the surface of shallow pools of water and seeking its food at the bottom. Begin with any one of these particularities of structure, and observe how the rest follow it. The web foot qualifies the bird for swimming; the spoon bill enables it to graze. But how is an animal, floating upon the surface of pools of water, to graze at the bottom, except by the mediation of a long neck? A long neck accordingly is given to it. Again, a warm-blooded animal, which was to pass its life upon water, required a defence against the coldness of that element. Such a defence is furnished to the swan, in the muff in which its body is wrapped. But all this outward apparatus would have been in vain, if the intestinal system had not been suited to the digestion of vegetable substances. I say, suited to the digestion of vegetable substances: for it is well known, that there are two intestinal systems found in birds, one with a membranous stomach and a gastric juice, capable of dissolving animal substances alone; the other with a crop and gizzard, calculated for the moistening, bruising and afterwards digesting, of vegetable aliment.

Or set off with any other distinctive part in he body of the swan; for instance, with the long neck The long neck, without the web foot, would have been an encumbrance to the bird; yet there is no necessary connexion between a long neck and a web foot. In fact they do not usually go together. How happens it, therefore, that they meet only when a particular design demands the aid of both?

II. This mutual relation, arising from a subserviency to a common purpose, is very observable also in the parts of a *mole*. The strong short legs of that animal, the palmated feet armed with sharp nails, the pig-like nose, the teeth, the velvet coat, the small external ear, the sagacious smell, the sunk protected eye, all conduce to the utilities or to the safety of its under-ground life. It is a special purpose, specially consulted throughout. The form of the feet fixes the character of the animal. They are so many shovels; they determine its action to that of rooting in the ground; and everything about its body agrees with this destination. The cylindrical figure of the mole, as well as the compactness of its form, arising from the terseness of its limbs, proportionably lessens its labor; because, according to its bulk, it thereby requires the least possible quantity of earth to be removed for its progress. It has nearly the same structure of the face and jaws as a swine, and the same office for them. The nose is sharp, slender, tendinous, strong; with a pair of nerves going down to the end of it. The plush covering, which, by the smoothness, closeness, and polish of the short piles that compose it, rejects the adhesion of almost every species of earth, defends the animal from cold and wet, and from the impediment which it would experience by the mould sticking to its body. From soils of all kinds the little pioneer comes forth bright and clean. Inhabiting dirt, it is, of all animals, the neatest.

But what I have always most admired in the mole is its eyes. This animal occasionally visiting the surface, and wanting, for its safety and direction, to be informed when it does so, or when it approaches it, a perception of light was necessary. I do not know that the clearness of sight depends at all upon the size of the organ. What is gained by the largeness or prominence of the globe of the eye is width in the field of vision. Such a capacity would be of no use to an animal which was to seek its food in the dark. The mole did not want to look about it; nor would a large advanced eye have been easily defended from the annoy-

nnce to which the life of the animal must constantly ex
pose it.   How indeed was the mole, working its way under ground, to guard its eyes at all?   In order to meet
this difficulty, the eyes are made scarcely larger than the
head of a corking-pin; and these minute globules are sunk
so deep in the skull, and lie so sheltered within the velvet
of its covering, as that any contraction of what may be
called the eye brows, not only closes up the apertures
which lead to the eyes, but presents a cushion, as it were,
to any sharp or pretruding substance, which might push
against them.   This aperture, even in its ordinary state, is
like a pin-hole in a piece of velvet, scarcely pervious to
loose particles of earth

Observe then, in this structure, that which we call relation.   There is no natural connexion between a small
sunk eye and a shovel palmated foot.   Palmated feet might
have been joined with goggle eyes; or small eyes might
have been joined with feet of any other form.   What was
it therefore which brought them together in the mole?
That which brought together the barrel, the chain, and the
fusee, in a watch; design: and design, in both cases, in-
ferred from the relation which the parts bear to one another in the prosecution of a common purpose.   As hath
already been observed, there are different ways of stating
the relation, according as we set out from a different part.
In the instance before us, we may either consider the
shape of the feet, as qualifying the animal for that mode
of life and inhabitation to which the structure of its eyes
co   es it; or we may consider the structure of the eye,
as the only one which would have suited with the action
to which the feet are adapted.   The relation is manifest,
whichever of the parts related we place first in the order
of our consideration.   In a word; the feet of the mole are
made for digging; the neck, nose, eyes, ears, and skin, are
peculiarly adapted to an under-ground life; and this is
what I call relation.   [Pl. XXX. fig. 1.]

CHAPTER XVI.

COMPENSATION.

COMPENSATION is a species of relation.   It is relation
when the *defects* of one part, or of one organ, are supplied

Ó

by the structure of another part, or of another organ Thus,

I. The short, unbending neck of the *elephant*, is compensated by the length and flexibility of his *proboscis*. He could not have reached the ground without it; or, if it be supposed that he might have fed upon the fruit, leaves, or branches of trees, how was he to drink? Should it be asked, why is the elephant's neck so short? it may be answered that the weight of a head so heavy could not have been supported at the end of a longer lever. To a form, therefore, in some respects necessary, but in some respects also inadequate to the occasion of the animal, a supplement is added, which exactly makes up the deficiency under which he labored.

If it be suggested that this proboscis may have been produced, in a long course of generations, by the constant endeavour of the elephant to thrust out his nose (which is the general hypothesis by which it has lately been attempted to account for the forms of animated nature,) I would ask, how was the animal to subsist in the meantime, during the process, *until* this elongation of snout was completed? What was to become of the individual, whilst the species was perfecting?

Our business at present is, simply to point out the relation which this organ bears to the peculiar figure of the animal to which it belongs And herein all things correspond. The necessity of the elephant's proboscis arises from the shortness of his neck; the shortness of the neck is rendered necessary by the weight of the head. Were we to enter into an examination of the structure and anatomy of the proboscis itself, we should see in it one of the most curious of all examples of animal mechanism. [Pl XXX. fig. 2, 3, 4, 5.] The disposition of the ringlets and fibres, for the purpose, first of forming a long cartilaginous pipe; secondly, of contracting and lengthening that pipe; thirdly, of turning it in every direction at the will of the animal; with the superaddition at the end, of a fleshy production, of about the length and thickness of a finger, and performing the office of a finger, so as to pick up a straw from the ground; these properties of the same organ, taken together, exhibit a specimen, no only of design, (which is attested by the advantage,) but of consummate art and, as I may say, of elaborate preparation, in accomplishing that design.

II The hook in the wing of a *bat* is strictly a mechanical, and also a *compensating* contrivance. [Pl XXX fig. 6] At the angle of its wing there is a bent claw, exactly in the form of a hook, by which the bat attaches itself to the sides of rocks, caves, and buildings, laying hold of crevices, joinings, chinks, and roughnesses It hooks itself by this claw; remains suspended by this hold; takes its flight from this position: which operations compensate for the decrepitude of its legs and feet. Without her hook, the bat would be the most helpless of all animals. She can neither run upon her feet, nor raise herself from the ground. These inabilities are made up to her by the contrivance in her wing: and in placing a claw on that part, the Creator has deviated from the analogy observed in winged animals.—A singular defect required a singular substitute

III. The *crane* kind are to live and seek their food amongst the waters; yet, having no web-feet, are incapable of swimming. To make up for this deficiency, they are furnished with long legs for wading, or long bills for groping; or usually with both. This is *compensation*. But I think the true reflection upon the present instance is, how every part of nature is tenanted by appropriate inhabitants. Not only is the surface of deep waters peopled by numerous tribes of birds that swim, but marshes and shallow pools are furnished with hardly less numerous tribes of birds that wade.

IV. The common *parrot* has, in the structure of its beak, both an inconveniency, and a *compensation* for it When I speak of an inconveniency, I have a view to a dilemma which frequently occurs in the works of nature, viz. that the peculiarity of structure by which an organ is made to answer one purpose, necessarily unfits it for some other purpose. This is the case before us. The upper bill of a parrot is so much hooked, and so much overlaps the lower, that if, as in other birds, the lower chap alone had motion, the bird could scarcely gape wide enough to receive its food: yet this hook and overlapping of the bill could not be spared, for it forms the very instrument by which the bird climbs, to say nothing of the use which it makes of it in breaking nuts and the hard substances upon which it feeds. How, therefore, has nature provided for the opening of this occluded mouth? By making the upper chap movable, [Pl. XXX. fig. 7,] as well as the lower. In most birds, the upper chap is connected, and makes but one piece with the skull; but in the parrot, the upper chap is joined to the bone of the head by a strong membrane placed on each side of it, which lifts and depresses it at pleasure.*

V. The *spider's web* is a *compensating* contrivance The spider lives upon flies, without wings to pursue them; a case, one would have thought, of great difficulty, yet provided for; and provided for by a resource, which no stratagem, no effort of the animal, could have produced, had not both its external and internal structure been specifica ly adapted to the operation.

VI. In many species of insects, the eye is fixed; and consequently without the power of turning the pupil to the object. This great defect is, however, perfectly *compensated*; and by a mechanism which we should not suspect. The eye is a multiplying glass, with a lens looking in every direction and catching every object. By which means, although the orb of the eye be stationary, the field of vision is as ample as that of other animals, and is commanded on every side. [Pl. XXX. fig. 8.] When this lattice-work was first observed, the multiplicity and minuteness of the surfaces must have added to the surprise of the discovery. Adams tells us, that fourteen hundred of these reticulations have been counted in the two eyes of a drone bee

In other cases the *compensation* is effected by the number and position of the eyes themselves. [Pl. XXX. fig. 9.] The spider has eight eyes, mounted upon different parts o' the head; two in front, two in the top of the head, two on each side. These eyes are without motion; but, by their situation, suited to comprehend every view which the wants or safety of the animal may render it necessary for it to take

VII. The Memoirs for the Natural History o' Animals, published by the French Academy, A. D. 1687, furnish us with some curious particulars in the eye of a chameleon. [Pl. XXXI. fig. 1.] Instead of two eyelids, it is covered by an eyelid with a hole in it. This singular structure ap-pears to be *compensatory*, and to answer to some other sin-gularities in the shape of the animal. The neck of the chameleon is inflexible. To make up for this, the eye is so prominent, as that more than half the ball stands out of the head. By means of which extraordinary projection, the pupil of the eye can be carried by the muscles in every direction, and is capable of being pointed towards every object. But then, so unusual an exposure of the globe of the eye requires, for its lubricity and defence, a more than

* Goldsmith's Nat. Hist. vol. v. p. 274.

linary protection of eyelid, as well as a more than ordinary supply of moisture; yet the motion of an eyelid.
formed according to the common construction, would be
impeded, as it should seem, by the convexity of the organ.
The aperture in the lid meets this difficulty. It enables
the animal to keep the principal part of the surface of the
eye under cover, and to preserve it in a due state of hu--
midity without shutting out the light; or without performing every moment a nictitation, which, it is probable, would
be more laborious to this animal than to others.

VIII. In another animal, and in another part of the
animal economy, the same Memoirs describe a most remarkable *substitution*. The reader will remember what
we have already observed concerning the *intestinal* canal;
that its length, so many times exceeding that of the body,
promotes the extraction of the chyle from the aliment, by
giving room for the lacteal vessels to act upon it through
a greater space. This long intestine, wherever it occurs,
is in other animals disposed in the abdomen from side to
side in returning folds. But, in the animal now under
our notice, the matter is managed otherwise. The same
intention is mechanically effectuated; but by a mechanism
of a different kind. The animal of which I speak is an
amphibious quadruped, which our authors call the alope-
cias, or sea-fox. [Pl. XXXI. fig. 2, 3.] The intestine
is straight from one end to the other: but in this straight
and consequently short intestine, is a winding, corkscrew,
spiral passage, through which the food, not without several
circumvolutions, and in fact by a long route, is conducted
to its exit. Here the shortness of the gut is *compensated*
by the obliquity of the perforation.

IX. But the works of the Deity are known by expedients. Where we should look for absolute destitution;
where we can reckon up nothing but wants, some contr
vance always comes in to supply the privation. A *snail*
without wings, feet, or thread, climbs up the stalks of
plants, by the sole aid of a viscid humour discharged from
her skin. She adheres to the stems, leaves, and fruits
of plants, by means of a sticking plaster. A *muscle*,
which might seem, by its helplessness, to lie at the mercy
of every wave that went over it, has the singular power of
spinning strong tendinous threads, by which she moors
her shell to rocks and timbers. A *cockle*, on the contrary,
by means of its stiff tongue, works for itself a shelter in the
sand. The provisions of nature extend to cases the most
desperate A *lobster* has in its constitution a difficulty so

O *

great, that one could hardly conjecture beforehand how nature would dispose of it. In most animals, the skin grows with their growth. If, instead of a soft skin, there be a shell, still it admits of a gradual enlargement. If the shell, as in the tortoise, consists of several pieces, the accession of substance is made at the sutures. Bivalve shells grow bigger by receiving an accretion at their edge; it is the same with spiral shells at their mouth. The simplici-y of their form admits of this. But the lobster's shell be-ing applied to the limbs of the body, as well as to the bod itself, allows not of either of the modes of growth whic. are observed to take place in other shells. Its hardness resists expansion; and its complexity renders it incapable of increasing its size by addition of substance to its edg How then was the growth of the lobster to be provided fo ? Was room to be made for it in the old shell, or was it) be successively fitted with new ones? If a change of sh ll became necessary, how was the lobster to extricate hims lf from his present confinement? How was he to uncase his buckler, or draw his legs out of his boots? The process, which fishermen have observed to take place, is as foll ws: At certain seasons, the shell of a lobster grows soft, the animal swells its body, the seams open, and the claws burst at the joints. When the shell has thus become loose upon the body, the animal makes a second effort, and by a tremulous, spasmodic motion, casts it off. In this state, the liberated but defenceless fish retires into holes in the rock. The released body now suddenly pushes its growth. In about eight and forty hours, a fresh concretion of hu-mour upon the surface, i. e. a new shell, is formed, adapted in every part to the increased dimensions of the animal This wonderful mutation is repeated every year.

If there be imputed defects without compensation, I should suspect that they were defects only in appearance. Thus, the body of the *sloth* has often been reproached for the slowness of its motions, which has been attributed to an imperfection in the formation of its limbs. But it ought to be observed, that it is this slowness which alone suspends the voracity of the animal. He fasts during his migration from one tree to another; and this fast may be necessary for the relief of his over-charged vessels, as well as to allow time for the concoction of the mass of coarse and hard food which he has taken into his stomach. The tardiness of his pace seems to have reference to the capac-ity of his organs, and to his propensities with respect to food, *i e* is calculated to counteract the effects of reple-tion.*

Or there may be cases in which a defect is artificial, and compensated by the very cause which produces it. Thus the *sheep*, in the domesticated state in which we see i , is destitute of the ordinary means of defence or escape; is incapable either of resistance or flight. But this is not so with the wild animal. The natural sheep is swift and active; and if it lose these qualities when it comes under the subjection of man, the loss is compensated by his pro-tection. Perhaps there is no species of quadruped what ever, which suffers so little as this does from the depreda-tion of animals of prey.

For the sake of making our meaning better understood, we have considered this business of compensation under certain *particularities* of constitution, in which it appears to be most conspicuous. Tl is view of the subject neces-sarily limits the instances to s.ngle species of animals. But there are compensations, perhaps not less certain, which extend over large classes, and to large portions of living nature.

I. In quadrupeds, the deficiency of teeth is usually *com-pensated* by the faculty of rumination. The sheep, deer, and ox tribe, are without fore-teeth in the upper jaw. These ruminate. The horse and ass are furnished with teeth in the upper jaw, and do not ruminate. In the former class, the grass and hay descend into the stomach nearly in the state in which they are cropped from the pasture, or gath-ered from the bundle. In the stomach, they are softened by the gastric juice, which in these animals is unusually copious. Thus softened and rendered tender, they are returned a second time to the action of the mouth, where the grinding teeth complete at their leisure the trituration

* Blumenbach states, in his Manual of Natural History, that he had conversed with many Hollanders who had lived in Guiana, and from them collected, that this apparently miserable animal is rather an en-viable one. First, he nourishes himself entirely from leaves, and, there-fore, when he has once climbed a tree, he can live on the same dish a quarter of a year. Secondly, he does not drink at all. Thirdly, on a tree he is exposed to but few enemies, and when the sloth marks that a tiger-cat is climbing up a branch, it goes softly to the end of the branch, and rocks it till the tiger-cat falls off, so that seldom is there an instance that a tiger-cat surprises one: even upon the ground, so powerful are the claws of the sloth, and so fearful its cries, that its enemies generally get the worst. So idle is Buffon's declamation against the goodness and wisdom of Providence, drawn from this beast.
Paxton

which is necessary, but which was before left imperfect. I say, the trituration which is necessary; for it appears from experiments, that the gastric fluid of sheep, for example, has no effec in digesting plants, unless they have been previously mas'icated; that it only produces a slight maceration, nearly as common water would do in a like degree of heat; but that when once vegetables are reduced to pieces by mastication, the fluid then exerts upon them its specific operation. Its first effect is to soften them, and to destroy their natural consistency; it then goes on to dissolve them; not sparing even the toughest parts, such as the nerves of the leaves.*

I think it very probable, that the gratification also of the animal is renewed and prolonged by this faculty. Sheep, deer, and oxen, appear to be in a state of enjoyment whilst they are chewing the cud. It is then, perhaps, that they best relish their food.

II. In birds, the *compensation* is still more striking They have no teeth at all. What have they then to make up for this severe want? I speak of granivorous and herbivorous birds; such as common fowls, turkeys, ducks, geese, pigeons, &c. for it is concerning these alone that the question need be asked. All these are furnished with a peculiar and most powerful muscle called the *gizzard*; the inner coat of which is fitted up with rough plates, which, by a strong friction against one another, break and grind the hard aliment as effectually, and by the same mechanical action, as a coffee-mill would do. It has been proved by the most correct experiments, that the gastric juice of these birds will not operate upon the *entire* grain; not even when softened by water or macerated in the crop. Therefore, without a grinding machine within its body, without the trituration of the gizzard, a chicken would have starved upon a heap of corn. Yet why should a bill and a gizzard go together? Why should a gizzard never be found where here are teeth?

Nor does the gizzard belong to birds as such. A gizzard is not found in birds of prey. *Their* food requires not to be ground down in a mill. The compensatory contrivance goes no farther than the necessity. In both classes of birds, however, the digestive organ within the body bears a strict and mechanical relation to the external instruments for procuring food. The soft membranous stomach, accompanies the hooked, notched beak; the short

* Spall. dis. III. Sect. 140.

muscular legs; the strong, sharp, crooked talons: The cartilaginous stomach attends that conformation of bill and toes, which restrains the bird to the picking of seeds, or the cropping of plants.

III. But to proceed with our *compensations.*—A very numerous and comprehensive tribe of terrestrial animals are entirely without feet; yet locomotive; and in a very considerable degree swift in their motion. How is the *want of feet* compensated? It is done by the disposition of the muscles and fibres of the trunk. In consequence of the just collocation, and by means of the joint action of longitudinal and annular fibres, that is to say, of strings and rings, the body and train of reptiles* are capable of being reciprocally shortened and lengthened, drawn up and stretched out. The result of this action is a progressive, and in some cases, a rapid movement of the whole body, in any direction to which the will of the animal determines it. The meanest creature is a collection of wonders. The play of the rings in an *earth-worm* as it crawls; the undulatory motion propagated along the body; the beards or prickles with which the annuli are armed, and which the animal can either shut up close to its body, or let out to lay hold of the roughness of the surface upon which it creeps; and the power arising from all these, of changing its place and position, affords, when compared with the provisions for motion in other animals, proofs of new and appropriate mechanism. Suppose that we had never seen an animal move upon the ground without feet, and that the problem was; muscular action, *i. e.* reciprocal contraction and relaxation being given, to describe how such an animal might be constructed, capable of voluntarily changing place. Something, perhaps, like the organization of reptiles might have been hit upon by the ingenuity of an artist; or might have been exhibited in an automaton, by the combination of springs, spiral wires, and ringlets; but to the solution of the problem would not be denied, surely, the

---

* Contraction and expansion is the mode of progression in *worms,* but not in *reptiles;* in the class of serpents locomotion consists simply of repeated horizontal undulations, viz. flexion and extension. Thus the head being the fixed point, the body and tail assume several curves; the tail then becomes the fixed point, the curvatures are straightened, and thus the animal advances with a *serpentine* motion. By these successive curvatures and right lines alternating, it moves forward at each *step* nearly the length of the whole body; the ribs, which Sir E. Home considers to act as feet, having nothing to do with locomotion unless as affording a fulcrum for the muscles.— *Paxton*

praise of invention and of successful thought: least of all could it ever be questioned, whether intelligence had been employed about it, or not.

———◆———

CHAPTER XVII.

THE RELATION OF ANIMATED BODIES TO INANIMATE NATURE

WE have already considered *relation*, and under different views; but it was the relation of parts to parts, of the parts of an animal to other parts of the same animal, or of another individual of the same species.

But the bodies of animals hold, in their constitution and properties, a close and important relation to natures altogether external to their own; to inanimate substances, and to the specific qualities of these; e. g. *they hold a strict relation to the* ELEMENTS *by which they are surrounded.*

I.   Can it be doubted, whether the *wings of birds* bear a relation to air, and the *fins of fish* to water? They are instruments of motion, severally suited to the properties of the medium in which the motion is to be performed: which properties are different. Was not this difference contemplated, when the instruments were differently constituted?

II.   The structure of the animal *ear* depends for its use, not simply upon being surrounded by a fluid, but upon the specific nature of that fluid. Every fluid would not serve: its particles must repel one another, it must form an elastic medium: for it is by the successive pulses of *such* a medium, that the undulations excited by the surrounding body are carried to the organ; that a communication is formed between the object and the sense; which must be done before the internal machinery of the ear, subtile as it is, can act at all.

III.   The *organs* of voice and respiration are, no less than the ear, indebted for the success of their operation to the peculiar qualities of the fluid in which the animal is immersed. They, therefore, as well as the ear, are constituted upon the supposition of such a fluid, i. e. of a fluid with such particular properties, being always present. Change the properties of the fluid, and the organ cannot act; change the organ, and the properties of the fluid would be lost. The structure therefore, of our organs, and the properties of our atmosphere are made for one another. Nor does it alter the relation, whether you allege the organ to be made for the element, (which seems the most natural way of considering it,) or the element as prepared for the organ.

IV. But there is another fluid with which we have to do, with properties of its own; with laws of acting, and of being acted upon, totally different from those of air and water. and that is *light*. To this new, this singular element; to qualities perfectly peculiar, perfectly distinct and remote from the qualities of any other substance with which we are acquainted, an organ is adapted, an instrument is correctly adjusted, not less peculiar amongst the parts of the body, not less singular in its form, and in the substance of which it is composed, not less remote from the materials, the model, and the analogy of any other part of the animal frame, than the element to which it relates is specific amidst the substances with which we converse. If this does not prove appropriation, I desire to know what would prove it.

Yet the element of light and the organ of vision, however related in their office and use, have no connexion whatever in their original. The action of rays of light upon the surfaces of animals, has no tendency to breed eyes in their heads. The sun might shine forever upon living bodies, without the smallest approach towards producing the sense of sight. On the other hand also, the animal eye does *not* generate or emit light.

V. Throughout the universe there is a wonderful *p o-portioning* of one thing to another. The size of animals, of the human animal especially, when considered with respect to other animals, or to the plants which grow around him, is such, as a regard to his conveniency would have pointed out. A giant or a pigmy could not have milked goats, reaped corn, or mowed grass; we may add, could not have rode a horse, trained a vine, shorn a sheep, with the same bodily ease as we do, if at all. A pigmy would have been lost amongst rushes, or carried off by birds of prey.

It may be mentioned likewise, that the model and the n.aterials of the human body being what they are, a much greater bulk would have broken down by its own weight The persons of men who much exceed the ordinary stature, betray this tendency.

VI. Again (and which includes a vast variety of particulars, and those of the greatest importance;) how close is

the *suitableness* of the earth and sea to their several in
nabitants; and of these inhabitants, to the places of their
appointed residence!

Take the *earth* as it is; and consider the correspondency of the powers of its inhabitants with the properties and
condition of the soil which they tread. Take the inhabitants as they are; and consider the substances which the
earth yields for their use. They can scratch its surface,
and its surface supplies all which they want. This is the
length of their faculties! and such is the constitution of
the globe, and their own, that this is sufficient for all their
occasions.

When we pass from the earth to the *sea*, from land to
water, we pass through a great change; but an adequate
change accompanies us of animal forms and functions, of
animal capacities and wants; so that *correspondency* remains.
The earth in its nature is very different from the sea, and
the sea from the earth; but one accords with its inhabitants
as exactly as the other.

VII. The last relation of this kind which I shall mention is that of *sleep* to *night*; and it appears to me to be
a relation which was expressly intended. Two points are
manifest: first, that the animal frame requires sleep; sec
ondly, that night brings with it a silence, and a cessation
of activity, which allows of sleep being taken without interruption, and without loss. Animal existence is made
up of action and slumber; nature has provided a season for
each. An animal which stood not in need of rest, would
always live in daylight. An animal which, though made
for action, and delighting in action, must have its strength
repaired by sleep, meets by its constitution the returns of
day and night. In the human species, for instance, were
the bustle, the labor, the motion of life, upheld by the
constant presence of light, sleep could not be enjoyed without being disturbed by noise, and without expense of that
time which the eagerness of private interest would not con-
tentedly resign. It is happy therefore for this part of the
creation, I mean that it is conformable to the frame and
wants of their constitution, that nature, by the very disposition of her elements, has commanded, as it were, and
imposed upon them, at moderate intervals, a general inter-
mission of their toils, their occupations, and pursuits.

But it is not for man, either solely or principally, that
night is made. Inferior, but less perverted natures, taste
its solace, and expect its return with greater exactness
and advantage than he does. I have often observed, and

never observed but to admire, the satisfaction no less than the regularity, with which the greatest part of the irrational world yield to this soft necessity, this grateful vicissitude: how comfortably the birds of the air, for example, address themselves to the repose of the evening; with what alertness they resume the activity of the day!

Nor does it disturb our argument to confess, that certain species of animals are in motion during the night, and at rest in the day. With respect even to them, it is still true, that there is a change of condition in the animal, and an external change corresponding with it. There is still the relation, though inverted. The fact is, that the repose of other animals sets these at liberty, and invites them to their food or their sport.

If the relation of *sleep* to *night*, and, in some instances, its converse, be real, we cannot reflect without amazement upon the extent to which it carries us. Day and night are things close to us; the change applies immediately to our sensations; of all the phenomena of nature, it is the most obvious and the most familiar to our experience; but in its cause, it belongs to the great motions which are passing in the heavens. Whilst the earth glides round her axle, she ministers to the alternate necessities of the animals dwelling upon her surface, at the same time that she obeys the influence of those attractions which regulate the order of many thousand worlds. The relation therefore of sleep to night, is the relation of the inhabitants of the earth to the rotation of their globe; probably it is more; it is a relation to the system, of which that globe is a part; and still farther, to the congregation of systems, of which theirs is only one. If this account be true, it connects the meanest individual with the universe itself: a chicken roosting upon its perch, with the spheres revolving in the firmament.

VIII. But if any one object to our representation, that the succession of day and night, or the rotation of the earth upon which it depends, is not resolvable into central attraction, we will refer him to that which certainly is,—to the change of the seasons. Now the constitution of animals susceptible of torpor, bears a relation to winter, similar to that which sleep bears to night. Against not only the cold, but the want of food which the approach of winter induces, the Preserver of the world has provided in many animals by migration, in many others by torpor. As one example out of a thousand; the bat, if it did not sleep through the winter, must have starved, as the moths and flying insects, upon which it feeds, disappear. But the

P

transition from summer to winter carries us i to the very midst of physical astronomy; that is to say, into the midst of those laws which govern the solar system at least and probably all the heavenly bodies.

CHAPTER XVIII.

INSTINCTS.

THE order may not be very obvious, by which I place *instincts* next to relations. But I consider them as a species of relation. They contribute, along with the animal organization, to a joint effect, in which view they are related to that organization. In many cases, they refer from one animal to another animal; and when this is the case, become strictly relations in a second point of view.

An INSTINCT is a propensity prior to experience, and independent of instruction. We contend, that it is by *instinct* that the sexes of animals seek each other; that animals cherish their offspring; that the young quadruped is directed to the teat of its dam; that birds build their nests, and brood with so much patience upon their eggs; that insects which do not sit upon their eggs, deposit them in those particular situations, in which the young, when hatched, find their appropriate food; that it is instinct which carries the salmon, and some other fish, out of the sea into rivers, for the purpose of shedding their spawn in fresh water.

We may select out of *this* catalogue the incubation of eggs. I entertain no doubt, but that a couple of sparrows hatched in an oven, and kept separate from the rest of their species, would proceed as other sparrows do, in every office which related to the production and preservation of their brood. Assuming this fact, the thing is inexplicable upon any other hypothesis than that of an instinct impressed upon the constitution of the animal. For, first, what should induce the female bird to prepare a nest before she lays her eggs? It is in vain to suppose her to be possessed of the faculty of reasoning; for no reasoning will reach the case. The fulness or distention which she might feel in a particular part of her body, from the growth and solidity of the egg within her, could not possibly inform her that she was about to produce something, which, when pro·

duced, was to be preserved and taken care of. Prior to experience, there was nothing to lead to this inference, or to this suspicion. The analogy was *all* against it; for, in every other instance, what issued from the body, was cast out and rejected.

But, secondly, let us suppose the egg to be produced into day; how should birds know that their eggs contain their young? there is nothing, either in the aspect, or in the internal composition of an egg, which could lead even the most daring imagination to conjecture, that it was hereafter to turn out from under its shell, a living, perfect bird. The form of the egg bears not the rudiments of a resemblance to that of the bird. Inspecting its contents, we find still less reason, if possible, to look for the result which actually takes place. If we should go so far, as, from the appearance of order and distinction in the disposition of the liquid substances which we noticed in the egg, to guess that it might be designed for the abode and nutriment of an animal, (which would be a very bold hypothesis,) we should expect a tadpole dabbling in the slime, much rather than a dry, winged, feathered creature; a compound of parts and properties impossible to be used in a state of confinement in the egg, and bearing no conceivable relation, either in quality or material, to anything observed in it. From the white of an egg, would any one look for the feather of a goldfinch? or expect from a simple uniform mucilage, the most complicated of all machines, the most diversified of all collections of substances? nor would the process of incubation, for sometime at least, lead us to suspect the event. Who that saw red streaks shooting in the fine membrane which divides the white from the yolk, would suppose that these were about to become bones and limbs? Who that espied two discolored points first making their appearance in the cicatrix, would have had the courage to predict, that these points were to grow into the heart and head of a bird? It is difficult to strip the mind of its experience. It is difficult to resuscitate surprise, when familiarity has once laid the sentiment asleep. But could we forget all that we know, and which *our* sparrows never knew, about oviparous generation: could we divest ourselves of every information, but what we derive from reasoning upon the appearance or quality discovered in the objects presented to us, I am convinced that Harlequin coming out of an egg upon the stage, is not more astonishing to a child, than the hatching of a chicken both would be and ought to be, to a philosopher.

But admit the sparrow by some means to know, that within that egg was concealed the principle of a future bird, from what chemist was she to learn, that *warmth* was necessary to bring it to maturity, or that the degree of warmth, imparted by the temperature of her own body, was the degree required?

To suppose, therefore, that the female bird acts in this process from a sagacity and reason of her own, is to suppose her to arrive at conclusions which there are no premises to justify. If our sparrow, sitting upon her eggs, expect young sparrows to come out of them, she forms, I will venture to say, a wild and extravagant expectation, in opposition to present appearances, and to probability. She must have penetrated into the order of nature, farther than any faculties of ours will carry us; and it hath been well observed, that this deep sagacity, if it be sagacity, subsists in conjunction with great stupidity, even in relation to the same subject. "A chemical operation," says Addison, "could not be followed with greater art or diligence, than is seen in hatching a chicken; yet is the process carried on without the least glimmering of thought or common sense. The hen will mistake a piece of chalk for an egg; is insensible of the increase or diminution of their number; does not distinguish between her own and those of another species; is frightened when her supposititious breed of ducklings take the water."

But it will be said, that what reason could not do for the bird, observation, or instruction, or tradition, might. Now, if it be true, that a couple of sparrows, brought up from the first in a state of separation from all other birds, would build their nest, and brood upon their eggs, then there is an end of this solution. What can be the traditionary knowledge of a chicken hatched in an oven?

Of young birds taken in their nests, a few species breed when kept in cages; and they which do so, build their nests nearly in the same manner as in the wild state, and sit upon their eggs. This is sufficient to prove an instinct, without having recourse to experiments upon birds hatched by artificial heat, and deprived from their birth of all communication with their species; for we can hardly bring ourselves to believe, that the parent bird informed her unfledged pupil of the history of her gestation, her timely preparation of a nest, her exclusion of the eggs, her long incubation, and of the joyful eruption at last of her expected offspring; all which the bird in the cage must have learned in her infancy, if we resolve her conduct into *institution*

Unless we will rather suppose, that she remembers her own escape from the egg; had attentively observed the conformation of the nest in which she was nurtured; and had treasured up her remarks for future imitation: which is not only extremely improbable, (for who, that sees a brood of callow birds in their nest, can believe that they are taking a plan of their habitation?) but leaves unaccounted for, one principal part of the difficulty, "the preparation of the nest before the laying of the egg." This she could not gain from observation in her infancy.

It is remarkable also, that the hen sits upon eggs which she has laid without any communication with the male, and which are therefore necessarily unfruitful; that secret she is not let into. Yet, if incubation had been a subject of instruction or of tradition, it should seem that this distinction would have formed part of the lesson; whereas the instinct of nature is calculated for a state of nature; the exception here alluded to taking place chiefly, if not solely, amongst domesticated fowls, in which nature is forced out of her course.

There is another case of oviparous economy, which is still less likely to be the effect of education than it is even in birds, namely that of *moths* and *butterflies*, which deposit their eggs in the precise substance, that of a cabbage for example, from which, not the butterfly herself, but the caterpillar which is to issue from her egg, draws its appropriate food. The butterfly cannot taste the cabbage Cabbage is no food for her; yet in the cabbage, not by chance, but studiously and electively, she lays her eggs There are, amongst many other kinds, the willow caterpillar, and the cabbage caterpillar: but we never find upon a willow the caterpillar which eats the cabbage; nor the converse. This choice, as appears to me, cannot in the butterfly proceed from instruction. She had no teacher in her caterpillar state. She never knew her parent I do not see, therefore, how knowledge, acquired by experience, if it ever were such, could be transmitted from one generation to another. There is no opportunity either for instruction or imitation. The parent race is gone, before the new brood is hatched. And if it be original reasoning in the butterfly, it is profound reasoning indeed. She must remember her caterpillar state, its tastes and habits; of which memory she shows no signs whatever. She must conclude from analogy, for here her recollection cannot serve her, that the little round body which drops from her abdomen, will at a future period produce a living creature. not like

herself, but like the caterpillar, which she remembers hers, (
once to have been.   Under the influence of these reflections,
she goes about to make provision for an order of things,
which she concludes will, sometime or other, take place.
And it is to be observed, that not a few out of many, but
that all butterflies argue thus, all draw this conclusion; all
act upon it.*

But suppose the address, and the selection, and the plan,
which we perceive in the preparations which many irrational animals make for their young, to be traced to some
probable origin; still there is left to be accounted for, that
which is the source and foundation of these phenomena,
that which sets the whole at work, the στοργη, the parental affection, which I contend to be inexplicable upon any
other hypothesis than that of instinct.

For we shall hardly, I imagine, in brutes, refer their
conduct towards their offspring to a sense of duty, or of
decency, a care of reputation, a compliance with public
manners, with public laws, or with rules of life built upon
a long experience of their utility.   And all attempts to account for the parental affection from association, I think,
fail.   With what is it associated?   Most immediately with
the throes of parturition, that is, with pain, and terror, and
disease.   The more remote, but not less strong association,
that which depends upon analogy, is all against it.   Everything else, which proceeds from the body, is cast away and
rejected.

In birds, is it the egg which the hen loves? or is it the
expectation which she cherishes of a future progeny, that
keeps her upon her nest?   What cause has she to expect
delight from her progeny?   Can any rational answer be
given to the question, why, prior to experience, the brood-
ing hen should look for pleasure from her chickens?   It
does not, I think, appear, that the cuckoo ever knows her

* The dragon-fly is an inhabitant of the air, and could not exist in
water; yet in this element, which is alone adapted for her young, she
drops her eggs.

Not less surprising is the parental instinct of the gad-fly, (Gastero-
philus equi) whose larvæ are destined to be nourished in the stomach
and intestines of the horse!   How shall the parent convey them there.
By a mode truly extraordinary—Flying round the animal she curiously
poises her body while she deposits her eggs on the hairs of his skin
Whenever therefore the horse chances to lick the part of his body to
which they are attached, they adhere to the tongue, and from thence pass
into the stomach and intestines.   And what increases our surprise is, that
the fly places her eggs almost exclusively on the knee and the shoulder
on those parts the horse is sure to lick.—Paxton.

young yet, in her way, she is as careful in making provision for them, as any other bird. She does not leave her egg in every hole.

The salmon suffers no surmountable obstacle to oppose her progress up the stream of fresh rivers. And what does she do there? She sheds a spawn, which she immediately quits, in order to return to the sea, and this issue of her body she never afterwards recognises in any shape whatever. Where shall we find a motive for her efforts and her perseverance? Shall we seek it in argumentation, or in instinct? The violet crab of Jamaica performs a fatiguing march of some months' continuance, from the mountains to the sea-side. When she reaches the coast, she casts her spawn into the open sea; and sets out upon her return home.

Moths and butterflies, as hath already been observed, seek out for their eggs those precise situations and substances, in which the offspring caterpillar will find its appropriate food. That dear caterpillar the parent butterfly must never see. There are no experiments to prove that she would retain any knowledge of it, if she did. How shall we account for her conduct? I do not mean for her art and judgment in selecting and securing a maintenance for her young, but for the impulse upon which she acts What should induce her to exert any art, or judgment, or choice, about the matter? The undisclosed grub, the animal which she is destined not to know, can hardly be the object of a particular affection, if we deny the influence of instinct. There is nothing, therefore, left to her, but that of which her nature seems incapable, an abstract anxiety for the general preservation of the species; a kind of patriotism; a solicitude lest the butterfly race should cease from the creation.

Lastly, the principle of association will not explain the discontinuance of the affection when the young animal is grown up. Association, operating in its usual way, would rather produce a contrary effect. The object would become more necessary by habits of society: whereas birds and beasts, after a certain time, banish their offspring; disown their acquaintance; seem to have even no knowledge of the objects which so lately engrossed the attention of their minds, and occupied the industry and labor of their bodies. This change, in different animals takes place at different distances of time from the birth, but the time always corresponds with the ability of the young animal to maintain itself; never anticipates it In the sparrow tribe, when it is perceived that the y g brood can fly and shift for themselves, then the parents forsake them forever; and though they continue to live together, pay them no more attention than they do to other birds in the same flock.*   I believe the same thing is true of all gregarious quadrupeds.

In this part of the case, the variety of resources, expedients, and materials, which animals of the same species are said to have recourse to, under different circumstances, and when differently supplied, makes nothing against the doctrine of instincts.   The thing which we want to account for, is the propensity.   The propensity being there, it is probable enough that it may put the animal upon different actions, according to different exigencies.   And this adaptation of resources may look like the effect of art and consideration, rather than of instinct; but still the propensity is nstinctive.   For instance, suppose what is related of the woodpecker to be true, that, in Europe, she deposits her eggs in cavities, which she scoops out in the trunks of soft or decayed trees, and in which cavities the eggs lie concealed from the eye, and in some sort safe from the hand of man; but that, in the forests of Guinea and the Brazils, which man seldom frequents, the same bird hangs her nest to the twigs of tall trees; thereby placing them out of the reach of *monkeys* and *snakes; i. e.* that in each situation she prepares against the danger which she has most occasion to apprehend: suppose, I say, this to be true, and to be alleged, on the part of the bird that builds these nests, as evidence of a reasoning and distinguishing precaution, still the question returns, whence the propensity to build at all?

Nor does parental affection accompany generation by any universal law of animal organization, if such a thing were intelligible.   Some animals cherish their progeny with the most ardent fondness, and the most assiduous attention; others entirely neglect them; and this distinction always meets the constitution of the young animal, with respect to its wants and capacities.   In many, the parental care extends to the young animal, in others, as in all oviparⁱ s fish, it is confined to the egg, and even, as to that, to tne disposal of it in its proper element.   Also, as there is generation without parental affection, so is there parental instinct, or what exactly resembles it, without generation In the bee tribe, the grub is nurtured neither by the fathe·

* Goldsmith's Nat. Hist. p. 244

nor the mother, but by the neutral bee. Probably the case is the same with ants.

I am not ignorant of the theory which resolves instinct into sensation; which asserts, that what appears to have a view and relation to the future, is the result only of the present disposition of the animal's body, and of pleasure or pain experienced *at the time*. Thus the incubation of eggs is accounted for by the pleasure which the bird is supposed to receive from the pressure of the smooth convex surface of the shells against the abdomen, or by the relief which the mild temperature of the egg may afford to the heat of the lower part of the body, which is observed at this time to be increased beyond its usual state. This present gratification is the only motive with the hen for sitting upon her nest; the hatching of the chickens, is with respect to her, an accidental consequence. The affection of viviparous animals for their young is, in like manner, solved by the relief, and perhaps the pleasure, which they receive from giving suck. The young animal's seeking, in so many instances, the teat of its dam, is explained from the sense of smell, which is attracted by the odour of milk. The salmon's urging its way up the stream of fresh water rivers, is attributed to some gratification or refreshment, which, in this particular state of the fish's body, she receives from the change of element. Now of this theory it may be said,

First, that of the cases which require solution, there are few to which it can be applied with tolerable probability, that there are none to which it can be applied without strong objections, furnished by the circumstances of the case. The attention of the cow to its calf, and of the ewe to its lamb, appear to be prior to their sucking. The attraction of the calf or lamb to the teat of the dam, is not explained by simply referring it to the sense of smell. What made the scent of milk so agreeable to the lamb, that it should follow it up with its nose, or seek with its mouth the place from which it proceeded? No observation, no experience, no argument could teach the new dropped animal, that the substance from which the scent issued, was the material of its food. It had never tasted milk before its birth. None of the animals, which are not designed for that nourishment, ever offer to suck, or to seek out any such food. What is the conclusion, but that the sugescent parts of animals are fitted for their use, and the knowledge of that use put into them?

We assert, secondly, that, even as to the cases in which the hypothesis has the fairest claim to consideration, it does not at all lessen the force of the argument for intention and design. The doctrine of instincts is that o. appetencies, *superadded* to the constitution of an animal, for the effectuating of a purpose beneficial to the species. The above-stated solution would derive these appetencies from organization; but then this organization is not less specifically, not less precisely, and, therefore, not less evidently adapted to the same ends, than the appetencies themselves would be upon the old hypothesis. In this way of considering the subject, sensation supplies the place of foresight; but this is the effect of contrivance on the part of the Creator. Let it be allowed, for example, that the hen is induced to brood upon her eggs by the enjoyment or relief which, in the heated state of her abdomen, she experiences from the pressure of round smooth surfaces, or from the application of a temperate warmth. How comes this extraordinary heat or itching, or call it what you will, which you suppose to be the cause of the bird's inclination, to be felt, just at the time when the inclination itself is wanted; when it tallies so exactly with the internal constitution of the egg, and with the help which that constitution requires in order to bring it to maturity? In my opinion, this solution, if it be accepted as to the fact, ought to increase, rather than otherwise, our admiration of the contrivance. A gardener lighting up his stoves, just when he wants to force his fruit, and when his trees require the heat, gives not a more certain evidence of design. So again; when a male and female sparrow come together, they do not meet to confer upon the expediency of perpetuating their species. As an abstract proposition, they care not the value of a barley-corn, whether the species be perpetuated or not: they follow their sensations; and all those consequences ensue, which the wisest counsels could have dictated, which the most solicitous care of futurity, which the most anxious concern for the sparrow world could have produced. But how do these consequences ensue? The sensations, and the constitution upon which they depend, are as manifestly directed to the purpose which we see fulfilled by them; and the train of intermediate effects, as manifestly laid and planned with a view to that purpose; that is to say, design is as completely evinced by the phe nomena, as it would be, even if we suppose the operations to begin, or to be carried on, from what some will allow to be alone properly called instincts, that is, from desires directed to a future end, and having no accomplishment or gratification distinct from the attainment of that end.

In a word; I should say to the patrons of this opinion, Be it so: be it, that those actions of animals which we refer to instinct, are not gone about with any view to their consequences, but that they are attended in the animal with a present gratification, and are pursued for the sake of that gratification alone; what does all this prove, but that the *prospection*, which must be somewhere, is not in the animal, but in the Creator?

In treating of the parental affection in brutes, our business lies rather with the origin of the principle, than with the effects and expressions of it. Writers recount these with pleasure and admiration. The conduct of many kinds of animals towards their young, has escaped no observer, no historian of nature. "How will they caress them," says Derham, "with their affectionate notes; lull and quiet them with their tender parental voice; put food into their mouths; cherish and keep them warm; teach them to pick, and eat, and gather food for themselves; and, in a word, perform the part of so many nurses, deputed by the sovereign Lord and Preserver of the world, to help such young and shiftless creatures!" Neither ought it, under this head, to be forgotten, how much the instinct *costs* the animal which feels it; how much a bird, for example, gives up, by sitting upon her nest; how repugnant it is to her organization, her habits, and her pleasures. An animal, formed for liberty, submits to confinement in the very season when everything invites her abroad: what is more; an animal delighting in motion, made for motion, all whose motions are so easy and so free, hardly a moment, at other times, at rest, is, for many hours of many days together, fixed to her nest, as close as if her limbs were tied down by pins and wires. For my part, I never see a bird in that situation, but I recognise an invisible hand, detaining the contented prisoner from her fields and groves, for the purpose, as the event proves, the most worthy of the sacrifice, the most important, the most beneficial.

But the loss of liberty is not the whole of what the procreant bird suffers. Harvey tells us, that he has often found the female wasted to skin and bone by sitting upon her eggs.

One observation more, and I will dismiss the subject. The *pairing* of birds, and the *non-pairing* of beasts, forms a distinction between the two classes, which shows that the conjugal instinct is modified with a reference to utility iounded on the condition of the offspring. In quadrupcds the young animal draws its nutriment from the body of th* dam. The male parent neither does, nor can contribute any part to its sustentation. In the winged race, the young bird is supplied by an importation of food, to procure *:d bring home which, in a sufficient quantity for the demand of a numerous brood, requires the industry of both parents. In this difference, we see a reason for the vagrant instinct of the quadruped, and for the faithful love of the feathered mate.

CHAPTER XIX.

OF INSECTS.

WE are not writing a system of natural history; therefore we have not attended to the classes into which the subjects of that science are distributed. What we had to observe concerning different species of animals, fell easily, for the most part, within the divisions which the course of our argument led us to adopt. There remain, however, some remarks upon the *insect* tribe, which could not properly be introduced under any of these heads; and which therefore, we have collected into a chapter by themselves.

The structure, and the use of the parts of insects, are less understood than that of quadrupeds and birds, not only by reason of their minuteness, or the minuteness of their parts (for that minuteness we can in some measure follow with glasses,) but also by reason of the remoteness of their manners and modes of life from those of larger animals. For instance: insects, under all their varieties of form, are endowed with *antennæ*, [Pl. XXXII. fig. 2, 3.] which is the name given to those long feelers that rise from each side of the head; but to what common use or want of the insect kind, a provision so universal is subservient, has not yet been ascertained: and it has not 'been ascertained, because it admits not of a clear, or very probable comparison, with any organs which we possess ourselves, or with the organs of animals which resemble ourselves in their functions and faculties, or with which we are better acquainted than we are with insects. We want a ground of analogy. This difficulty stands in our way as to some particulars in the insect constitution which we might wish to be acquainted with. Nevertheless, there are many contrivances in the bodies of insects, neither dubious in their use, nor obscure in their structure, and most properly mechanical. These form parts of *our* argument.

I. The *elytra*, or scaly wings of the genus of scarabæus or beetle, furnish an example of this kind. The true wing of the animal is a light transparent membrane, finer than the finest gauze, and not unlike it. It is also, when expanded, in proportion to the size of the animal, very large. In order to protect this delicate structure, and perhaps also to preserve it in a due state of suppleness and humidity, a strong hard case is given to it, in the shape of the horny wing which we call the elytron. When the animal is at rest, the gauze wings lie folded up under this impenetrable shield. When the beetle prepares for flying, he raises the integument, and spreads out his thin membrane to the air. And it cannot be observed without admiration, what a tissue of cordage, *i. e.* of muscular tendons, must run in various and complicated, but determinate directions along this fine surface, in order to enable the animal, either to gather it up into a certain precise form, whenever it desires to place its wings under the shelter which nature hath given to them; or to expand again their folds, when wanted for action. [Pl. XXXII. fig. 1.]

In some insects, the elytra cover the whole body; in others, half; in others, only a small part of it; but in all, they completely hide and cover the true wings. [Pl. XXXII fig. 2.]

Also, many or most of the beetle species lodge in holes in the earth, environed by hard rough substances, and have frequently to squeeze their way through narrow passages; in which situation, wings so tender, and so large, could scarcely have escaped injury, without both a firm covering to defend them, and the capacity of collecting themselves up under its protection.

II. Another contrivance, equally mechanical and equally clear, is the *awl* or borer, fixed at the tails of various species of flies; and with which they pierce, in some cases, plants; in others, wood; in others, the skin and flesh of animals; in others, the coat of the chrysalis of insects of a different species from their own; and in others, even lime, mortar, and stone. I need not add, that having pierced the substance, they deposit their eggs in the hole. The descriptions which naturalists give of this organ, are such as the following: it is a sharp-pointed instrument, which, in its inactive state, lies concealed in the extremity of the abdomen, and which the animal draws out at pleasure, for the purpose of making a puncture in the leaves, stem, or bark, of the particular plant which is suited to the nourishment of its young. In a sheath which divides and opens whenever the organ is used, there is enclosed a compact, solid, dentated stem, along which runs a *gutter* or *groove*, by which groove, after the penetration is effected, the egg, assisted in some cases by a peristaltic motion, passes to its destined lodgement.* In the œstrus or gad-fly, the wimble *draws out* like the pieces of a spy-glass; the last piece is armed with three hooks, and is able to bore through the hide of an ox. Can anything more be necessary to display the mechanism, than to relate the fact? [Pl. XXXII, fig. 3, 4.]

III. The *stings* of insects, though for a different purpose, are, in their structure, not unlike the piercer. The sharpness to which the point in all of them is wrought; the temper and firmness of the substance of which it is composed; the strength of the muscles by which it is darted out, compared with the smallness and weakness of the insect, and with the soft and friable texture of the rest of the body; are properties of the sting to be noticed, and not a little to be admired. The sting of a *bee* will pierce through a goat-skin glove. It penetrates the human flesh more readily than the finest point of a needle. The *action* of the sting affords an example of the union of chemistry and mechanism, such as, if it be not a proof of contrivance, nothing is. First, as to the chemistry; how highly concentrated must be the *venom*, which, in so small a quantity, can produce such powerful effects! And in the bee we may observe, that this venom is made from *honey*, the only food of the insect, but the last material from which I should have expected that an exalted poison could, by any process or digestion whatsoever, have been prepared. In the next place, with respect to the mechanism, the sting is not a simple, but a compound instrument. The visible sting, though drawn to a point exquisitely sharp, is, in strictness, only a sheath; for, near to the extremity may be perceived by the microscope two minute orifices, from which orifices, in the act of stinging, and, as it should seem, after the point

* There are numerous variations in the structure of this organ; an example of the one just mentioned is seen in the ovipositor of the *buprestis*, Fig. 9. It consists of three long and sharp laminæ, the two lateral ones forming a sheath to the intermediate one, which is the tube which conveys the egg. In some cases the instrument forms a saw, or what Pa ey here calls a dentated stem, which conveys the eggs. as in the *tenthredo, cici'æ timbrx,* &c.—*Paxton.*

of the main sting has buried itself in the flesh, are launch-
ed out two subtile rays, which may be called the true or
proper stings, as being those through which the poison is
infused into the puncture already made by the exterior sting.
I have said, that chemistry and mechanism are here *united*
by which observation I meant, that all this machinery,
would have been useless, *telum imbelle*, if a supply of
poison, intense in quality, in proportion to the smallness of
the drop, had not been furnished to it by the chemical
elaboration which was carried on in the insect's body; and
that, on the other hand, the poison, the result of this process, could not have attained its effect, or reached its
enemy, if, when it was collected at the extremity of the
abdomen, it had not found there a machinery, fitted to conduct it to the external situations in which it was to operate,
viz. an awl to bore a hole, and a syringe to inject the fluid.
Yet these attributes, though combined in their action, are
independent in their origin. The venom does not breed
the sting; nor does the sting concoct the venom. [Pl
XXXII. fig. 5.]

IV. The *proboscis*, with which many insects are endowed, comes next in order to be considered. [Pl. XXXII.
fig. 6, 7, 8.] It is a tube attached to the head of the animal.
In the bee, it is composed of two pieces connected by a
joint; for if it were constantly extended, it would be too
much exposed to accidental injuries; therefore, in its indolent state, it is doubled up by means of the joint, and
in that position lies secure under a scaly penthouse. In
many species of the butterfly, the proboscis, when not in
use, is coiled up like a watch spring. In the same bee,
the proboscis serves the office of the mouth, the insect
having no other: and how much better adapted it is, than
a mouth would be, for collecting of the proper nourishment of the animal, is sufficiently evident. The food of
the bee is the nectar of flowers; a drop of syrup, lodged
deep in the bottom of the corollæ, in the recesses of the
petals, or down the neck of a monopetalous glove. Into
these cells the bee thrusts its long narrow pump, through
the cavity of which it sucks up this precious fluid, inaccessible to every other approach. It is observable also, that
the plant is not the worse for what the bee does to it. The
harmless plunderer rifles the sweets, but leaves the flower
uninjured. The ringlets of which the proboscis of the bee
is composed, the muscles by which it is extended and
contracted, form so many microscopical wonders The
agility also with which it is moved, can hardly fail to ex-

cite admiration   But it it enough for our purpose to observe in general, the suitableness of the structure to the
use, of the means to the end, and especially the wisdom
by which nature has departed from its most general analogy (for animals being furnished with mouths are such,)
when the purpose could be better answered by the deviation.

In some insects, the proboscis, or tongue, or trunk, is
shut up in a sharp-pointed sheath, which sheath, being of
a much firmer texture than the proboscis itself, as well as
sharpened at the point, pierces the substance which contains the food, and then *opens within the wound*, to allow
the enclosed tube, through which the juice is extracted, to
perform its office.   Can any mechanism be plainer than
this is; or surpass this?

V.   The *metamorphosis* of insects from grubs into moths
and flies, is an astonishing process.   A hairy caterpillar
is transformed into a butterfly.   Observe the change.   We
have four beautiful wings, where there were none before;
a tubular proboscis, in the place of a mouth with jaws and
teeth; six long legs, instead of fourteen feet.   In another
case, we see a white, smooth, soft worm, turned into a
black, hard, crustaceous beetle, with gauze wings.   These,
as I said, are astonishing processes, and must require, as
it should seem, a proportionably artificial apparatus.   The
hypothesis which appears to me most probable is, that, in
the grub; there exist at the same time three animals, one
within another, all nourished by the same digestion, and
by a communicating circulation; but in different stages of
maturity.   The latest discoveries made by naturalists seem
to favour this supposition.   The insect already equip-
ped with wings, is descried under the membranes, both
of the worm and nymph.   In some species, the proboscis,
the antennæ, the limbs and wings of the fly, have been
observed to be folded up within the body of the caterpillar;
and with such nicety as to occupy a small space only under
the two first wings.   This being so, the outermost animal,
which, besides its own proper character, serves as an integument to the other two, being the farthest advanced, dies,
as we suppose, and drops off first.   The second, the pupa
or chrysalis, then offers itself to observation.   This also,
in its turn, dies; its dead and brittle husk falls to pieces.
and makes way for the appearance of the fly or moth
Now, if this be the case, or indeed whatever explication
be adopted, we have a prospective contrivance of the most
curious kind; we have organizations *three deep.* yet a vas-

ular system, which supplies nutrition, growth, and life, to
a l of them together.

VI. Almost all insects are oviparous. Nature keeps
her butterflies, moths, and caterpillars, locked up during
the winter in their egg state; and we have to admire the
various devices to which, if we may so speak, the same
nature hath resorted, for the *security* of the egg. Many
insects enclose their eggs in a silken web; others cover
them with a coat of hair torn from their own bodies; some
glue them together; and others, like the moth of the silk
worm, glue them to the leaves upon which they are depos
ited, that they may not be shaken off by the wind, or washed away by rain: some again make incisions into leaves,
and hide an egg in each incision; whilst some envelope
their eggs with a soft substance, which forms the first aliment of the young animal: and some again make a hole in
the earth, and having stored it with a quantity of proper
food, deposit their eggs in it. In all which we are to observe, that the expedient depends, not so much upon the
address of the animal, as upon the physical resources of
his constitution.

The art also with which the young insect is *coiled up* in
the egg, presents, where it can be examined, a subject of
great curiosity. The insect, furnished with all the members
which it ought to have, is rolled up into a form which
seems to contract it into the least possible space; by which
contraction, notwithstanding the smallness of the egg, it has
room enough in its apartment, and to spare. This folding
of the limbs appears to me to indicate a special direction,
for, if it were merely the effect of compression, the collocation of the parts would be more various than it is. In
the same species, I believe, it is always the same.

These observations belong to the whole insect tribe, or
to a great part of them. Other observations are limited
to fewer species; but not, perhaps, less important or satis·
factory.

1. The organization in the abdomen of the *silkworm*,
or *spider*, whereby these insects form their *thread*, is as
incontestably mechanical as a wire-drawer's mill. In the
body of the silkworm are two bags, remarkable for their
form, position, and use. [Pl. XXXIII. fig. 1.] They wind
round the intestine; when drawn out, they are ten inches
in length, though the animal itself be only two. Within
these bags is collected a glue; and communicating with
the bags, are two paps or outlets, perforated, like a grater
by a number of small holes. The glue or gum, being pass-

Q*

ed through these minute apertures, form hairs of a most imperceptible fineness; and these hairs, when joined, compose the silk which we wind off from the cone, in which the silkworm has wrapped itself up: in the spider, the web is formed from this thread. In both cases, the extremity of the thread, by means of its adhesive quality, is first attached by the animal to some external hold; and the end being now fastened to a point, the insect, by turning round its body, or by receding from that point, draws out the thread through the holes above described, by an operation, as hath been observed, exactly similar to the drawing of wire. The thread, like the wire, is formed by the hole hrough which it passes. In one respect there is a difference. The wire is the metal unaltered, except in figure. In the animal process, the nature of the substance is somewhat changed as well as the form; for, as it exists within the insect, it is a soft clammy gum or glue. The thread acquires, it is probable, its firmness and tenacity from the action of the air upon its surface, in the moment of exposure; and a thread so fine is almost all surface. This property, however, of the paste is part of the contrivance [Pl. XXXIII. fig. 2.]

The mechanism itself consists of the bags or reservoirs into which the glue is collected, and of the external holes communicating with these bags: and the action of the machin is seen in the forming of a thread, as wire is formed, by forcing the material already prepared through holes of proper dimensions. The secretion is an act too subtile for our discernment, except as we perceive it by the produce. But one thing answers to another; the secretory glands to the q lity and consistence required in the secreted substance; the bag to its reception: the outlets and orifices are constructed, not merely for relieving the reservoirs of their burden, but for manufacturing the contents into a form as ! texture, of great external use, or rather indeed of future necessity to the life and functions of the insect.

II. *Bees*, under one character or other, have furnished every naturalist with a set of observations. I shall in this place confine myself to one; and that is, the *relatior* which obtains between the wax and the honey. No person who has inspected a bee-hive, can forbear remarking how commodiously the honey is bestowed in the comb, and amongst other advantages, how effectually the fermenta tion of the honey is prevented by distributing it into smal. ce ls The fact is, that when the honey is separated from the comb, and put into jars, it runs into fermentation, with a much less degree of heat than what takes place in a hive. This may be reckoned a nicety; but, independently of any nicety in the matter, I would ask, what could the bee do with the honey if it had not the wax? how, at least, could it store it up for winter? The wax, therefore, answers a purpose with respect to the honey; and the honey constitutes that purpose with respect to the wax. This is the relation between them. But the two substances, though together of the greatest use, and without each other of little, come from a different origin. The bee finds the honey, but makes the wax. The honey is lodged in the nectaria of flowers, and probably undergoes little alteration; is merely collected: whereas the wax is a ductile, tenacious paste, made out of a dry powder, not simply by kneading it with a liquid, but by a digestive process in the body of the bee. What account can be rendered of facts so circumstanced, but that the animal, being intended to feed upon honey, was, by a peculiar external configuration, enabled to procure it? that, moreover, wanting the honey when it could not be procured at all, it was farther endued with the no less necessary faculty of constructing repositories for its preservation? which faculty, it is evident, must depend primarily, upon the capacity of providing suitable materials. Two distinct functions go to make up the ability. First, the power in the bee, with respect to wax, of loading the farina of flowers upon its thighs. Microscopic observers speak of the spoon-shaped appendages with which the thighs of bees are beset for this very purpose; but, inasmuch as the art and will of the bee may be supposed to be concerned in this operation, there is, secondly, that which doth not rest in art or will—a digestive faculty which converts the loose powder into a stiff substance. This is a just account of the honey and the honey-comb, and this account, through every part, carries a creative intelligence along with it.

The *sting* also of the bee has this relation to the honey, that it is necessary for the protection of a treasure which invites so many robbers.

III. Our business is with mechanism. In the *panorpa* tribe of insects, there is a forceps in the tail of the male insect, with which he catches and holds the female. [Pl. XXXIII. fig. 3.] Are a pair of pincers more mechanical than this provision in its structure? or is any structure more clear and certain in its design?

IV St. Pierre tells us,* that in a fly with six feet, (I do not remember that he describes the species,) the pair next the head and the pair next the tail, have brushes at their extremities, with which the fly dresses, as there may be occasion, the anterior or the posterior part of its body; but that the middle pair have no such brushes, the situation of these legs not admitting of the brushes, if they were there, being converted to the same use. This is a very exact mechanical distinction

V. If the reader, looking to our distributions of science, wish to contemplate the chemistry, as well as the mechanism of nature, the insect creation will afford him an example. I refer to the light in the tail of a *glow-worm.* Two points seem to be agreed upon by naturalists concerning it: first, that it is phosphoric; secondly, that its use is to attract the male insect. The only thing to be inquired after, is the singularity, if any such there be, in the natural history of this animal, which should render a provision of this kind more necessary for it than for other insects. That singularity seems to be the difference which subsists between the male and the female; which difference is greater than what we find in any other species of animal whatever. The glow-worm is a female *caterpillar*; the male of which is a *fly*; lively, comparatively small, dissimilar to the female in appearance, probably also as distinguished from her in habits, pursuits, and manners, as he is unlike in form and external constitution. [Pl. XXXIII. fig. 4, 5.] Here then is the adversity of the case. The caterpillar cannot meet her companion in the air. The winged rover disdains the ground. They might never therefore be brought together, did not this radiant torch direct the volatile mate to his sedentary female.

In this example, we also see the resources of art anticipated. One grand operation of chemistry is the making of phosphorus: and it was thought an ingenious devise, to make phosphoric matches supply the place of lighted tapers. Now this very thing is done in the body of the glow-worm. The phosphorus is not only made, but kindled; and caused to emit a steady and genial beam, for the purpose which is here stated, and which I believe to be the true one

VI. Nor is the last the only instance that entomology affords, in which our discoveries, or rather our projects, turn out to be imitations of nature. Some years ago, a plan was suggested, o producing propulsion by reaction in this way: By the force of a steam-engine, a stream of water was to be shot out of the stern of a boat; the impulse of which stream upon the water in the river, was to push the boat itself forward; it is, in truth, the principle by which sky-rockets ascend in the air. Of the use or practicability of the plan, I am not speaking; nor is it my concern to praise its ingenuity: but it is certainly a contrivance. Now, if naturalists are to be believed, it is exactly the device which nature has made use of, for the motion of some species of aquatic insects. The larva of the *dragon-fly*, according to Adams, swims by ejecting water from its tail; is driven forward by the reaction of water in the pool upon the current issuing in a direction backward from its body. [Pl. XXXIII. fig. 6.]

VII. Again: Europe has lately been surprised by the elevation of bodies in the air by means of a balloon. The discovery consisted in finding out a manageable substance, which was, bulk for bulk, lighter than air; and the application of the discovery was, to make a body composed of this substance bear up, along with its own weight, some heavier body which was attached to it. This expedient, so new to us, proves to be no other than what the author of nature has employed in the *gossamer spider*. We frequently see this spider's thread floating in the air, and extended from hedge to hedge, across a road or brook of four or five yards width. The animal which forms the thread has no wings wherewith to fly from one extremity to the other of this line; nor muscles to enable it to spring or dart to so great a distance: yet its Creator hath laid for it a path in the atmosphere; and after this manner. Though the animal itself be heavier than air, the thread which it spins from its bowels is specifically lighter. This is its *balloon*. The spider, left to itself, would drop to the ground; but being tied to its thread, both are supported. We have here a very peculiar provision: and to a contemplative eye it is a gratifying spectacle, to see this insect wafted on her thread, sustained by a levity not her own, and traversing regions, which, if we examined only the body of the animal, might seem to have been forbidden to its nature.

I must now crave the reader's permission to introduce into this place, for want of a better, an observation or two upon the tribe of animals, whether belonging to land or water, which are covered by *shells*.

I. The *shells* of *snails* are a wonderful, a mechanical

and, if one might so speak concerning the works of nature, an original contrivance. Other animals have their proper retreats, their hybernacula also, or winter-quarters, but the snail carries these about with him. He travels with his tent; and this tent, though, as was necessary, both light and thin, is completely impervious either to moisture or air. The young snail comes out of its egg with the shell upon its back; and the gradual enlargement which the shell receives, is derived from the slime excreted by the animal's skin. Now the aptness of this excretion to the purpose, its property of hardening into a shell, and the action, whatever it be, of the animal, whereby it avails itself of its gift, and of the constitution of its glands, (to say nothing of the work being commenced before the animal is born,) are things which can, with no probability, be referred to any other cause than to express design; and that not on the part of the animal alone, in which design, though it might build the house, could not have supplied the material. The will of the animal could not determine the quality of the excretion. Add to which, that the shell of a snail, with its pillar and convolution, is a very artificial fabric; whilst a snail, as it should seem, is the most numb and unprovided of all artificers. In the midst of variety, there is likewise a regularity, which would hardly be expected. In the same species of snail, the number of turns is usually, if not always, the same. The sealing up of the mouth of the shell by the snail, is also well calculated for its warmth and security; but the cerate is not of the same substance with the shell.

II. Much of what has been observed of snails belongs to *shell-fish* and their *shells*, particularly to those of the univalve kind; with the addition of two remarks: one of which is upon the great strength and hardness of most of these shells. I do not know whether, the weight being given, art can produce so strong a case as are some of these shells. Which defensive strength suits well with the life of an animal, that has often to sustain the dangers of a stormy element, and a rocky bottom, as well as the attacks of voracious fish. The other remark is, upon the property, in the animal excretion, not only of congealing, but of congealing, or, as a builder would call it, *setting*, in water, and into a cretaceous substance, firm and hard. This property is much more extraordinary, and, chemically speaking, more specific, than that of hardening in the air; which may be reckoned a kind of exsiccation, like the drying of clay into bricks.

III. In the *bivalve* order of shell-fish, cockles, muscles, oysters, &c. what contrivance can be so simple or so clear, as the insertion at the back, of a tough, tendinous substance, that becomes at once the ligament which binds the two shells together, and the *hinge* upon which they open and shut.

IV. The shell of a lobster's tail, in its articulations and overlapping, represents the jointed part of a coat of mail; or rather, which I believe to be the truth, a coat of mail is an imitation of a lobster's shell. The same end is to be answered by both; the same properties, therefore, are required in both, namely, hardness and flexibility, a covering which may guard the part without obstructing its motion. For this double purpose, the art of man, expressly exercised upon the subject, has not been able to devise anything better than what nature presents to his observation. Is not this, therefore, mechanism, which the mechanic, having a similar purpose in view, adopts? Is the structure of a coat of mail to be referred to art? Is the same structure of the lobster, conducing to the same use, to be referred to anything less than art?

Some, who may acknowledge the imitation, and assent to the inference which we draw from it in the instance before us, may be disposed, possibly, to ask, why such imitations are not more frequent than they are, if it be true, as we allege, that the same principle of intelligence, design, and mechanical contrivance, was exerted in the formation of natural bodies, as we employ in the making of the various instruments by which our purposes are served? The answers to this question are, first, that it seldom happens that precisely the same purpose, and no other, is pursued in any work which we compare, of nature and of art; secondly, that it still more seldom happens, that we *can* imitate nature, if we would. Our materials and our workmanship are equally deficient. Springs and wires, and cork and leather, produce a poor substitute for an arm or a hand. In the example which we have selected, I mean a lobster's shell compared with a coat of mail, these difficulties stand less in the way, than in almost any other that can be assigned: and the consequence is, as we have seen, that art gladly borrows from nature her contrivance, and imitates it closely.

But to return to insects. I think it is in this class of animals above all others, especially when we take in the

multitude of species which the microscope discovers, that
we are struck with what Cicero has called "the *insatiable*
variety of nature." There are said to be six thousand
species of flies; seven hundred and sixty butterflies; each
different from all the rest, (St. Pierre.)   The same writer
tells us, from his own observation, that thirty-seven species
of winged insects, with distinctions well expressed, visited
a single strawberry plant in the course of three weeks.*
Ray observed, within the compass of a mile or two of his
own house, two hundred kinds of butterflies, noctural and
diurnal.   He likewise asserts, but I think without any
grounds of exact computation, that the number of species
of insects, reckoning all sorts of them, may not be short
of ten thousand.†   And in this vast variety of animal forms
(for the observation is not confined to insects, though more
applicable perhaps to them than to any other class) we are
sometimes led to take notice of the different methods, or
rather of the studiously diversified methods, by which
one and the same purpose is attained.   In the article of
breathing, for example, which was to be provided for in
some way or other, besides the ordinary varieties of lungs,
gills, and breathing-holes (for insects in general respire,
not by the mouth, [Pl. XXXIII. fig. 7,] but through holes
in the sides,) the nymphæ of gnats have an apparatus to
raise their *backs* to the top of the water, and so take breath
[Pl. XXXIII. fig. 8.]   The hydrocanthari do the like by
thrusting their *tails* out of the water.‡   The maggot of the
eruca labra [Pl. XXXIII. fig. 9,] has a long tail, one part
sheathed within another, (but which it can draw out at
pleasure,) with a starry tuft at the end, by which *tuft*,
when expanded upon the surface, the insect both supports
itself in the water, and draws in the air which is necessary.
In the article of natural clothing, we have the skins of animals invested with scales, hair, feathers, mucus, froth; or
itself turned into a shell or crust: in the no less necessary
article of offence and defence, we have teeth, talons, beaks,
horns, stings, prickles, with (the most singular expedient
for the same purpose) the power of giving the electric

* Vol. i. p. 3.
† Wisdom of God, p. 23.   The number of species of insects known
to entomologists, and preserved in cabinets, is at present not less than
forty thousand.   This number, however, must probably form a small
proportion of the whole number which exist upon the earth.—*See Kirby
and Spence's Entomology.*—Ed.
† Derham, p 7

shock,* and, as is credibly related of some animals, of driving away their pursuers by an intolerable fœtor, or of blackening the water through which they are pursued.† The consideration of these appearances might induce us to believe, that *variety* itself, distinct from every other reason, was a motive in the mind of the Creator, or with the agents of his will.

To this great variety in organized life. the Deity has given, or perhaps there arises out of it, a corresponding variety of anima¹ *appetites.* For the final cause of this we have not far to seek. Did all animals covet the same element, retreat, or food, it is evident how much fewer could be supplied and accommodated, than what at present live conveniently together, and find a plentiful subsistence. What one nature rejects, another delights in. Food which is nauseous to one tribe of animals, becomes, by that very property which makes it nauseous, an alluring dainty to another tribe. Carrion is a treat to dogs, ravens, vultures, fish. The exhalations of corrupted substances attract flies by crowds. Maggots revel in putrefaction.

CHAPTER XX.

OF PLANTS.

I THINK a designed and studied mechanism to be, in general, more evident in animals than in *plants;* and it is unnecessary to dwell upon a weaker argument, where a

---

* The *raja torpedo, gymnotus electricus,* and some other fish, have a curious apparatus of nerves, which in its effects may be compared to an electrical battery. In the first named fish, the electrical organs are situated between the head and the pectoral fins. When the integuments are raised the organ appears, consisting of some hundred pentagonal and hexagonal cells, filled with a glairy fluid. Minute blood-vessels are dispersed over it, and its nerves are of extraordinary size. When the hand is applied to the electrical organs, a benumbing effect is instantly felt in the fingers and the arm. When caught in a net, it has been known to give a violent shock to the hands of the fisherman who ventures to seize it. *Phil. Trans.* 1816, p. 120. Ibid. 1817, p. 32.—*Paxton.*

† The several species of *sepiæ* or *cuttle fish* have this faculty. They possess a bag situated on, or near the liver, called the *ink-bag,* from its containing a black fluid, the contents of which are discharged by a muscular sheath compressing the body of the animal. By this singular evacuation the creature renders the surrounding element so black and bitter, when in danger of being attacked, that an enemy will not pursue it.—*Ib.*

stronger is at hand.   There are, however, a few observations upon the vegetable kingdom, which lie so directly in
our way, that it would be improper to pass by them without notice.

The one great intention of nature in the structure of
plants, seems to be the perfecting of the *seed;* and, what
is part of the same intention, the preserving of it until it
be *perfected.* This intention shows itself, in the first place,
by the care which appears to be taken, to protect and ripen,
by every advantage which can be given to them of situation in the plant, those parts which most immediately contribute to fructification, viz. the antheræ, the stamina, and
the stigmata.   These parts are usually lodged in the centre, the recesses, or the labyrinths of the flower; during
their tender and immature state, are shut up in the stalk,
or sheltered in the bud: as soon as they have acquired
firmness of texture sufficient to bear exposure, and are
ready to perform the important office which is assigned to
them, they are disclosed to the light and air, by the bursting of the stem, or the expansion of the petals; after which,
they have, in many cases, by the very form of the flower
during its blow, the light and warmth reflected upon them
from the concave side of the cup.   What is called also the
sleep * of plants, is the leaves or petals disposing themselves

---

* "The periodical change in the direction of leaves, which has been
called the 'Sleep of Plants,' is undeniably connected with the stimulating
operation of light.   It is established, that during the clear light of the
sun, the leaves become erect, and move their upper surface to the light,
whilst, on the contrary, during the absence of light, they either hang
downwards, and turn to the horizon, or they take an upright position, so
that the under surface of the leaves is turned more outward.   On account
of this particular position of what has been called 'Sleeping Plants,' we
cannot properly ascribe this direction to sleep, because the leaves do
sometimes even raise themselves during this state with greater energy,
and press upon the stem or leaf-stalk, for the purpose of turning their
lower surface outwards.   This change is much rather, therefore, the consequence of the contest between the activity of the plant, and the great
activity of nature.   This change is the more evident, and the sleep of
leaves the more striking, the finer and more compounded the organization of the leaves are.   We hence most frequently observe it in the pin-
nated leaves of leguminous plants, although also in some others, as in
atriplex.
That an internal and self-dependent activity is to be taken into account in this sleep of plants, is plain from the fact that this sleep does
not equally follow from a short withdrawing of the light, but only from
its complete and long-continued removal; as also from this other circumstance, that leaves fall asleep or awake at fixed hours, whether
the sky be serene or troubled, exactly as happens with regard to animals.   Other stimula, too, and especially heat, have a great influence

in such a manner as to shelter the young stems, buds, or fruit. They turn up, or they fall down, according as this purpose renders either change or position requisite. In the growth of corn, whenever the plant begins to shoot, the two upper leaves of the stalk join together, embrace the ear, and protect it till the pulp has acquired a certain degree of consistency. In some water plants, the flowering and fecundation are carried on *within* the stem, which afterwards opens to let loose the impregnated seed.* The *pea* or papilionaceous tribe, enclose the parts of fructification within a beautiful folding of the internal blossom, sometimes called, from its shape, the boat or keel; itself also protected under a penthouse formed by the external petals. This structure is very artificial; and what adds to the value of it, though it may diminish the curiosity, very general. It has also this farther advantage, (and it is an advantage strictly mechanical,) that all the blossoms turn their *backs* to the wind, whenever the gale blows strong enough to endanger the delicate parts upon which the seed depends. I have observed this a hundred times in a field of peas in blossom. It is an aptitude which results from the figure of the flower, and, as we have said, is strictly mechanical; as much so as the turning of a weather-board or tin cap upon the top of a chimney. Of the *poppy*, and of many similar species of flowers, the head, while it is growing, hangs down, a rigid curvature in the upper part of the stem giving to it that position; and in that position it is impenetrable by rain or moisture. When the head has acquired its size, and is ready to open, the stalk *erects* itself, for the purpose, as it should seem, of presenting the flower, and with the flower, the instruments of fructification, to the genial influence of the sun's rays. This always struck me as a curious property; and specifically as well as originally, provided for in the constitution of the plant, for, if the stem be only bent by the weight of the head, how comes it to straighten itself when the head is the heaviest? These instances show the attention of nature to this principal object, the safety and maturation of the parts upon which the seed depends.

In *trees*, especially in those which are natives of colder climates, this point is taken up earlier. Many of these trees (observe in particular the *ash* and the *horse-chestnut*) pro-

upon this phenomenon, because, in the cold, leaves awaken later, and fall more easily asleep, notwithstanding the influence of light." **Vide** Elements of the Philosophy of Plants by Decandolle.—*Paxton*

* Phil. Trans. par. i. 1796; p. 502

duce the embryos of the leaves and flowers in one year
and bring them to perfection the following. There is a
winter therefore to be gotten over. Now what we are to remark is, how nature has prepared for the trials and sever-
ities of that season. These tender embryos are, in the
first place, wrapped up with a compactness which no art
can imitate; in which state they compose what we call the
bud. This is not all. The bud itself is enclosed in scales;
which scales are formed from the remains of past leaves,
and the rudiments of future ones. Neither is this the
whole. In the coldest climates a third preservative is added, by the bud having a *coat* of gum or resin, which, being
congealed, resists the strongest frosts. On the approach
of warm weather, this gum is softened, and ceases to be a
hinderance to the expansion of the leaves and flowers. All
this care is part of that system of provisions, which has for
its object and consummation the production and perfecting
of the seeds.

The SEEDS themselves are packed up in a *capsule*, a
vessel composed of coats, [Pl. XXXIV. fig. 1,] which,
compared with the rest of the flower, are strong and tough.
From this vessel projects a tube, through which tube the
farina, or some subtile fecundating effluvium that issues
from it, is admitted to the seed. And here also occurs a
mechanical variety, accommodated to the different circumstances under which the same purpose is to be accomplished. In flowers which are erect, the pistil is shorter than
the stamina; [Pl. XXXIV. fig. 2,] and the pollen, shed
from the antheræ into the cup of the flower, is caught in
its descent by the head of the pistil, called the stigma. But
how is this managed when the flowers hang down, (as
does the crown imperial, for instance,) and in which position the farina, in its fall, would be carried from the stigma, and not towards it? The relative length of the parts
is now inverted. The pistil in these flowers is usually
longer instead of shorter than the stamina, [Pl. XXXIV.
fig. 3,] that its protruding summit may receive the pollen
as it drops to the ground. In some cases (as in the *nigella*,) [Pl. XXXIV. fig. 4,] where the shafts of the pistils
or styles are disproportionably long, they bend down their
extremities upon the antheræ, that the necessary approxi
mation may be effected.*

* Amongst the various means which nature has provided for the pur
pose of assisting the impregnation of plants, that afforded by the agency
of insects is not one of the least. In the spring and summer month

But (to pursue this great work in its progress) the impregnation, to which all this machinery relates, being completed, the other parts of the flower fade and drop off, whilst the *gravid seed-vessel*, on the contrary, proceeds to increase its bulk, always to a great, and in some species (in the gourd, for example, and melon,) to a surprising comparative size; assuming in different plants an incalculable variety of forms, but all evidently conducing to the security of the seed. By virtue of this process, so necessary but so diversified, we have the seed at length, in stone-fruits

numerous species of these lively little beings may be seen in almost every expanded flower; and whether they are in search of honey, which is contained in the nectaries of many flowers, or whatever may be the object of their attraction, by being continually on the move, they, no doubt, further the dispersion of the pollen, and thus, in a great measure, contribute to the fertility of the plants they visit.

In many plants, as those which belong to the Linnæan class *diœcia*, where the stamens and pistils are in separate flowers, and those flowers situated on two separate plants of the same species, the operation of insects, or the efficacy of winds, is indispensably necessary to the perfecting the fruit, by transporting the pollen of the one to the stigma of the other.

Some plants, indeed, that have perfect, or united flowers, have the anthers so situated that it is almost impossible the pollen can, of itself, reach the stigma; in this case insects generally become the auxiliaries to the fertilization of the seed. An instance of this may be seen in the *aristolochia clematitis.* "According to Professor Willdenow, the flower of this plant is so formed, that the anthers of themselves cannot impregnate the stigma; but this important affair is devolved upon a particular species of *tipula.* (*T. pennicornis.*) The throat of the flower is lined with dense hair, pointing downward so as to form a kind of funnel, or entrance like that of some kinds of mouse-traps, through which the insects may easily enter but not return: several creep in, and, uneasy at their confinement, are constantly moving to and fro, and so deposit the pollen upon the stigma: but when the work intrusted to them is completed, and impregnation has taken place, the hair which prevented their escape shrinks, and adheres closely to the sides of the flower, and these little go-betweens of Flora at length leave their prison. A writer, however, in the Annual Medical Review (ii. 400,) doubts the accuracy of this fact, on the ground that he could never find *T. pennicornis*, though *A. clematitis* has produced fruit two years at Brompton." *Introduction to Entomology, by Kirby and Spence*, vol. i. p. 298.

That the *tipula pennicornis* does enter the flowers of *aristolochia clematitis*, as recorded by Professor Willdenow, I can confidently affirm, from having observed them in great plenty in the inflated base of the corolla every year, for these last fifteen years, in the Oxford Botanic Garden, where the plant generally forms fruit. The first time I found this insect in the flowers of the above species of *aristolochia*, was on the 12th of July, 1812, at Godstow, near Oxford, where the plant was then growing in a wild state near the ruins of the nunnery.

For the above observations the editor is indebted to an excellent botanist, Mr W. Baxter.--*Paxton.*

R*

and nuts, incased in a strong shell, the shell itself enclosed in a pulp or husk, by which the seed within is, or hath been, fed; or, more generally, (as in grapes, oranges, and the numerous kinds of berries,) plunged over head in a glutinous sirup, contained within a skin or bladder: at other times (as in apples and pears) embedded in the heart of a firm fleshy substance; or (as in strawberries) pricked into the surface of a soft pulp.

These and many other varieties exist in what we call *fruits.** In pulse, and grain, and grasses; in trees, and shrubs, and flowers; the variety of the seed-vessels is incomputable. We have the seeds (as in the pea tribe) regularly disposed in parchment pods, which, though soft and membranous, completely exclude the wet, even in the heaviest rains! the pod also, not seldom (as in the bean) lined with a fine down; at other times (as in the senna) distended like a blown bladder: or we have the seed enveloped in wool (as in the cotton plant,) lodged (as in pines) between the hard and compact scales of a cone, or barricadoed (as in the artichoke and thistle) with spikes

* From the conformation of fruits alone, one might be led, even without experience, to suppose, that part of this provision was destined for the utilities of animals. As limited to the plant, the provision itself seems to go beyond its object. The flesh of an apple, the pulp of an orange, the meat of a plum, the fatness of the olive, appear to be *more* than sufficient for the nourishing of the seed or kernel. The event shows, that this redundancy, if it be one, ministers to the support and gratification of animal natures; and when we observe a provision to be more than sufficient for one purpose, yet wanted for another purpose, it is not unfair to conclude, that both purposes were contemplated together. It favors this view of the subject to remark, that fruits are not (which they might have been) ready altogether, but that they ripen in succession throughout a great part of the year; some in summer; some in autumn: that some require the slow maturation of the winter, and supply the spring; also that the coldest fruits grow in the hottest places. Cucumbers, pine-apples, melons, are the natural produce of warm climates, and contribute greatly, by their coolness, to the refreshment of the inhabitants of those countries.

" The eatable part of the cherry or peach first serves the purposes of perfecting the seed or kernel, by means of vessels passing through the stone, and which are very visible in a peach-stone. After the kernel is perfected, the stone becomes hard, and the vessels cease their functions. But the substance surrounding the stone is not then thrown away as useless. That which was before only an instrument for perfecting the kernel now receives and retains to itself the whole of the sun's influence, and thereby becomes a grateful food to man. Also, what an evident mark of design is the stone protecting the kernel ! The intervention of the stone prevents the second use from interfering with the first."

Paxton.

and prickles; in mushrooms, placed under a penthouse; in ferns, within slits in the back part of the leaf; or (which is the most general organization of all) we find them covered by strong, close tunicles, and attached to the stem according to an order appropriated to each plant, as is seen in the several kinds of grain, and of grasses.

In which enumeration, what we have first to notice is, unity of purpose under variety of expedients. Nothing can be more *single* than the design; more *diversified* than the means. Pellicles, shells, pulps, pods, husks, skin, scales, armed with thorns, are all employed in prosecuting the same intention. Secondly; we may observe, that, ir all these cases, the purpose is fulfilled within a just and *limited* degree. We can perceive, that if the seeds of plants were more strongly guarded than they are, their greater security would interfere with other uses. Many species of animals would suffer, and many perish, if they could not obtain access to them. The plant would overrun the soil; or the seed be wasted for want of room to sow itself. It is sometimes as necessary to destroy particular species of plants, as it is at other times to encourage their growth. Here, as in many cases, a balance is to be maintained between opposite uses. The provisions for the preservation of seeds appear to be directed, chiefly, against the inconstancy of the elements, or the sweeping destruction of inclement seasons. The depredation of animals, and the injuries of accidental violence, are allowed for in the abundance of the increase. The result is, that out of the many thousand different plants which cover the earth, not a single species, perhaps, has been lost since the creation.

When nature has perfected her seeds, her next care is to disperse them. The seed cannot answer its purpose while it remains confined in the capsule. After the seeds therefore are ripened, the pericarpium opens to let them out: and the opening is not like an accidental bursting, but, for the most part, is according to a certain rule in each plant. What I have always thought very extraordinary; nuts and shells, which we can hardly crack with our teeth, divide and make way for the little tender sprout which proceeds from the kernel. Handling the nut, I could hardly conceive how the plantule was ever to get out of it There are cases, it is said, in which the seed-vessel, by an elastic jerk at the moment of its explosion, casts the seed to a distance. We all however know, that many seeds (those of the most composite flowers, as of the thistle, dandelion, &c) are endowed with what are not improperly called *wings* that is, downy appendages, by which they are enabled to float in the air, and are carried oftentimes by the wind to great distances from the plant which produces them. It is the swelling also of this downy tuft within the seed-vessel, that seems to overcome the resistance of its coats, and to open a passage for the seed to escape.

But the *constitution* of seeds is still more admirable than either their preservation or their dispersion. In the body of the seed of every species of plant, or nearly of every one, provision is made for two grand purposes; first, for the safety of the *germ*; secondly, for the temporary support of the future plant. The sprout, as folded up in the seed, is delicate and brittle beyond any other substance. It cannot be touched without being broken. Yet, in beans, peas, grass-seeds, grain, fruits, it is so fenced on all sides, so shut up and protected, that, whilst the seed itself is rudely handled, tossed into sacks, shovelled into heaps, the sacred particle, the miniature plant, remains unhurt. It is wonderful also, how long many kinds of seeds, by the help of their integuments, and perhaps of their oils, stand out against decay. A grain of mustard seed has been known to lie in the earth for a hundred years; and, as soon as it hath acquired a favorable situation, to shoot as vigorously as if just gathered from the plant. Then, as to the second point, the temporary support of the future plant, the matter stands thus. In grain, and pulse, and kernels, and pippins, the germ composes a very small part of the seed. The rest consists of a nutritious substance, from which the sprout draws its aliment for some considerable time after it is put forth; viz. until the fibres, shot out from the other end of the seed, are able to imbibe juices from the earth, in a sufficient quantity for its demand. It is owing to this constitution, that we see seeds sprout, and the sprouts make a considerable progress without any earth at all. It is an economy also, in which we remark a close analogy between the seeds of plants, and the eggs of animals. The same point is provided for, in the same manner, in both. In the egg, the residence of the living principle, the cicatrix, forms a very minute part of the contents. The white, and the white only, is expended in the formation of the chicken. The yolk, very little altered, or diminished, is wrapped up in the abdomen of the young bird when it quits the shell, and serves for its nourishment, till it have learned to pick its own food. This perfectly resembles the first nutrition of a plant. In the plant, as well as in the animal, the structure has every character of contrivance

belonging to i.: in both, it breaks the transition from pre
pared to unprepared aliment; in both, it is prospective and
compensatory. In animals which suck, this intermediate
nourishment is supplied by a different source

In all subjects, the most common observations are the
best, when it is their truth and strength which have made
them common. There are, of this sort *two* concerning
plants, which it falls within our plan to notice. The *first*
relates to what has already been touched upon, their ger
mination. When a grain of corn is cast into the ground,
this is the change which takes place. From one end o.
the grain issues a green sprout; from the other, a number of
white fibrous threads. [Pl. XXXIV. fig. 5.] How can this
be explained? Why not sprouts from both ends? Why not
fibrous threads from both ends? To what is the difference
to be referred, but to design; to the different uses which
the parts are thereafter to serve; uses which discover
themselves in the sequel of the process? The sprout, or
plumule, struggles into the air; and becomes the plant, of
which, from the first, it contained the rudiments: the fibres
shoot into the earth; and thereby both fix the plant to the
ground, and collect nourishment from the soil for its support.* Now, what is not a little remarkable, the parts

* " The *seed*, the last production of vigorous vegetation, is wonder
fully diversified in form. Being of the highest importance to the resources of nature, it is defended above all other parts of the plant, by soft,
pulpy substances, as in the esculent fruits, by thick membranes, as in the
leguminous vegetables, and by hard shells, or a thick epidermis, as in the
palms and grasses.

" In every seed there is to be distinguished, first, the *organ of nourishment;* secondly, the nascent plant, or the *plume;* thirdly, the nascent
root, or the *radicle.*

" In the common garden bean, the organ of nourishment is divided into two lobes called *cotyledons;* the plume is the small white point between the upper part of the lobes; and the radicle is the small curved cone
at their base.

" In wheat, and in many of the grasses, the organ of nourishment is a
single part, and these plants are called *monocotyledonous.* In other
cases it consists of more than two parts, when the plants are called *polye-
otyledonous.* In the greater number of instances it is, however, simply
divided into two, and is *dicotyledonous.*

" The matter of the seed, when examined in its common state, appears
dead and inert; it exhibits neither the forms nor the functions of life
But let it be acted upon by moisture, heat, and air, and its organized
powers are soon distinctly developed. The cotyledons expand, the
membranes burst, the radicle acquires new matter, descends into the
soil, and the plume rises towards the free air. By degrees, the organs
of nourishment of dicotyledonous plants become vascular, and are con
verted into seed leaves, and the perfect plant appears above the soil

issuing from the seed take their respective directions, into whatever position the seed itself happens to be cast. If the seed be thrown into the wrongest possible position, that is, if the ends point in the ground the reverse of what they ought to do, everything, nevertheless, goes on right. The sprout, after being pushed down a little way, makes a bend, and turns upwards: the fibres, on the contrary, after shooting at first upwards, turn down Of this extraordinary vegetable fact, an account has lately been attempted to be given: " The plumule, (it is said,) is stimulated by the *air* into action, and elongates itself when it is thus most excited; the radicle is stimulated by *moisture*, and elongates itself when *it* is thus most excited. Whence one of these grows upward in quest of its adapted object, and the other downward "* Were this account better verified by experiment† than it is, it only shifts the con-

Nature has provided the elements of germination on every part of the surface; water and pure air and heat are universally active, and the means for the preservation and multiplication of life, are at once simple and grand." *Sir H. Davy's Elements of Agricultural Chemistry*, i ed. p. 70.—*Paxton.*

* Darwin's Phytologia, p. 144.

† " Gravitation has a very important influence on the growth of plants and it is rendered probable, by the experiments of Mr. Knight, that they owe the peculiar direction of their roots and branches almost entirely to its force.

" That gentleman fixed some seeds of the garden bean on the circumference of a wheel, which in one instance was placed vertically, and in the other horizontally, and made to revolve, by means of another wheel worked by water, in such a manner, that the number of the revolutions could be regulated; the beans were supplied with moisture, and were placed under circumstances favorable to germination. The great velocity of motion given to the wheel was such, that it performed 250 revolutions in a minute. It was found that in all cases the beans grew, and that the direction of the roots and stems was influenced by the motion of the wheel. When the centrifugal force was made superior to the force of gravitation, which was supposed to be done when the vertical wheel performed 150 revolutions in a minute, all the radicles, in whatever way they were protruded from the position of the seeds, turned their points outwards from the circumference of the wheel, and in their subsequent growth receded nearly at right angles from its axis; the germens (plumules) on the contrary, k the opposite direction, and in a few days their points all met in the ce.. e of the wheel.

"When the centrifugal force was made merely to modify the force of gravitation in the horizontal wheel, where the greatest velocity of revolution was given, the radicles pointed downwards about ten degrees below, and the germens (plumules) as many degrees above the horizontal line of the wheel's motion; and the deviation from the perpendicular was less in proportion, as the motion was less rapid.

" These facts afford a rational solution of this curious problem, respect

:rivance. It does not disprove the contrivance; it only removes it a little farther back. Who, to use our author's own language, "*adapted* the objects?" Who gave such a quality to these connate parts, as to be susceptible of *different* "stimulation;" as to be "excited" each only by its own element, and precisely by that which the success of the vegetation requires? I say, "which the success of the *vegetation* requires:" for the toil of the husbandman would have been in vain; his laborious and expensive preparation of the ground in vain; if the event must, after all, depend upon the position in which the scattered seed was sown. Not one seed out of a hundred would fall in a right direction.

Our *second* observation is upon a general property of climbing plants, which is strictly mechanical. In these plants, from each knot or joint, or as botanists call it, axilla, of the plant, issue, close to each other, two shoots, one bearing the flower and fruit; the other, drawn out into a wire, a long, tapering, spiral tendril, that twists itself round anything which lies within its reach. Considering, that in this class two purposes are to be provided for, (and together,) fructification and support, the fruitage of the plant, and the sustentation of the stalk, what means could be used more effectual, or, as I have said, more mechanical, than what this structure presents to our eyes? Why, or how, without a view to this double purpose, do two shoots, of such different and appropriate forms, spring from the same joint, from contiguous points of the same stalk? It never happens thus in robust plants, or in trees. "We see not, (says Ray,) so much as one tree, or shrub, or herb, that hath a firm and strong stem, and that is able to mount up and stand alone without assistance, *furnished with these tendrils.*" Make only so simple a comparison

---

ing which, different philosophers have given such different opinions; some referring it to the nature of the sap, as De la Hire, others as Darwin, to the living powers of the plant, and the stimulus of air upon the leaves, and of moisture upon the roots. The effect is now shown to be connected with mechanical causes; and there seems no other power in nature to which it can with propriety be referred but gravity, which acts universally, and which must tend to dispose the parts to take a uniform direction.

"The direction of the radicles and germens (plumules) is such, that both are supplied with food, and acted upon by those external agents which are necessary for their developement and growth. The roots come in contact with the fluids in the ground; the leaves are exposed to light and air; and the same grand law which preserves the planets in their orbits is thus essential to the functions of vegetable life."—Davy's El. Agr Chem. E. Ed. p. 32 —*Paxton.*

as that between a pea and a bean. Why does the pea pu.
forth tendrils, the bean not; but because the stalk of the
pea cannot support itself, the stalk of the bean can? We
may add also, as a circumstance not to be overlooked, that
in the pea tribe these clasps do not make their appearance
till they are wanted; till the plant has grown to a height
to stand in need of support.

'This word " support " suggests to us a reflection upon
the property of grasses, of corn, and canes. The hollow
stems of these classes of plants are set, at certain intervals,
with joints. These joints are not found in the trunks of
trees, or in the solid stalks of plants. There may be other
uses of these joints; but the fact is, and it appears to be
at least one purpose designed by them, that they *corrobo-
rate* the stem; which, by its length and hollowness, would
otherwise be too liable to break or bend.

Grasses are Nature's care. With these she clothes the
earth; with these she sustains its inhabitants. Cattle feed
upon their leaves; birds upon their smaller seeds; men
upon the larger: for few readers need be told, that the
plants which produce our bread-corn belong to this class.
In those tribes, which are more generally considered as
grasses, their extraordinary means and powers of preserva
tion and increase, their hardness, their almost unconquer-
able disposition to spread, their faculties of reviviscence,
coincide with the intention of nature concerning them
They thrive under a treatment by which other plants are de·
stroyed. The more their leaves are consumed, the more
their roots increase. The more they are trampled upon,
the thicker they grow., Many of the seemingly dry and
dead leaves of grasses revive, and renew their verdure, in
the spring. In lofty mountains, where the summer heats
are not sufficient to ripen the seeds, grasses abound, which
are viviparous, and consequently able to propagate them·
selves without seed. It is an observation, likewise, which
has often been made, that herbivorous animals attach them·
selves to the leaves of grasses; and, if at liberty in their
pastures to range and choose, leave untouched the straws
which support the flowers.*

The GENERAL properties of vegetable nature, or proper
ties common to large portions of that kingdom, are almost
all which the compass of our argument allows to bring forward. It is impossible to follow plants into their several
species We may be allowed, however, to single out three

* With. Bot. Ar vol. i. p. 28. ed. 2d.

or four of these species as worthy of a particular notice either by some singular mechanism, or by some peculiar provision, or by both.

I. In Dr Darwin's Botanic Garden (1. 395, note,) is the following account of the *vallisneria*, as it has been observed in the river Rhone.—[Pl. XXXV. fig. 1, 2, 3.] "They have roots at the bottom of the Rhone. The flowers of the *female plant* float on the surface of the water, and are furnished with an *elastic, spiral stalk*, which extends or contracts as the water rises or falls; this rise or fall, from the torrents which flow into the river, often amounting to many feet in a few hours. The flowers of the *male plant* are produced under water; and as soon as the fecundating farina is mature, they separate themselves from the plant, rise to the surface, and are wafted by the air, or borne by the currents, to the female flowers." Our attention in this narrative will be directed to two particulars; first to the mechanism, the "elastic spiral stalk," which lengthens or contracts itself according as the water rises or falls; secondly, to the provision which is made for bringing the male flower, which is produced *under* water, to the female flower which floats upon the surface.

II. My second example I take from Withering. (Arrang. vol. ii. p. 209. ed. 3.) "The *cuscuta Europæa* is a parasitical plant. [Plate XXXVI.] The seed opens and puts forth a *little spiral body*, which does NOT seek the earth to take root, but *climbs* in a spiral direction, from right to left, up other plants, from which, by means of vessels, it draws its nourishment." The "little spiral body" proceeding from the seed, is to be compared with the fibres which seeds send out in ordinary cases: and the comparison ought to regard both the form of the threads and the direction They are straight; this is spiral. They shoot downwards; this points upwards. In the rule, and in the exception, we equally perceive design.

III. A better known parasitical plant is the evergreen shrub, called the *mistletoe*. What we have to remark in it is a singular instance of *compensation*. No art has yet made these plants take root in the earth. Here therefore might seem to be a mortal defect in their constitution. Let us examine how this defect is made up to them. The seeds are endued with an adhesive quality, so tenacious, that, if they be rubbed upon the smooth bark of almost any tree, they will stick to it. And then what follows? Roots springing from these seeds, insinuate their fibers into the woody substance of the tree; and the event is, that a mistletoe plant is produced next winter;* of no other plant do the roots refuse to shoot in the ground; of no other plant do the seeds possess this adhesive, generative quality, when applied to the bark of trees.

IV. Another instance of the *compensatory* system is in the autumnal crocus, or meadow saffron, (*colchicum autumnale.*) [Pl. XXXVII.] I have pitied this poor plant a thousand times. Its blossom rises out of the ground in the most forlorn condition possible; without a sheath, a fence, a calyx, or even a leaf to protect it; and that, not in the spring, not to be visited by summer suns, but under all the disadvantages of the declining year. When we come, however, to look more closely into the structure of this plant, we find that, instead of its being neglected, nature has gone out of her course to provide for its security, and to make up to it for all its defects. The seed-vessel, which in other plants is situated within the cup of the flower, or just beneath it, in this plant lies buried ten or twelve inches under ground within the bulbous root. The tube of the flower, which is seldom more than a few tenths of an inch long, in this plant extends down to the root. The stiles in all cases reach the seed-vessel; but it is in this, by an elongation unknown to any other plant. All these singularities contribute to one end. " As this plant blossoms late in the year, and probably would not have time to ripen its seeds before the access of winter, which would destroy them, Providence has contrived its structure such, that this important office may be performed at a depth in the earth out of reach of the usual effects of frost."† That is to say, in the autumn nothing is done above ground but the business of impregnation; which is an affair between the antheræ and the stigmata, and is probably soon over. The maturation of the impregnated seed, which in other plants proceeds within a capsule, exposed together with the rest of the flower to the open air, is here carried on, and during the whole winter, within the heart, as we may say, of the earth, that is "out of the reach of the usual effects of frost." But then a new difficulty presents itself. Seeds, though perfected, are known not to vegetate at this depth in the earth. Our seeds, therefore, though so safely lodged, would after all, be lost to the purpose for which all seeds are intended. Lest this should be the case, " a second admirable provision is made to raise them above the surface when they are perfected, and to sow them at a proper dis

---

* Withering, Bot. Arr. vol. i. p. 203, ed. 2d.
† Withering's Botanical Arrangement, p. 360.

tance;" viz. the germ grows up *in the spring*, upon a fruit stalk, accompanied with leaves. The seeds now, in common with those of other plants, have the benefit of the summer, and are sown upon the surface. The order of vegetation externally is this:—The plant produces its flowers ir September; its leaves and fruits in the spring following.

V. I give the account of the *dionæa muscipula*, [Plate XXXVIII.] an extraordinary American plant, as some late authors have related it: but whether we be yet enough acquainted witu the plant, to bring every part of this account to the test of repeated and familiar observation, I am unable to say. Its leaves are jointed, and furnished with two rows of strong prickles; their surfaces covered with a number of minute glands, which secrete a sweet liquor that allures the approach of flies. When these parts are touched by the legs of flies, the two lobes of the leaf instantly spring up, the rows of prickles lock themselves fast together, and squeeze the unwary animal to death."* Here, under a new model, we recognise the ancient plan of nature, viz. the relation of parts and provisions to one another, to a common office, and to the utility of the organized body to which they belong. The attracting sirup, the rows of strong prickles, their position so as to interlock the joints of the leaves; and what is more than the rest, that singular irritability of their surfaces, by which they close at a touch; all bear a contributory part in producing an effect, connected either with the defence, or with the nutrition of the plant.

CHAPTER XXI

THE ELEMENTS.

WHEN we come to the elements, we take leave of our mechanics; because we come to those things, of the organization of which, if they be organized, we are confessedly ignorant. This ignorance is implied by their name. To say the truth, our investigations are stopped long before we arrive at this point. But then it is for our comfort to find, that a knowledge of the constitution of the elements is not necessary for us. For instance, as Addison has well observed, " we know *water* sufficiently, when we

* Smellie's Phil. of Nat. His v. l. p. 5.

know how to boil, how to freeze, how to evaporate, how to make it fresh, how to make it run or spout out in what quantity and direction we please, without knowing what water is." The observation of this excellent writer has more propriety in it now, than it had at the time it was made: for the constitution, and the constituent parts of water, appear in some measure to have been lately discovered; yet it does not, I think, appear, that we can make any better or greater use of water since the discovery, than we did before it.

We can never think of the elements, without reflecting upon the number of distinct uses which are *consolidated* in the same substance. The *air* supplies the lungs, supports fire, conveys sound, reflects light, diffuses smells, gives rain, wafts ships, bears up birds. 'Εξ υδατος τα παντα *water*, besides maintaining its own inhabitants, is the universal nourisher of plants, and through them of terrestrial animals; is the basis of their juices and fluids; dilutes their food; quenches their thirst; floats their burdens *Fire* warms, dissolves, enlightens; is the great promoter of vegetation and life, if not necessary to the support of both.

We might enlarge, to almost any length we pleased, upon each of these uses; but it appears to me almost sufficient to state them. The few remarks which I judge it necessary to add, are as follow:

I. *Air* is essentially different from earth. There appears to be no necessity for an atmosphere's investing our globe; yet it does invest it: and we see how many, how various, and how important are the purposes which it answers to every order of animated, not to say of organized beings, which are placed upon the terrestrial surface. I think that every one of these uses will be understood upon the first mention of them, except it be that of *reflecting* light, which may be explained thus —If I had the power of seeing only by means of rays coming directly from the sun, whenever I turned my back upon the luminary, I should find myself in darkness. If I had the power of seeing by reflected light, yet by means only of light reflected from solid masses, these masses would shine, indeed, and glisten, but it would be in the dark. The hemisphere, the sky, the world, could only be *illuminated*, as it is illuminated, by the light of the sun being from all sides, and in every direction, reflected to the eye by particles, as numerous, as thickly scattered, and as widely diffused, as are those of the air

Another general quality of the atmosphere is the power of evaporating fluids. The adjustment of this quality to our use is seen in its action upon the sea. In the sea, water and salt are mixed together most intimately; yet the atmosphere raises the water, and leaves the salt. Pure and fresh as drops of rain descend, they are collected from brine. If evaporation be solution, (which seems to be probable,) then the air dissolves the water, and not the salt. Upon whatever it be founded, the distinction is critical, so much so, that when we attempt to imitate the process by art, we must regulate our distillation with great care and nicety, or, together with the water, we get the bitterness, or, at least, the distastefulness, of the marine substance: and, after all, it is owing to this original elective power in the air, that we can effect the separation which we wish, by any art or means whatever.

By evaporation, water is carried up into the air; by the converse of evaporation, it falls down upon the earth. And how does it fall? Not by the clouds being all at once reconverted into water, and descending like a sheet; not in rushing down in columns from a spout; but in moderate drops, as from a colander. Our watering-pots are made to imitate showers of rain. Yet, *à priori*, I should have thought either of the two former methods more likely to have taken place than the last.

By respiration, flame, putrefaction, air is rendered unfit for the support of animal life. By the constant operation of these corrupting principles, the whole atmosphere, if there were no restoring causes, would come at length to be deprived of its necessary degree of purity Some of these causes seem to have been discovered, and their efficacy ascertained by experiment. And so far as the discovery has proceeded, it opens to us a beautiful and a wonderful economy. *Vegetation* proves to be one of them. A sprig of mint corked up with a small portion of foul air placed in the light, renders it again capable of supporting life or flame Here, therefore, is a constant circulation of benefits maintained between the two great provinces of organized nature. The plant purifies what the animal has poisoned; in return, the contaminated air is more than ordinarily nutritious to the plant. *Agitation with water* turns out to be another of these restoratives. The foulest air, shaken in a bottle with water for a sufficient length of time, recovers a great degree of its purity. Here then again, allowing for the scale upon which nature works, we see the salutary effects of *storms* and *tempests*. The yesty

s*

waves which confound the heaven and the sea are doing the very thing which was done in the bottle. Nothing can be of greater importance to the living creation, than the salubrity of their atmosphere. It ought to reconcile us, therefore, to these agitations of the elements, of which we sometimes deplore the consequences, to know, that they tend powerfully to restore to the air that purity, which so many causes are constantly impairing.

II. In water, what ought not a little to be admired, are those negative qualities which constitute its *purity*. Had it been vinous, or oleaginous, or acid; had the sea been filled, or the rivers flowed, with wine or milk; fish, con stituted as they are, must have died; plants, constituted as they are, would have withered; the lives of animals which feed upon plants, must have perished. Its very *in-sipidity*, which is one of those negative qualities, renders it the best of all menstrua. Having no taste of its own, it becomes the sincere vehicle of every other. Had there been a taste in water, be it what it might, it would have infected everything we ate or drank, with an importunate repetition of the same flavor.

Another thing in this element, not less to be admired, is the constant *round* which it travels; and by which, with out suffering either adulteration or waste, it is continually offering itself to the wants of the habitable globe. From the sea are exhaled those vapors which form the clouds; these clouds descend in showers, which, penetrating into the crevices of the hills, supply springs; which springs flow in little streams into the valleys; and there, uniting, become rivers; which rivers, in return, feed the ocean. So there is an incessant circulation of the same fluid; and not one drop probably more or less now than there was at the creation. A particle of water takes its departure from the surface of the sea, in order to fulfil certain important offi ces to the earth; and, having executed the service whic was assigned to it, returns to the bosom which it left.

Some have thought, that we have too much water upon the globe, the sea occupying above three quarters of its whole surface. But the expanse of ocean, immense as i is, may be no more than sufficient to fertilize the earth. Or, independently of this reason, I know not why the sea may not have as good a right to its place as the land. It may proportionably support as many inhabitants; minister to as large an aggregate of enjoyment. The land only af fords a habitable surface; the sea is habitable to a great depth.

III Of fire, we have said that it *dissolves* The only idea probably which this term raised in the reader's mind, was that of fire melting metals, resins, and some other substances, fluxing ores, running glass, and assisting us in ma..y of our operations, chemical or culinary. Now these are only uses of an occasional kind, and give us a very imperfect notion of what fire does for us. The grand importance of this dissolving power, the great office indeed of fire in the economy of nature, is keeping things in a state o.' solution, that is to say, in a state of fluidity. Were it not for the presence of heat, or of a certain degree of it, al. fluids would be frozen. The ocean itself would be a quar-·y of ice; universal nature stiff and dead.

We see, therefore, that the elements bear not only a strict relation to the constitution of organized bodies, but a relation to each other. Water could not perform its office to the earth without air; nor exist, as water, without fire.

IV. Of light, (whether we regard it as of the same substance with fire, or as a different substance,) it is altogether superfluous to expatiate upon the use. No man disputes it. The observations, therefore, which I shall offer, respect that little which we seem to know of its constitution.

Light travels from the sun at the rate of twelve million of miles in a minute. Urged by such a velocity, with what *force* must its particles drive against, (I will not say the eye, the tenderest of animal substances, but) every substance, animate or inanimate, which stands in its way! It might seem to be a force sufficient to shatter to atoms the hardest bodies.

How then is this effect, the consequence of such prodigious velocity, guarded against? By a proportionable *minuteness* of the particles of which light is composed. It is impossible for the human mind to imagine to itself anything so small as a particle of light. But this extreme exility, though difficult to conceive, it is easy to prove. A drop of tallow, expended in the wick of a farthing candle, shall send forth rays sufficient to fill a hemisphere of a mile diameter; and to fill it so full of these rays, that an aperture not larger than the pupil of an eye, wherever it be placed within the hemisphere, shall be sure to receive some of them. What floods of light are continually poured from the sun, we cannot estimate; but the immensity of the sphere which is filled with its particles, even if it reached no farther than the orbit of the earth, we can in some sort compute; and we have reason to believe, that throughout th s whole region, the particles of light lie, in latitude at least, near to one another. The spissitude of the sun's rays at the earth is such, that the number which falls upon a burning glass of an inch diameter, is sufficient, when concentrated, to set wood on fire.

The tenuity and the velocity of particles of light, as ascertained by separate observations, may be said to be proportioned to each other; both surpassing our utmost stretch of comprehension; but proportioned. And it is this proportion alone which converts a tremendous element into a welcome visiter.

It has been observed to me by a learned friend, as having often struck his mind, that if light had been made by a common artist, it would have been of one uniform *color*; whereas, by its present composition, we have that variety of colors which is of such infinite use to us for the distinguishing of objects; which adds so much to the beauty of the earth, and augments the stock of our innocent pleasures

With which may be joined another reflection, viz. that, considering light as compounded of rays of seven different colors, (of which there can be no doubt, because it can be resolved into these rays by simply passing it through a prism,) the constituent parts must be well mixed and blended together, to produce a fluid so clear and colorless as a beam of light is, when received from the sun.

—◆—

CHAPTER XXII.

ASTRONOMY.*

My opinion of astronomy has always been, that it is *not* the best medium through which to prove the agency of an intelligent Creator; but that, this being proved, it shows, beyond all other sciences, the magnificence of his operations. The mind, which is once convinced, it raises to sublimer views of the Deity than any other subject affords; but it is not so well adapted as some other subjects are to the purpose of argument. We are destitute of the means of examining the constitution of the heavenly bodies. The very simplicity of their appearance is against them. We

* For the articles in this chapter marked with an asterisk, I am indebted to some obliging communications received (through the hands of the Lord Bishop of Elphin) from the Rev. J. Brinkle· D D. Andrew's Professor of Astronomy in the University of Dublin.

see nothing but bright points, luminous circles, or the phases of spheres reflecting the light which falls upon them. Now we deduce design from relation, aptitude, and correspondence of *parts*. Some degree therefore of *complexity* is necessary to render a subject fit for this species of argument. But the heavenly bodies do not, except perhaps in the instance of Saturn's ring, present themselves to our observation as compounded of parts at all. This, which may be a perfection in them, is a disadvantage to us, as inquirers after their nature They do not come within our mechanics.

And what we say of their forms, is true of their *motions* Their motions are carried on without any sensible intermediate apparatus; whereby we are cut off from one principal ground of argumentation—analogy. We have nothing wherewith to compare them; no invention, no discovery, no operation or resource of art, which, in this respect, resembles them. Even those things which are made to imitate and represent them, such as orreries, planetaria, celestial globes, &c. bear no affinity to them, in the cause and principle by which their motions are actuated. I can assign for this difference a reason of utility, viz. a reason why though the action of *terrestrial* bodies upon each other be, in almost all cases, through the intervention of solid or fluid substances, yet central attraction does not operate in this manner. It was necessary that the intervals between the planetary orbs should be devoid of any *inert* matter either fluid or solid, because such an intervening substance would, by its resistance, destroy those very motions which attraction is employed to preserve. This may be a final cause of the difference; but still the difference destroys the analogy.*

Our ignorance, moreover, of the *sensitive* natures by which other planets are inhabited, necessarily keeps from us the knowledge of numberless utilities, relations, and subserviencies, which we perceive upon our own globe.

After all; the real subject of admiration is, that we understand so much of astronomy as we do. That an animal confined to the surface of one of the planets; bearing a

---

* The moon has no perceptible atmosphere: and as no effects have been observed like those which would be produced by vapors or exhalations from its surface, it is possible that there are no fluids upon it There is no reason, however, from these circumstances, for denying the existence of sensitive beings upon it, although they must be very differently constituted from ourselves to whom air and water are essentially necessary.— *Paxton.*

less proportion to it than the smallest microscopic insect *
does to the plant it lives upon; that this little, busy, in
quisitive creature, by the use of senses which were given
to it for its domestic necessities, and by means of the assistance of those senses which it has had the art to procure,
should have been enabled to observe the whole system of
worlds to which its own belongs; the changes of place
of the immense globes which compose it; and with such
accuracy, as to mark out, beforehand, the situation in the
heavens in which they will be found at any future point of
time, and that these bodies, after sailing through regions
of void and trackless space, should arrive at the place where
they were expected. not within a minute, but within a few
seconds of a minute, of the time prefixed and predicted: all
this is wonderful, whether we refer our admiration to the
constancy of the heavenly motions themselves, or to the
perspicacity and precision with which they have been noticed by mankind.   Nor is this the whole, nor indeed the
chief part of what astronomy teaches.   By bringing reason
to bear upon observation, (the acutest reasoning upon the
exactest observation) the astronomer has been able, out
of the confusion (for such it is) under which the motions
of the heavenly bodies present themselves to the eye of
a mere gazer upon the skies, to elicit their order and their
real paths.

Our knowledge, therefore, of astronomy is admirable,
though imperfect; and, amidst the confessed desiderata and
desideranda which impede our investigation of the wisdom
of the Deity, in these the grandest of his works, there are
to be found, in the phenomena, ascertained circumstances
and laws, sufficient to indicate an intellectual agency in
three of its principal operations, viz. in choosing, in determining, in regulating: in *choosing*, out of a boundless variety of suppositions which were equally possible, that
which is beneficial; in *determining*, what, left to itself, had
a thousand chances against conveniency, for one in its
favor; in *regulating* subjects, as to quantity and degree,
which, by their nature, were unlimited with respect to

* Hooke describes a minute animalcule, which he discovered with a microscope, upon a vine.   From his data an estimate may be made of its
bulk; but it is not so easy to fix upon any determinate quantity for the
size of the plant.   However, to put the case strongly, let the bulk of it
be taken as equal to that of a cylinder one inch in diameter and a mile in
length.   Such a cylinder would contain above 345 cubic feet, and yet it
would be many million times less when compared with the animalcule.
than the earth is when compared with the bulk of a man.—*Parten.*

eitber   It will be our business to offer, under each of these heads, a few instances, such as best admit of a popular explication.

1. Amongst proofs of choice, one is, fixing the source of light and heat in the *centre* of the system. The sun is ignited and luminous; the planets which move round him, cold and dark. There seems to be no antecedent necessity for this order. The sun might have been an opaque mass; some one, or two, or more, or any, or all the planets, globes of fire. There is nothing in the nature of the heavenly bodies, which requires that those which are stationary should be on fire, that those which move should be cold; for, in fact, comets are bodies on fire,* or at least capable of the most intense heat, yet revolve round a centre; nor does this order obtain between the primary planets and their secondaries, which are all opaque. When we consider, therefore, that the sun is one; that the planets going round it are at least seven;† that it is indifferent to their nature, which are luminous and which are opaque, and also, in what order, with respect to each other, these two kinds of bodies are disposed; we may judge of the improbability of the present arrangement taking place by chance.

If, by way of accounting for the state in which we find the solar system, it be alleged (and this is one amongst the guesses of those who reject an intelligent Creator) that the planets themselves are only cooled or cooling masses, and were once, like the sun, many thousand times hotter than red-hot iron; then it follows, that the sun also himself must be in his progress towards growing cold; which puts an end to the possibility of his having existed, as he is.

* It may be reasonably doubted whether comets are ever absolutely " on fire," and yet some of them, from their near approach to the sun, must certainly be " capable of intense heat." If we conceive the earth's distance from the sun to be divided into 1000 parts, the comet of 1680 was, at one time, not more distant than six of those parts from the sun. From hence Sir I Newton calculated that it was exposed to a heat which was 2000 times greater than that of a red-hot iron.—*Paxton.*

† The seven planets here alluded to are Mercury, Venus, the Earth, Mars, Jupiter, Saturn, and the Georgium Sidus : we now know that there are four more, Ceres, Pallas, Juno, and Vesta; the first of these was discovered in 1801, the second was observed in March, 1802, the third was not discovered till 1804, nor the last till 1807. Now Dr. Paley's dedication is dated July, 1802; it is very possible, therefore that this 22d chapter was written before he had heard of Pallas, and even while it was yet doubtful whether Ceres was a comet or a planet. This will explain the reason for his having qualified the expression, and having said " at least seven."

from eternity. This consequence arises out of the hypoth
esis with still more certainty, if we make a part of it, what
the philosophers who maintain it have usually taught, that
the planets were originally masses of matter, struck off in
a state of fusion from the body of the sun by the percus-
sion of a comet, or by a shock from some other cause, with
which we are not acquainted: for, if these masses, partak-
ing of the nature and substance of the sun's body, have in
process of time lost their heat, that body itself, in time
likewise, no matter in how much longer time, must lose its
heat also, and therefore be incapable of an eternal duration in the state in which we see it, either for the time to
come, or the time past.

The preference of the present to any other mode of distributing luminous and opaque bodies, I take to be evident
It requires more astronomy than I am able to lay before
the reader, to show, in its particulars, what would be the
effect to the system, of a dark body at the centre, and of
one of the planets being luminous; but I think it manifest,
without either plates or calculation, first, that supposing
he necessary proportion of magnitude between the central
and the revolving bodies to be preserved, the ignited planet
would not be sufficient to illuminate and warm the rest of
the system; secondly, that its light and heat would be imparted to the other planets much more irregularly than
light and heat are now received from the sun.

(*) II. Another thing, in which a choice appears to be
exercised, and in which, amongst the possibilities out o
which the choice was to be made, the number of those
which were wrong bore an infinite proportion to the num
ber of those which were right, is in what geometricians
call the *axis of rotation*. This matter I will endeavour
to explain. The earth, it is well known, is not an exac
globe, but an oblate spheroid, something like an orange.
Now the axes of rotation, or the diameters upon which such
a body may be made to turn round, are as many as can be
drawn through its centre to opposite points upon its whole
surface: but of these axes none are *permanent*, except
either its shortest diameter, i. e. that which passes through
the heart of the orange from the place where the stalk is
inserted into it, and which is but one; or its longest diameters, at right angles with the former, which must all terminate in the single circumference which goes round the
thickest part of the orange. The shortest diameter is
that upon which in fact the earth turns; and it is, as the
reader sees, what it ought to be, a permanent axis; where-

is, had blind chance, had a casual impulse, had a stroke or push at random, set the earth a-spinning, the odds were infinite, but that they had sent it round upon a wrong axis And what would have been the consequence? The difference between a permanent axis and another axis is this When a spheroid in a state of rotatory motion gets upon a permanent axis, it keeps there; it remains steady and faithful to its position; its poles preserve their direction with respect to the plane and to the centre of its orbit: but whilst it turns upon an axis which is *not* permanent, (and the number of those we have seen infinitely exceeds the number of the other,) it is always liable to shift and vacillate from one axis to another, with a corresponding change in the inclination of its poles. Therefore, if a planet once set off revolving upon any other than its shortest, or one of its longest axis, the poles on its surface would keep perpetually changing, and it never would attain a permanent axis of rotation. The effect of this unfixedness and instability would be, that the equatorial parts of the earth might become the polar, or the polar the equatorial; to the utter destruction of plants and animals, which are not capable of interchanging their situations, but are respectively adapted to their own. As to ourselves, instead of rejoicing in our temperate zone, and annually preparing for the moderate vicissitude, or rather the agreeable succession of seasons which we experience and expect, we might come to be locked up in the ice and darkness of the arctic circle, with bodies neither inured to its rigors, nor provided with shelter or defence against them. Nor would it be much better, if the trepidation of our pole, taking an opposite course, should place us under the heats of a vertical sun. But if it would fare so ill with the human inhabitant, who can live under greater varieties of latitude than any other animal; still more noxious would this translation of climate have proved to life in the rest of the creation; and most perhaps of all, in plants. The habitable earth, and its beautiful variety, might have been destroyed by a simple mischance in the axis of rotation.*

* The earth being an oblate spheroid, we may suppose it to be cut by a plane passing through A B, Fig. 3, Plate XXXIX, which may represent its axis, and the common section of this plane with the spheroid will be an ellipse like A D B E; of this ellipse A B will be an axis; and, from the property of the curve, it will also be the shortest line which can be drawn through the centre C. If now the diameter D E be drawn at right angles to A B, it will be the longest line which can be drawn in the ellipse, and it will represent a diameter of the equator. As the plane

III. All this, however, proceeds upon a supposition of the earth having been formed at first an oblate spheroid There is another supposition; and perhaps our limited in formation will not enable us to decide between them. The second supposition is, that the earth, being a mixed mass somewhat fluid, took, as it might do, its present form, by the joint action of the mutual gravitation of its parts and its rotatory motion. This, as we have said, is a point in the history of the earth which our observations are not sufficient to determine. For a very small depth below the surface (but extremely small, less, perhaps, than an eight-thousandth† part, compared with the depth of the centre) we find vestiges of ancient fluidity. But this fluidity must have gone down many hundred times farther than we can penetrate, to enable the earth to take its present oblate form; and whether any traces of this kind exist to that depth, we are ignorant. Calculations were made a few years ago, of the mean density of the earth, by comparing the force of its attraction with the force of attraction of a rock of granite, the bulk of which could be ascertained. and the upshot of the calculation was, that the earth upon an average, through its whole sphere, has twice the density of granite, or about five times that of water. Therefore it cannot be a hollow shell, as some have formerly supposed; nor can its internal parts be occupied by central fire, or by water. The solid parts must greatly exceed the fluid parts; and the probability is, that it is a solid mass throughout, composed of substances more ponderous the deeper we go. Nevertheless, we may conceive the present face of the earth to have originated from the revolution of a sphere covered by a surface of a compound mixture; the fluid and solid parts separating, as the surface becomes quiescent Here then comes in the *moderating* hand of the Creator If the water had exceeded its present proportion, even but by a trifling quantity compared with the whole globe, all

passing through A B is not confined to one situation more than another, D E may represent any " one of the longest axes of the spheroid," and will, as well as A B, always be a " permanent axis of rotation." But if any other diameter, as G H, is taken, the earth could not continue to revolve permanently about it.—*Paxton.*

† The " deep St. John," one of the deepest mines in the Hartz, was found by M. Deluc to sink 1359 feet. This was in 1778, and it may, since that time, have been carried lower, but probably not to the depth of the mine of Valenciana in New Spain, the bottom of which, according to Humboldt, is 1681 feet below the surface. Now the diameter of the earth being about 7912 miles, " the eight-thousandth part of the depth of the centre" must be 2611 feet, or nearly half a mile.—*Ibid.*

he land would have been covered: had there been much
ess than there is, there would not have been enough to
fertilize the continent.* Had the exsiccation been progressive, such as we may suppose to have been produced
by an evaporating heat, how came it to stop at the point at
which we see it? Why did it not stop sooner; why at all?
The mandate of the Deity will account for this; nothing
else will.

IV. OF CENTRIPETAL FORCES. By virtue of the simplest
law that can be imagined, viz. that a body *continues* in
the state in which it is, whether of motion or rest; and if in
motion, goes on in the line in which it was proceeding,
and with the same velocity, *unless* there be some cause for
change: by virtue, I say, of this law, it comes to pass
(what may appear to be a strange consequence) that cases
arise, in which attraction, incessantly drawing a body towards a centre, never brings, nor ever will bring, the body
to that centre, but keep it in eternal circulation round it.
If it were possible to fire off a cannon ball with a velocity
of five miles in a second, and the resistance of the air could
be taken away, the cannon ball would forever wheel round
the earth, instead of falling down upon it.† This is the
principle which sustains the heavenly motions. The Deity,
having appointed this law to matter, (than which, as we
have said before, no law could be more simple,) has turned
it to a wonderful account in constructing planetary systems.

The actuating cause in these systems, is an attraction,
which varies reciprocally as the square of the distance·
that is, at double the distance, has a quarter of the force,
at half the distance four times the strength; and so on.
Now, concerning this law of variation, we have three
things to observe: First; that attraction, for anything we
know about it, was just as capable of one law of variation

* Nearly three quarters of the earth's surface are covered by the sea.
Now evaporation is proportionate to the surface of the fluid, and consequently a less expanse of waters would not have afforded a sufficient supply of rain, which does not now fall upon the whole, in greater quantities
than are required " to fertilize the earth."—*Paxton.*

† If a body be projected horizontally from a station A, Fig. 6, Plate
XXXIX, which is at a certain height, its weight or the force of gravity
will draw it towards the earth. It may be supposed to come down,
for example, at B. But from the tendency which the body has to con
tinue in the state of motion which is communicated to it, it will be carri
ed farther before it falls, if it is projected with a greater force. Hence,
if this force be increased it may be made to reach C by a greater increase,
it may be carried to D; or even round to A, from whence it originally
se out - *Ibid.*

as of another: Secondly; that out of an infinite number of possible laws, those which were admissible for the purpose of supporting the heavenly motions, lay within certain narrow limits· Thirdly; that of the admissible laws, or those which come within the limits prescribed, the law that actually prevails is the most beneficial. So far as these propositions can be made out, we may be said, I think, to prove *choice* and *regulation;* choice, out of boundless variety; and regulation, of that which, by its own nature, was, in respect of the property regulated, indifferent and indefinite

First then, attraction, for anything we know about it, was originally indifferent to all laws of variation depending upon change of distance, *i. e.* just as susceptible of one law as of another. It might have been the same at all distances; it might have increased as the distance increased: or it might have diminished with the increase of the distance, yet in ten thousand different proportions from he present; it might have followed no stated law at all If attraction be what Cotes, with many other Newtonians, have thought it to be, a primordial property of matter, not dependent upon, or traceable to, any other material cause; then, by the very nature and definition of a primordial property, it stood indifferent to all laws. If it be the agency of something immaterial, then also, for anything we know of it, it was indifferent to all laws. If the revolution of bodies round a centre depend upon vortices, neither are these limited to one law more than another.

There is, I know, an account given of attraction, which should seem, in its very cause, to assign to it the law which we find it to observe; and which, therefore, makes that law, a law, not of choice, but of necessity: and it is the account, which ascribes attraction to an *emanation* from the attracting body. It is probable, that the influence of such an emanation will be proportioned to the spissitude of the rays of which it is composed; which spissitude, supposing the rays to issue in right lines on all sides from a point, will be reciprocally as the square of the distance.*

* Let the light of a candle fall upon a square object like A B C D, Fig. 4, Plate XXXIX, and if a screen be placed parallel to the object and at double the distance, the shadow E F G H, received upon it, will be four times the size of the object itself. For the rays passing in straight lines by the angles A, B, C, D, the sides E F, F G, G H, H E, must be each double of A B, B C, C D, D A: therefore the shadow may be divided into four squares each equal in size to the object. At three times the distance from the candle. the sides of the shadow would each be three times as large as the sides of the object, and its area would. therefore. contain

The mathematics of this solution we do not call in question the question with us is, whether there be any sufficient reason to believe, that attraction is produced by an emanation. For my part, I am totally at a loss to comprehend how particles streaming *from* a centre should draw a body *towards* it. The impulse, if impulse it be, is all the other way. Nor shall we find less difficulty in conceiving a conflux of particles, incessantly flowing to a centre, and carrying down all bodies along with it, that centre also itself being in a state of rapid motion through absolute space: for by what source is the stream fed, or what becomes of the accumulation? Add to which, that it seems to imply a contrariety of properties, to suppose an ethereal fluid to *act*, but not to *resist;* powerful enough to carry down bodies with great force towards a centre, yet, inconsistently with the nature of inert matter, powerless and perfectly yielding with respect to the motions which result from the projectile impulse. By calculations drawn from ancient notices of eclipses of the moon, we can prove that, if such a fluid exist at all, its resistance has had no sensible effect upon the moon's motion for two thousand five hundred years. The truth is, that, except this one circumstance of the variation of the attracting force at different distances agreeing with the variation of the spissitude, there is no reason whatever to support the hypothesis of an emanation; and, as it seems to me, almost insuperable reasons against it.

(*) II. Our second proposition is, that whilst the possible laws of variation were infinite, the *admissible* laws, or the laws compatible with the preservation of the system, lie within narrow limits. If the attracting force had varied according to any *direct* law of the distance, let it have been what it would, great destruction and confusion would have taken place. The direct simple proportion of the distance would, it is true, have produced an ellipse, out the perturbing forces would have acted with so much advantage, as to be continually changing the dimensions of the ellipse, in a manner inconsistent with our terrestrial

nine times the space. For the same reason if the distance be increased four, five, or six times, the area of the shadow will contain sixteen, twenty-five, or thirty-six squares, each equal to the object. Now the quantity of light which falls upon the object would, if it had not been intercepted, have spread over that part of the screen, which is occupied by the shadow; and as the surface is increased, over which a certain quantity of rays is spread, in the same ratio their spissitude or density will be diminished consequently this spissitude will be reciprocally as the squares of the distances —*Paxton.*

T*

creation For instance; if the planet Saturn, so large and so remote, had attracted the earth, both in proportion to the quantity of matter contained in it, which it does; and also in any proportion to its distance; *i. e.* if it had pulled the harder for being the farther off, (instead of the reverse of it,) it would have dragged out of its course the globe which we inhabit, and have perplexed its motions, to a degree incompatible with our security, our enjoyments, and probably our existence. Of the *inverse* laws, if the centripetal force had changed as the cube of the distance, or in any higher proportion, that is (for I speak to the unlearned,) if, at double the distance, the attractive force had been diminished to an eighth part, or to less than that, the consequence would have been, that the planets, if they once began to approach the sun, would have fallen into his body; if they once, though by ever so little, increased their distance from the centre, would forever have receded from it. The laws, therefore, of attraction, by which a system of revolving bodies could be upholden in their motions, lie within narrow limits, compared with the possible laws. I much underrate the restriction, when I say that, in a scale of a mile, they are confined to an inch. All direct ratios of the distance are excluded, on account of danger from perturbing forces; all reciprocal ratios, except what lie beneath the cube of the distance, by the demonstrable consequence, that every the least change of distance would, under the operation of such laws, have been fatal to the repose and order of the system. We do not know, that is, we seldom reflect, how interested we are in this matter. Small irregularities may be endured; but changes within these limits being allowed for, the permanency of our ellipse is a question of life and death to our whole sensitive world.

(*) III. That the subsisting law of attraction falls within the limits which utility requires, when these limits bear so small a proportion to the range of possibilities upon which chance might equally have cast it, is not, with any appearance of reason, to be accounted for by any other cause than a regulation proceeding from a designing mind But our next proposition carries the matter somewhat farther. We say, in the third place, that, out of the different laws which lie within the limits of admissible laws, the *best* is made choice of; that there are advantages in this particular law which cannot be demonstrated to belong to any other law; and, concerning some of which, it can be demonstrated that they do no belong to any other

(*) 1. Whilst this law prevails between each particle of matter, the *united* attraction of a sphere, composed of that matter, observes the same law. This property of the law is necessary, to render it applicable to a system composed of spheres, but it is a property which belongs to no other law of attraction that is admissible. The law of variation of the united attraction is in no other case the same as the law of attraction of each particle, one case excepted, and that is of the attraction varying directly as the distance; * the inconveniency of which law, in other respects, we have already noticed.

We may follow this regulation somewhat farther, and still more strikingly perceive that it proceeded from a designing mind. A law both admissible and convenient was requisite. In what way is the law of the attracting globes obtained? Astronomical observations and terrestrial experiments show, that the attraction of the globes of the system is made up of the attraction of their parts; the attraction of each globe being compounded of the attractions of its parts. Now, the admissible and convenient law which exists, could not be obtained in a system of bodies gravitating by the united gravitation of their parts, unless each particle of matter were attracted by a force varying by one particular law viz. varying inversely as the square of the distance; for, if the action of the particles be according to any other law whatever, the admissible and convenient law which is adopted could not be obtained. Here then are clearly shown regulation and design. A law both admissible and convenient was to be obtained: the mode chosen for obtaining that law was by making *each* particle of matter act. After this choice was made, then farther attention was to be given to each particle of matter, and one, and one only particular law of action to be assigned to it. No other law would have answered the purpose intended.

(*) 2. All systems must be liable to *perturbations*. And therefore, to guard against these perturbations, or rather to guard against their running to destructive lengths, is perhaps the strongest evidence of care and foresight that can be given. Now we are able to demonstrate of our law of

* Let A, Fig. 5, Plate XXXIX, represent a sphere composed of particles, which mutually attract each other with a force, which varies reciprocally as the squares of the distances ; their united attraction, on a similar particle P without the sphere, will be according to the same law that is, the particle will be attracted towards the sphere with a force, which will also vary reciprocally as the square of C P, its distance from the centre of the sphere.—*Paxton.*

attraction, what can be demonstrated of no other, and what qualifies the dangers which arise from cross but unavoidable influences, that the action of the parts of our system upon one another will not cause permanently increasing irregularities, but merely periodical or vibratory ones; that is, they will come to a limit, and then go back again. This we can demonstrate only of a system, in which the following properties concur, viz. that the force shall be inversely as the square of the distance; the masses of the revolving bodies small, compared with that of the body at the centre; the orbits not much inclined to one another; and their eccentricity little. In such a system the grand points are secure. The mean distances and periodic times, upon which depend our temperature and the regularity of our year, are constant. The eccentricities, it is true, will still vary, but so slowly, and to so small an extent, as to produce no inconveniency from fluctuation of temperature and season. The same as to the obliquity of the planes of the orbits. For instance, the inclination of the ecliptic to the equator will never change above two degrees, (out of ninety,) and that will require many thousand years in performing.

It has been rightly also remarked, that if the great planets, Jupiter and Saturn, had moved in lower spheres, their influences would have had much more effect, as to disturbing the planetary motions, than they now have. While they revolve at so great distances from the rest, they act almost equally on the sun and on the inferior planets; which has nearly the same consequence as not acting at all upon either.

If it be said that the planets might have been sent round the sun in exact circles, in which case, no change of distance from the centre taking place, the law of variation of the attracting power would have never come in question, one law would have served as well as another; an answer to the scheme may be drawn from the consideration of these same perturbing forces. The system retaining in other respects its present constitution, though the planets had been at first sent round in exact circular orbits, they could not have kept them: and if the law of attraction had not been what it is, or, at least, if the prevailing law had transgressed the limits above assigned, every evagation would have been fatal: the planet once drawn, as drawn it necessarily must have been, out of its course, would have wandered in endless error.

(*) V. What we have seen in the law of the centripetal force, viz. a choice guided by views of utility, and a choice of one aw out of thousands which might equally have taken p ace, we see no less in the *figures* of the planetary orbits. It was not enough to fix the law of the centripetal force, though by the wisest choice; for even under that law, it was still competent to the planets to have moved in paths possessing so great a degree of eccentricity, as, in the course of every revolution, to be brought very near to the sun, and carried away to immense distances from him. The comets actually move in orbits of this sort; and had the planets done so, instead of going round in orbits near ly circular, the change from one extremity of temperature to another must, in ours at least, have destroyed every animal and plant upon its surface. Now, the distance from the centre at which a planet sets off, and the absolute force of attraction at that distance, being fixed, the figure of his orbit, its being a circle, or nearer to, or farther off from a circle, viz. a rounder or a longer oval, depends upon two things, the velocity with which, and the direction in which, the planet is projected. And these, in order to produce a right result, must be both brought within certain narrow limits. One, and only one, velocity united with one, and only one, direction, will produce a perfect circle And the velocity must be near to this velocity, and the direction also near to this direction, to produce orbits, such as the planetary orbits are, nearly circular; that is, ellipses with small eccentricities. The velocity and the direction must *both* be right. If the velocity be wrong, no direction will cure the error; if the direction be in any considerable degree oblique, no velocity will produce the orbit required. Take for example the attraction of gravity at the surface of the earth. The force of that attraction being what it is, out of all the degrees of velocity, swift and slow, with which a ball might be shot off, none would answer the purpose of which we are speaking, but what was nearly that of five miles in a second.* If it were less than that, the body

* The moon describes in one second of time nearly two-thirds of a mile in its orbit round the earth: and if its distance were diminished it might still continue to revolve nearly in a circle round the same centre, if its velocity were increased so as to compensate for the greater attraction, which would now draw it constantly out of the rectilinear direc tion, in which it would otherwise move. This distance may be supposed to be diminished till the moon is brought near to the earth's surface, and t would, under these circumstances, still continue to complete its revolution, if its velocity were increased to about five miles in a second. Now for the description of such a revolution, there is no difference between the moon and any other material substance at the same distance; for they would bo r be drawn down through the same space in the same time by

wou d not get round at all, but would come to the ground, if it were in any considerable degree more than that, the body would take one of those eccentric courses, those long ellipses of which we have noticed the inconveniency.* If the velocity reached the rate of seven miles in a second, or went beyond that, the ball would fly off from the earth, and never be heard of more. In like manner with respect to the *direction;* out of the innumerable angles in which he ba'l might be sent off, (I mean angles formed with a line drawn to the centre,) none would serve but what was nearly a right one; out of the various directions in which the cannon might be pointed, upwards and downwards, every one would fail, but what was exactly or nearly hori-

the force of attraction towards the earth's centre; and therefore a cannon ball projected parallel to the horizon with this velocity would (if there were no resistance from the air or other accidental circumstance) complete its circular revolution, and come back to the place from which it had set out, in a few minutes less than an hour and a half, which is equivalent to the velocity of about five miles in a second.—*Paxton.*

* The ball is supposed to be fired from a place not far from the earth's surface, it can therefore be easily conceived that if its direction is much depressed below the horizon, it must be soon brought down to the ground; but it is not equally obvious that an elevation of any magnitude would likewise prevent its completing its revolution round the earth. Abstracting from the air's resistance, and of course omitting the supposition of a projectile force sufficient to carry the ball off into infinite space, it will move in the curve of an ellipse, of which one of the foci is situated in the centre of the earth. Now a body moving uninterruptedly in an ellipse must return in time to the same point from which it set out. The body therefore which, when projected from A, Fig. 6, Pl. XXXIX, comes down to the earth at C, would have continued its course along the dotted line and returned to A, if the mass of matter in the earth had been collected together at its centre, so as not to interfere with the motion of the projectile. Let us now conceive the body to be projected back from C, with the velocity which it had acquired in its fall, and with the direction in which it reached the earth, it would then pass through A, and come down on the other side of A I, in just the same curve, in which it had fallen from A to C. The same would apply to bodies projected upwards from B or D; and if the velocities of projection were less or greater than what would have been acquired in falling from A, the bodies would still turn, but at some less or more distant point. The longest diameter, however, of the ellipsis in which they move must always pass through the earth's centre, and if the bo lies rise on one side of this diameter they must fall down on the other. Now it will be seen that the curves at B, C, and D, make the angles ABI, ACI, ADI less, as the body is supposed to go farther and farther before it falls, and that the curves, in which the body can complete a revolution near the surface, will in all its parts be nearly parallel to it. Hence the cannon ball fired upwards will come back again to the ground and not be able completely to go round the earth upon any other supposition except that of its being fired in nearly an horizontal direction.—*Paxton.*

zontal. The same thing holds true o he planets; of our own among the rest. We are entitled therefore, to ask, and to urge the question, Why did the projectile velocity and projectile direction of the earth happen to be nearly those which would retain it in a *circular* form? Why not one of the infinite number of velocities, one of the infinite number of directions, which would have made it approach much nearer to, or recede much farther from, the sun?

The planets going round, all in the same direction, and all nearly in the same plane, afforded to Buffon a ground for asserting, that they had all been shivered from the sun by the same stroke of a comet, and by that stroke projected into their present orbits. Now, besides that this is to attribute to chance the fortunate concurrence of velocity and direction which we have been here noticing, the hypothesis, as I apprehend, is inconsistent with the physical laws by which the heavenly motions are governed. If the planets were struck off from the surface of the sun, they would return to the sun again. Nor will this difficulty be got rid of, by supposing that the same violent blow which shattered the sun's surface, and separated large fragments from it, pushed the sun himself out of his place; for the consequence of this would be, that the sun and system of shattered fragments would have a progressive motion, which indeed may possibly be the case with our system; but then each fragment would, in every revolution, return to the surface of the sun again. The hypothesis is also contradicted by the vast difference which subsists between the *diameters* of the planetary orbits. The distance of Saturn from the sun (to say nothing of the Georgium Sidus` is nearly twenty-five times that of Mercury; a disparity which it seems impossible to reconcile with Buffon's scheme Bodies starting from the same place, with whatever difference of direction or velocity they could set off, could not have been found, at these different distances from the centre, still retaining their nearly circular orbits. They must have been carried to their proper distances before they were projected.*

* " If we suppose the matter of the system to be accumulated in the centre by its gravity, *no* mechanical principles, with the assistance of this power of gravity could separate the vast mass into such parts as the sun and planets; and after carrying them to their different distances, project them in their several directions, preserving still the equality of action and reaction, or the state of the centre of gravity of the system. Such an exquisite structure of things could only arise from the contrivance and

To conclude: In astronomy, the great thing is to raise the imagination to the subject, and that oftentimes in opposition to the impression made upon the senses. An allusion, for example, must be gotten over, arising from the distance at which we view the heavenly bodies, viz. the apparent *slowness* of their motions. The moon shall take some hours in getting half a yard from a star which it touched. A motion so deliberate, we may think easily guided. But what is the fact? The moon, in fact, is, all this while, driving through the heavens, at the rate of considerably more than two thousand miles in an hour; which is more than double of that with which a ball is shot off from the mouth of a cannon. Yet is this prodigious rapidity as much under government, as if the planet proceeded ever so slowly, or were conducted in its course inch by inch. It is also difficult to bring the imagination to conceive (what yet, to judge tolerably of the matter, it is necessary to conceive) how *loose*, if we may so express it, the heavenly bodies are. Enormous globes, held by nothing, confined by nothing, are turned into free and boundless space, each to seek its course by the virtue of an invisible principle; but a principle, one, common, and the same in all; and ascertainable. To preserve such bodies from being lost, from running together in heaps, from hindering and distracting one another's motions, in a degree inconsistent with any continuing order; *i. e.* to cause them to form planetary systems, systems that, when formed, can be upheld, and more especially, systems accommodated to the organized and sensitive natures which the planets sustain, as we know to be the case, where alone we can know what the case is, upon our earth: all this requires an intelligent interposition, because it can be demonstrated concerning it, that it requires an adjustment of force, distance, direction, and velocity, out of the reach of chance to have produced; an adjustment, in its view to utility, similar to that which we see in ten thousa.. subjects of nature which are nearer to us, but in power, and in extent of space through which that power is exerted, stupendous.

But many of the heavenly bodies, as the sun and fixed stars, are *stationary*. Their rest must be the effect of an

powerful influences of an intelligent, free, and most potent agent. The same powers, therefore, which at present govern the material universe, and conduct its various motions, are *very different* from those which were necessary to have produced it from nothing, or to have disposed it in the admirable form in which it now proceeds."— *Maclaurin's Account of Newton's Phil.* p. 407, ed. 3.

absence or of an equilibrium of attractions. It proves also, that a projectile impulse was originally given to some of the heavenly bodies, and not to others. But farther; if attraction act at all distances, there can be only one quiescent centre of gravity in the universe: and all bodies whatever must be approaching this centre, or revolving round it According to the first of these suppositions, if the duration of the world had been long enough to allow of it, all its parts, all the great bodies of which it is composed, must have been gathered together in a heap round this point. No changes, however, which have been observed, afford us the smallest reason for believing, that either the one su* position or the other is true: and then it will follow, that attraction itself is controlled or suspended by a superior agent: that there is a power above the highest of the powers of material nature; a will which restrains and circumscribes the operations of the most extensive *

CHAPTER XXIII.

OF THE PERSONALITY OF THE DEITY

CONTRIVANCE, if established, appears to me to prove everything which we wish to prove. Amongst other things, it proves the *personality* of the Deity, as distinguished from what is sometimes called nature, sometimes called a prin-

* It must here, however, be stated, that many astronomers deny that any of the heavenly bodies are absolutely stationary. Some of the brightest of the fixed stars have certainly small motions; and of the rest the distance is too great, and the intervals of our observation too short, to enable us to pronounce with certainty that they may not have the same. The motions in the fixed stars which have been observed, are considered either as proper to each of them, or as compounded of the motion of our system, and of motions proper to each star. By a comparison of these motions, a motion in our system is supposed to be discovered. By continuing this anology to other, and to all systems, it is possible to suppose that attraction is unlimited, and that the whole material universe is revolving round some fixed point within its containing sphere or space.—*Paley.*

The milky way is known to derive its appearance from a congeries of very small stars, but there are luminous spots in the heaven, which cannot be separated into distinct stars by the most powerful telescopes; these have been observed in some instances to alter their form, which Sir W. Herschell attributed to the mutual attraction of the luminous particles which composed them.

ciple: which terms, in the mouths of those who use them philosophically, seem to be intended to admit and to express an efficacy, but to exclude and to deny a personal agent. Now that which can contrive, which can design, must be a person. These capacities constitute personality, for they imply consciousness and thought. They require that which can perceive an end or purpose; as well as the power of providing means, and of directing them to their end * They require a centre in which perceptions unite, and from which volitions flow; which is mind. The acts of a mind prove the existence of a mind; and in whatever a mind resides, is a person. The seat of intellect is a person We have no authority to limit the properties of mind to any particular corporeal form, or to any particular circum-scription of space. These properties subsist in created nature under a great variety of sensible forms. Also every animated being has its *sensorium;* that is, a certain portion of space, within which perception and volition are exerted. This sphere may be enlarged to an indefinite extent; may comprehend the universe; and, being so imagined, may serve to furnish us with as good a notion as we are capable of forming, of the *immensity* of the Divine Nature, *i. e.* of a Being, infinite, as well in essence as in power yet nevertheless a person.

" No man hath seen God at any time." And this, I be lieve, makes the great difficulty. Now it is a difficulty which chiefly arises from our not duly estimating the state of our faculties. The Deity, it is true, is the object of none of our senses: but reflect what limited capacities an imal senses are. Many animals seem to have but one sense, or perhaps two at the most; touch and taste. Ought such an animal to conclude against the existence of odors, sounds, and colors? To another species is given the sense of smelling. This is an advance in the knowledge of the powers and properties of nature: but, if this favored animal should infer from its superiority over the class last described, that it perceived everything which was per-ceptible in nature, it is known to us, though perhaps not

Some of the fixed stars appear double, and even multiple when highly magnified. The same great astronomer, whom we have just mentioned was induced to believe that these were separate systems, and his son, assisted by Mr. South, has established that some of them have undoubt edly a revolution round a common centre of gravity analogous to the notions of the sun and planets.—*Paxton.*

* Priestley's Letters to a Philosophical Unbeliever, p. 153, ed. 2

suspected by the animal itself, that it proceeded upon a false and presumptuous estimate of its faculties. To another is added the sense of hearing; which lets in a class of sensations entirely unconceived by the animal before spoken of; not only distinct, but remote from any which it had ever experienced, and greatly superior to them. Yet this last animal has no more ground for believing that its senses comprehend all things, and all properties of things which exist, than might have been claimed by the tribes of animals beneath it; for we know that it is still possible to possess another sense, that of sight, which shall disclose to the percipient a new world. This fifth sense makes the animal what the human animal is: but to infer, that possibility stops here; that either this fifth sense is the last sense, or that the five comprehend all existence, is just as unwarrantable a conclusion, as that which might have been made by any of the different species which possessed fewer, or even by that, if such there be, which possessed only one. The conclusion of the one-sense animal, and the conclusion of the five-sense animal, stand upon the same authority. There may be more and other senses than those which we have. There may be senses suited to the perception of the powers, properties, and substance of spirits. These may belong to higher orders of rationa. agents: for there is not the smallest reason for supposing that we are the highest, or that the scale of creation stops with us.

The great *energies* of nature are known to us only by their effects. The substances which produce them, are as much concealed from our senses as the divine essence itself. *Gravitation*, though constantly present, though constantly exerting its influence, though everywhere around us, near us, and within us; though diffused throughout all space, and penetrating the texture of all bodies with which we are acquainted, depends, if upon a fluid, upon a fluid which, though both powerful and universal in its operation, is no object of sense to us; if upon any other kind of substance or action, upon a substance and action from which *we* receive no distinguishable impressions. Is it then to be wondered at, that it should, in some measure, be the same with the Divine Nature?

Of this, however, we are certain, that whatever the Deity be, neither the *universe*, nor any part of it which we see, can be He. The universe itself is merely a collective name: its parts are all which are real; or which are *things*. Now inert matter is out of the question and organized

substances include marks of contrivance. But whateve
includes marks of contrivance, whatever, in its constitution,
testifies design, necessarily carries us to something beyond
itself, to some other being, to a designer prior to, and out
of itself.   No animal, for instance, can have contrived its
own limbs and senses; can have been the author to itself
of the design with which they were constructed. That
supposition involves all the absurdity of self-creation, *i. e*
of acting without existing.   Nothing can be God, which is
ordered by a wisdom and a will which itself is void of,
which is indebted for any of its properties to contrivance
ab extra. The *not* having that in his nature which requires
the exertion of another prior being (which property is
sometimes called self-sufficiency, and sometimes self-com-
prehension,) appertains to the Deity, as his essential distinction, and removes his nature from that of all things
which we see.   Which consideration contains the answer
to a question that has sometimes been asked, namely: Why,
since something or other must have existed from eternity,
may not the present universe be that something?   The
contrivance perceived in it proves that to be impossible.
Nothing contrived can, in a strict and proper sense, be
eternal, forasmuch as the contriver must have existed before
the contrivance.

Wherever we see marks of contrivance, we are led for
its cause to an *intelligent* author.   And this transition of
the understanding is founded upon uniform experience.
We see intelligence constantly contriving; that is, we see
intelligence constantly producing effects, marked and distinguished by certain properties; not certain particular
properties, but by a kind and class of properties, such as
relation to an end, relation of parts to one another, and to
a common purpose.   We see, wherever we are witnesses
to the actual formation of things, nothing except intelligence producing effects so marked and distinguished. Furnished with this experience, we view the productions of
nature.   We observe *them* also marked and distinguished
in the same manner.   We wish to account for their origin.
Our experience suggests a cause perfectly adequate to this
account.   No experience, no single instance or example,
can be offered in favor of any other.   In this cause, therefore, we ought to rest; in this cause the common sense of
mankind has, in fact, rested, because it agrees with that
which in all cases is the foundation of knowledge   -the
undeviating course of their experience.   The reasoning is
the same as that by which we conclude any ancient ap-

pearances to have been the effects of volcanoes or inunda-
tions, namely, because they resemble the effects which fire
and water produce before our eyes; and because we have
never known these effects to result from any other operation. And this resemblance may subsist in so many circumstances, as not to leave us under the smallest doubt
in forming our opinion. Men are not deceived by this
reasoning: for whenever it happens, as it sometimes does
happen, that the truth comes to be known by direct information, it turns out to be what was expected. In like
manner, and upon the same foundation (which in truth is
that of experience) we conclude that the works of nature
proceeded from intelligence and design, because, in the
properties of relation to a purpose, subserviency to a use,
they resemble what intelligence and design are constantly
producing, and what nothing except intelligence and design ever produce at all. Of every argument, which
would raise a question as to the safety of this reasoning,
it may be observed, that if such argument be listened to,
it leads to the inference, not only that the present order
of nature is insufficient to prove the existence of an intelligent Creator, but that no imaginable order would be sufficient to prove it; that *no* contrivance, were it ever so mechanical, ever so precise, ever so clear, ever so perfectly
like those which we ourselves employ, would support this
conclusion. A doctrine to which, I conceive, no sound
mind can assent.

The force, however, of the reasoning is sometimes sunk
by our taking up with mere names. We have already noticed,* and we must here notice again, the misapplication
of the term " law," and the mistake concerning the idea
which that term expresses in physics, whenever such idea
is made to take the place of power, and still more of an intelligent power, and, as such, to be assigned for the cause
of anything, or of any property of anything, that exists
This is what we are secretly apt to do, when we speak of or
ganized bodies (plants for instance, or animals,) owing their
production, their form, their growth, their qualities, their
beauty, their use, to any law or laws of nature; and when
we are contented to sit down with that answer to our inquiries concerning them. I say once more, that it is a perversion of language to assign any law as the efficient operative cause of anything. A law presupposes an agent, for
it is only the mode according to which an agent proceeds,

* Chap. I. sec. vv
U*

t implies a power, for it is the order according to which
that power acts. Without this agent, without this power,
which are both distinct from itself, the "law" does nothing—is nothing.

What has been said concerning "law," holds true cf
mechanism. Mechanism is not itself power. Mechanism,
without power, can do nothing. Let a watch be contrived
and constructed ever so ingeniously; be its parts ever so
many, ever so complicated, ever so finely wrought, or artificially put together, it cannot *go* without a weight or spring,
i. e. without a force independent of, and ulterior to, its mechanism. The spring acting at the centre, will produce
different motions and different results, according to the
variety of the intermediate mechanism. One and the selfsame spring, acting in one and the same manner, viz. by
simply expanding itself, may be the cause of a hundred different, and all useful, movements, if a hundred different and
well-devised sets of wheels be placed between it and the
final effect; *e. g.* may point out the hour of the day, the
day of the month, the age of the moon, the position of the
planets, the cycle of the years, and many other serviceable
notices: and these movements may fulfil their purposes
with more or less perfection, according as the mechanism
is better or worse contrived, or better or worse executed,
or in a better or worse state of repair ; *but in all cases, it
is necessary that the spring act at the centre.* The course
of our reasoning upon such a subject would be this: by
inspecting the watch, even when standing still, we get a
proof of contrivance, and of a contriving mind having been
employed about it. In the form and obvious relation of its
parts, we see enough to convince us of this. If we pull
the works in pieces, for the purpose of a closer examination,
we are still more fully convinced. But when we see the
watch *going,* we see proof of another point, viz. that there
is a power somewhere and somehow or other, applied to
it; a power in action;—that there is more in the subject
han the mere wheels of the machine;—that there is a
secret spring, or a gravitating plummet;—in a word, that
there is force and energy, as well as mechanism.

So then, the watch in motion establishes to the observer
two conclusions: One; that thought, contrivance, and design, have been employed in the forming, proportioning,
and arranging of its parts; and that whoever or wherever
he be, or were, such a contriver there is, or was: The other,
that force or power, distinct from mechanism, is at this
present time acting upon it If I saw a hand-mill even a

rest, I should see contrivance; but if I saw it grinding, I should be assured that a hand was at the windlass, though in another room. It is the same in nature. In the works of nature we trace mechanism; and this alone proves contrivance: but living, active, moving, productive nature proves also the exertion of a power at the centre; for, wherever the power resides may be denominated the centre.

The intervention and disposition of what are called "second causes," fall under the same observation. This disposition is or is not mechanism, according as we can or cannot trace it by our senses and means of examination

That is all the difference there is; and it is a difference which respects our faculties, not the things themselves. Now, where the order of second causes is mechanical, what is here said of mechanism strictly applies to it. But it would be always mechanism (natural chemistry, for instance, would be mechanism) if our senses were acute enough to descry it. Neither mechanism, therefore, in the works of nature, nor the intervention of what are called second causes, (for I think that they are the same thing,) excuses the necessity of an agent distinct from both.

If, in tracing these causes, it be said, that we find certain general properties of matter which have nothing in them that bespeaks intelligence, I answer, that still the *managing* of these properties, the pointing and directing them to the uses which we see made of them, demands intelligence in the highest degree. For example: suppose animal secretions to be elective attraction, and that such and such attractions universally belong to such and such substances; in all which there is no intellect concerned; still the choice and collocation of these substances, the fixing upon right substances, and disposing them in right places, must be an act of intelligence. What mischief would follow, were there a single transposition of the secretory organs; a single mistake in arranging the glands which compose them!

There may be many second causes, and many courses of second causes, one behind another, between what we observe of nature and he Deity; but there must be intelligence somewhere; there must be more in nature than what we see; and, amongst the things unseen, there must be an intelligent, designing author. The philosopher beholds with astonishment the production of things around him. Unconscious particles of matter take their stations, and severally range themselves in an order, so as to become collectively plants or animals, i e organized bodies, with

parts bearing strict and evident relation to one another
and to the utility of the whole: and it should seem that
these particles could not move in any other way than as
they do; for they testify not the smallest sign of choice, or
liberty, or discretion.   There may be particular intelligent
beings guiding these motions in each case; or they may
be the result of trains of mechanical dispositions, fixed
beforehand by an intelligent appointment, and kept in action by a power at the centre.   But, in either case, there
must be intelligence.

The minds of most men are fond of what they call a
principle, and of the appearance of simplicity, in accounting for phenomena.   Yet this principle, this simplicity,
resides merely in the *name;* which name, after all, comprises, perhaps, under it a diversified, multifarious, or progressive operation, distinguishable into parts.   The power
in organized bodies, of producing bodies like themselves,
is one of these principles.   Give a philosopher this, and
he can get on.   But he does not reflect, what this mode of
production, this principle (if such he choose to call it) requires; how much it presupposes; what an apparatus of instruments, some of which are strictly mechanical, is necessary to its success; what a train it includes of operations and
changes, one succeeding another, one related to another,
one ministering to another; all advancing, by intermediate,
and frequently, by sensible steps, to their ultimate result.
Yet, because the whole of this complicated action is wrapped up in a single term, *generation,* we are to set it down
as an elementary principle; and to suppose, that when we
have resolved the things which we see into this principle,
we have sufficiently accounted for their origin, without the
necessity of a designing, intelligent Creator.   The truth is,
generation is not a principle, but a *process.*   We might
as well call the casting of metals a principle; we might, so
far as appears to me, as well call spinning and weaving
principles: and then, referring the texture of cloths, the
fabric of muslins and calicoes, the patterns of diapers and
damasks, to these, as principles, pretend to dispense with
intention, thought, and contrivance, on the part of the artist; or to dispense, indeed, with the necessity of any artist
at all, either in the manufacturing of the article, or in the
fabrication of the machinery by which the manufacture
was carried on.

And after all, how, or in what sense, is it true, that animals produce their *like?*   A butterfly, with a broboscis instead of a mouth, with four wings and six legs, produces a

hairy caterpillar, with jaws and teeth, and fourteen feet
A frog produces a tadpole. A black beetle with gauze
wings, and a crusty covering, produces a white, smooth,
soft worm; an ephemeron fly, a cod-bait maggot. These,
by a progress through different stages of life, and action,
and enjoyment, (and in each state provided with implements and organs appropriated to the temporary nature
which they bear,) arrive at last at the form and fashion of
the parent animal. But all this is process, not principle;
and proves, moreover, that the property of animated bodies,
of producing their like, belongs to them, not as a primordial
property, not by any blind necessity in the nature of things,
but as the effect of economy, wisdom, and design; because
the property itself assumes diversities, and submits to deviations dictated by intelligible utilities, and serving distinct
purposes of animal happiness.

The opinion, which would consider "generation" as a
principle in nature; and which would assign this principle
as a cause, or endeavour to satisfy our minds with such a
cause, of the existence of organized bodies, is confuted, in
my judgment, not only by every mark of contrivance discoverable in those bodies, for which it gives us no contriver,
offers no account whatever; but also by the farther consideration, that things generated possess a clear relation to
things *not* generated. If it were merely one part of a generated body bearing a relation to another part of the same
body, as the mouth of an animal to the throat, the throat
to the stomach, the stomach to the intestines, those to the
recruiting of the blood, and by means of the blood, to the
nourishment of the whole frame; or if it were only one
generated body bearing a relation to another generated
body, as the sexes of the same species to each other,
animals of prey to their prey, herbivorous and granivorous animals to the plants or seeds upon which they feed,
it might be contended, that the whole of this correspondency was attributable to generation, the common origin
from which these substances proceeded. But what shall
we say to agreements which exist between things generated and things *not generated?* Can it be doubted, was it
ever doubted, but that the *lungs* of animals bear a relation
to the *air*, as a permanently elastic fluid? They act in it
and by it, they cannot act without it. Now, if generation
produced the animal, it did not produce the air; yet their
properties correspond. The *eye* is made for *light*, and light
for the eye. The eye would be of no use without light,
and light perhaps of litt without eyes yet one is produc-

ed by generation; the other not.   The *ear* depends upon *undulations* of air.   Here are two sets of motions: first, of the pulses of the air; secondly, of the drum, bones, and nerves of the ear: sets of motions bearing an evident reference to each other: yet the one, and the apparatus for the one, produced by the intervention of generation; the other altogether independent of it.

If it be said, that the air, the light, the elements, the world itself, is *generated*; I answer, that I do not comprehend the proposition.   If the term mean anything similar to what it means when applied to plants or animals, the proposition is certainly without proof; and, I think, draws as near to absurdity as any proposition can do, which does not include a contradiction in its terms.   I am at a loss to conceive, how the formation of the world can be compared to the generation of an animal.   If the term generation signify something quite different from what it signifies on ordinary occasions, it may, by the same latitude, signify anything.   In which case, a word or phrase taken from the language of Otaheite, would convey as much theory concerning the origin of the universe, as it does to talk of its being generated.

We know a cause (intelligence) adequate to the appearances which we wish to account for; we have this cause continually producing similar appearances; yet, rejecting this cause, the sufficiency of which we know, and the action of which is constantly before our eyes, we are invited to resort to suppositions destitute of a single fact for their support, and confirmed by no analogy with which we are acquainted.   Were it necessary to inquire into the *motives* of men's opinions, I mean their motives separate from their arguments, I should almost suspect, that, because the proof of a Deity drawn from the constitution of nature is not only popular but vulgar, (which may arise from the cogency of the proof, and be indeed its highest recommendation,) and because it is a species almost of *puerility* to take up with it; for these reasons, minds, which are habitually in search of invention and originality, feel a resistless inclination to strike off into other solutions and other expositions. The truth is, that many minds are not so indisposed to anything which can be offered to them, as they are to the *flatness* of being content with common reasons; and, what is most to be lamented, minds conscious of superiority are the most liable to this repugnancy

The "suppositions" here alluded to, all agree in one character: they all endeavour to dispense with the necessty in nature, of a particular personal intelligence, that is to say, with the exertion of an intending, contriving mind, in the structure and formation of the organized constitution which the world contains. They would resolve all productions into *unconscious* energies, of a like kind, in that respect, with attraction, magnetism, electricity, &c. without anything farther.

In this the old system of atheism and the new agree And I much doubt, whether the new schemes have advanced anything upon the old, or done more than changed the terms of the nomenclature. For instance, I could never see the difference between the antiquated system of atoms, and Buffon's organic molecules. This philosopher, having made a planet by knocking off from the sun a piece of melted glass, in consequence of the stroke of a comet; and having set it in motion by the same stroke, both round its own axis and the sun, finds his next difficulty to be, how to bring plants and animals upon it. In order to solve this difficulty, we are to suppose the universe replenished with particles endowed with life, but without organization or senses of their own; and endowed also with a tendency to marshal themselves into organized forms. The concourse of these particles, by virtue of this tendency, but without intelligence, will, or direction, (for I do not find that any of these qualities are ascribed to them,) has produced the living forms which we now see.

Very few of the conjectures which philosophers hazard upon these subjects, have more of pretension in then than the challenging you to show the direct impossibility of the hypothesis. In the present example, there seemed to be a positive objection to the whole scheme upon the very face of it; which was that, if the case were as here represented, *new* combinations ought to be perpetually taking place; new plants and animals, or organized bodies which were neither, ought to be starting up before our eyes every day. For this, however, our philosopher has an answer Whilst so many forms of plants and animals are already in existence, and, consequently, so many "internal moulds," as he calls them, are prepared and at hand, the organic particles run into these moulds, and are employed in supplying an accession of substance to them, as well for their growth, as for their propagation. By which means things keep their ancient course. But, says the same philosopher, should any general loss or destruction of the present constitution of organized bodies take place, the particles, for want of "moulds" into which they might enter would run into different combinations, and replenish the waste with new species of organized substances.

Is there any history to countenance this notion? Is it known, that any destruction has been so repaired? any desert thus repeopled?

So far as I remember, the only natural appearance mentioned by our author, by way of fact whereon to build his hypothesis, the only support on which it rests, is the formation of *worms* in the intestines of animals, which is here ascribed to the coalition of superabundant organic particles. floating about in the first passages; and which have combined themselves into these simple animal forms, for want of internal moulds, or of vacancies in those moulds, into which they might be received. The thing referred to, is rather a species of facts, than a single fact; as some other cases may, with equal reason, be included under it But to make it a fact at all, or in any sort applicable to the question, we must begin with asserting an *equivocal* generation, contrary to analogy, and without necessity: contrary to an analogy, which accompanies us to the very limits of our knowledge or inquiries; for wherever, either in plants or animals, we are able to examine the subject we find procreation from a parent form: without necessity, for I apprehend that it is seldom difficult to suggest me thods, by which the eggs, or spawn, or yet invisible rudiments of these vermin, may have obtained a passage into the cavities in which they are found.* Add to this, that their *constancy to their species*, which, I believe, is as regular in these as in the other vermes, decides the question against our philosopher, if in truth any question remained upon the subject.

Lastly; these wonder-working instruments, these "internal moulds," what are they after all? what, when examined, but a name without signification; unintelligible. if not self-contradictory; at the best, differing in nothing from the "essential forms" of the Greek philosophy? One short sentence of Buffon's work exhibits his scheme as follows: "When this nutritious and prolific matter, which is diffused throughout all nature, passes through the *internal mould* of an animal or vegetable, and finds a proper matrix, or receptacle, it gives rise to an animal or vegetable of the same species." Does any reader annex a meaning to the expres-

---

* I trust I may be excused for not citing, as another fact which is to confirm the hypothesis, a grave assertion of this writer, that the branches of trees upon which the stag feeds, break out again in his horns Such *facts* merit no discussion.

sion "internal mould," in this sentence? Ought it then to be said that though we have little notion of an internal mould, we have not much more of a designing mind? The very contrary of this assertion is the truth. When we speak of an artificer or an architect, we talk of what is comprehensible to our understanding, and familiar to our experience. We use no other terms, than what refer us for their meaning to our consciousness and observation; what express the constant objects of both; whereas names, like that we have mentioned, refer us to nothing; excite no idea: convey a sound to the ear, but I think do no more.

Another system, which has lately been brought forward, and with much ingenuity, is that of *appetencies*. The principle, and the short account of the theory, is this: Pieces of soft, ductile matter, being endued with propensities or appetencies for particular actions, would, by continual endeavours, carried on through a long series of generations, work themselves gradually into suitable forms; and at length acquire, though perhaps by obscure and almost imperceptible improvements, an organization fitted to the action which their respective propensities led them to exert. A piece of animated matter, for example, that was endued with a propensity to *fly*, though ever so shapeless, though no other we will suppose than a round ball, to begin with, would, in a course of ages, if not in a million of years, perhaps in a hundred millions of years, (for our theorists, having eternity to dispose of, are never sparing in time,) acquire *wings*. The same tendency to locomotion in an aquatic animal, or rather in an animated lump which might happen to be surrounded by water, would end in the production of *fins*; in a living substance, confined to the solid earth, would put out *legs* and *feet*; or, if it took a different turn, would break the body into ringlets, and conclude by *crawling* upon the ground.

Although I have introduced the mention of this theory into this place, I am unwilling to give to it the name of an *atheistic* scheme, for two reasons: first, because, so far as I am able to understand it, the original propensities, and the numberless varieties of them (so different, in this respect, from the laws of mechanical nature, which are few and simple,) are, in the plan itself, attributed to the ordination and appointment of an intelligent and designing Creator; secondly, because, likewise, that large postulatum, which is all along assumed and presupposed, the faculty in living bodies of producing other bodies organized like themselves, seems to be referred to the same cause; at

W

least is not attempted to be accounted for by any other. In one important respect, however, the theory before us coincides with atheistic systems, viz. in that, in the formation of plants and animals, in the structure and use of their parts, it does away final causes. Instead of the parts of a plant or animal, or the particular structure of the parts, having been intended for the action or the use to which we see them applied, according to this theory, they have themselves grown out of that action, sprung from that use. The theory therefore dispenses with that which we insist upon, the necessity, in each particular case, of an intelligent, designing mind, for the contriving and determining of the forms which organized bodies bear. Give our philosopher these appetencies; give him a portion of living irritable matter (a nerve, or the clipping of a nerve) to work upon; give also to his incipient or progressive forms, the power, in every stage of their alteration, of propagating their like; and, if he is to be believed, he could replenish the world with all the vegetable and animal productions which we at present see in it.

The scheme under consideration is open to the same objection with other conjectures of a similar tendency, viz. a total defect of evidence. No changes, like those which the theory requires, have ever been observed. All the changes in Ovid's Metamorphoses might have been effected by these appetencies, if the theory were true: yet not an example, nor the pretence of an example, is offered of a single change being known to have taken place. Nor is the order of generation obedient to the principle upon which this theory is built. The mammæ * of the male have not vanished by inusitation; *nec curtorum, per multa sæcula Judæorum propagini deest præputium.* It is easy to say, and it has been said, that the alterative process is too slow to be perceived; that it has been carried on through tracts of immeasurable time; and that the present order of things is the result of a gradation, of which no human records can trace the steps. It is easy to say this; and yet it is still true, that the hypothesis remains destitute of evidence.

The *analogies* which have been alleged, are of the following kind The *bunch* of a camel is said to be no other than the effect of carrying burdens; a service in which

* I confess myself totally at a loss to guess at the reason, either final or efficient, for this part of the animal frame, unless there be some foundation for an opinion, of which I draw the hint from a paper of Sir Everard Home's, (Phil. Transac. 1799, p. 2,) viz. that the mammæ of the fœtus may be formed before the sex is determined.

the species has been employed from the most ancient times of the world The first race, by the daily loading of the back, would probably find a small grumous tumour to be formed in the flesh of that part. The next progeny would bring this tumour into the world with them. The life to which they were destined would increase it. The cause which first generated the tubercle being continued, it would go on, through every succession, to augment its size, till it attained the form and the bulk under which it now appears This may serve for one instance: another, and that also of the passive sort, is taken from certain species of birds Birds of the *crane* kind, as the crane itself, the heron, bittern, stork, have, in general, their thighs bare of feathers This privation is accounted for from the habit of wading in water, and from the effect of that element to check the growth of feathers upon these parts; in consequence of which, the health and vegetation of the feathers declined through each generation of the animal; the tender down, exposed to cold and wetness, became weak, and thin, and rare, till the deterioration ended in the result which we see, of absolute nakedness. I will mention a third instance, because it is drawn from an active habit, as the two last were from passive habits; and that is the *pouch* of the pelican. The description, which naturalists give of this organ, is as follows: " From the lower edges of the under chap hangs a bag, reaching from the whole length of the bill to the neck, which is said to be capable of containing fifteen quarts of water. This bag the bird has a power of wrinkling up into the hollow of the under chap. When the bag is empty, it is not seen; but when the bird has fished with success, it is incredible to what an extent it is often dilated The first thing the pelican does in fishing, is to fill the bag; and then it returns to digest its burden at leisure. The bird preys upon large fishes, and hides them by dozens in its pouch. When the bill is opened to its widest extent, a person may run his head into the bird's mouth, and conceal it in this monstrous pouch, thus adapted for very singular purposes."* Now this extraordinary conformation is nothing more, say our philosophers, than the result of habit; not of the habit or effort of a single pelican, or of a single race of pelicans, but of a habit perpetuated through a long series of generations. The pelican soon found the conveniency of reserving in its mouth, when its appetite was glutted the remainder of its prey, which is fish. The ful-

* Goldsmith, vol. vi. p. 52

ness produced by this attempt, of course stretched the skin which lies between the under chaps, as being the most yielding part of the mouth. Every distension increased the cavity. The original bird, and many generations which succeeded him, might find difficulty enough in making the pouch answer this purpose: but future pelicans, entering upon life with a pouch derived from their progenitors, of considerable capacity, would more readily accelerate its advance to perfection, by frequently pressing down the sack with the weight of fish which it might now be made to contain.

These, or of this kind, are the analogies relied upon. Now, in the first place, the instances themselves are unauthenticated by testimony; and, in theory, to say the least of them, open to great objections. Who ever read of camels without bunches, or with bunches less than those with which they are at present usually formed? A bunch, not unlike the camel's, is found between the shoulders of the buffalo; of the origin of which it is impossible to give the account which is here given. In the second example; Why should the application of water, which appears to promote and thicken the growth of feathers upon the bodies and breasts of geese and swans, and other water-fowls, have divested of this covering the thighs of cranes? The third instance, which appears to me as plausible as any that can be produced, has this against it, that it is a singularity restricted to the species; whereas, if it had its commencement in the cause and manner which have been assigned, the like conformation might be expected to take place in other birds which feed upon fish. How comes it to pass, that the pelican alone was the inventress, and her descendants the only inheritors, of this curious resource?

But it is the less necessary to controvert the instances themselves, as it is a straining of analogy beyond all limits of reason and credibility, to assert that birds, and beasts, and fish, with all their variety and complexity of organization, have been brought into their forms, and distinguished into their several kinds and natures, by the same process (even if that process could be demonstrated, or had it ever been actually noticed) as might seem to serve for the gradual generation of a camel's bunch, or a pelican's pouch

The solution, when applied to the works of nature *generally*, is contradicted by many of the phenomena, and totally inadequate to others. The *ligaments* or strictures, by which the tendons are tied down at the angles of the joints *could* by no possibility be formed by the motion or exer cise of the tendons themselves; by any appetency exciting these parts into action; or by any tendency arising therefrom. The tendency is all the other way; the *conatus* in constant opposition to them. Length of time does not help the case at all, but the reverse. The *valves* also in the blood-vessels, could never be formed in the manner which our theorist proposes. The blood, in its right and natural course, has no tendency to form them. When obstructed or refluent, it has the contrary. These parts could not grow out of their use, though they had eternity to grow in.

The *senses* of animals appear to me altogether incapable of receiving the explanation of their origin which this theory affords. Including under the word "sense" the organ and the perception, we have no account of either. How will our philosopher get at *vision*, or make an eye? How should the blind animal effect sight, of which blind animals, we know, have neither conception nor desire? Affecting it, by what operation of its will, by what endeavour to see, could it so determine the fluids of its body, as to inchoate the formation of an eye; or suppose the eye formed, would the perception follow? The same of the other senses And this objection holds its force, ascribe what you will to the hand of time, to the power of habit, to changes too slow to be observed by man, or brought within any comparison which he is able to make of past things with the present: concede what you please to these arbitrary and unattested suppositions, how will they help you? Here is no inception. No laws, no course, no powers of nature which prevail at present, nor any analogous to these, could give commencement to a new sense. And it is in vain to inquire how that might proceed, which could never *begin*.

I think the senses to be the most inconsistent with the hypothesis before us, of any part of the animal frame. But other parts are sufficiently so. The solution does not apply to the parts of animals which have little in them of motion. If we could suppose joints and muscles to be gradually formed by action and exercise, what action or exercise could form a skull, or fill it with brains? No effort of the animal could determine the clothing of its skin. What *conatus* could give prickles to the porcupine or hedgehog, or to the sheep its fleece?

In the last place: What do these appetencies mean when applied to plants? I am not able to give a signification to the term, which can be transferred from animals to plants, or which is common to both Yet a no less successful or-

w*

ganization is found in plants, than what obtains in animals
A solution is wanted for one as well as the other.

Upon the whole; after all the schemes and struggles of a
reluctant philosophy, the necessary resort is to a Deity
The marks of *design* are too strong to be gotten over
Design must have had a designer. That designer mus
have been a person. That person is GOD

CHAPTER XXIV

OF THE NATURAL ATTRIBUTES OF THE DEITY.

IT is an immense conclusion, that there is a God; a
perceiving, intelligent, designing Being; at the head of creation, and from whose will it proceeded. The *attributes* of
such a Being, suppose his reality to be proved, must be
adequate to the magnitude, extent, and multiplicity of his
operations: which are not only vast beyond comparison with
those performed by any other power, but, so far as respects
our conceptions of them, infinite, because they are unlimited on all sides.

Yet the contemplation of a nature so exalted, however
surely we arrive at the proof of its existence, overwhelms
our faculties. The mind feels its powers sink under the
subject. One consequence of which is, that from painful
abstraction the thoughts seek relief in sensible images.
Whence may be deduced the ancient, and almost universal propensity to idolatrous substitutions. They are the
resources of a laboring imagination. False religions usually fall in with the natural propensity; true religions, or
such as have derived themselves from the true, resist it.

It is one of the advantages of the revelations which we
acknowledge, that whilst they reject idolatry with its many
pernicious accompaniments, they introduce the Deity to
human apprehension, under an idea more personal, more
determinate, more within its compass, than the theology
of nature can do. And this they do by representing him
exclusively under the relation in which he stands to ourselves; and, for the most part, under some precise character, resulting from that relation, or from the history of his
providences. Which method suits the span of our intellects
much better than the universality which enters into the
idea of God, as deduced from the views of nature. When
therefore, these representations are well founded in point

of a sthority, (for all depends upon that,) they afford a con descension to the state of our faculties, of which, they who have most reflected upon the subject, will be the first to acknowledge the want and the value.

Nevertheless, if we be careful to imitate the documents of our religion, by confining our explanations to what concerns ourselves, and do not affect more precision in our ideas than the subject allows of, the several terms which are employed to denote the attributes of the Deity, may be made, even in natural religion, to bear a sense consistent with truth and reason, and not surpassing our comprehension.

These terms are, omnipotence, omniscience, omnipresence, eternity, self-existence, necessary existence, spirituality.

"Omnipotence," "omniscience," "infinite" power "infinite" knowledge, are *superlatives*; expressing our conception of these attributes in the strongest and most elevated terms which language supplies. We ascribe power to the Deity under the name of "omnipotence," the strict and correct conclusion being, that a power which could create such a world as this is, must be, beyond all comparison, greater than any which we experience in ourselves, than any which we observe in other visible agents; greater also than any which we can want, for our individual protection and preservation, in the Being upon whom we depend. It is a power, likewise, to which we are not authorised, by our observation or knowledge, to assign any limits of space or duration.

Very much of the same sort of remark is applicable to the term, "omniscience," infinite knowledge, or infinite wisdom. In strictness of language, there is a difference between knowledge and wisdom; wisdom always supposing action, and action directed by it. With respect to the first, viz. *knowledge*, the Creator must know, intimately, the constitution and properties of the things which he created; which seems also to imply a foreknowledge of their action upon one another, and of their changes; at least, so far as the same result from trains of physical and necessary causes. His omniscience also, as far as respects things present, is deducible from his nature, as an intelligent being, joined with the extent, or rather the universality, of his operations. Where he acts, he is; and where he is, he perceives. The *wisdom* of the Deity, as testified in the works of creation, surpasses all idea we have of wisdom, drawn from the highest intellectual operations of the highest

class of intelligent beings with whom we are acquainted,
and, which is of the chief importance to us, whatever be its
compass or extent, which it is evidently impossible that we
should be able to determine, it must be adequate to the
conduct of that order of things under which we live.   And
his is enough.   It is of very inferior consequence, by what
terms we express our notion, or rather our admiration of
this attribute.   The terms, which the piety and the usage
of language have rendered habitual to us, may be as proper as any other.   We can trace this attribute much beyond
what is necessary for any conclusion to which we have
occasion to apply it.   The degree of knowledge and power,
requisite for the formation of created nature, cannot, with
respect to us, be distinguished from infinite.

The divine "omnipresence" stands, in natural theology,
upon this foundation:—In every part and place of the universe, with which we are acquainted, we perceive the exertion of a power, which we believe, mediately or immediately, to proceed from the Deity.   For instance: in what part
or point of space, that has ever been explored, do we not
discover attraction?   In what regions do we not find light?
In what accessible portion of our globe do we not meet
with gravity, magnetism, electricity? together with the
properties also and powers of organized substances, of vegetable or of animated nature?   Nay, farther, we may ask,
what kingdom is there of nature, what corner of space, in
which there is anything that can be examined by us, where
we do not fall upon contrivance and design?   The only reflection perhaps which arises in our minds from this view
of the world around us is, that the laws of nature everywhere prevail; that they are uniform and universal.   But
what do we mean by the laws of nature, or by any law?
Effects are produced by power, not by laws.   A law cannot
execute itself.   A law refers us to an agent.   Now an
agency so general, as that we cannot discover its absence,
or assign the place in which some effect of its continued
energy is not found, may, in popular language at least,
and, perhaps, without much deviation from philosophical
strictness, be called universal: and, with not quite the
same, but with no inconsiderable propriety, the person, or
Being, in whom that power resides, or from whom it is derived, may be taken to be *omnipresent*.   He who upholds
all things by his power, may be said to be everywhere
present.

This is called a virtual presence.   There is also what
metaphysicians denominate an essential ubiquity;   and

which idea the language of Scripture seems to favor: but the former, I think, goes as far as natural theology carries us.

"Eternity" is a negative idea, clothed with a positive name. It supposes, in that to which it is applied, a present existence; and is the negation of a beginning or an end of that existence. As applied to the Deity, it has not been controverted by those who acknowledge a Deity at all. Most assuredly, there never was a time in which nothing existed, because that condition must have continued. The universal *blank* must have remained; nothing could rise up out of it; nothing could ever have existed since: nothing could exist now. In strictness, however, we have no concern with duration prior to that of the visible world. Upon this article, therefore, of theology, it is sufficient to know, that the contriver necessarily existed before the contrivance.

"Self-existence" is another negative idea, viz. the negation of a preceding cause, as of a progenitor, a maker, an author, a creator.

"Necessary" existence means demonstrable existence

"Spirituality" expresses an idea, made up of a negative part, and of a positive part. The negative part consists in the exclusion of some of the known properties of matter, especially of solidity, of the *vis inertiae*, and of gravitation. The positive part comprises perception, thought, will, power, *action*; by which last term is meant, the origination of motion; the quality, perhaps, in which resides the essential superiority of spirit over matter, "which cannot move, unless it be moved; and cannot but move, when impelled by another."* I apprehend that there can be no difficulty in applying to the Deity both parts of this idea.

------◆------

CHAPTER XXV

THE UNITY OF THE DEITY.

Of the "Unity of the Deity," the proof is, the *uniformity* of plan observable in the universe. The universe itself is a system; each part either depending upon other parts, or being connected with other parts by some common law of motion, or by the presence of some common substance

---

* Bishop Wilkin's Principles of Nat. Rel. p. 106

One principle of gravitation causes a stone to drop towards the earth, and the moon to wheel round it. One law of attraction carries all the different planets about the sun. This philosophers demonstrate. There are also other points of agreement amongst them, which may be considered as marks of the identity of their origin, and of their intelligent Author. In all are found the conveniency and stability derived from gravitation. They all experience vicissitudes of days and nights, and changes of season. They all, at least Jupiter, Mars, and Venus, have the same advantages from their atmosphere as we have. In all the planets, the axes of rotation are permanent. Nothing is more probable, than that the same attracting influence, acting according to the same rule, reaches to the fixed stars: but, if this be only probable, another thing is certain, viz. that the same element of light does. The light from a fixed star affects our eyes in the same manner, is refracted and reflected according to the same laws, as the light of a candle The velocity of the light of the fixed stars is also the same as the velocity of the light of the sun, reflected from the satellites of Jupiter. The heat of the sun, in kind, differs nothing from the heat of a coal fire.

In our own globe, the case is clearer. New countries are continually discovered, but the old laws of nature are always found in them: new plants perhaps, or animals, but always in company with plants and animals which we already know: and always possessing many of the same general properties. We never get among such original, or totally different, modes of existence, as to indicate, that we are come into the province of a different Creator, or under the direction of a different will. In truth, the same order of things attends us wherever we go. The elements act upon one another, electricity operates, the tides rise and fall, the magnetic needle elects its position in one region of the earth and sea as well as in another. One atmosphere invests all parts of the globe, and connects all; one sun illuminates; one moon exerts its specific attraction upon all parts. If there be a variety in natural effects, as, e. g. in the tides of different seas, that very variety is the result of the same cause, acting under different circumstances. In many cases this is proved; in all, is probable.

The inspection and comparison of *living* forms, add to this argument examples without number. Of all large terrestrial animals, the structure is very much alike; their senses nearly the same; their natural functions and passions nearly the same; their viscera nearly the same, both in substance, shape, and office: digestion, nutrition, circulation, secretion, go on, in a similar manner, in all. The great circulating fluid is the same; for, I think, no difference has been discovered in the properties of *blood*, from whatever animal it be drawn. The experiment of transfusion proves, that the blood of one animal will serve for another. The *skeletons* also of the larger terrestrial animals, show particular varieties, but still under a great general affinity. The resemblance is somewhat less, yet sufficiently evident, between quadrupeds and birds. They are all alike in five respects, for one in which they differ.

In *fish*, which belong to another department, as it were of nature, the points of comparison become fewer. But we never lose sight of our analogy, e. g. we still meet with a stomach, a liver, a spine; with bile and blood; with teeth; with eyes,—(which eyes are only slightly varied from our own, and which variation, in truth, demonstrates, not an interruption, but a continuance of the same exquisite plan; for it is the adaptation of the organ to the element, viz. to the different refraction of light passing into the eye out of a denser medium.) The provinces, also, themselves of water and earth, are connected by the species of animals which inhabit both; and also by a large tribe of aquatic animals, which closely resemble the terrestrial in their internal structure; I mean the cetaceous tribe, which have hot blood, respiring lungs, bowels, and other essential parts, like those of land animals. This similitude, surely, bespeaks the same creation and the same Creator.

Insects and *shell-fish* appear to me to differ from other classes of animals the most widely of any. Yet even here, beside many points of particular resemblance, there exists a general relation of a peculiar kind. It is the relation of inversion; the law of contrariety: namely, that whereas, in other animals, the bones, to which the muscles are attached, lie *within* the body; in insects and shell-fish they lie on the *outside* of it. The shell of a lobster performs to the animal the office of a *bone*, by furnishing to the tendons that fixed basis or immovable fulcrum, without which, mechanically, they could not act. The crust of an insect is its shell, and answers the like purpose. The shell also of an oyster stands in the place of a *bone*; the bases of the muscles being fixed to it, in the same manner as, in other animals, they are fixed to the bones. All which (under wonderful varieties, indeed, and adaptations of form) confesses an imitation, a remembrance, a carrying on, of the same plan.

The observations here made are equally applicable to plants; but, I think, unnecessary to be pursued.

It is a very striking circumstance, and alone sufficient to prove all which we contend for, that in this part likewise of organized nature, we perceive a continuation of the *sexual* system.

Certain however it is, that the whole argument for the divine unity, goes no farther than to a unity of counsel.

It may likewise be acknowledged, that no arguments which we are in possession of, exclude the ministry of subordinate agents. If such there be, they act under a presiding, a controlling will; because they act according to certain general restrictions, by certain common rules, and, as it should seem, upon a general plan: but still such agents, and different ranks, and classes, and degrees of them, may be employed.

CHAPTER XXVI.

THE GOODNESS OF THE DEITY

THE proof of the *divine goodness* rests upon two propositions, each, as we contend, capable of being made out by observations drawn from the appearances of nature.

The first is, "that in a vast plurality of instances in which contrivance is perceived, the design of the contrivance is *beneficial*."

The second, "that the Deity has superadded *pleasure* to animal sensations, beyond what was necessary for any other purpose, or when the purpose, so far as it was necessary, might have been effected by the operation of pain."

First, " in a vast plurality of instances in which contrivance is perceived, the design of the contrivance is *beneficial*."

No productions of nature display contrivance so manifestly as the parts of animals; and the parts of animals have all of them, I believe, a real, and, with very few exceptions, all of them a known and intelligible, subserviency to the use of the animal. Now, when the multitude of animals is considered, the number of parts in each, their figure and fitness, the faculties depending upon them, the variety of species, the complexity of structure, the success, in so many cases, and felicity of the result, we can never reflect, without the profoundest adoration, upon the character of that Being from whom all these things have proceeded: we cannot help acknowledging, what an exertion of benevoence creation was; of a benevolence how minute in its care, how vast in its comprehension!

When we appeal to the parts and faculties of animals and to the limbs and senses of animals in particular, we state, I conceive, the proper medium of proof for the conclusion which we wish to establish. I will not say that the insensible parts of nature are made solely for the sensitive parts; but this I say, that, when we consider the benevolence of the Deity, we can only consider it in relation to sensitive be ng. Without this reference, or referred to anything else, the attribute has no object; the term has no meaning. Dead matter is nothing. The parts, therefore, especially the limbs and senses of animals, although they constitute, in mass and quantity, a small portion of the material creation, yet, since they alone are instruments of perception, they compose what may be called the whole of visible nature, estimated with a view to the disposition of its Author. Consequently, it is in *these* that we are to seek his character. It is by these that we are to prove, that the world was made with a benevolent design.

Nor is the design abortive It is a happy world after all. The air, the earth, the water, teem with delighted existence. In a spring noon, or a summer evening, on whichever side I turn my eyes, myriads of happy beings crowd upon my view. "The insect youth are on the wing." Swarms of new-born *flies* are trying their pinions in the air. Their sportive motions, their wanton mazes, their gratuitors activity, their continual change of place without use or purpose, testify their joy, and the exultation which they feel in their lately discovered faculties. A *bee* amongst the flowers in spring, is one of the most cheerful objects that can be looked upon. Its life appears to be all enjoyment; so busy, and so pleased: yet it is only a specimen of insect life, with which, by reason of the animal being half domesticated, we happen to be better acquainted than we are with that of others. The *whole* winged insect tribe, it is probable, are equally intent upon their proper employments, and under every variety of constitution, gratified, and perhaps equally gratified, by the offices which the Author of their nature has assigned to them. But the atmosphere is not the only scene of enjoyment for the insect race. Plants are covered with aphides, greedily sucking their juices, and constan'ly, as it should seem, in the act of sucking I'

X

cannot be doubted but that this is a state of gratification
What else should fix them so close to the operation, and
so long? Other species are *running about*, with an alacr'ty
in their motions, which carries with it every mark of pleasure. Large patches of ground are sometimes ha.f covered
with these brisk and sprightly natures. If we look to what
the *waters* produce, shoals of the fry of fish frequent the
margins of rivers, of lakes, and of the sea itself. These
are so happy, that they know not what to do with themselves
Their attitudes, their vivacity, their leaps out of the water,
their frolics in it, (which I have noticed a thousand times
with equal attention and amusement,) all conduce to show
their excess of spirits, and are simply the effects of that
excess. Walking by the seaside, in a calm evening, upon
a sandy shore, and with an ebbing tide, I have frequently
remarked the appearance of a dark cloud, or rather, very
thick mist, hanging over the edge of the water, to the
height, perhaps, of half a yard, and of the breadth of two
or three yards, stretching along the coast as far as the eye
could reach, and always retiring with the water. When
this cloud came to be examined, it proved to be nothing
else than so much space, filled with young *shrimps*, in the
act of bounding into the air from the shallow margin of the
water, or from the wet sand. If any motion of a mute animal could express delight, it was this: if they had meant
to make signs of their happiness, they could not have done
it more intelligibly. Suppose then, what I have no doub
of, each individual of this number to be in a state of posi
tive enjoyment; what a sum, collectively, of gratificatio
and pleasure have we here before our view!

The *young* of all animals appear to me to receive plea-
ure simply from the exercise of their limbs and bodily fac
ulties, without reference to any end to be attained, or any
use to be answered by the exertion. A child, withou'
knowing anything of the use of language, is in a high de
gree delighted with being able to speak. Its incessan:
repetition of the few articulate sounds, or perhaps of the
single word which it has learned to pronounce, proves this
point clearly. Nor is it less pleased with its first successful endeavours to walk, or rather to run, (which precedes
walking,) although entirely ignorant of the importance of
the attainment to its future life, and even without applying it to any present purpose. A child is delighted with
speaking, without having anything to say; and with walking, without knowing where to go. And, prior to both
these I am disposed to believe, that the waking hours of

infancy are agreeably taken up with the exercise of vision, or perhaps, more properly speaking, with learning to see

But it is not for youth alone that the great Parent of creation hath provided. Happiness is found with the purring cat, no less than with the playful kitten; in the armed chair of dozing age, as well as in either the sprightliness of the dance, or the animation of the chase. To novel ty, to acuteness of sensation, to hope, to ardor of pursuit, succeeds what is, in no inconsiderable degree, an equivalent for them all, "perception of ease." Herein is the exact difference between the young and the old. The young are not happy, but when enjoying pleasure; the old are happy, when free from pain. And this constitution suits with the degrees of animal power which they respectively possess. The vigor of youth was to be stimulated to action by impatience of rest; whilst, to the imbecility of age, quietness and repose become positive gratifications. In one important respect the advantage is with the old. A state of ease is, generally speaking, more attainable than a state of pleasure. A constitution, therefore, which can enjoy ease, is preferable to that which can taste only pleasure. The same perception of ease oftentimes renders old age a condition of great comfort; especially when riding at its anchor after a busy or tempestuous life. It is well described by Rousseau, to be the interval of repose and enjoyment, between the hurry and the end of life. How far the same cause extends to other animal natures cannot be judged of with certainty. The appearance of satisfaction, with which most animals, as their activity subsides, seek and enjoy rest, affords reason to believe, that this source of gratification is appointed to advanced life, under all, or most, of its various forms. In the species with which we are best acquainted, namely, our own, I am far, even as an observer of human life, from thinking that youth is its happiest season, much less the only happy one: as a Christian, I am willing to believe that there is a great deal of truth in the following representation given by a very pious writer, as well as an excellent man.* "To the intelligent and virtuous, old age presents a scene of tranquil enjoyments, of obedient appetite, of well-regulated affections, of maturity in knowledge, and of calm preparation for immortality. In this serene and dignified state, placed as it were on the confines of two worlds, the mind of a good man reviews what is past with the complacency of an approving conscience; and looks forward with humble confidence in

* Father's instructions; by Dr. Percival of Manchester, p. 317

the mercy of God, and with devout aspirations towards his eternal and ever increasing favor."

What is seen in different stages of the same life, is still more exemplified in the lives of different animals. Animal enjoyments are infinitely *diversified*. The modes of life to which the organization of different animals respectively determines them, are not only of various but of opposite kinds. Yet each is happy in its own. For instance; animals of prey live much alone; animals of a milder constitution, in society. Yet the herring, which lives in shoals, and the sheep, which live in flocks, are not more happy in a crowd, or more contented amongst their companions, than is the pike, or the lion, with the deep solitudes of the pool, or the forest.

But it will be said, that the instances which we have here brought forward, whether of vivacity or repose, or of apparent enjoyment derived from either, are picked and favorable instances. We answer, first, that they are instances, nevertheless, which comprise large provinces of sensitive existence; that every case which we have described, is the case of millions. At this moment, in every given moment of time, how many myriads of animals are eating their food, gratifying their appetites, ruminating in their holes, accomplishing their wishes, pursuing their pleasures, taking their pastimes! In each individual, how many things must go right for it to be at ease; yet how large a proportion out of every species is so in every assignable instant! Secondly, we contend, in the terms of our original proposition, that throughout the whole of life, as it is diffused in nature, and as far as we are acquainted with it, looking to the average of sensations, the plurality and the preponderancy is in favor of happiness by a vast excess. In our own species, in which perhaps the assertion may be more questionable than in any other, the prepollency of good over evil, of health, for example, and ease, over pain and distress, is evinced by the very notice which calamities excite. What inquiries does the sickness of our friends produce! What conversation their misfortunes! This shows that the common course of things is in favor of happiness; that happiness is the rule, misery the exception. Were the order reversed, our attention would be called to examples of health and competency, instead of disease and want.

One great cause of our insensibility to the goodness of the Creator, is the very *extensiveness* of his bounty. We prize but little what we share only in common with the rest, or with the generality of our species. When we hear of blessings, we think forthwith of successes, of prosperou. fortunes, of honors, riches, preferments, *i. e.* of those ad· vantages and superiorities over others, which we happen either to possess, or to be in pursuit of, or to covet. The common benefits of our nature entirely escape us. Yet these are the great things. These constitute what most properly ought to be accounted blessings of Providence; what alone, if we might so speak, are worthy of its care Nightly rest and daily bread, the ordinary use of our limbs, and senses, and understandings, are gifts which admit of no comparison with any other. Yet, because almost every man we meet with possesses these, we leave them out of our enumeration. They raise no sentiment: they move no gratitude. Now herein is our judgment perverted by our selfishness. A blessing ought in truth to be the *more* satisfactory, the bounty at least of the donor is rendered more conspicuous, by its very diffusion, its commonness, its cheapness; by its falling to the lot, and forming the happiness, of the great bulk and body of our species, as well as of ourselves. Nay, even when we do not possess it, it ought to be matter of thankfulness that others do. But we have a different way of thinking. We court distinction. That is not the worst; we *see* nothing but what has distinction to recommend it. This necessarily contracts our views of the Creator's beneficence within a narrow compass; and most unjustly. It is in those things which are so common as to be no distinction, that the amplitude of the divine benignity is perceived.

But pain, no doubt, and privations exist, in numerous instances, and to a degree, which, collectively, would be very great, if they were compared with any other thing than with the mass of animal fruition. For the application, herefore, of our proposition to that *mixed* state of things which these exceptions induce, two rules are necessary, and both, I think, just and fair rules. One is, that we regard those effects alone which are accompanied with proofs of intention: The other, that when we cannot resolve all appearances into benevolence of design, we make the few give place to the many; the little to the great; that we take our judgment from a large and decided preponderancy, if there be one.

I crave leave to transcribe into this place, what I have said upon this subject in my Moral Philosophy:—

" When God created the human species, either he wished ed their happiness, or he wished their misery, or he was indifferent and unconcerned about either

x*

" If he had wished our misery, he might have made sure of his purpose, by forming our senses to be so many sores and pains to us, as they are now instruments of gratification and enjoyment: or by placing us amidst objects so ill suited to our perceptions, as to have continually offended us, instead of ministering to our refreshment and delight He might have made, for example, everything we tasted, bitter; everything we saw, loathsome· everything we ouched, a sting; every smell, a stench; and every sound, a discord

" If he had been indifferent about our happiness or mis-ry, we must impute to our good fortune (as all design by his supposition is excluded) both the capacity of our senses to receive pleasure, and the supply of external objects fitted to produce it.

" But either of these, and still more both of them, being too much to be attributed to accident, nothing remains but the first supposition, that God, when he created the human species, wished their happiness; and made for them the provision which he has made, with that view and for that purpose.

" The same argument may be proposed in different terms; thus: Contrivance proves design: and the predominant tendency of the contrivance indicates the disposition of the designer. The world abounds with contrivances: and all the contrivances which we are acquainted with, are directed to beneficial purposes. Evil, no doubt, exists; but is never, that we can perceive, the *object* of contrivance. Teeth are contrived to eat, not to ache; their aching now and then is incidental to the contrivance, perhaps inseparable from it: or even, if you will, let it be called a defect in the contrivance; but it is not the object of it. This is a distinction which well deserves to be attended to. In describing implements of husbandry, you would hardly say of the sickle, that it is made to cut the reaper's hand; though, from the construction of the instrument, and the manner of using it, this mischief often follows. But if you had occasion to describe instruments of torture or execution: this engine, you would say, is to extend the sinews; this to dislocate the joints; this to break the bones; this to scorch the soles of the feet. Here pain and misery are the very objects of the contrivance. Now, nothing of this sort is to be found in the works of nature. We never discover a train of contrivance to bring about an evil purpose. No anatomist ever discovered a system of organization calculate! to produce pain and disease; o. in explaining the parts of the human body, ever said, this is to irritate, this to inflame; this duct is to convey the gravel to the kidneys; this gland to secrete the humour which forms the gout: if by chance he come at a part of which he knows not the use, the most he can say is, that it is useless; no one ever suspects that it is put there to incommode, to annoy, or to torment."

The TWO CASES which appear to me to have the most of difficulty in them, as forming the most of the appearance of exception to the representation here given, are those of *venomous* animals, and of animals *preying* upon one another These properties of animals, wherever they are found, must, I think, be referred to design; because there is, in all cases of the first, and in most cases of the second, an express and distinct organization provided for the producing of them. Under the first head, the fangs of vipers, the stings of wasps and scorpions, are as clearly intended for their purpose, as any animal structure is for any purpose the most incontestably beneficial. And the same thing must, under the second head, be acknowledged of the talons and beaks of birds, of the tusks, teeth, and claws of beasts of prey, of the shark's mouth, of the spider's web, and of numberless weapons of offence belonging to different tribes of voracious insects. We cannot, therefore, avoid the difficulty by saying, that the effect was not intended. The only question open to us is, whether it be ultimately evil. From the confessed and felt imperfection of our knowledge, we ought to presume, that there may be consequences of this economy which are hidden from us: from the benevolence which pervades the general designs of nature, we ought also to presume, that these consequences, if they could enter into our calculation, would turn the balance on the favorable side. Both these I contend to be reasonable presumptions Not reasonable presumptions, if these two cases were the only cases which nature presented to our observation; but reasonable presumptions under the reflection, that the cases in question are combined with a multitude of intentions, all proceeding from the same author, and all, except these, directed to ends of undisputed utility. Of the vindications, however, of this economy, which we are able to assign, such as most extenuate the difficulty, are the following.

With respect to *venomous* bites and stings, it may be observed,—

1. That the animal itself being regarded, the faculty complained of is *good:* being conducive, in all cases, to the defence of the animal, in some cases, to the subduing

of its prey; and in some, probably, to the killing of it, when caught, by a mortal wound, inflicted in the passage to the stomach, which may be no less merciful to the victim than salutary to the devourer. In the viper, for instance, the poisonous fang may do that which, in other animals of prey, is done by the crush of the teeth. Frogs and mice might be swallowed alive without it.

2 But it will be said, that this provision, when it comes to the case of bites, deadly even to human bodies and to those of large quadrupeds, is greatly *overdone;* that it might have fulfilled its use, and yet have been much less deleterious than it is. Now I believe the case of bites, which produce death in large animals (of stings I think there are none,) to be very few. The experiments of the Abbé Fontana, which were numerous, go strongly to the proof of this point. He found that it required the action of five exasperated vipers to kill a dog of a moderate size; but that, to the killing of a mouse or a frog, a single bite was sufficient; which agrees with the use which we assign to the faculty. The Abbé seemed to be of opinion, that the bite even of the rattlesnake would not usually be mortal; allowing, however, that in certain particularly unfortunate cases, as when the puncture had touched some very tender part, pricked a principal nerve for instance, or, as it is said, some more considerable lymphatic vessel, death might speedily ensue.

3. It has been, I think, very justly remarked, concerning serpents, that, whilst only a few species possess the venomous property, that property guards the whole tribe. The most innocuous snake is avoided with as much care as a viper. Now the terror with which large animals regard this class of reptiles, is its protection; and this terror is founded in the formidable revenge, which a few of the number, compared with the whole, are capable of taking. The species of serpents, described by Linnæus, amount to two hundred and eighteen, of which thirty-two only are poisonous.

4. It seems to me, that animal constitutions are provided, not only for each element, but for each state of the elements, *i. e.* for every climate, and for every temperature; and that part of the mischief complained of, arises from animals (the human animal most especially) occupying situations upon the earth which do not belong to them, nor were ever intended for their habitation. The folly and wickedness of mankind, and necessities proceeding from these causes, have driven multitudes of the species to seek a refuge amongst burning sands whilst countries, blessed

with hospitable skies, and with the most fertile soils, remain almost without a human tenant. We invade the ter-
ritories of wild beasts and venomous reptiles, and then com
plain that we are infested by their bites and stings. Some
accounts of Africa place this observation in a strong point
of view. "The deserts," says Adanson, "are entirely barren, except where they are found to produce serpents; and
in such quantities, that some extensive plains are almost
entirely covered with them." These are the natures appropriated to the situation. Let them enjoy their existence; let them have their country. Surface enough will
be left to man, though his numbers were increased a hundred fold, and left to him, where he might live exempt
from these annoyances.

The SECOND CASE, viz. that of animals *devouring* one
another, furnishes a consideration of much larger extent.
To judge whether, as general provision, this can be deemed an *evil*, even so far as we understand its consequences,
which, probably, is a partial understanding, the following
reflections are fit to be attended to.

1. Immortality upon this earth is out of the question
Without death there could be no generation, no sexes, no
parental relation, *i. e.* as things are constituted, no animal
happiness. The particular duration of life, assigned to different animals, can form no part of the objection; because,
whatever that duration be, whilst it remains finite and limited, it may always be asked, why it is no longer. The
natural age of different animals varies, from a single day
to a century of years. No account can be given of this;
nor could any be given, whatever other proportion of life
had obtained amongst them.

The term then of life in different animals being the same
as it is, the question is, what mode of taking it away is the
best even for the animal itself?

Now, according to the established order of nature, (which
we must suppose to prevail, or we cannot reason at all upon
the subject,) the three methods by which life is usually put
an end to, are acute diseases, decay, and violence. The
simple and natural life of *brutes*, is not often visited by acute
distempers; nor could it be deemed an improvement of
their lot, if they were. Let it be considered, therefore, in
what a condition of suffering and misery a brute animal is
placed, which is left to perish by *decay*. In human sickness
or infirmity, there is the assistance of man's rational fellow creatures, if no to alleviate his pains, at least to min-

ster to his necessities, and to supply the place of his own activity. A brute, in his wild and natural state, does every hing for himself. When his strength therefore, or his speed, or his limbs, or his senses fail him, he is delivered over, either to absolute famine, or to the protracted wretchedness of a life slowly wasted by the scarcity of food. Is it then to see the world filled with drooping, superannuated, half starved, helpless, and unhelped animals, that you would alter the present system of pursuit and prey?

2 Which system is also to them the spring of motion and activity on both sides. The pursuit of its prey forms the employment, and appears to constitute the pleasure, of a considerable part of the animal creation. The using of the means of defence, or flight, or precaution, forms also the business of another part. And even of this latter tribe, we have no reason to suppose, that their happiness is much molested by their fears. Their danger exists continually; and in some cases they seem to be so far sensible of it, as to provide in the best manner they can against it; but it is only when the attack is actually made upon them, that they appear to suffer from it. To contemplate the insecurity of heir condition with anxiety and dread, requires a degree of reflection, which (happily for themselves) they do not possess. A *hare*, notwithstanding the number of its dangers and its enemies, is as playful an animal as any other.

3. But, to do justice to the question, the system of animal *destruction* ought always to be considered in strict connexion with another property of animal nature, viz. *superfecundity*. They are countervailing qualities. One subsists by the correction of the other. In treating, therefore, of the subject under this view, (which is, I believe, the true one,) our business will be, first, to point out the advantages which are gained by the powers in nature of a superabundant multiplication; and then to show, that these advantages are so many reasons for appointing that system of animal hostilities, which we are endeavouring to account for.

In almost all cases, nature produces her supplies with profusion. A single cod-fish spawns, in one season, a greater number of eggs than all the inhabitants of England amount to. A thousand other instances of prolific generation might be stated, which, though not equal to this, would carry on the increase of the species with a rapidity which outruns calculation, and to an immeasurable extent. The advantages of such a constitution are two: first that it tends

to keep the world always full: whilst, seccnlly, it allows
the proportion between the several species of animals to be
differently modified, as different purposes require, or as
different situations may afford for them room and food
Where this vast fecundity meets with a vacancy fitted to
receive the species, there it operates with its whole effect,
here it pours in its numbers, and replenishes the waste
We complain of what we call the exorbitant multiplication
of some troublesome insects; not reflecting that large portions of nature might be left void without it.   If the ac
counts of travellers may be depended upon, immense tracts
of forest in North America would be nearly lost to sensitivo
existence, if it were not for *gnats*.   "In the thinly inhab
ited regions of America, in which the waters stagnate and
the climate is warm, the whole air is filled with crowds ot
these insects."   Thus it is, that where we look for solitude
and deathlike silence, we meet with animation, activity,
enjoyment; with a busy, a happy, and a peopled world.
Again; hosts of *mice* are reckoned amongst the plagues of
the northeast part of Europe; whereas vast plains in Sibe-
ria, as we learn from good authority, would be lifeless without them.   The Caspian deserts are converted by their
presence into crowded warrens.   Between the Volga and
the Yaik, and in the country of Hyrcania, the ground, says
Pallas, is in many places *covered* with little hills, raised by
the earth cast out in forming the burrows.   Do we so
envy these blissful abodes, as to pronounce the fecundity
by which they are supplied with inhabitants, to be an evil;
a subject of complaint, and not of praise?   Farther; by
virtue of this same superfecundity, what we term destruction, becomes almost instantly the parent of life.   What we
call blights, are oftentimes legions of animated beings,
claiming their portion in the bounty of nature.   What cor-
rupts the produce of the earth to us, prepares it for them.
And it is by means of their rapid multiplication, that they
take possession of their pasture; a slow propagation would
not meet the opportunity.

But in conjunction with the occasional use of this fruitfulness, we observe, also, that it allows the proportion between the several species of animals, to be differently modified, as different purposes of utility may require.   When
the forests of America come to be cleared, and the swamps
drained, our gnats will give place to other inhabitants.   If
the population of Europe should spread to the north and
the east, the mice will retire before the husbandman and

the shepherd, and yield their station to herds and flocks. In what concerns the human species, it may be a part of the scheme of Providence, that the earth should be inhabited by a shifting, or perhaps a circulating population. In this economy, it is possible that there may be the following advantages: When old countries are become exceedingly corrupt, simpler modes of life, purer morals, and better institutions, may rise up in new ones, whilst fresh soils reward the cultivator with more plentiful returns. Thus the different portions of the globe come into use in succession as the residence of man; and, in his absence, entertain other guests, which, by their sudden multiplication, fill the chasm. In domesticated animals, we find the effect of their fecundity to be, that we can always command *numbers*; we can always have as many of any particular species as we please, or as we can support. Nor do we complain of its excess; it being much more easy to regulate abundance, than to supply scarcity.

But then this *superfecundity*, though of great occasional use and importance, exceeds the ordinary capacity of nature to receive or support its progeny. All superabundance supposes destruction, or must destroy itself. Perhaps there is no species of terrestrial animals whatever, which would not overrun the earth, if it were permitted to multiply in perfect safety; or of fish, which would not fill the ocean: at least, if any single species were left to their natural increase without disturbance or restraint, the food of other species would be exhausted by their maintenance. It is necessary, therefore, that the effects of such prolific faculties be curtailed. In conjunction with other checks and limits, all subservient to the same purpose, are the *thinnings* which take place among animals, by their action upon one another. In some instances we ourselves experience, very directly, the use of these hostilities. One species of insects rids us of another species; or reduces their ranks. A third species, perhaps, keeps the second within bounds; and birds or lizards are a fence against the inordinate increase by which even these last might infest us. In other more numerous, and possibly more important instances, this disposition of things, although less necessary or useful to us, and of course less observed by us, may be necessary and useful to certain other species; or even for the preventing of the loss of certain species from the universe: a misfortune which seems to be studiously guarded against. Though there may be the appearance of failure in some of the details of Nature's works, in her great purposes there never are. Her species never fail. The provision which was originally made for continuing the replenishment of the world, has proved itself to be effectual through a long succession of ages.

What farther shows, that the system of destruction amongst animals holds an express relation to the system of fecundity; that they are parts indeed of one compensatory scheme; is, that in each species the fecundity bears a proportion to the smallness of the animal, to the weakness, to the shortness of its natural term of life, and to the dangers and enemies by which it is surrounded. An elephant produces but one calf: a butterfly lays six hundred eggs Birds of prey seldom produce more than two eggs: the sparrow tribe, and the duck tribe, frequently sit upon a dozen. In the rivers, we meet with a thousand minnows for one pike; in the sea, a million of herrings for a single shark. Compensation obtains throughout. Defencelessness and devastation are repaired by fecundity.

We have dwelt the longer upon these considerations, because the subject to which they apply, namely, that of animals *devouring* one another, forms the chief, if not the only instance, in the works of the Deity, of an economy, stamped by marks of design, in which the character of utility can be called in question. The case of *venomous* animals is of much inferior consequence to the case of prey, and in some degree, is also included under it. To both cases, it is probable that many more reasons belong, than those of which we are in possession

Our FIRST PROPOSITION, and that which we have hitherto been defending, was, "that, in a vast plurality of in stances in which *contrivance* is perceived, the design of the contrivance is beneficial."

Our SECOND PROPOSITION is, "that the Deity has added *pleasure* to animal sensations, beyond what was necessary for any other purpose, or when the purpose, so far as it was necessary, might have been effected by the opera tion of pain."

This proposition may be thus explained: The capacities which, according to the established course of nature, are *necessary* to the support or preservation of an animal, however manifestly they may be the result of an organization contrived for the purpose, can only be deemed an act or a part of the same will, as that which decreed the existence of the animal itself; because, whether the creation proceeded from a benevolent or a malevolent being those capacities must have been given, if the animal existed a all. Animal properties therefore, which fall under this description, do not strictly prove the goodness of God: they may prove the existence of the Deity; they may prove a high degree of power and intelligence: but they do not prove his goodness: forasmuch as they must have been found in any creation which was capable of continuance, although it is possible to suppose, that such a creation might have been produced by a being, whose views rested upon misery

But there is a class of properties, which may be said to be superadded from an intention expressly directed to happiness; an intention to give a happy existence distinct from the general intention of providing the means of existence, and that is, of capacities for pleasure, in cases wherein, so far as the conservation of the individual or of the species is concerned, they were not wanted, or wherein the purpose might have been secured by the operation of pain. The provision which is made of a variety of objects, not necessary to life, and ministering only to our pleasures; and the properties given to the necessaries of life themselves, by which they contribute to pleasure as well as preservation; show a farther design than that of giving existence.*

A single instance will make all this clear. Assuming the necessity of food for the support of animal life; it is requisite, that the animal be provided with organs, fitted for the procuring, receiving, and digesting of its food. It may also be necessary, that the animal be impelled by its sensations to exert its organs. But the pain of hunger would do all this. Why add pleasure to the act of eating; sweetness and relish to food? Why a new and appropriate sense for the perception of the pleasure? Why should the juice of a peach, applied to the palate, affect the part so differently from what it does when rubbed upon the palm of the hand? This is a constitution, which, so far as appears to me, can be resolved into nothing but the pure benevolence of the Creator. Eating is necessary; but the pleasure attending it is not necessary; and that this pleasure depends not only upon our being in possession of the sense of taste, which is different from every other, but upon a particular

* See this topic considered in Dr. Balguy's Treatise upon the Divine Benevolence. This excellent author, first, I think, proposed it; and nearly in the terms in which it is here stated. Some other observations also under this head, are taken from that treatise.

state of the organ in which it resides, a felicitous adaptation of the organ to the object, will be confessed by any
one, who may happen to have experienced that vitiation of
taste which frequently occurs in fevers, when every taste is
irregular, and every one bad.

In mentioning the gratifications of the palate, it may be
said, that we have made choice of a trifling example. I am
not of that opinion. They afford a share of enjoyment to
man: but to brutes, I believe that they are of very great
importance. A horse at liberty passes a great part of his
waking hours in eating. To the ox, the sheep, the deer,
and other ruminating animals, the pleasure is doubled
Their whole time almost is divided between browsing upon
their pasture and chewing their cud. Whatever the pleasure be, it is spread over a large portion of their existence
If there be animals, such as the lupous fish, which swallow
their prey whole, and at once, without any time, as it should
seem, for either drawing out, or relishing the taste in the
mouth, is it an improbable conjecture, that the seat of taste
with them is in the stomach? or, at least, that a sense of
pleasure, whether it be taste or not, accompanies the dissolution of the food in that receptacle, which dissolution in
general is carried on very slowly? If this opinion be right
they are more than repaid for their defect of palate. The
feast lasts as long as the digestion.

In seeking for argument, we need not stay to insist upon
the comparative importance of our example; for the observation holds equally of all, or of three at least, of the other
senses. The necessary purposes of hearing might have
been answered without harmony; of smell, without fragrance; of vision, without beauty. Now, "If the Deity
had been indifferent about our happiness or misery, we
must impute to our good fortune (as all design by this supposition is excluded) both the capacity of our senses to receive
pleasure, and the supply of external objects fitted to excite
it." I allege these as *two* felicities, for they are different
things, yet both necessary: the sense being formed, the
objects which were applied to it might not have suited it,
the objects being fixed, the sense might not have agreed
with them. A coincidence is here required, which no accident can account for. There are three possible suppositions
upon the subject, and no more. The first, that the sense
by its original constitution, was made to suit the object. the
second, that the object, by its original constitution, was
made to suit the sense: the third, that the sense is so con-

stituted, as to be able, either universally, or with.n c⟨ ⟩in limits, by habit and familiarity, to render every cojec. pleasant. Whichever of these suppositions we adopt, the effect evinces, on the part of the Author of Nature, a studious benevolence. If the pleasures which we derive from any of our senses depend upon an original congruity between the sense and the properties perceived by it, we know by experience, that the adjustment demanded, with respect to the qualities which were conferred upon the objects that surround us, not only choice and selection, out of a boundless variety of possible qualities, with which these objects might have been endued, but a *proportioning also of degree*, because an excess or defect of intensity spoils the perception, as much almost as an error in the kind and nature of the quality. Likewise the degree of dulness or acuteness in the sense itself, is no arbitrary thing, but in order to preserve the congruity here spoken of, requires to be in an exact or near correspondency with the strength of the impression. The dulness of the senses forms the complaint of old age. Persons in fevers, and, I believe, in most maniacal cases, experience great torment from their preternatural acuteness. An increased, no less than an impaired sensibility, induces a state of disease and suffering.

The doctrine of a specific congruity between animal senses and their objects, is strongly favored by what is observed of insects in the selection of their food. Some of these will feed upon one kind of plant or animal, and upon no other: some caterpillars upon the cabbage alone; some upon the black currant alone. The species of caterpillar which eats the vine, will starve upon the elder: nor will that which we find upon fennel, touch the rosebush. Some insects confine themselves to two or three kinds of plants or animals. Some again show so strong a preference, as to afford reason to believe, that, though they may be driven by hunger to others, they are led by the pleasure of taste to a few particular plants alone: and all this, as it should seem, independently of habit or imitation.

But should we accept the third hypothesis, and even carry it so far, as to ascribe everything which concerns the question to habit, (as in certain species, the human species most particularly, there is reason to attribute something,) we have then before us an animal capacity, not less perhaps to be admired than the native congruities which the other scheme adopts. It cannot be shown to result from any fixed necessity in nature, that what is frequently applied to the senses should of course become agreeable to them. It is, so far as it subsists, a power of accommodation provided in these senses by the Author of their structure, and forms a part of their perfection.

In whichever way we regard the senses, they appear to be specific gifts, ministering, not only to preservation, but to pleasure. But what we usually call the *senses* are probably themselves far from being the only vehicles of enjoyment, or the whole of our constitution, which is calculated for the same purpose. We have many internal sensations of the most agreeable kind, hardly referable to any of the five senses. Some physiologists have holden, that all secretion is pleasurable; and that the complacency which in health, without any external assignable object to excite it, we derive from life itself, is the effect of our secretions going on well within us. All this may be true; but if true, what reason can be assigned for it, except the will of the Creator? It may reasonably be asked, why is anything a pleasure? and I know of no answer which can be returned to the question, but that which refers it to appointment. We can give no account whatever of our pleasures in the simple and original perception; and, even when physical sensations are assumed, we can seldom account for them in the secondary and complicated shapes in which they take the name of diversions. I never yet met with a sportsman, who could tell me in what the sport consisted; who could resolve it into its principle, and state that principle. I have been a great follower of fishing myself, and in its cheerful solitude have passed some of the happiest hours of a sufficiently happy life; but to this moment, I could never trace out the source of the pleasure which it afforded me.

The " quantum in rebus inane!" whether applied to our amusements or, to our graver pursuits, (to which in truth it sometimes equally belongs,) is always an unjust complaint. If trifles engage, and if trifles make us happy, the true reflection suggested by the experiment, is upon the tendency of nature to gratification and enjoyment; which is, in other words, the goodness of its Author toward his sensitive creation.

Rational natures also, as such, exhibit qualities which help to confirm the truth of our position. The degree of understanding found in mankind, is usually much greater than what is necessary for mere preservation. The pleasure of choosing for themselves, and of prosecuting the object

y*

of their choice, should seem to be an original source of enjoyment. The pleasures received from things, great beautiful, or new, from imitation, or from the liberal arts are in some measure, not only superadded, but unmixed, gratifications, having no pains to balance them.*

I do not know whether our attachment to *property* be not something more than the mere dictate of reason, or even than the mere effect of association. Property communicates a charm to whatever is the object of it. It is the first of our abstract ideas; it cleaves to us the closest and the longest. It endears to the child its plaything, to the peasant his cottage, to the landholder his estate. It supplies the place of prospect and scenery. Instead of coveting the beauty of distant situations, it teaches every man to find it in his own. It gives boldness and grandeur to plains and fens, tinge and coloring to clays and fallows.

All these considerations come in aid of our *second* proposition. The reader will now bear in mind what our two propositions were. They were, firstly, that in a vast plurality of instances in which contrivance is perceived, the design of the contrivance is beneficial: secondly, that the Deity has added pleasure to animal sensations beyond what was necessary for any other purpose; or when the purpose, so far as it was necessary, might have been effected by the operation of pain.

Whilst these propositions can be maintained, we are authorised to ascribe to the Deity the character of benevolence: and what is benevolence at all, must in him be *infinite* benevolence, by reason of the infinite, that is to say, the incalculably great, number of objects upon which it is exercised.

Of the ORIGIN OF EVIL, no universal solution has been discovered; I mean, no solution which reaches to all cases of complaint. The most comprehensive is that which arises from the consideration of *general rules*. We may, I think, without much difficulty, be brought to admit the four following points: first, that important advantages may accrue to the universe from the order of nature proceeding according to general laws: secondly, that general laws, however well set and constituted, often thwart and cross one another: thirdly, that from these thwartings and crossings, frequent particular inconveniences will arise: and, fourth

* Balguy on the Divine Benevolence.

ly that it agrees with our observation to suppose, that some degree of these inconveniences takes place in the works of nature. These points may be allowed; and it may also be asserted, that the general laws with which we are acquainted, are directed to beneficial ends. On the other hand, with many of these laws we are not acquainted at all, or we are totally unable to trace them in their branches, and in their operation; the effect of which ignorance is, that they cannot be of importance to us as measures by which to regulate our conduct. The conservation of them may be of importance in other respects, or to other beings, but we are uninformed of their value or use; uninformed, consequently, when, and how far, they may or may not be suspended, or their effects turned aside, by a presiding and benevolent will, without incurring greater evils than those which would be avoided. The consideration, therefore, of general laws, although it may concern the question of the origin of evil very nearly, (which I think it does,) rests in views disproportionate to our faculties, and in a knowledge which we do not possess. It serves rather to account for the obscurity of the subject, than to supply us with distinct answers to our difficulties. However, whilst we assent to the above stated propositions as principles, whatever uncertainty we may find in the application, we lay a ground for believing, that cases of apparent evil, for which *we* can suggest no particular reason, are governed by reasons, which are more general, which lie deeper in the order of second causes, and which on that account are removed to a greater distance from us.

The doctrine of *imperfections*, or, as it is called, of evils of imperfection, furnishes an account, founded, like the former, in views of universal nature. The doctrine is briefly this:—It is probable, that creation may be better replenished by sensitive beings of different sorts, than by sensitive beings all of one sort. It is likewise probable, that it may be better replenished by different orders of beings rising one above another in gradation, than by beings possessed of equal degrees of perfection. Now, a gradation of such beings, implies a gradation of imperfections No class can justly complain of the imperfections which belong to its place in the scale, unless it were allowable for it to complain, that a scale of being was appointed in nature; for which appointment there appear to be reasons of wisdom and goodness.

In like manner, *finiteness*, or what is resolvable into

finiteness, in inanimate subjects, can never be a just subject of complaint, because if it were ever so, it would be
always so: we mean, that we can never reasonably demand that things should be larger or more, when the same
demand might be made, whatever the quantity or number
was.

And to me it seems, that the sense of mankind has so
far acquiesced in these reasons, as that we seldom complain
of evils of this class, when we clearly perceive them to be
such. What I have to add, therefore, is, that we ought not
to complain of some other evils which stand upon the same
foot of vindication as evils of confessed imperfection. We
never complain, that the globe of our earth is too small;
nor should we complain, if it were even much smaller. But
where is the difference to us, between a less globe, and
part of the present being uninhabitable? The inhabitants
of an island may be apt enough to murmur at the sterility
of some parts of it, against its rocks, or sands, or swamps;
but no one thinks himself authorised to murmur, simply
because the island is not larger than it is. Yet these are
the same griefs.

The above are the two metaphysical answers which have
been given to this great question. They are not the worse
for being metaphysical, provided they be founded (which I
think they are) in right reasoning: but they are of a nature too wide to be brought under our survey, and it is often difficult to apply them in the detail. Our speculations,
therefore, are perhaps better employed when they confine
themselves within a narrower circle.

The observations which follow, are of this more limited,
but more determinate, kind.

Of *bodily pain*, the principal observation, no doubt, is
that which we have already made, and already dwelt upon,
viz. "that it is seldom the object of contrivance; that when
it is so, the contrivance rests ultimately in good."

To which, however, may be added, that the annexing of
pain to the means of destruction is a salutary provision,
inasmuch as it teaches vigilance and caution; both give
notice of danger, and excites those endeavours which may
be necessary to preservation. The evil consequence which
sometimes arises from the want of that timely intimation of
danger which pain gives, is known to the inhabitants of
cold countries by the example of frost-bitten limbs. I have
conversed with patients who have lost toes and fingers by
this cause. They have in general told me, that they were

totally unconscious of any local uneasiness at the time
Some I have heard declare, that whilst they were about
their employment, neither their situation, nor the state ot
the air was unpleasant. They felt no pain; they suspected no mischief; till, by the application of warmth, they
discovered, too late, the fatal injury which some of their extremities had suffered. I say that this shows the use of pain,
and that we stand in need of such a monitor. I believe
also, that the use extends farther than we suppose, or can
now trace; that to disagreeable sensations we, and all animals, owe, or have owed, many habits of action which are
salutary, but which are become so familiar, as not easily to
be referred to their origin.

Pain also itself is not without its *alleviations*. It may be
violent and frequent; but it is seldom both violent and long
continued: and its pauses and intermissions become posi
tive pleasures. It has the power of shedding a satisfaction
over intervals of ease, which I believe few enjoyments ex
ceed. A man resting from a fit of the stone or gout, is, for
the time, in possession of feelings which undisturbed health
cannot impart. They may be dearly bought, but still they
are to be set against the price. And, indeed, it depends
upon the duration and urgency of the pain, whether they be
dearly bought or not. I am far from being sure, that a man
is not a gainer by suffering a moderate interruption of bodily ease for a couple of hours out of the four-and-twenty.
Two very common observations favor this opinion: one is,
that remissions of pain call forth, from those who experience them, stronger expressions of satisfaction and of gratitude towards both the author and the instruments of their
relief, than are excited by advantages of any other kind:
the second is, that the spirits of sick men do not sink in
proportion to the acuteness of their sufferings; but rather
appear to be roused and supported, not by pain, but by the
high degree of comfort which they derive from its cessation, or even its subsidency, whenever that occurs; and
which they taste with a relish that diffuses some portion of
mental complacency over the whole of that mixed state of
sensations in which disease has placed them.

In connexion with bodily pain may be considered bodily
disease, whether painful or not. Few diseases are fatal
I have before me the account of a dispensary in the neigh-
bourhood which states six years' experience as follows:
"admitted 6,420—*cured* 5,476—dead 234." And this I
suppose nearly to agree with what other similar institutions

exhib t.   Now, in all these cases, some disorder must have been felt, or the patients would not have applied for a rem edy; yet we see how large a proportion of the maladies which were brought forward, have either yielded to proper treatment, or, what is more probable, ceased of their own accord.   We owe these frequent recoveries, and where recovery does not take place, this patience of the human constitutio · under many of the distempers by which it is visited, to two benefactions of our nature.   One is, that she works within certain limits; allows of a certain latitude within which health may be preserved, and within the confines of which it only suffers a graduated diminution.   Different quantities of food, different degrees of exercise, different portions of sleep, different states of the atmosphere are compatible with the possession of health.   So likewis ': is with the secretions and excretions, with many internal functions of the body, and with the state, probably, of most of its internal organs.   They may vary considerably, not only without destroying life, but without occasioning any high degree of inconveniency.   The other property of our nature, to which we are still more beholden, is its constant endeavour to restore itself, when disordered, to its regular course.   The fluids of the body appear to possess a power of separating and expelling any noxious substance which may have mixed itself with them.   This they do in eruptive fevers, by a kind of despumation, as Sydenham calls it, analogous in some measure to the intestine action by which fermenting liquors work the yeast to the surface The solids, on their part, when their action is obstructed, not only resume that action, as soon as the obstruction is removed, but they struggle with the impediment.   They take an action as near to the true one, as the difficulty and the disorganization, with which they have to contend, will allow of.

Of *mortal* diseases, the great use is to reconcile us to death.   The horror of death proves the value of life.   But it is in the power of disease to abate, or even extinguish, this horror; which it does in a wonderful manner, and oftentimes by a mild and imperceptible gradation.   Every man who has been placed in a situation to observe it, is surprised with the change which has been wrought in himself, when he compares the view which he entertains of death upon a sick-bed, with the heart-sinking dismay with which he should some time ago have met it in health There is no similitude between the sensations of a man ed to execution, and the calm expiring of a patient at the close of his disease. Death to him is only the last of a long train of changes; in his progress through which, it is possible that he may experience no shocks or sudden tran-sitions.

Death itself, as a mode of removal and of succession, is so connected with the whole order of our animal world, that almost everything in that world must be changed, to be able to do without it. It may seem likewise impossible to separate the fear of death from the enjoyment of life, or the perception of that fear from rational natures. Brutes are, in a great measure, delivered from all anxiety on this account by the inferiority of their faculties; or rather, they seem to be armed with the apprehension of death just suf-iciently to put them upon the means of preservation, and no farther. But would a human being wish to purchase this immunity, at the expense of those mental powers which enable him to look forward to the future?

Death implies *separation:* and the loss of those whom we love must necessarily be accompanied with pain. To the brute creation, nature seems to have stepped in with some secret provision for their relief, under the rupture of their attachments. In their instincts towards their off-spring, and of their offspring to them, I have often been surprised to observe how ardently they love, and how soon they forget. The pertinacity of human sorrow (upon which, time also, at length, lays its softening hand) is probably, therefore, in some manner connected with the qualities of our rational or moral nature. One thing how-ever is clear, viz. that it is better that we should possess affections, the sources of so many virtues and so many joys, although they be exposed to the incidents of life, as well as the interruptions of mortality, than, by the want of them, be reduced to a state of selfishness, apathy, and quietism.

Of other external evils, (still confining ourselves to what are called physical or natural evils,) a considerable part come within the scope of the following observation: The great principle of human satisfaction is *engagement* It is a most just distinction, which the late Mr. Tucker has dwelt upon so largely in his works, between pleasures in which we are passive, and pleasures in which we are ac-tive. And, I believe, every attentive observer of human life will assent to his position, that however grateful the sensations may occasionally be in which we are passive, it is not these, but the latter class of our pleasures, which constitute satisfaction; which supply that regular stream of moderate and miscellaneous enjoyments, in which happiness, as distinguished from voluptuousness, consists. Now for rational occupation, which is, in other words, for the very material of contented existence, there would be no place left, if either the things with which we had to do were absolutely impracticable to our endeavours, or if they were too obedient to our uses. A world, furnished with advantages on one side, and beset with difficulties, wants, and inconveniencies on the other, is the proper abode of free, rational, and active natures, being the fittest to stimulate and exercise their faculties. The very *refractoriness* of the objects they have to deal with, contributes to this purpose. A world in which nothing depended upon ourselves, however it might have suited an imaginary race of beings, would not have suited mankind. Their skill, prudence, industry; their various arts, and their best attainments, from the application of which they draw, if not their highest, their most permanent gratifications, would be insignificant, if things could be either moulded by our volitions, or, of their own accord, conformed themselves to our views and wishes. Now it is in this refractoriness that we discern the seed and principle of *physical* evil, as far as i arises from that which is external to us.

Civil evils, or the evils of civil life, are much more easily disposed of than physical evils; because they are, in truth, of much less magnitude, and also because they result, by a kind of necessity, not only from the constitution of our nature, but from a part of that constitution which no one would wish to see altered. The case is this: Mankind will in every country *breed up* to a certain point of distress. That point may be different in different countries or ages according to the established usages of life in each. It will also shift upon the scale, so as to admit of a greater or less number of inhabitants, according as the quantity of provision, which is either produced in the country, or supplied to it from other countries, may happen to vary. But there must always be such a point, and the species will always breed up to it. The order of generation proceeds by something like a geometrical progression. The increase of provision, under circumstances even the most advantageous, can only assume the form of an arithmetic series. Whence it follows, that the population will always overtake the provision, will pass beyond the line of plenty, and will continue to increase till checked by the difficulty of procuring subsistence.* Such difficulty therefore, along with its attendant circumstances, must be found in every old country: and these circumstances constitute what we call poverty, which necessarily imposes labor, servitude, restraint.

It seems impossible to people a country with inhabitants who shall be all in easy circumstances. For suppose the thing to be done, there would be such marrying and giving in marriage amongst them, as would in a few years change the face of affairs entirely; i. e. as would increase the consumption of those articles, which supplied the natural or habitual wants of the country, to such a degree of scarcity, as must leave the greatest part of the inhabitants unable to procure them without toilsome endeavours, or, out of the different kinds of these articles, to procure any kind except that which was most easily produced. And this, in fact, describes the condition of the mass of the community in all countries; a condition unavoidably, as it should seem, resulting from the provision which is made in the human, in common with all animal constitutions, for the perpetuity and multiplication of the species.

It need not however dishearten any endeavours for the public service, to know that population naturally treads upon the heels of improvement. If the condition of a people be meliorated, the consequence will be, either that the mean happiness will be increased, or a greater number partake of it; or, which is most likely to happen, that both effects will take place together. There may be limits fixed by nature to both; but they are limits, not yet attained, nor even approached, in any country of the world.

And when we speak of limits at all, we have respect only to provisions for animal wants. There are sources, and means, and auxiliaries, and augmentations of human happiness, communicable without restriction of numbers; as capable of being possessed by a thousand persons as by one. Such are those which flow from a mild, contrasted with a tyrannic government, whether civil or domestic; those which spring from religion; those which grow out of a sense of security; those which depend upon habits of virtue, sobriety, moderation, order; those, lastly, which are found in the possession of well-directed tastes and desires, compared with the dominion of tormenting, pernicious, contradictory, unsatisfied, and unsatisfiable passions

*See ‖ of this subject, in a late treatise upon population.

Z

The *distinctions* of civil life are ap enough to be re garded as evils, by those who sit under them: but, in my opinion, with very little reason.

In the first place, the advantages which the higher con ditions of life are supposed to confer, bear no proportion in value to the advantages which are bestowed by nature The gifts of nature always surpass the gifts of fortune How much, for example, is activity better than attendance; beauty than dress; appetite, digestion, and tranquil bowe.s, than all the studies of cookery, or than the most costly compilation of forced or far-fetched dainties?

Nature has a strong tendency to equalisation. Habit. the instrument of nature, is a great leveller; the familiari- ty which it induces, taking off the edge both of our plea- sures and our sufferings. Indulgencies which are habitual keep us in ease, and cannot be carried much farther. So that, with respect to the gratifications of which the senses are capable, the difference is by no means proportionable to the apparatus. Nay, so far as superfluity generates fastidiousness, the difference is on the wrong side.

It is not necessary to contend, that the advantages de- rived from wealth are none, (under due regulations they are certainly considerable,) but that they are not greater than they ought to be. *Money* is the sweetener of human toil, the substitute for coercion, the reconciler of labor with liberty. It is, moreover, the stimulant of enterprise in all projects and undertakings, as well as of diligence in the most beneficial arts and employments. Now did afflu- ence, when possessed, contribute nothing to happiness, or nothing beyond the mere supply of necessaries; and the secret should come to be discovered; we might be in dan- ger of losing great part of the uses which are at present derived to us through this important medium. Not only would the tranquillity of social life be put in peril by the want of a motive to attach men to their private concerns; but the satisfaction which all men receive from success in their respective occupations, which collectively constitutes the great mass of human comfort, would be done away in its very principle.

With respect to *station*, as it is distinguished from rich- es, whether it confer authority over others, or be invested with honors which apply solely to sentiment and imagina- tion, the truth is, that what is gained by rising through the ranks of life, is not more than sufficient to draw forth the exertions of those who are engaged in the pursuits which lead to advancement, and which in general are such as ought to be encouraged. Distinctions of this sort are subjects much more of competition than of enjoyment: and in that competition their use consists. It is not, as hath been rightly observed, by what the *Lord Mayor* feels in his coach, but by what the *apprentice* feels who gazes at him, that the public is served.

As we approach the summits of human greatness, the comparison of good and evil, with respect to personal comfort, becomes still more problematical; even allowing to ambition all its pleasures. The poet asks, "What is grandeur, what is power?" The philosopher answers, " Constraint and plague: et in maximâ quâque fortuna minimum licere." One very common error misleads the opinion of mankind upon this head, viz. that universally, authority is pleasant, submission painful. In the general course of human affairs, the very reverse of this is nearer to the truth Command is anxiety, obedience ease.

Artificial distinctions sometimes promote real equality. Whether they be hereditary, or be the homage paid to office, or the respect attached by public opinion to particular professions, they serve to *confront* that grand and unavoidable distinction which arises from property, and which is most overbearing where there is no other. It is of the nature of property, not only to be irregularly distributed, but to run into large masses. Public laws should be so constructed as to favor its diffusion as much as they can. But all that can be done by laws consistently with that degree of government of his property which ought to be left to the subject, will not be sufficient to counteract this tendency. There must always therefore be the difference between rich and poor; and this difference will be the more grinding, when no pretension is allowed to be set up against it.

So that the evils, if evils they must be called, which spring either from the necessary subordinations of civil life, or from the distinctions which have, naturally, though not necessarily, grown up in most societies, so long as they are unaccompanied by privileges injurious or oppressive to the rest of the community, are such as may, even by the most depressed ranks, be endured with very little prejudice to their comfort.

The mischiefs of which mankind are the occasion to one another, by their private wickednesses and cruelties; by tyrannical exercises of power; by rebellions against just authority; by wars, by national jealousies and competitions operating to the destruction of their countries, or by other instances of misconduct either in individuals or societies, are all to be resolved into the character of man as a *free agent*. Free agency in its very essence contains liability to abuse. Yet, if you deprive man of his free agency, you subvert his nature. You may have order from him and regularity, as you may from the tides or the trade-winds, but you put an end to his moral character, to virtue, to merit, to accountableness, to the use indeed of reason. To which must be added the observation, that even the bad qualities of mankind have an origin in their good ones. The case is this: human passions are either necessary to human welfare, or capable of being made, and, in a great majority of instances, in fact made, conducive to its happiness. These passions are strong and general; and perhaps would not answer their purpose unless they were so. But strength and generality, when it is expedient that particular circumstances should be respected, become, if left to themselves, excess and misdirection. From which excess and misdirection, the vices of mankind (the causes no doubt of much misery) appear to spring. This account, whilst it shows us the principle of vice, shows us, at the same time, the province of reason and of self-government; the want also of every support which can be procured to either from the aids of religion; and it shows this, without having recourse to any native gratuitous malignity in the human constitution. Mr. Hume, in his posthumous dialogues, asserts indeed of *idleness*, or aversion to labor (which he states to lie at the root of a considerable part of the evils which mankind suffer,) that it is simply and merely bad. But how does he distinguish idleness from the love of ease? or is he sure, that the love of ease in individuals is not the chief foundation of social tranquillity? It will be found, I believe, to be true, that in every community there is a large class of its members, whose idleness is the best quality about them, being the corrective of other bad ones. If it were possible, in every instance, to give a right determination to industry, we could never have too much of it. But this is not possible, if men are to be free. And without this, nothing would be so dangerous as an incessant, universal, indefatigable activity. In the civil world, as well as in the material, it is the *vis inertiæ* which keeps things in their places.

NATURAL THEOLOGY has ever been pressed with this question: Why, under the regency of a supreme and benevolent Will, should there be, in the world, so much as there is of the appearance of *chance?*

The question in its whole compass lies beyond our reach: but there are not wanting, as in the origin of evil, answers which seem to have considerable weight in particular cases, and also to embrace a considerable number of cases.

I. There must be *chance* in the midst of design: by which we mean, that events which are not designed, necessarily arise from the pursuit of events which are designed. One man travelling to York, meets another man travelling to London. Their meeting is by chance, is accidental, and so would be called and reckoned, though the journeys which produced the meeting were, both of them, undertaken with design and from deliberation. The meeting, though accidental, was nevertheless hypothetically necessary, (which is the only sort of necessity that is intelligible:) for, if the two journeys were commenced at the time, pursued in the direction, and with the speed, in which and with which they were in fact begun and performed, the meeting could not be avoided. There was not, therefore, the less necessity in it for its being by chance Again, the rencounter might be most unfortunate, though the errands, upon which each party set out upon his journey, were the most innocent or the most laudable. The by effect may be unfavorable, without impeachment of the proper purpose, for the sake of which the train, from the operation of which these consequences ensued, was put in motion. Although no cause acts without a good purpose, accidental consequences, like these, may be either good or bad.

II. The *appearance of chance* will always bear a proportion to the ignorance of the observer. The cast of a die as regularly follows the laws of motion, as the going of a watch; yet, because we can trace the operation of those laws through the works and movements of the watch, and cannot trace them in the shaking and throwing of the die, (though the laws be the same, and prevail equally in both cases,) we call the turning up of the number of the die chance, the pointing of the index of the watch machinery, order, or by some name which excludes chance. It is the same in those events which depend upon the will of a free and rational agent. The verdict of a jury, the sentence of

z*

a judge, the resolution of an assembly, the issue of a con
tested election, will have more or less of the appearance
of chance, might be more or less the subject of a wager,
according as we were less or more acquainted with the
reasons which influenced the deliberation. The difference resides in the information of the observer, and not
in the thing itself; which, in all the cases proposed,
proceeds from intelligence, from mind, from counsel, from
design.

Now when this one cause of the appearance of chance,
viz. the ignorance of the observer, comes to be applied to
the operations of the Deity, it is easy to foresee how fruitful it must prove of difficulties, and of seeming confusion.
It is only to think of the Deity, to perceive, what variety
of objects, what distance of time, what extent of space
and action, his counsels may, or rather must, comprehend.
Can it be wondered at, that, of the purposes which dwell in
such a mind as this, so small a part should be known to
us? It is only necessary, therefore, to bear in our thought,
that in proportion to the inadequateness of our information,
will be the quantity, in the world, of apparent chance.

III. In a great variety of cases, and of cases comprehending numerous subdivisions, it appears, for many reasons, to be better that events rise up by *chance*, or, more
properly speaking, with the appearance of chance, than according to any observable rule whatever. This is not seldom the case even in human arrangements. Each person's
place and precendency in a public meeting, may be determined by *lot*. Work and labor may be *allotted*. Tasks
and burdens may be *allotted*:—

———Operumque laborem
Partibus æquabat justis, aut *sorte* trahebat.

Military service and station may be *allotted*. The distribution of provision may be made by *lot*, as it is in a sail-
or's mess; n some cases also, the distribution of favors
may be made by *lot*. In all these cases, it seems to be acknowledged, that there are advantages in permitting events
to chance, superior to those which would or could arise
from regulation. In all these cases, also, though events
rise up in the way of chance, it is by appointment that they
do so.

In other events, and such as are independent of human
will, the reasons for this preference of uncertainty to rule,
appear to be still stronger. For example, it seems to be
expedient that the period of human life should be *uncertain*

Did mortality follow any fixed rule, it would produce a security in those that were at a distance from it, which would lead to the greatest disorders; and a horror in those who approached it, similar to that which a condemned prisoner feels on the night before his execution. But, that death be uncertain, the young must sometimes die, as well as the old. Als , were deaths never *sudden*, they who are in health would be too confident of life. The strong and the active, who want most to be warned and checked, would live without apprehension or restraint. On the other hand, were sudden deaths very frequent, the sense of constant jeopardy would interfere too much with the degree of ease and enjoyment intended for us; and human life be too precarious for the business and interests which belong to it. There could not be dependence either upon our own lives, or the lives of those with whom we are connected, sufficient to carry on the regular offices of human society. The manner, therefore, in which death is made to occur, conduces to the purposes of admonition, without overthrowing the necessary stability of human affairs.

Disease being the forerunner of death, there is the same reason for its attacks coming upon us under the appearance of chance, as there is for uncertainty in the time of death itself.

The *seasons* are a mixture of regularity and chance. They are regular enough to authorise expectation, whilst their being in a considerable degree irregular, induces, on the part of the cultivators of the soil, a necessity for personal attendance, for activity, vigilance, precaution. It is this necessity which creates farmers; which divides the profit of the soil between the owner and the occupier; which, by requiring expedients, by increasing employment, and by rewarding expenditure, promotes agricultural arts and agricultural life, of all modes of life the best, being the most conducive to health, to virtue, to enjoyment. I believe it to be found in fact, that where the soil is the most fruitful, and the seasons the most constant, there the condition of the cultivators of the earth is the most depressed. Uncertainty, therefore, has its use, even to those who sometimes complain of it the most. Seasons of scarcity themselves are not without their advantages. They call forth new exertions; they set contrivance and ingenuity at work; they give birth to improvements in agriculture and economy; they promote the investigation and management of public resources

Again; there are strong intelligible reasons, why there should exist in human society great disparity of *wealth* and *station;* not only as these things are acquired in different degrees, but at the first setting out of life.   In order for instance, to answer the various demands of civil life, there ought to be amongst the members of every civil society a diversity of education, which can only belong to an original diversity of circumstances.   As this sort of disparity, which ought to take place from the beginning of life, must, *ex hypothesi,* be previous to the merit or demerit of the persons upon whom it falls, can it be better disposed of than by chance?   *Parentage* is that sort of chance: yet it is the commanding circumstance which in general fixes each man's place in civil life, along with everything which appertains to its distinctions.   It may be the result of a beneficial rule that the fortunes or honors of the father devolve upon the son; and, as it should seem, of a still more necessary rule, that the low or laborious condition of the parent be communicated to his family; but with respect to the successor himself, it is the drawing of a ticket in a lottery.   Inequalities therefore of fortune, at least the greatest part of them, viz. those which attend us from our birth, and depend upon our birth, may be left, as they are left, to *chance,* without any just cause for questioning the regency of a supreme Disposer of events.

But not only the donation, when by the necessity of the case they must be gifts, but even the *acquirability* of civil advantages, ought perhaps, in a considerable degree, to lie at the mercy of chance.   Some would have all the virtuous rich, or at least removed from the evils of poverty, without perceiving, I suppose, the consequence, that all the poor must be wicked.   And how such a society could be kept in subjection to government, has not been shown; for the poor, that is, they who seek their subsistence by constant manual labor, must still form the mass of the community; otherwise the necessary labor of life could not be carried on; the work would not be done, which the wants of mankind, in a state of civilisation, and still more in a state of refinement, require to be done.

It appears to be also true, that the exigencies of social life call not only for an original diversity of *external* circumstances, but for a mixture of different faculties, tastes, and tempers.   Activity and contemplation, restlessness and quiet, courage and timidity, ambition and contentedness, not to say even indolence and dulness, are all wanted in the world, all conduce to the well going on of human affairs, just as the rudder, the sails, and the ballast of a ship, all perform their part in the navigation. Now, since these characters require for their foundation different original talents, different dispositions, perhaps also different bodily constitutions; and since, likewise, it is apparently expedient, that they be promiscuously scattered amongst the different classes of society; can the distribution of talents, dispositions, and the constitutions upon which they depend be better made than by *chance?*

The *opposites* of apparent chance are, constancy and sensible interposition; every degree of *secret* direction being consistent with it. Now, of *constancy*, or of fixed and known rules, we have seen in some cases the inapplicability; and inconveniences which we do not see, might attend their application in other cases.

Of *sensible* interposition we may be permitted to remark, that a Providence, always and certainly distinguishable, would be neither more nor less than miracles rendered frequent and common. It is difficult to judge of the state into which this would throw us. It is enough to say, that it would cast us upon a quite different dispensation from that under which we live. It would be a total and radical change. And the change would deeply affect, or perhaps subvert, the whole conduct of human affairs. I can readily believe, that, other circumstances being adapted to it, such a state might be better than our present state. It may be the state of other beings; it may be ours hereafter. But the question with which we are now concerned is, how far it would be consistent with our condition, supposing it in other respects to remain as it is? And in this question there seems to be reasons of great moment on the negative side. For instance; so long as bodily labor continues, on so many accounts, to be necessary for the bulk of mankind, any dependency upon supernatural aid, by unfixing those motives which promote exertion, or by relaxing those habits which engender patient industry, might introduce negligence, inactivity, and disorder, into the most useful occupations of human life; and thereby deteriorate the condition of human life itself.

As moral agents, we should experience a still greater alteration; of which more will be said under the next article.

Although therefore the Deity, who possesses the power of winding and turning, as he pleases, the course of causes which issue from himself, do in fact interpose to alter or intercept effects, which without such interposition would have taken place; yet it is by no means incredible, that his Providence, which always rests upon final good, may have made a *reserve* with respect to the manifestation of his interference, a part of the very plan which he has appointed for our terrestrial existence, and a part conformable with, or in some sort required by, other parts of the same plan. It is at any rate evident, that a large and ample province remains for the exercise of Providence, without its being naturally perceptible by us; because obscurity, when applied to the interruption of laws, bears a necessary proportion to the imperfection of our knowledge when applied to the laws themselves, or rather to the effects which these laws, under their various and incalculable combinations, would of their own accord produce. And if it be said, that the doctrine of Divine Providence, by reason of the ambiguity under which its exertions present themselves, can be attended with no *practical* influence upon our conduct; that, although we believe ever so firmly that there is a Providence, we must prepare, and provide, and act, as if there were none; I answer that this is admitted; and that we farther allege, that so to prepare, and so to provide, is consistent with the most perfect assurance of the reality of a Providence: and not only so, but that it is probably, one advantage of the present state of our information, that our provisions and preparations are not disturbed by it. Or if it be still asked, of what use at all then is the doctrine, if it neither alter our measures nor regulate our conduct? I answer again, that it is of the greatest use, but that it is a doctrine of sentiment and piety, not (immediately at least) of action or conduct; that it applies to the consolation of men's minds, to their devotions, to the excitement of gratitude, the support of patience, the keeping alive and the strengthening of every motive for endeavouring to please our Maker; and that these are great uses.

OF ALL VIEWS under which human life has ever been considered, the most reasonable, in my judgment, is that which regards it as a state of *probation*. If the course of the world were separated from the contrivances of nature, I do not know that it would be necessary to look for any other account of it than what, if it may be called an account, is contained in the answer, that events rise up by chance. But since the contrivances of nature decidedly evince *intention*; and since the course of the world and the contrivan ces of nature have the same author; we are, by the force of this connexion, led to believe, that the appearance under which events take place, is reconcilable with the supposition of design on the part of the Deity. It is enough that they be reconcilable with this supposition, and it is undoubtedly true, that they may be reconcilable, though we cannot reconcile them. The mind, however, which contemplates the works of nature, and in those works sees so much of means directed to ends, of beneficial effects brought about by wise expedients, of concerted trains of causes terminating in the happiest results; so much, in a word, of counsel, intention, and benevolence; a mind, I say, drawn into the habit of thought which these observations excite, can hardly turn its view to the condition of our own species, without endeavouring to suggest to itself some purpose, some design, for which the state in which we are placed is fitted, and which it is made to serve. Now we assert the most probable supposition to be, that it is a state of moral probation; and that many things in it suit with this hypothesis, which suit no other. It is not a state of unmixed happiness, or of happiness simply: it is not a state of designed misery, or of misery simply: it is not a state of retribution: it is not a state of punishment. It suits with none of these suppositions. It accords much better with the idea of its being a condition calculated for the production, exercise, and improvement of moral qualities, with a view to a future state, in which these qualities, after being so produced, exercised, and improved, may, by a new and more favoring constitution of things, receive their reward, or become their own. If it be said, that this is to enter upon a religious rather than a philosophical consideration, I answer, that the name of religion ought to form no objection, if it shall turn out to be the case, that the more religious our views are, the more probability they contain The degree of beneficence, of benevolent intention, and of power, exercised in the construction of sensitive beings, goes strongly in favor, not only of a creative, but of a continuing care, that is, of a ruling Providence. The degree of chance which appears to prevail in the world, requires to be reconciled with this hypothesis. Now it is one thing to maintain the doctrine of Providence along with that of a future state, and another thing without it. In my opinion, the two doctrines must stand or fall together. For although more of this apparent chance may perhaps upon other principles, be accounted for, than is generally supposed, yet

a future state alone rectifies all disorders: and if it can be
shown, that the appearance of disorder is consistent with
ne uses of life as a *preparatory* state, or that in some respects it promotes these uses, then, so far as this hypothesis may be accepted, the ground of the difficulty is done
away.

In the wide scale of human condition, there is not per-
.aps one of its manifold diversities which does not bear
upo the design here suggested. Virtue is infinitely various   There is no situation in which a rational being is
placed, from that of the best instructed Christian down to
the condition of the rudest barbarian, which affords not
room for moral agency; for the acquisition, exercise, and
display of voluntary qualities, good and bad.   Health and
sickness, enjoyment and suffering, riches and poverty,
knowledge and ignorance, power and subjection, liberty
and bondage, civilisation and barbarity, have all their offices and duties, all serve for the *formation* of character: for
when we speak of a state of trial, it must be remembered
that characters are not only tried, or proved, or detected
but that they are generated also, and *formed* by circumstan
ces.   The best dispositions may subsist under the most depressed, the most afflicted fortunes.   A West Indian slave,
who, amidst his wrongs, retains his benevolence, I, for my
part, look upon, as amongst the foremost of human candi-
dates for the rewards of virtue.   The kind master of such
a slave, that is, he who, in the exercise of an inordinate
authority, postpones in any degree his own interest to his
slaves' comfort, is likewise a meritorious character: but
still he is inferior to his slave.   All however which I con
.end for is, that these destinies, opposite as they may be
in every other view, are both *trials*; and equally such.
The observation may be applied to every other condition;
to the whole range of the scale, not excepting even its
lowest extremity.   *Savages* appear to us all alike; but it
is owing to the distance at which we view savage life, that
we perceive in it no discrimination of character.   I make
no doubt, but that moral qualities, both good and bad, are
called into action as much, and that they subsist in as
great a variety in these inartificial societies as they are, or
do, in polished life.   Certain at least it is, that the good
or ill treatment which each individual meets with, depends
more upon the choice and voluntary conduct of those about
him, than it does, or ought to do, under regular civil institutions, and the coercion of public laws.   So again, to turn

our eyes to the other end of the scale, namely, that part of it which is occupied by mankind enjoying the benefits of learning, together with the lights of revelation, there also, the advantage is all along *probationary.* Christianity itself, I mean the revelation of Christianity, is not only a blessing, but a trial. It is one of the diversified means by which the character is exercised: and they who require of Christianity, that the revelation of it should be universal, may possibly be found to require, that one species of probation should be adopted, if not to the exclusion of others, at least to the narrowing of that variety which the wisdom of the Deity hath appointed to this part of his moral economy.*

New if this supposition be well founded; that is, if it be true that our ultimate, or most permanent happiness will depend, not upon the temporary condition into which we are cast, but upon our behavior in it; then is it a much more fit subject of *chance* than we usually allow or apprehend it to be, in what manner the variety of external circumstances which subsist in the human world, is distributed amongst the individuals of the species. "This life being a state of probation, it is immaterial," says Rousseau, "what kind of trials we experience in it, provided they produce their effects." Of two agents who stand indifferent to the moral Governor of the universe, one may be exercised by riches, the other by poverty. The treatment of these two shall appear to be very opposite, whilst in truth it is the same: for though, in many respects, there be great disparity between the conditions assigned, in one main article there may be none, viz. in that they are alike trials; have both their duties and temptations, not less arduous or less dangerous in one case than the other; so that if the final award follow the character, the original distribution of the circumstances under which that character is formed, may be defended upon principles not only of justice but of equality. What hinders, therefore, but that mankind may draw lots for their condition? They take their

---

* The reader will observe, that I speak of the revelation of Christianity as distinct from Christianity itself. That *dispensation* may already be universal. That part of mankind which never heard of Christ's name, may nevertheless be redeemed, that is, be placed in a better condition, with respect to their future state, by his intervention; may be the objects of his benignity and intercession, as well as of the propitiatory virtue of his passion. But this is not " natural theology," therefore I will not dwell longer upon it.

portion of faculties and opportunities, as any unknown cause, or concourse of causes, or as causes acting for other purposes, may happen to set them out: but the event is governed by that which depends upon themselves, the application of what they have received. In dividing the talents, no rule was observed; none was necessary: In rewarding the use of them, that of the most correct justice. The chief difference at last appears to be, that the right use of more talents, *i. e.* of a greater trust, will be more highly rewarded, than the right use of fewer talents, *i. e.* of a less trust And since, for other purposes, it is expedient that there be an inequality of concredited talents here, as well, probably, as an inequality of conditions hereafter, though all remuneratory; can any rule, adapted to that inequality, be more agreeable, even to our apprehensions of distributive justice than this is?

We have said that the appearance of *casualty*, which attends the occurrences and events of life, not only does not interfere with its uses, as a state of probation, but that it promotes these uses.

Passive virtues, of all others the severest and the most sublime; of all others, perhaps, the most acceptable to the Deity; would, it is evident, be excluded from a constitution, in which happiness and misery regularly followed virtue and vice. Patience and composure under distress, affliction, and pain; a steadfast keeping up of our confidence in God, and of our reliance upon his final goodness, at the time when everything present is adverse and discouraging; and (what is no less difficult to retain) a cordial desire for the happiness of others, even when we are deprived of our own: these dispositions, which constitute, perhaps, the perfection of our moral nature, would not have found their proper office and object in a state of avowed retribution; and in which, consequently, endurance of evil would be only submission to punishment.

Again: One man's sufferings may be another man's trial. The family of a sick parent is a school of filial piety. The charities of domestic life, and not only these but all the social virtues, are called out by distress But then, misery, to be the proper object of mitigation, or of that benevolence which endeavours to relieve, must be really or apparently casual. It is upon such sufferings alone that benevolence can operate. For were there no evils in the world, but what were punishments, properly and intelligibly such, benevolence would only stand in the way of

,ustice. Such evils, consistently with the administration of moral government, could not be prevented or alleviated that is to say, could not be remitted in whole or in part except by the authority which inflicted them, or by an appellate or superior authority. This consideration, which is founded in our most acknowledged apprehensions of the nature of penal justice, may possess its weight in the Divine counsels. Virtue perhaps is the greatest of all ends. In human beings, relative virtues form a large part of the whole. Now relative virtue presupposes, not only the existence of evil, without which it could have no object, no material to work upon, but that evils be, apparently at least, *misfortunes;* that is, the effects of apparent chance. It may be in pursuance, therefore, and in furtherance of the same scheme of probation, that the evils of life are made *so* to present themselves.

I have already observed, that, when we let in religious considerations, we often let in light upon the difficulties of nature. So in the fact now to be accounted for, the *degree* of happiness which we usually enjoy in this life, may be better suited to a state of trial and probation, than a greater degree would be. The truth is, we are rather too much delighted with the world, than too little. Imperfect, broken, and precarious as our pleasures are, they are more than sufficient to attach us to the eager pursuit of them. A regard to a *future* state can hardly keep its place as it is. If we were designed, therefore, to be influenced by that regard, might not a more indulgent system, a higher, or more uninterrupted state of gratification, have interfered with the design? At least it seems expedient, that mankind should be susceptible of this influence, when presented to them. that the condition of the world should not be such as to exclude its operation, or even to weaken it more than it does. In a religious view (however we may complain of them in every other,) privation, disappointment, and satiety. are not without the most salutary tendencies.

C IAPTER XXVII.

CONCLUSION.

I.r all cases, wherein the mind feels itself in danger of being confounded by variety, it is sure to rest upon a few strong points, or perhaps upon a single instance. Amongst a multitude of proofs, it is *one* that does the business. If we observe in any argument, that hardly two minds fix upon the same instance, the diversity of choice shows the strength of the argument, because it shows the number and competition of the examples. There is no subject in which the tendency to dwell upon select or single topics is so usual, because there is no subject, of which, in its full extent, the latitude is so great, as that of natural history applied to the proof of an intelligent Creator. For my part, I take my stand in human anatomy; and the examples of mechanism I should be apt to draw out from the copious catalogue which it supplies, are the pivot upon which the head turns the ligament within the socket of the hip-joint, the pulley or trochlear muscles of the eye, the epiglottis, the bandages which tie down the tendons of the wrist and instep, the slit or perforated muscles at the hands and feet, the knitting of the intestines to the mesentery, the course of the chyle into the blood, and the constitution of the sexes as extended throughout the whole of the animal creation. To these instances the reader's memory will go back, as they are severally set forth in their places; there is not one of the number which I do not think decisive; not one which is not strictly mechanical; nor have I read or heard of any solution of these appearances, which, in the smallest degree, shakes the conclusion that we build upon them.

But, of the greatest part of those, who, either in this book or any other, read arguments to prove the existence of a God, it will be said, that they leave off only where they began; that they were never ignorant of this great truth, never doubted of it; that it does not, therefore, appear what is gained by researches from which no new opinion is learned, and upon the subject of which no proofs were wanted. Now I answer, that, by *investigation*, the following points are always gained, in favor of doctrines even the most generally acknowledged, (supposing them to be true,) viz. stability and impression. Occasions will arise to try the firmness of our most habitual opinions. And upon these occasions, it is a matter of incalculable use to feel our foundation; to find a support in argument for what we had taken up upon authority. In the present case, the arguments upon which the conclusion rests, are exactly such as a truth of universal concern ought to rest upon. "They are sufficiently open to the views and capacities of the unlearned, at the same time that they acquire new strength and lustre from the discoveries of the learned." If they had been altogether abstruse and recondite, they would not have found their way to the understandings of the mass of mankind; if they had been merely popular, they might have wanted solidity.

But, secondly, what is gained by research in the stability of our conclusion, is also gained from it in *impression*. Physicians tell us, that there is a great deal of difference between taking a medicine, and the medicine getting into the constitution. A difference not unlike which, obtains with respect to those great moral propositions, which ought to form the directing principles of human conduct. It is one thing to assent to a proposition of this sort; and another, and a very different thing, to have properly imbibed its influence. I take the case to be this: Perhaps almost every man living has a particular train of thought, into which his mind glides and falls, when at leisure from the impressions and ideas that occasionally excite it; perhaps, also, the train of thought here spoken of, more than any other thing, determines the character. It is of the utmost consequence, therefore, that this property of our constitution be well regulated. Now it is by frequent or continued meditation upon a subject, by placing a subject in different points of view, by induction of particulars, by variety of examples, by applying principles to the solution of phenomena, by dwelling upon proofs and consequences, that mental exercise is drawn into any particular channel. It is by these means, at least, that we have any power over it. The train of spontaneous thought, and the choice of that train, may be directed to different ends, and may appear to be more or less judiciously fixed, according to the purpose, in respect of which we consider it: but, in a *moral view*, I shall not, I believe, be contradicted when I say, that, if one train of thinking be more desirable than another, it is that which regards the phenomena of nature with a constant reference to a supreme intelligent Author. To have made this the ruling, the habitual sentiment of our minds, is to have laid the foundation of everything which is religious. The world thenceforth

Aa*

becomes a temple, and life itself one continued act of adoration.   The change is no less than this that whereas formerly God was seldom in our thoughts, we can now scarcely
look upon anything without perceiving its relation to him.
Every organized natural body, in the provisions which it
contains for its sustentation and propagation, testifies a
care, on the part of the Creator, expressly directed to these
purposes.   We are on all sides surrounded by such bodies,
examined in their parts, wonderfully curious; compared
with one another, no less wonderfully diversified.   So that
the mind, as well as the eye, may either expatiate in vari
ety and multitude, or fix itself down to the investigation
of particular divisions of the science.   And in either case
it will rise up from its occupation, possessed by the subject,
in a very different manner, and with a very different degree
of influence, from what a mere assent to any verbal proposition which can be formed concerning the existence of
the Deity, at least that merely complying assent with which
those about us are satisfied, and with which we are too
apt to satisfy ourselves, will or can produce upon the
thoughts.   More especially may this difference be perceived, in the degree of admiration and of awe with which
the Divinity is regarded, when represented to the understanding by its own remarks, its own reflections, and its
own reasonings, compared with what is excited by any
language that can be used by others.   The works of nature
want only to be contemplated.   When contemplated, they
have everything in them which can astonish by their greatness: for, of the vast scale of operation through which our
discoveries carry us, at one end we see an intelligent Power arranging planetary systems, fixing, for instance, the
trajectory of *Saturn*, or constructing a ring of two hundred
thousand miles diameter to surround his body, and be suspended like a magnificent arch over the heads of his inhabitants; and, at the other, bending a hooked tooth, con-
certing and providing an appropriate mechanism, for the
clasping and reclasping of the filaments of the feather of the
humming bird.   We have proof, not only of both these
works proceeding from an intelligent agent, but of their
proceeding from the same agent: for, in the first place, we
can trace an identity of plan, a connexion of system, from
Saturn to our own globe: and when arrived upon our globe,
we can, in the second place, pursue the connexion through
all the organized, especially the animated, bodies which it
supports.   We can observe marks of a common relation

as well to one another as to the elements of which their habitation is composed Therefore one mind hath planned or at least hath prescribed, a general plan for all these productions One Being has been concerned in all.

Under this stupendous Being we live. Our happiness, our existence, is in his hands. All we expect must come from him. Nor ought we to feel our situation insecure. In every nature, and in every portion of nature, which we can descry, we find attention bestowed upon even the minutest parts. The hinges in the wings of an *earwig*, and the joints of its antennæ, are as highly wrought, as if the Creator had nothing else to finish. We see no signs of diminution of care by multiplicity of objects, or of distraction of thought by variety. We have no reason to fear, therefore, our being forgotten, or overlooked, or neglected.

The existence and character of the Deity, is, in every view, the most interesting of all human speculations. In none, however, is it more so, than as it facilitates the belief of the fundamental articles of *Revelation.* It is a step to have it proved, that there must be something in the world more than what we see. It is a farther step to know, that amongst the invisible things of nature, there must be an intelligent mind, concerned in its production, order, and support. These points being assured to us by Natural Theology, we may well leave to Revelation the disclosure of many particulars, which our researches cannot reach, respecting either the nature of this Being as the original cause of all things, or his character and designs as a moral governor; and not only so, but the more full confirmation of other particulars, of which, though they do not lie altogether beyond our reasonings and our probabilities, the certainty is by no means equal to the importance. Tho true theist will be the first to listen to *any* credible communication of Divine knowledge. Nothing which he has learned from Natural Theology, will diminish his desire of farther instruction, or his disposition to receive it with humility and thankfulness. He wishes for light: he rejoices in light. His inward veneration of this great Being, will incline him to attend with the utmost seriousness, not only to all that can be discovered concerning him by researches into nature, but to all that is taught by a revelation, which gives reasonable proof of having proceeded from him.

But above every other article of revealed religion, does the anterior belief of a Deity bear with the strongest force upon that grand point, which gives indeed interest and importance to all the rest—the resurrection of the human dead. The thing might appear hopeless, did we not see a power at work adequate to the effect, a power under the guidance of an intelligent will, and a power penetrating the inmost recesses of all substance. I am far from justifying the opinion of those, who "thought it a thing incredible that God should raise the dead:" but I admit, that it is first necessary to be persuaded, that there *is* a God to do so. This being thoroughly settled in our minds, there seems to be nothing in this process (concealed and mysterious as we confess it to be) which need to shock our belief. They who have taken up the opinion, that the acts of the human mind depend upon *organization*, that the mind itself indeed consists in organization, are supposed to find a greater difficulty than others do, in admitting a transition by death to a new state of sentient existence, because the old organization is apparently dissolved. But I do not see that any impracticability need be apprehended even by these; or that the change, even upon their hypothesis, is far removed from the analogy of some other operations, which we know with certainty that the Deity is carrying on. In the ordinary derivation of plants and animals from one another, a particle, in many cases, minuter than all assignable, all conceivable dimension; an aura, an effluvium, an infinitesimal, determines the organization of a future body; does no less than fix, whether that which is about to be produced shall be a vegetable, a merely sentient, or a rational being; an oak, a frog, or a philosopher; makes all these differences, gives to the future body its qualities, and nature, and species. And this particle, from which springs, and by which is determined a whole future nature, itself proceeds from, and owes its constitution to, a prior body; nevertheless, which is seen in plants most decisively, the incepted organization, though formed within, and through, and by a preceding organization, is not corrupted by its corruption, or destroyed by its dissolution; but, on the contrary, is sometimes extricated and developed by those very causes survives and comes into action, when the purpose for which it was prepared requires its use. Now an economy which nature has adopted, when the purpose was to transfer an organization from one individual to another, may have something analogous to it, when the purpose is to transmit an organization from one state of being to another state: and they who found thought in organization, may see something in this analogy applicable to their difficulties, for, whatever can transmit a similariy of organization will answer their purpose, because, according even to their own theory, it may be the vehicle of consciousness; and because con sciousness carries identity and individuality along with it through all changes of form or of visible qualities. In the most general case, that, as we have said, of the derivation of plants and animals from one another, the latent organi zation is either itself similar to the old organization, or has the power of communicating to new matter the old organic form. But it is not restricted to this rule. There are other cases, especially in the progress of insect life, in which the dormant organization does not much resemble that which encloses it, and still less suits with the situation in which the enclosing body is placed, but suits with a different situation to which it is destined. In the larva of the libellula, which lives constantly, and has still long to live, under water, are descried the wings of a fly, which two years afterwards is to mount into the air. Is there nothing in this analogy?—It serves at least to show, that even in the observable course of nature, organizations are formed one beneath another; and, amongst a thousand other in stances, it shows completely, that the Deity can mould and fashion the parts of material nature, so as to fulfil any purpose whatever which he is pleased to appoint.

They who refer the operations of mind to a substance totally and essentially different from matter, (as most certainly these operations, though affected by material causes, hold very little affinity to any properties of matter with which we are acquainted,) adopt perhaps a juster reasoning and a better philosophy; and by these the considerations above suggested are not wanted, at least in the same de. gree. But to such as find, which some persons do find, an insuperable difficulty in shaking off an adherence to those analogies which the corporeal world is continually suggest- ing to their thoughts; to such, I say, every consideration will be a relief, which manifests the extent of that intelli- gent power which is acting in nature, the fruitfulness of its resources, the variety, and aptness, and success of its means; most especially every consideration which tei ds to show, that, in the translation of a conscious existence, there is no even in their own way of regarding it, any- thing greatly beyond, or totally unlike, what takes place

in such parts (probably small parts) of the order of nature
as are accessible to our observation.

Again; if there be those who think, that the contracted
ness and debility of the human faculties in our present
state, seem ill to accord with the high destinies which the
expectations of religion point out to us, I would only ask
them, whether any one, who saw a child two hours after its
birth, could suppose that it would ever come to understand
fluxions;* or who then shall say, what farther amplification
of intellectual powers, what accession of knowledge, what
advance and improvement, the rational faculty, be its constitution what it will, may not admit of, when placed amidst
new objects, and endowed with a sensorium adapted, as it
undoubtedly will be, and as our present senses are, to the
perception of those substances, and of those properties of
things, with which our concern may lie.

Upon the whole; in everything which respects this awful,
but, as we trust, glorious change, we have a wise and
powerful Being (the author, in nature, of infinitely various
expedients, for infinitely various ends) upon whom to rely
for the choice and appointment of means, adequate to the
execution of any plan which his goodness or his justice
may have formed, for the moral and accountable part of his
terrestrial creation.   That great office rests with *him:* be
it *ours* to hope and to prepare, under a firm and settled
persuasion, that, living and dying, we are his; that life is
passed in his constant presence, that death resigns us to
his merciful disposal.

* See Search's Light of Nature, passim.

VOCABULARY

A

Abdomen, the cavity of the belly.

Accretion, a growth; increase in size or extent

Adipose, fatty, containing fat

Alkalies, a peculiar class of chemical substances which have the property of combining with and neutralizing the properties of acids.

Anconæus, the name of one of the muscles which extend the elbow joint.

Anal, a term applied to one of the fins of fish, situated near the anus or vent.

Anhelation, breathing hard or panting.

Annular, in the form of a ring.

Annuli, rings—applied to the muscular fibres which surround the bodies of some animals like rings.

Antennae, organs of touch, situated near the mouths of insects having many joints.

Antherae, small bodies which contain the pollen or fertilizing dust of flowers ; the antherae are fixed generally on the ends of slender filaments, and surround the germ or seed vessel.

Aorta, the main artery of the body, which receives the blood directly from the heart and distributes it to the body.

Auricle, a cavity of the heart. Its external shape gives it the appearance of an appendage to the organ, and its name is derived from its supposed resemblance to an ear, (auricula.)

Automaton, a machine having a power of motion within itself, but destitute of life.

B.

Buccinator, the principal muscle of the cheek.

Biceps, one of the muscles which bend the elbow-joint.

Bivalve, consisting of two valves or shells, as in shell-fish—e g the oyster.

Brachiæus, the name of two muscles moving the arm.

Brevis, short.

C.

Calyx, the flower cup ; the external or outermost part of the flower, generally resembling the leaves in color, and containing the other parts of the flower within it. It is often wanting.

Camera obscura, or dark chamber. An optical instrument in which the rays of light from external objects are made to pass through a convex lens into a dark box where they are received upon a screen, and produce a representation of external objects.

Capsule, the seed vessel of plants.

Carnivorous, feeding or living on flesh.

Carotid, the name of the arteries which pass up the neck on each side of the windpipe, and convey the blood to the head.

Cartilaginous, gristly; formed from or consisting of gristle.

Cellular, consisting of cells.

Centripetal, having a tendency towards the centre. All bodies on the surface, have a tendency to fall towards the centre of the earth.

Cetaceous, of the whale kind.

Chrysalis, an insect in the second stage of its metamorphosis.

Cicatrix, a scar.

Comminuted, broken up into small pieces.

Conatus, attempt, endeavour, effort.

Condyles, prominences at the ends of some of the bones which are intended to afford surfaces for the formation of joints.

Congeries, a heap or pile of bodies accumulated together.

Connate, produced or being born together; having their origin at the same time, and from the same cause.

Convolution, the turning, rolling, or winding of anything. The convolutions of a snail's shell are the spiral windings of the tube in which it exists around a central pillar or basis.

Cornea, the transparent coat at the front part of the eye, through which we see the pupil and the iris.

Corolla. This term includes what are commonly called the leaves of the flower, viz. the various colored leaves which give their beauty and fragrance to most flowers.

Cretaceous, formed of, or consisting of chalk. It is applied not merely to substances consisting of chalk, commonly so called, but to a variety of others, which resemble it merely in having the same chemical composition, such as the shells of shell-fish, &c.

Cubital, an anatomical term used to designate parts in, and relating to the cubit or fore-arm, which extends from the elbow to the hand.

D.

Deglutition, the act of swallowing.

Diaphragm, a muscular membrane which is stretched completely across the cavity of the body like a curtain, and divides the chest from the belly, and by its contraction performs an important part in the act of respiration.

Dioptric, a term applied to that part of the science of optics which treats of the passage of light through, and its refraction by means of, transparent substances.

Dorsal, appertaining to the back.

Ductus arteriosus, a duct or canal leading from the pulmonary artaries to the aorta, by which the blood is before birth conveyed from the pulmonary arteries to the aorta without passing through the lungs. It is closed after birth.

Duodenum, the first of the small intestines, being the next in order to the stomach, and receiving the food from it.

E.

Elytra, the external, hard, scaly wings of many insects, such as the beetles.

Entomology, the science relating to insects.

Epiglottis, a valve which covers the passage from the mouth into the windpipe.

Eruca labra, the name of an insect.

Eustachian, applied to parts first discovered by Eustachius.

Exility, slenderness, smallness.

Exuviae, the cast off skins, shells, or other coverings of animals

Exsiccation, drying, parting with moisture to air or heat.

Evagation, wandering, deviation from an appointed course.

F.

Farina. This word is sometimes used instead of pollen for the fertili
zing dust produced from the stamens and anthers of flowers, and col
lected by bees. It is so used by our author.

Fibula, a small long bone, extending from the knee to the ankle-joint,
parallel to and connected with the tibia or principal bone of the leg or
its outside. The lower end of it forms the outer ankle.

Foramen ovale, or oval hole, an opening in the foetal state, between
the two ventricles of the heart, permitting the passage of blood from
one to the other. It is closed after birth.

Fusee, see Plate of the parts of the watch.

G.

Gallinaceous Birds of a particular order, living generally upon grains
or seeds of plants, of a stately aspect, and confined powers of flight.
Such are the common domestic fowl, the turkey, the peacock, &c.

Gestation, the art of carrying the young within the body of the parent,
whether in the state of the egg or of the living foetus.

Graminivorous, living or feeding upon grass.

Granivorous, living or feeding upon grains and seeds.

Gregarious, herding together—flocking together—assembling in herds
and companies.

H.

Halitus, the watery vapor which is thrown out from the lungs with the
air at every act of respiration.

Hemiplegia, a paralysis or palsy of one half of the body, consisting in a
loss of the sense of feeling, or of the power of voluntary motion; or of
both.

Herbivorous, living upon herbs, or rather upon vegetable substances in
general. A term used in contra-distinction to carnivorous.

Homologous, having the same relation or proportions. Lines drawn
through any two similar bodies of different sizes, are said to be homologous when they are drawn through corresponding parts of each.

Hybernacula, the habitations, coverings, or retreats in which animals
pass the winter. Animals when residing in them are generally in a
torpid state.

Hydrocanthari, a name of insects

I.

Ignited, a chemical term applied to a body raised to a high degree of
heat.

Inertia, a property of all matter which disposes it to remain in the state
in which it is, whether of motion or rest.

Iris, plural *Irides;* the colored ring surrounding the pupil of the eye.

L.

Lachrymal, appertaining to or relating to the tears, or to the apparatus
for their production.

Lacteals, capillary or hair-like vessels opening upon the internal surface of the intestines, absorbing the chyle or nutritious fluid prepared by the digestive organs from the food, and conveying it through the mesentery to the thoracic duct and thence into the circulating mass of the blood.

Lamella, a thin plate or edge.

Laminae, thin plates or layers.

Larynx, the upper part of the windpipe, including the organs of voice

Lens, a circular glass whose surfaces are either convex or concave. It is also applied to any other transparent body of the same shape, as ice, crystal, or diamond.

Levitation, the making an object lighter ; giving to it a buoyant tendency.

Longus, long. A name applied to several muscles of the body on account of their length when compared with other muscles.

Lubricity, facility of the slipping or gliding of one surface over another without friction, whether in consequence of the smoothness of the surfaces, or the interposition of some soft, slippery fluid, or substance.

Lubricate, to give lubricity.

Luxation, dislocation of a bone, throwing a bone out of joint.

Lymphatics, small vessels in the bodies of animals carrying lymph.

M.

Masseter, a strong muscle which closes the jaw in chewing, situated at the back part of the cheek towards the ear. It may be felt in chewing.

Mediastinum, a fold of the membrane lining the chest, by which it is divided into two cavities.

Medullary, formed or consisting of marrow. Applied to the substance of the brain and nerves, and to that in the cavities of some of the bones.

Menstruum, any liquid or fluid in which another body is dissolved.

Mesentery, a double fold of the membrane lining the abdomen and covering the intestines, by which the latter are suspended, and are connected to the walls of the cavity. It gives passage to vessels, nerves, and to the lacteals.

Monopetalous, applied to flowers consisting of a single petal or flower cup.

N.

Nectaria, that part of the corolla of plants which produces honey.

Nictitating, winking. Applied generally to the third eyelid of birds and some other animals.

Nigella, the name of a plant.

Nymphae, insects in the second preparatory state, before their final transformation.

O

Oblate. A sphere flattened at the poles is said to be oblate.

Oesophagus, the tube or canal which conveys food from the mouth to the stomach.

Omentum, the caul; a kind of apron formed of fat and membrane which hangs down and covers the intestines within the abdomen.

Os hyoides, the bone of the tongue and throat.

Os pubis, the bone which arches forward from the pelvis, and supports the lower part of the belly.

Ossification, a change of structure into bone.

Oviparous, bringing forth or bearing young by means of eggs.

P.

Palmated, having a palm like that of the hand.

Pancreas, a gland within the abdomen, just below the stomach, and providing a fluid to assist in digestion.

Papillae, little projections on the surface of organs, as on the tongue which are the seats of sensation.

Papilionaceous, of or resembling butterflies. Applied to a certain tribe of flowers on account of their resemblance in shape to those insects.

Pectoral, of or relating to the chest.

Pelvis, the broad flat basin, constituting the lower part of the abdomen, composed principally of the broad flat bones usually called the hip and haunch bones.

Peritonaeum, a membrane lining the cavity of the abdomen and giving a close covering to all its contents.

Peristaltic, applied to the crawling, worm-like motion of the intestines.

Pericardium, the bag containing the heart.

Pericarpium, a kind of seed vessels of plants.

Periosteum, the membrane which adheres to, and closely invests the surface of bones.

Petals, the flower leaves, or leaves of the corolla of plants.

Pharynx, the cavity at the back part of the mouth which receives the food just before swallowing, and transmits it to the oesophagus.

Phosphoric, of or resembling phosphorus.

Pistil, the part of a flower intended to receive the pollen or fertilizing dust of the stamens.

Piston, a movable cylinder in the tube of some machines, intended to take off by its motion the pressure of the air, or to receive the impulse from steam as in the pump and steam-engine.

Plantule, a little plant. Applied to the part which first sprouts from the seed when it begins to grow. It refers to the same part with *Plumule*.

Pleura, the membrane lining the chest.

Plumule, see plantule.

Pneumatic, of or relating to the air or wind.

Pollen, the fertilizing dust of flowers, produced by the stamens, and falling upon the pistils in order to render a flower capable of producing seed or fruit.

Primordial, original.

R.

Radicle, the little root which is first sent out by a seed when it begins to grow.

Refraction, generally applied to the change of direction which takes place when a ray of light moves from one medium into another of a different density.

Renitency, resistance.

Retina, a very sensible and delicate membrane at the back part of the eye, intended to receive the images of objects like the screen of a camera obscura. Supposed to be an expansion of the nerve of the eye.

Rictus, the extent of the mouth when opened widely as in gaping

S.

Sanguiferous, carrying blood.

Sensorium, the seat or centre of sensations, to which all the impressions made upon the external organs of sense are transmitted, and where they are perceived.

Spheroid, approaching in form to, or resembling a sphere.

Spiculae, spines or sharp projections.

Sternum, the breast bone.

Stigma, plural, *stigmata;* the extremity of the pistil of plants.

Storgee, the sentiment or instinct of parental affection.

Stum, an unfermented mass of liquor.

Subclavian, a term applied to parts which are situated beneath the clavi cle or collar bone as the subclavian artery, &c.

Sugescent, employed in sucking.

Sui generis, of a peculiar kind or character.

Sutures, the union of bones by their edges, without movable joints, as in the flat bones of the skull. The edges in this case are often notched like the teeth of a saw, and the line of union resembles a seam. Whence called a suture.

Synovia, the liquid which lubricates the internal surfaces of the joints to give facility of motion.

T.

Telum imbelle, a harmless weapon.

Thorax, the chest.

Tibia, the main bone of the leg, extending from the knee to the foot Its projecting extremity forms the inner ankle, and its ends enter into the formation of both the knee and ankle joints.

Trachea, the windpipe.

Tubercle, a swelling or prominence.

U.

Umbilical, proceeding from or relating to the navel or umbilicus.

Univalve, consisting of a single valve or shell, such as the snail, cockle.

Urachus, a vessel leading from the bladder to the navel before birth, which is converted into a ligament after birth.

Ureter, the tube conveying the urine from the kidneys to the bladder

V.

Vallisneria, the name of a plant.

Valvulae conniventes, folds formed by the internal membrane of the intestines, constituting partial valves, and intended to retard the passage of the food.

Vascular, containing or consisting of vessels.

Vena cava, one of the great veins which brings the blood from the extremities of the body to the heart.

Ventral, of or appertaining to the belly.

Ventricle, a term applied to several small internal cavities in the body, as the ventricles of the brain and of the heart.

Vertebrae, the separate bones constituting the back bone.

Viscus, plural *Viscera;* the internal organs of the body, as lungs, heart, stomach, liver, brain, &c.

Viviparous, producing or bringing forth young alive.

Vortex, plural *Vortices;* anything whirled round. The heavenly bodies have been formerly supposed to be carried around in their orbits by certain vortices or whirlpools which were imagined to exist.

PAXTON'S ILLUSTRATIONS,

WITH

DESCRIPTIONS.

INDEX TO THE PLATES.

CHAPTER 1.

PLATE 1. — THE WATCH.

Fig. 1. The *box*, or *barrel*, containing the main spring, which is the first power; and the *chain*, which communicates the power to—

Fig. 2. The *fusee* and *great* wheel. The fusee is tapered at the top to correct the irregular recoil of the spring. The great wheel turns—

Fig. 3. The *centre* wheel and pinion, which makes one revolution in an hour, carries the minute hand, and turns—

Fig. 4. The *third* wheel and pinion, which turns the contrite wheel.

Fig. 5. The *contrite* wheel, which makes one revolution in a minute, and turns the balance or escape wheel.

Fig. 6. The *balance* wheel, which acts upon the pallats of the verge, and escapes or drops from one pallat to another alternately, thereby keeping the balance in constant vibration.

Fig. 7. The *balance verge* and *balance* or *pendulum spring*, which regulates the whole machine.

Fig. 8. The *cannon pinion*, affixed to the centre wheel arbour, on which the minute hand is placed.

Fig. 9. The *minute* wheel.

Fig. 10. The *hour* wheel. The two last mentioned wheels are turned by the cannon pinion, and having a greater number of teeth, move much slower than the cannon pinion, and mark the hour by the hand on the dial.

The above is a description of the several wheels alluded to by Paley. Their relative situation, and combined movement, may be seen by the simple inspection of a watch.

PLATE I.

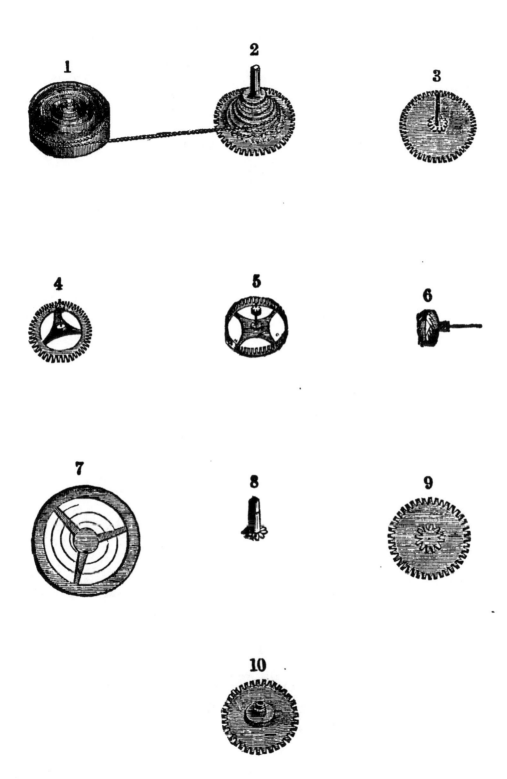

PLATE II.

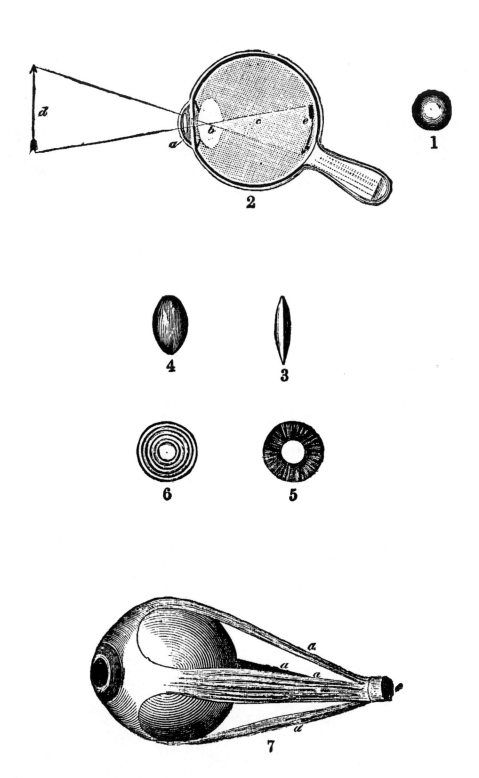

CHAPTER III.

PLATE II. — THE EYE.

FIG. 1. The *crystalline lens of a fish;* it is proportionably larger than in other animals, and perfectly spherical.

FIG. 2. A section of the human eye. It is formed of various *coats,* or membranes, containing pellucid humours of different degrees of density, and calculated for collecting the rays of light into a focus, upon the nerve situated at the bottom of the eye-ball.

The external membrane, called *sclerotic,* is strong and firm, and is the support of the spherical figure of the eye: it is deficient in the centre, but that part is supplied by the *cornea,* which is transparent and projects like the segment of a small globe from one of larger size. The interior of the sclerotic is lined by the *choroid,* which is covered by a dark mucous secretion, termed *pigmentum nigrum,* intended to absorb the superfluous rays of light. The *choroid* is represented in the plate by the black line. The third and inner membrane, which is marked by the white line, is the *retina,* the expanded optic nerve.

Within these coats of the eye, are the *humours.* *a,* the *aqueous* humour, a thin fluid like water; *b,* the *crystalline lens,* of a dense texture; *c,* the *vitreous* humour, a very delicate gelatinous substance, named from its resemblance to melted glass. Thus the crystalline is more dense than the vitreous, and the vitreous more dense than the aqueous humour: they are all perfectly transparent, and together make a compound lens, which refracts the rays of light issuing from an object, *d,* and delineates its figure *e,* in the focus upon the retina, inverted.

FIG. 3. The *lens of the telescope.*

FIG. 4. The crystalline *lens,* or, as it has been called, the crystalline *humour,* of the eye.

FIG. 5, 6. A plan of the circular and radiated fibres which the *iris* is supposed to possess; the former contracts, the latter dilates the pupil, or aperture formed by the inner margin of the iris.

FIG. 7. *a, a, a, a,* the four *straight* muscles, arising from the bottom of the orbit, where they surround, *c,* the optic nerve; and are inserted by broad, thin tendons at the fore part of the globe of the eye into the tunica sclerotica.

311

CHAPTER III.

PLATE III.—THE EYE OF BIRDS AND OF THE EEL.

FIG. 1, 2. The *flexible rim*, or *hoop*, of the eye of birds, consisting of bony plates, which occupy the front of the sclerotic; lying close together and overlapping each other. These bony plates in general form a slightly convex ring, Fig. 1, but in the *accipitres* they form a concave ring, as in Fig. 2, the bony rim of a hawk.

FIG. 3, 4, 6. Exhibit the *marsupium*; it arises from the back of the eye, proceeding apparently through a slit in the retina; it passes obliquely into the vitreous humour, and terminates in that part, as in the eagle. Fig. 3, a section of the eye of the falco chrysaetos. In some species it reaches the lens, and is attached to it as in Fig. 4, 6. In the plate the marsupium is marked with a *.

FIG. 5. The head of an *eel*; the skin is represented turned back; and as the *transparent, horny covering* of the eye, *a, a,* is a cuticular covering, it is separated with it. Other fish have a similar, insensible, dense, and thick adnata, which is designed to protect the eye; and it seems especially necessary, as fish have no eyelids.

312

PLATE III.

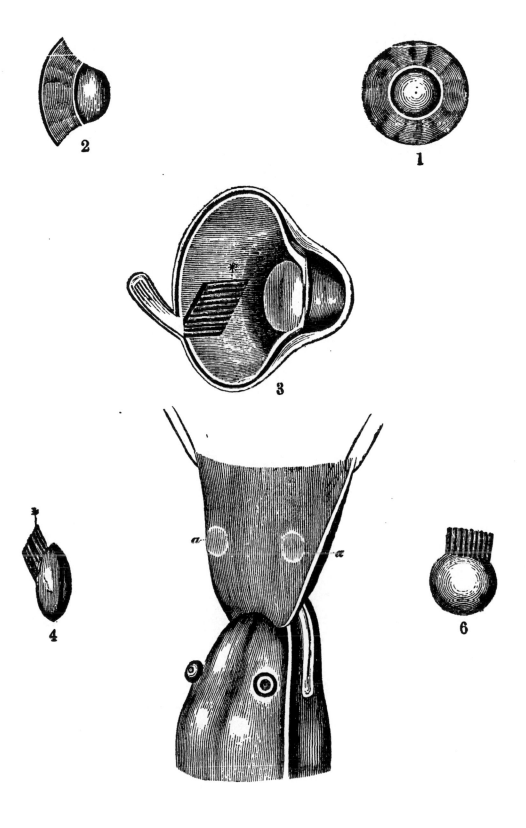

PLATE IV.

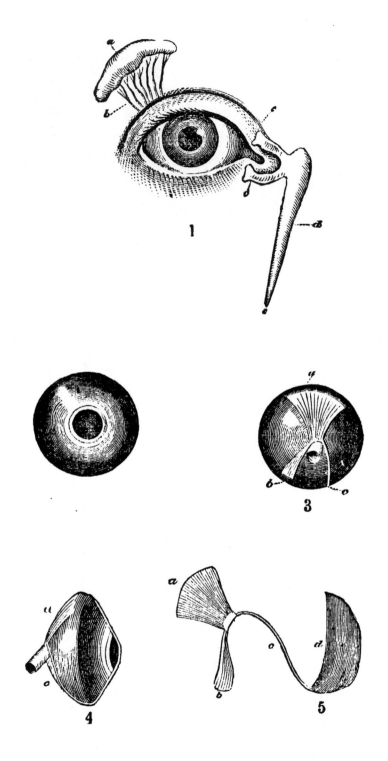

CHAPTER III.

PLATE IV.—THE LACHRYMAL APPARATUS AND NICTITATING MEMBRANE.

FIG. 1. *a*, is the organ which supplies this fluid, called the *lachry-nal gland*, it is situated at the outer and upper part of the orbit of the eye. This is the gland which secretes or separates the tears from the blood. There are five or six ducts or tubes, *b*, which convey this fluid to the globe of the eye, for the purpose of keeping it moist, and for facilitating its movements; the motion of the eyelid diffuses the tears, and *c, c*, the *puncta lachrymalia*, take up the superfluous moisture, which passes through *d*, the *lachrymal sac and duct* into the nostril at *e*.

FIG. 2. The *nictitating membrane*, or third eyelid; it is a thin semi-transparent fold of the conjunctive, which, in a state of rest, lies in the inner corner of the eye, with its loose edge nearly vertical, but can be drawn out so as to cover the whole front of the globe. In this figure it is represented in the act of being drawn over the eye. By means of this membrane, according to Cavier, the eagle is enabled to look at the sun.

FIG. 3. The two muscles of the nictitating membrane are very singular in their form and action; they are attached to the back of the sclerotica; one of them, *a*, which from its shape is called *quadratus*, has its origin from the upper and back part of the sclerotica; its fibres descend towards the optic nerve, and terminate in a curved margin with a cylindrical canal in it. The other muscle, *b*, which is called *pyramidalis*, arises from the lower and back part of the sclerotica. It has a long tendinous chord, *c*, which passes through the canal of the quadratus, *a*, as a pulley, and having arrived at the lower and exterior part of the eye-ball, is inserted into the loose edge of the nictitating membrane. This description refers also to Fig. 4, a profile of the eye, and Fig. 5, the membrane and its muscles detached from the eye.

CHAPTER III.

PLATE **V.**— THE HUMAN EAR, AND TYMPANUM OF THE ELEPHANT

FIG. 1. The organ of hearing; *a*, the *external ear* ; *b*, the *meatus auditorius externus*, or outward passage of the ear; leading to *c*, the *membrana tympani*, or drum ; *d*, the *ossicula auditus*, or little bones of the ear; *e*, the *semicircular canals* ; *f*, the *cochlea* ; *g*, a section of the *eustachian tube*, which extends from the cavity of the tympanum, to the back of the mouth or fauces.

FIG. 2. The bones of the ear magnified. *a*, the *malleus*, or mallet, connected by a process to the tympanum; the round head is lodged in the body of, *b*, the *incus*, or anvil, and the incus is united to, *c*, the *os orbiculare*, or round bone, and this to, *d*, the *stapes*, or the stirrup. These bones are named from their shape, and the names assist in conveying an idea of their form. They are united by ligaments, and form an uninterrupted chain to transmit the vibrations of the atmosphere.

FIG. 3. The *labyrinth*, so named from the intricacy of its cavities ; it is situated in the petrous part of the temporal bone, and consists of the *vestibule*, or *central cavity*, three *semicircular canals*, and *cochlea*, so named from its resemblance to the windings of a snail shell, and is best explained by the plate, Fig. 1, and 3.

The vibrations of sounds, striking against the membrana tympani, are propagated by the intervention of these four little bones, to the *water* contained within the cavities of the labyrinth; and by means of this water the impression is conveyed to the extremities of the *auditory nerve*, and finally to the brain.

Fish require no tympanum, nor external opening to the ear; the fluid in which they live is the medium for conducting sounds through the bones of the head.

FIG. 4. The tympanum of the *elephant*, of its natural size, showing its radiated fibres, supposed to be muscular.

318

PLATE V.

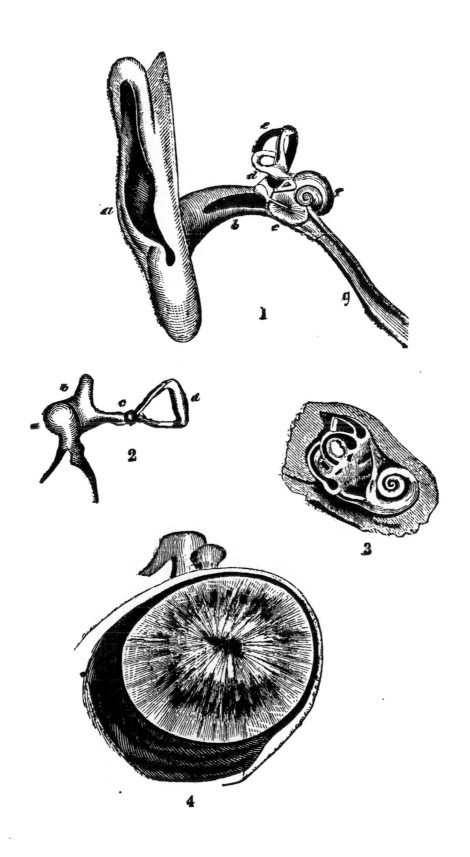

PLATE VI.

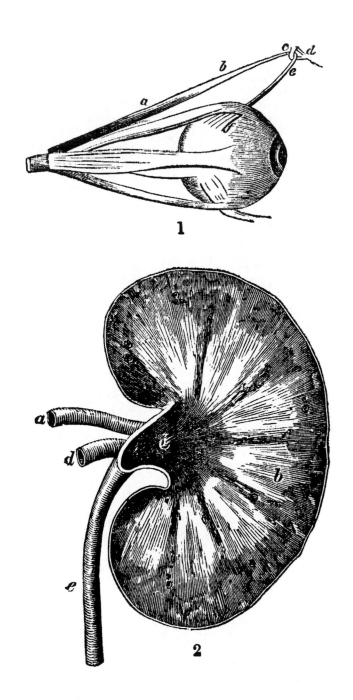

1

2

CHAPTER VII.

PLATE VI. - TROCHLEAR MUSCLE OF THE EYE, AND KIDNEY.

FIG. 1. The *trochlear* or *superior oblique* muscle, arises with the straight muscles from the bottom of the orbit. *Its* muscular portion, *a*, is extended over the upper part of the eye-ball, and gradually assumes the form of a smooth, round tendon *b*, which passes through the pulley, *c*, and is fixed to the inner edge of the orbit, *d*, then returning backwards and downwards, *e* is inserted into, *f*, the sclerotic membrane. The use of this muscle is to bring the eye forwards, and to turn the pupil downwards and upwards.

FIG. 2. A section of the *human kidney; a*, the *emulgent artery*, which conveys the blood to, *b*, the *papillæ*, where the peculiar fluid is secreted; from whence it passes by tubes into, *c*, the *pelvis; e*, the *ureter*, or tube, which conducts the secretion to its receptacle; *d*, the *emulgent vein*, for returning the blood, after it has been submitted to the action of the gland.

323

CHAPTER V II.

PLATE VII.—VERTEBRÆ OF THE HUMAN NECK.

Fig. 1. A representation of the head and the neck; the latter is composed of seven bones called *vertebræ*.

Fig. 2. Exhibits the first and second vertebræ, with their mode of connexion. The uppermost vertebra, termed the *atlas*, from its supporting the globe of the head, has an oval *concave* surface on either side, *a, a*, for the reception of two corresponding *convex* surfaces placed on the lower part of the head, in such a manner as only to admit of the action of bending and raising the head

Fig. 3. The *atlas*.

Fig. 4. The second vertebra, called *dentata*, has two plane sur faces, *a, a*, adapted to the planes, *a, a*, Fig. 3, of the atlas: and this manner of articulation provides for the turning of the head laterally in almost every direction. Fig. 2. and 4, *b, b*, show the *tooth-like process* which affords a firm pivot for the production of the lateral motion just described. This process is received into a corresponding *indentation* of the atlas, Fig. 3, *b*, and a strong ligament passes behind it, serving as an effectual security against dislocation, and consequent compression of the spinal marrow. Fig. 4, *d*, marks the situation for the spinal marrow, which passes through the ring of each vertebra. The letter, *c*, indicates a perforation in the lateral process; and, as there is a corresponding perforation in each lateral, or as it is termed, *transverse* process of the seven *cervical* vertebræ, a conti..uous passage is thus formed for the protection of two important blood-vessels destined to supply the brain.

324

PLATE VII.

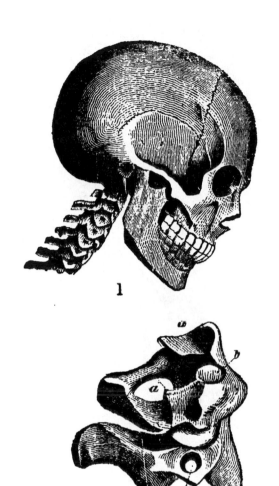

1

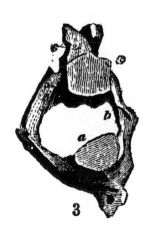

3

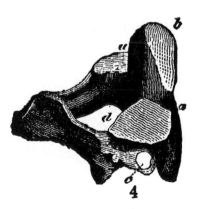

2

4

PLATE VIII.

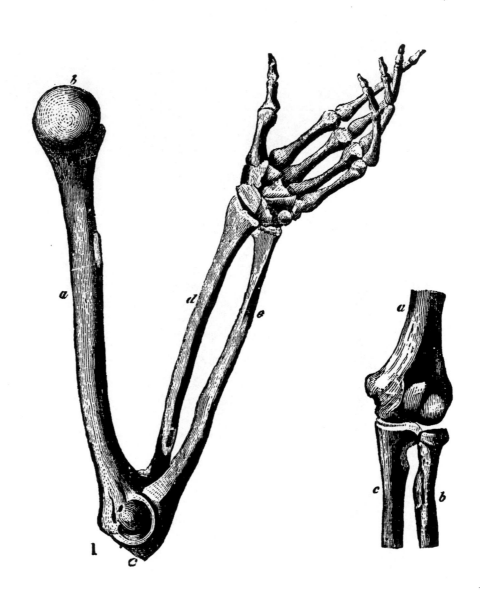

CHAPTER VIII.

PLATE VIII.—BONES OF THE ARM.

FIG. 1. *a*, the *humerus*; the head, *b*, is a portion of a sphere, and exhibits an example of the *ball and socket*, or universal joint; *c.* the *hinge-joint*, instanced in the elbow; *d*, the *radius*; *e*, the *ulna.* The radius belongs more peculiarly to the wrist, being the bone which supports the hand, and which turns with it in all its revolving motions. The ulna principally belongs to the elbow-joint, for by it we perform all the actions of bending or extending the arm.

FIG. 2. *a*, the humerus: *b*, shows the connexion of the radius with *c*, the ulna, at the elbow. The mode of articulation at the wrist is seen, Fig. 1.

Dd*   329

CHAPTER VIII.

PLATE IX. — THE SPINE.

FIG. 1. The *human spine*, so named from the series of sharp pro cesses projecting from the posterior part of the vertebræ. The spine consists of *seven* vertebræ of the neck, distinguished by the perforations in their transverse processes; of *twelve* belonging to the back, and marked by depressions for the heads of the ribs; and, lastly, of *five* belonging to the loins, which are larger than the other vertebræ.

FIG. 2. A separated *dorsal vertebra:* *a*, the body of the vertebra *b*, the ring through which the spinal marrow passes: *c, c*, the articulating surfaces to which the ribs are united.

FIG. 3. The vertebra of a very large serpent, drawn from a spe cimen belonging to the Anatomy School of Christ Church, Oxford. This figure shows the socket of the vertebra.

FIG. 4. The ball or rounded joint, evidently calculated for extensive motion.

FIG. 5. A part of the spine of the same reptile; it is exceedingly strong. each bone being united to the other by fifteen surfaces of articulation.

330

PLATE IX.

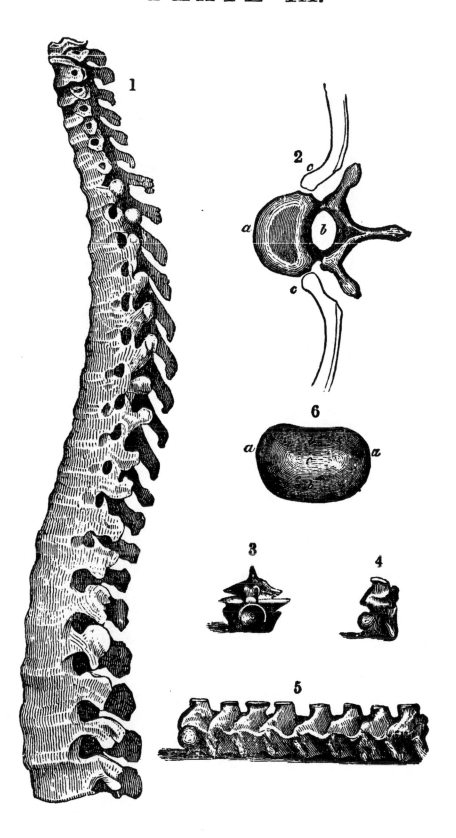

PLATE X.

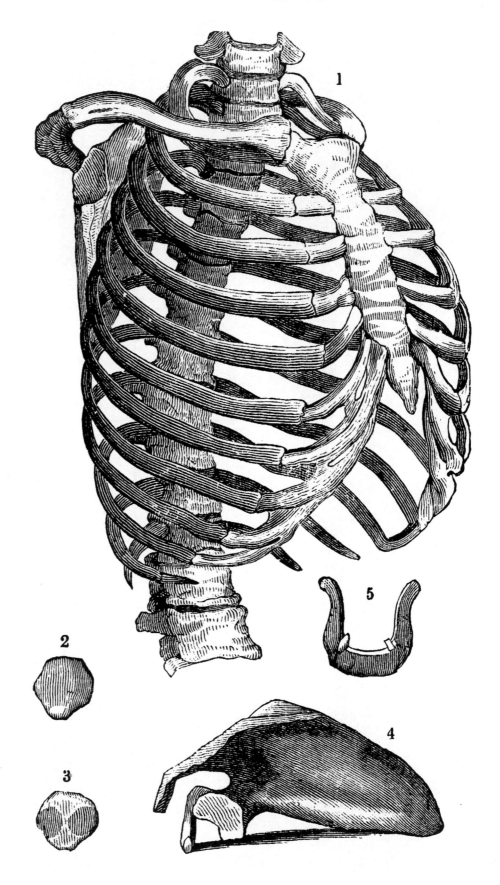

CHAPTER VIII.

PLATE X. — THE CHEST, PATELLA, AND SHOULDER-BLADE.

FIG. 1. The *spine*, *ribs*, and *sternum*, constitute the frame work of the *chest* or *thorax*. Referring, however, to the plate, or to nature, we observe that the ribs are not continued throughout from the spine to the sternum, but intervening *cartilages* complete the form of the chest, by connecting the end of the first ten ribs to the breast bone. This is a farther provision, relative to the mechanical function of the lungs, deserving notice. The muscles of respiration enlarge the capacity of the chest by elevating the ribs; and during the momentary interval of muscular action, the cartilages, from their great *elasticity*, restore the ribs to their former position.

FIG. 2. Represents the true shape of the *patella*, the *anterior surface convex*. FIG. 3, the *posterior surface*, which has two concave depressions adapted to the condyles of the thigh bone. The projection of the patella, as a lever, or pulley, removes the acting force from the centre of motion, by which means the muscles have a greater advantage in extending the leg. That this bone is " un like any other in the body," is a mistake ; such bones are numerous, though less obvious, for they do not exceed the size of a pea: these are called *sesamoid bones*, and are formed in the flexor tendons of the thumb, and sometimes in the fingers. They are frequently found under the tendons of some of the muscles. Two of these sort of bones are constantly found under the articulation of the great toe with the foot : some also are discovered, though not so constant ly, under the corresponding joints of the other toes. The sesamoid bones, like the patella, remove their tendons from the centre of mo tion, facilitate their glidings over the bone, and protect their artic- ulations.

FIG. 4. The shoulder-blade (*scapula*) is joined to the collar bone by ligaments, and to the thorax by powerful muscles which are ca- pable of sustaining immense weights, and whose action gives the various directions to the arm, and enables it freely to revolve at the shoulder-joint.

FIG 5. The *os hyoides*, a small bone situated at the root of the tongue. It serves as a lever or point for attaching the muscles of he tongue, larynx, and those of deglutition.

335

CHAPTER VIII.

PLATE XI —THE HIP, KNEE AND ANKLE JOINTS

Fig. 1. The capsular ligament is here opened in order to show the ligament of the hip, named the *round ligament*. It allows considerable latitude of motion, at the same time that it is the great safeguard against dislocation.

Fig. 2 and 4. The *crucial* or *internal ligaments* of the knee-joint arise from each side of the depression between the condyles of the thigh-bone; the anterior is fixed into the centre, the posterior into the back of the articulation of the tibia. This structure properly limits the motions of the joint, and gives the firmness requisite for violent exertions. Viewing the form of the bones, we should consider it one of the weakest and most superficial, but the strength of its ligaments and the tendons passing over it, render it the most secure, and the least liable to dislocation of any joint in the whole body.

Fig. 3. One of the *interarticular* cartilages of the knee, from their shape called *semilunar;* it is also represented *in situ,* Fig. 2. The outer edge of each cartilage is thick, the inner concave edge thin the sockets for the condyles of the thigh-bone are thus rendered deeper, and the cartilages are so fixed as to allow a little play on the tibia, by which the joint moves with great freedom.

A moving cartilage is not common, but is peculiar to those joints whose motions are very frequent, or which move under a great weight. It is a contrivance found at the jaw-bone, the inner head of the collar-bone and the articulation of the wrist, as well as at the knee. The obvious use is to lessen friction and facilitate motion.

Fig. 4. *a,* the *fibula; b,* the *tibia,* the lower extremities of which, *c, d,* form the outer and inner ankle, and receive, *e,* the great articulating bone of the foot, called the astragalus between them. When the foot sustains the weight of the body the joint is firm, but when raised it easily runs on the ends of these bones, so that the toe is directed to the place on which we intend to step.

336

PLATE XI.

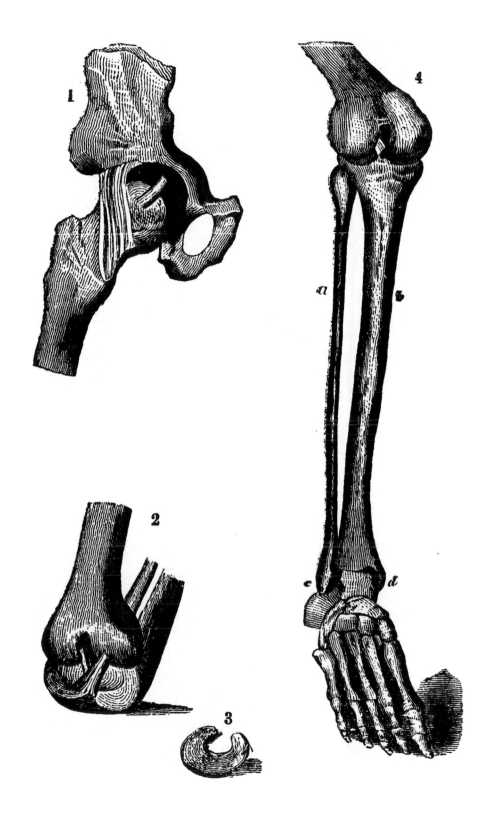

PLATE XII.

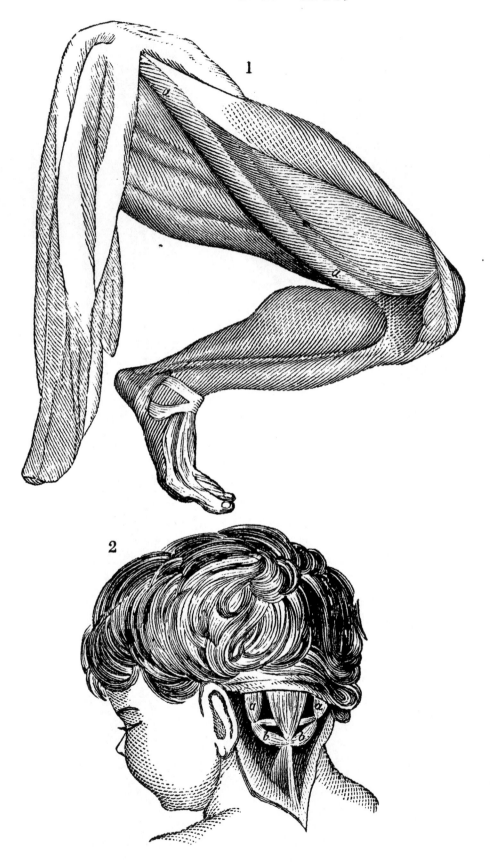

CHAPTER IX.

PLATE XII. — THE SARTORIUS AND OBLIQUE MUSCLES OF THE HEAD.

FIG. 1. *a, a,* the *sartorius,* is the longest muscle of the whole fabric: it is extended obliquely across the thigh from the fore part of the hip, to the inner side of the tibia. Its office is to bend the knee, and bring the leg inwards.

FIG. 2. There are two pairs of oblique muscles; *a, a,* the *obliquus capitis superior,* arising from the transverse process of the atlas, and inserted into the occipital bone; *b, b,* the *obliquus capitis inferior* arising from the spinous process of the dentata, and inserted into the transverse process of the atlas. These muscles roll the head on one side, and draw it backwards.

Ee*   341

CHAPTER XI

PLATE XIII.—THE MUSCLES OF THE ARM.

FIG. 1. *a*, the *biceps*, (biceps flexor cubiti) arise by two portions from the scapula; they form a thick mass of flesh in the middle of the arm, which is finally inserted into the upper end of the radius; *b*, the *brachiæus internus*, arises from the middle of the *os humeri*, and is inserted into the ulna. Both these muscles bend the fore-arm. *c*, the *longus et brevis brachiæus externus*; these are better named as one muscle, *triceps extensor cubiti*. It is attached to the inferior edge of the scapula, and to the os humeri, by three distinct heads, which unite and invest the whole back part of the bone, becoming a strong tendon which is implanted into the elbow. It is a powerful extensor of the fore-arm. *d*, the *anconæus*, a small triangular muscle, situated at the outer side of the elbow: it assists the last muscle.

FIG. 1 and 2. *e, e*, the *annular ligament* of the wrist, under which pass the tendons of the muscles of the fingers.

F   *f*, tne *deltoid muscle*; the muscle at the shoulder by   arm is raised.

342

PLATE XIII.

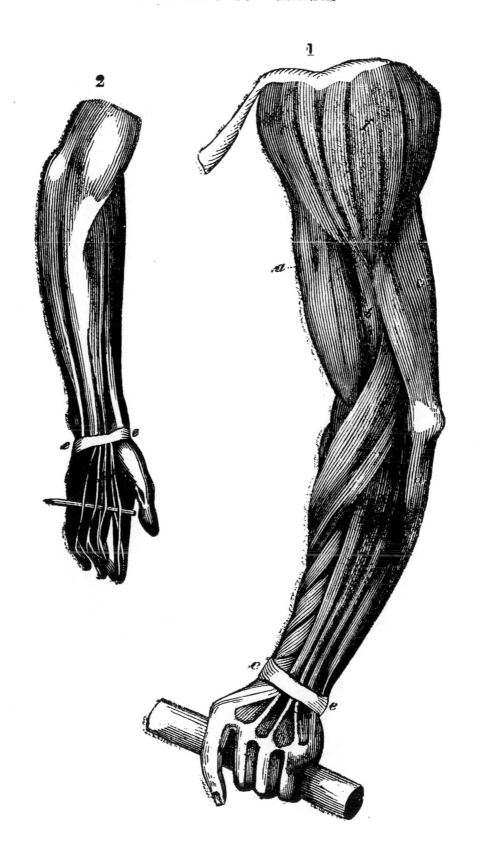

PLATE XIV.

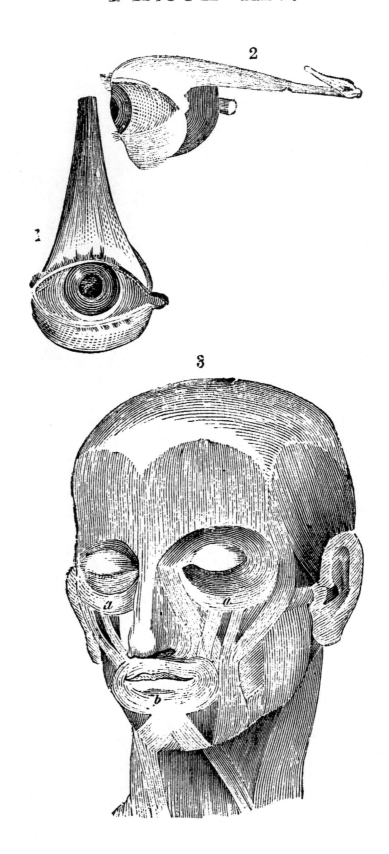

CHAPTER IX

PLATE **XIV** — THE MUSCLES THAT RAISE THE EYE-LIDS AND SPHINCTER OR CIRCULAR MUSCLES.

FIG. 1. A front view of this muscle, named *levator palpebræ superioris:* Fig. 2. a profile of the same in its natural position. This muscle arises within the orbit, and is inserted by a broad tendon into the upper eye-lid. Its name is expressive of its use.

FIG. 3. Exhibits examples of *sphincter* muscles: *a, a,* the *orbicularis palpebrarum*, encircling the eyelid; it closes the eye, and compresses it with spasmodic force, when injured by particles of dust, &c. *b,* the *orbicularis oris,* surrounding the mouth: its chief use is to contract the lips.

341

CHAPTER IX.

PLATE XV.—THE DIGASTRIC MUSCLE.

FIG. 1 and 2. The *digastric muscle* has its origin, *a*, at the lower part of the temporal bone; it runs downwards and forwards, and forms a strong, round tendon, *b*, which passes through a perforation in the stylo-hyoideus muscle, *f;* it is then fixed by a strong ligament, *c*, to the os hyoides, *d;* it again becomes fleshy, runs upwards, and is inserted into, *e*, the chin. This description differs from Dr. Paley's, and it will be found by reference to dissections or the plate that the os hyoides furnishes a *stay* or *brace* instead of a pulley, and that the loop or *ring* is in the stylo-hyoideus muscle.

PLATE XV.

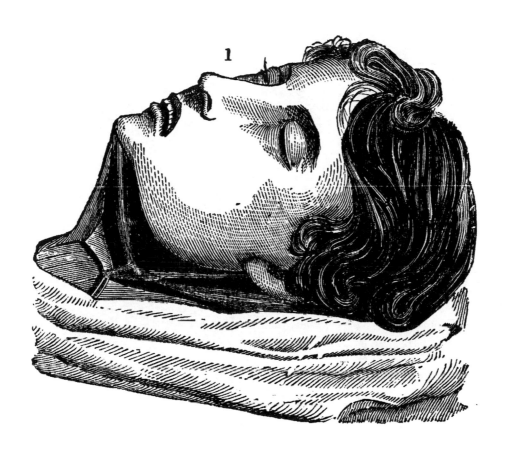

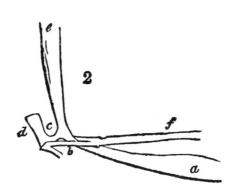

PLATE XVI.

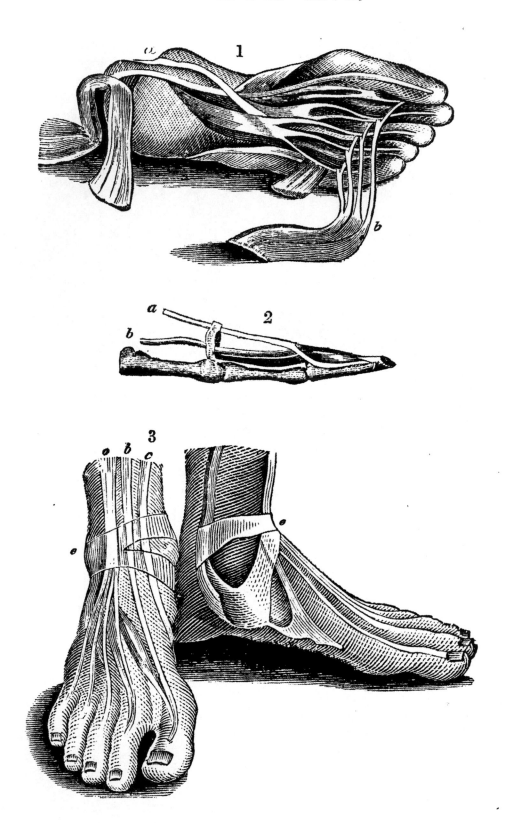

CHAPTER IX.

PLATE XVI. — THE TENDONS OF THE TOES.

Fig. 1. *a,* the tendon of the *long flexor of the toes,* which divides about the middle of the foot into four portions, passing through the slits in, *b,* the *short flexor tendons.* Fig. 2. explains a similar contrivance belonging to each finger: *a,* a tendon of the *flexor sublimis* ; *b,* a tendon of the *flexor profundus,* passing through it.

Fig. 3. *a, b,* tendons of the extensor muscles of the toes; *c.* a tendon of a flexor of the foot. These are bound down and retained *in situ* by, *e,* the *annular ligament* of the instep, which consists of two distinct cross bands, going from the outer ankle to the inner ankle and neighbouring bones.

Ff*

353

CHAPTER X.

PLATE XVII. — THE HEART.

FIG. 1. A section of the human heart; *a, a,* the *superior* and *inferior vena cava,* the veins which convey the blood to the, *b, right auricle;* and thence into, *c,* the corresponding *ventricle;* from this ventricle the blood is impelled through, *e,* the *pulmonary artery,* into the lungs; and returning by *f, f,* the *pulmonary veins,* it is received into, *g,* the *left auricle;* it flows next into, *h,* the *left ventricle;* which by its contraction distributes the blood through the general arterial system:— *j,* the *aorta,* the great artery which transmits blood to the different parts of the body, from whence it is returned by veins to the *cavæ; k,* the *right subclavian; l,* the *right carotid* arteries, originating from one common trunk; *m,* the *left carotid : n,* the *left subclavian; d,* the *valves* of the right; *i,* the *valves* of the left ventricle.

FIG. 2. The valves of the right side (*tricuspid valves*) separated from the heart; *a, a, a,* the *carnaæ columnæ,* or muscular fibres of the valves; *b, b, b,* the *chordæ tendineæ,* or tendinous filaments which are attached to, *c,* the valves.

FIG. 3. Exhibits the *artery* cut open with the form of the *semilunar valves.*

FIG. 4. A portion of the artery filled, showing how effectually the valves prevent the retrograde motion of the blood in the aorta and pulmonary artery.

FIG. 5, 6. A section of a cutting and grinding tooth, showing the apertures at the root and the cavities for the vessels and nerves, which supply the bony part of the teeth, the enamel not being an organized substance.

354

PLATE XVII.

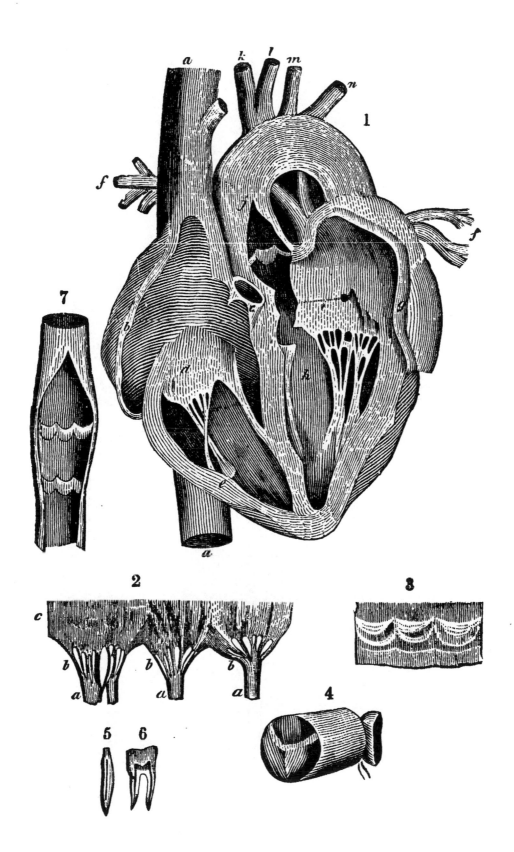

PLATE XVIII.

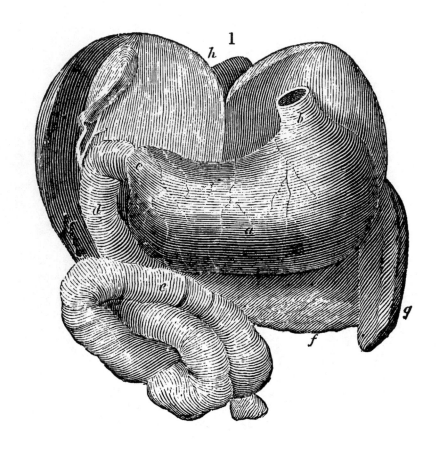

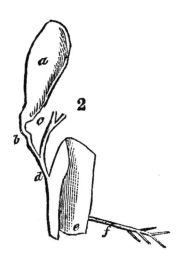

CHAPTER X.

PLATE XVIII. — THE STOMACH, GALL-BLADDER, &c.

FIG. 1. *a*, the *stomach; b*, the *cardia; c*, the *pylorus.* The *gastric nice* is a secretion derived from the inner membrane of the stomach, and digestion is principally performed by it. In the various orders of animated beings it differs, being adapted to the food on which they are accustomed to subsist. The food, when properly masticated, is dissolved by the gastric fluid, and converted into *hyme ;* so that most kinds of the ingesta lose their specific qualities · and the chemical changes to which they would otherwise be liable, as putridity and rancidity, &c. are thus prevented.

In this plate, *h*, the *liver* is turned up, in order to show the *gall-bladder* which is attached to its concave surface ; *d*, the *duodenum; e*, part of the small *intestines ; f*, the *pancreas ;* and *g*, ine *spleen.*

FIG. 2. Explains the several ducts and their communication with the *duodenum ; a*, the *gall-bladder ; b*, the *ductus cysticus;* which uniting with, *c*, the *ductus hepaticus*, forms, *d*, the *ductus communus ;* which, after passing between the muscular and inner coats of the intestine, opens into it at *e. f*, the *pancreatic duct.* The bile is said to become more viscid, acrid, and bitter, from the thinner parts being absorbed during its retention in the gall-bladder.

359

CHAPTER X.

PLATE XIX. — THE LACTEALS, AND THORACIC DUCT.

The figure in this plate represents the course of the food, from its entrance at the mouth to its assimilation with the blood ; *a*, the *œsoph-agus*, extending from the *pharynx* to, *b*, the *stomach* ; where the alimentary matter, having undergone the digestive process, is converted into *chyme*, a soft, homogeneous substance, and escapes at *c*, the *pylorus*, into, *d*, the *intestines*. In this plate a large portion of the latter is spread out to show a part of the absorbent system, called *lacteals :* these collect and imbibe the *chyle*, or milky juice from the chyme, and transmit it through *e, e*, the *mesenteric glands*, into one general receptacle, *f*, (*receptaculum chyli*,) from which, *g*, the *thoracic duct* ascends in a more or less tortuous direction to the lower vertebræ of the neck, and after forming an arch, it descends and enters *h*, the left *subclavian vein*, at the point where that vein is united with the *internal jugular*. The absorbents of the right side frequently form a trunk, which enters the *right subclavian vein*.

360

PLATE XIX.

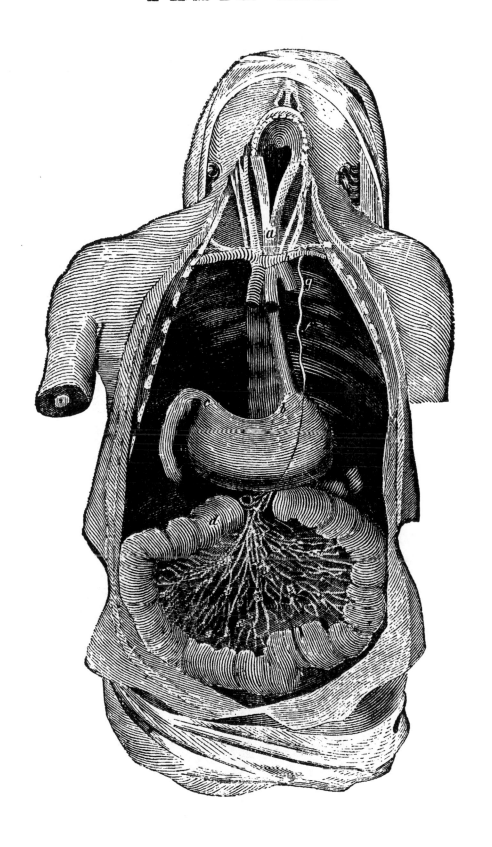

PLATE XX.

CHAPTER A.

PLATE XX.— THE PAROTID GLAND.

FIG. 1. A dissection to exhibit the *parotid gland.*

FIG. 2. Explains the former ; *a, a,* the integuments turned back ; *b,* the *parotid gland ; c,* its *pipe* or *duct* passing over the *masseter* then perforating, *d,* the *buccinator muscle,* and opening into the mouth opposite the second molar tooth. The flow of saliva into the mouth is incessant, and it is one of the most useful digestive fluids. It is favorable to the maceration and division of the food, it assists it in deglutition and transformation into chyme ; it also renders more easy the motions of the tongue in speech and singing.

Gg*

CHAPTER A.

PLATE XXI. — THE LARYNX.

FIG. 1 The *larynx, pharynx*, &c. *a*, the *os hyoides, b*, the *epiglottu* pressed down, thus covering the *glottis*, or opening of the *larynx*; as it does in the act of deglutition.

FIG. 2. Exhibits the *larynx*, and *trachea*; which is a continuation of the former; *b*, the *epiglottis*; *g*, the *arytenoid cartilages*; *e* the *thyroid cartilage*, exceedingly strong, for the protection of the upper part of the air tube; *d*, the *cartilaginous ringlets* of the *trachea* or *wind-pipe*, each forming nearly two-thirds of a circle, and com pleted by *f*, a soft *membrane*, which, from its apposition to, *e*, Fig. 1, the *œsophagus*, accommodates itself to tne substances passing into the stomach.

FIG. 3. The *larynx* or *upper* part of the wind-pipe of a bird This is called the *inferior larynx*, where the vocal organ is formed by a compression of the trachea, for it is here contracted into a narrow chink, and divided into two openings by a slender bone. or tense membrane, which, in producing sounds, resembles the mechanism of a musical instrument. In the plate this part of the larynx is a little turned up to show the *tendinous band* at this extremity stretched across it, which is furnished from the surrounding parts with muscles to modulate the tone.

366

PLATE XXI.

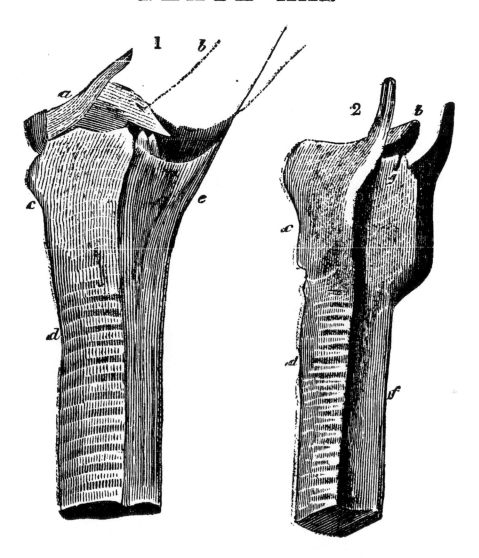

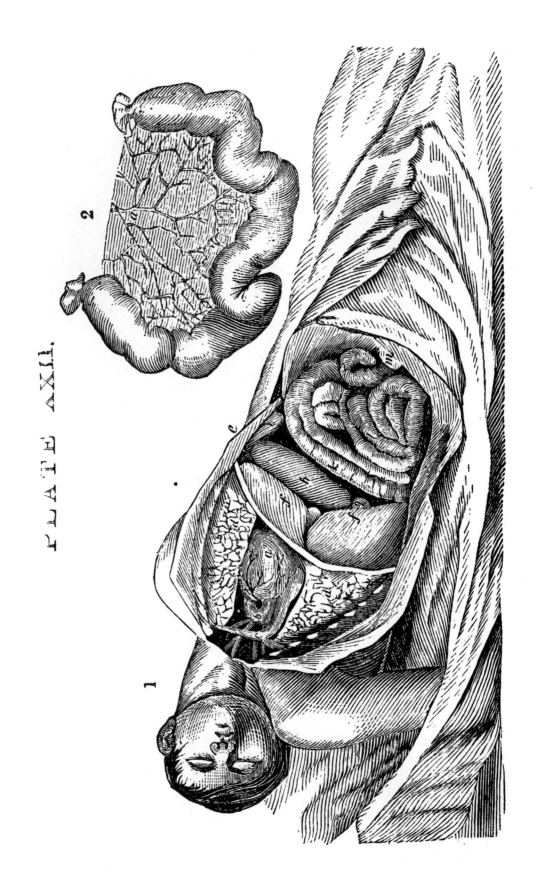

PLATE XXII.

CHAPTER XI.

PLATE XXII.— PACKAGE OF THE VISCERA, AND MESENTERY.

Fig 1. In this plate the parietes of the chest and abdomen, with the omentum, are removed to show the viscera *in situ*; *a*, the *heart*; *b*, the *aorta*; *c*, the *descending vena cava*; *d*, the *lungs* divided by the mediastinum into two portions; three lobes belong to the right, and two to the left portion of the lungs; *e*, the *diaphragm*, or that muscle which separates the thorax from the abdomen; *f*, the *liver*; *g*, the *gall-bladder*; *h*, the *stomach*; *i*, the *spleen*; *k*, the *large intestines*; *l*, the *small intestines*; *m*, the *bladder*.

The viscera of the thorax and abdomen, *i. e.* the viscera of *organic life*, are *irregularly* disposed. The *agents of volition* are double, but the instruments of *involuntary motion*, namely, the interior life, are single, and at least are irregular in their form.

The several viscera are correctly described in the Theology, and sufficient is said for the purposes for which they are introduced. To the supposed use of the *spleen* only an objection must be taken: various hypotheses have been entertained as to its office, but none are conclusive; the most probable is, that it is a source of supply of blood for furnishing the gastric secretion, or that the blood undergoes some important change in it.

Fig. 2. The *mesentery*. This membrane is formed by a reflection of the *peritonæum* from each side of the vertebræ; it connects the intestines loosely to the spine, to allow them a certain degree of motion, yet retains them in their places; and furnishes their exterior covering. Between the laminæ of, *a*, the *mesentery*, are received the *glands, vessels*, and *nerves*; and its extent admits of a proper distribution of each.

371

CHAPTER XII.

PLATE XXIII. — NERVES OF THE BILL OF A DUCK, VALVULÆ
CONNIVENTES. CHAP. XIII. AIR-BLADDER OF A FISH, AND
FANG OF THE VIPER.

Fig. 1. The upper *mandible* of the duck, on which are distributed the first and second branches of the fifth pair of nerves; the former passing through the orbit to the extremity of the bill, and, together with the latter, supplying the whole palatine surface. This gustatory sensibility is the more necessary to those races of birds called palmipedes, such as penguins, the wild goose, ducks, &c. and the grallæ, such as water-hens, curlews, woodcocks, &c. their sight being of no assistance to them in finding their prey in the mire.

Fig. 2. A small portion of the human intestine cut open in order to show the *valvulæ conniventes*. It may be questioned, whether these extremely soft rugæ or folds of the villous coat of the intestine can in the least retard the passage of the food through its canal; nor does the erect attitude of man require them; for, since there are as many of the convolutions of the intestines ascending as there are descending, the weight of the food can have no influence in the action of the intestine: it is certain, however, that this arrangement of the internal coat, affords *a more extensive surface for the lacteals and secreting vessels*; and this appears to be the real use of the *valvulæ conniventes*.

Fig. 3. The *air-bladder* in the roach. This vessel differs in size and shape, in different species of fish; generally communicating, by one or more ducts, either with the œsophagus or stomach; by which means the fish receives or expels the air, thus sinking or rising without effort: but as some are destitute of this organ, it is considered as an accessary instrument of motion. Such fish live almost uniformly at the bottom of the water.

Fig. 4. The head of a viper of the natural size.

Fig. 5. The *fang* magnified, at the root of which is the gland which secretes the venom: a hair is represented in the tube through which the poison is ejected.

Fig. 6, 7 See note, p. 126.

PLATE XXIII.

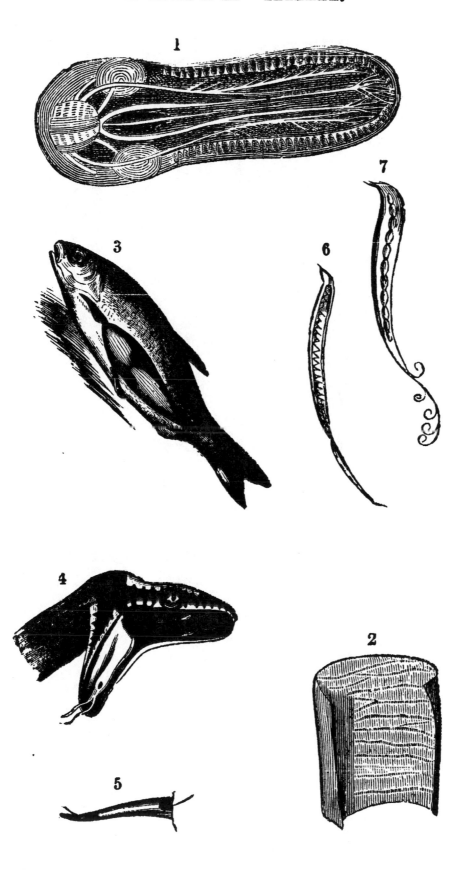

PLATE XXIV.

CHAPTER XXI.

PLATE XXIV. — THE OPOSSUM.

FIG. 1. The American opossum; (*didelphis marsupialis virginiana.*) The body of the animal is of a grayish yellow color, some hairs entirely black, with others entirely white; the tail furnished with scales; the hands, nose, and ears naked. The female has the whole length of the belly cleft or slit, and appears like a person's waistcoat buttoned only at the top and bottom. This cavity the animal has the power of firmly closing. Within are thirteen teats, extremely small, one in the centre, and the rest ranged round it.

FIG. 2. One of the young of the opossum.

FIG. 3. The pelvis of the opossum; *a, a,* the two bones (*ossa marsupialia*) placed on the anterior part called the *ossa pubis.*

The kangaroo and several other animals of New Holland have a similar structure.

Hh*   377

CHAPTER XIII.

PLATE **XXV.** — CLAW OF THE HERON, AND BILL OF THE SOLAND GOOSE.

Fig 1. The *middle claw of the heron.*

Fig. 2. The head of the *Soland goose,* (*pelicanus bassanus*) drawn from a specimen in the Ashmolean Museum, Oxford. This owl inhabits the coldest parts of Great Britain, more especially the northern isles of Scotland. The inhabitants of St. Kilda make it their principal article of food, and are said to consume annually nea 90,000 young birds, beside an amazing quantity of eggs.

378

PLATE XXV.

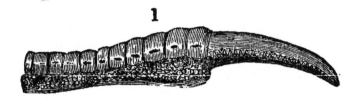

1

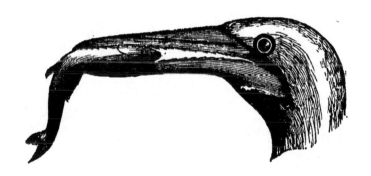

PLATE· XXVI.

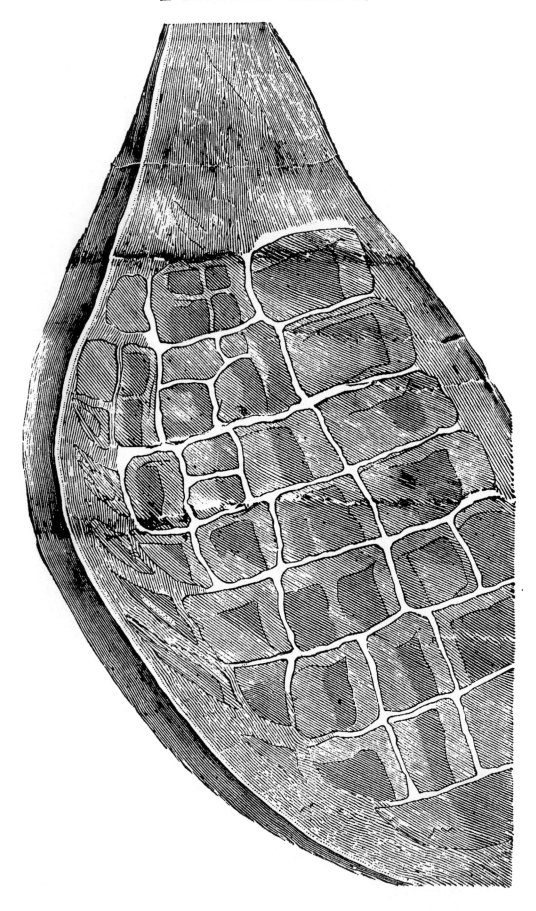

CHAPTER XIII.

PLATE XXVI. — STOMACH OF THE CAMEL.

The figure in this plate exhibits the *cells in the stomach of the camel*, from a preparation in the museum of the Royal College of Surgeons, London. In the camel, dromedary, and lama, there are four stomachs, as in horned ruminants; but the structure, in some respects, differs from those of the latter. The camel tribe have in the first and second stomach numerous cells, several inches deep, formed by bands of muscular fibres crossing each other at right angles; these are constructed so as to retain the water, and completely exclude the food. In a camel dissected by Sir E. Home, the cells of the stomach were found to contain two gallons of water; but in consequence of the muscular contraction, which had taken place immediately after death, he was led to conclude this was a quantity much less than these cavities were capable of receiving in the living animal. See Lectures on Comparative Anatomy, by Sir E. Home, vol. 1. p. 168.

Mr. Bruce states, in his Travels, that he procured four gallons of water from a camel, which from necessity he slaughtered in Upper Egypt.

383

CHAPTER XIII.

PLATE XXVII. — TONGUE OF THE WOODPECKER, AND SKULL) THE BABYROUESSA.

Fig. 1. The *head of the woodpecker, (picus viridis.)*

Fig. 2. The *tongue,* the natural size.

Fig. 3. The claw of the same bird, referred to in Chap. V.

Fig. 4. The *skull of the babyrouessa,* from a specimen in the Anatomy School, Christ Church, Oxford.

This animal is nearly the size of the common hog, and instead of bristles, is covered with fine short and woolly hair, of a deep brown or black color. It is also distinguished by the extraordinary position and form of the *upper tusks,* which are not situated on the edge of the jaw, as in other animals, but are placed externally, perforating the skin of the snout, and turning upwards towards the forehead.

The babyrouessa is found in large herds in many parts of Java Amboina, and other Indian islands, and feeds on vegetables.

384

PLATE XXVII.

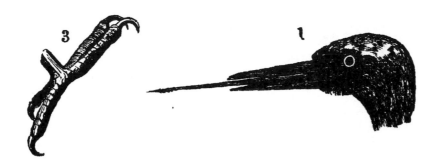

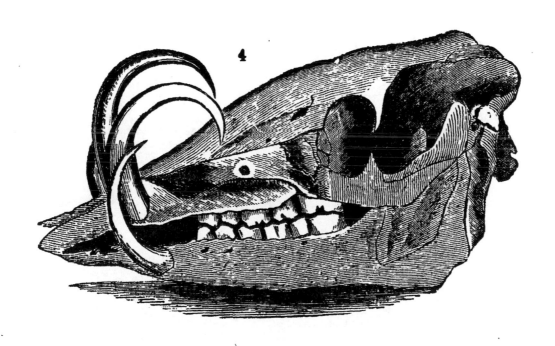

PLATE XXVIII.

1

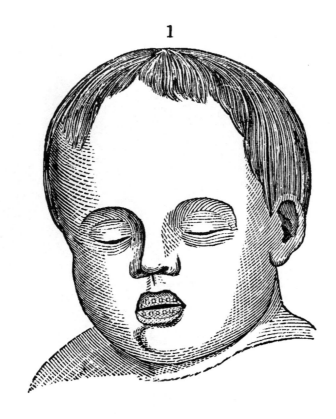

2

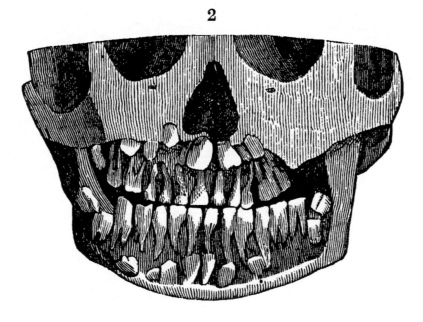

CHAPTER XIV.

Plate XXVIII.— temporary and permanent teeth.

Fig. 1. The gums and outer plate of the bone are removed showing the teeth of the infant, as they exist at the time of its birth they are without roots, and contained in a capsule within the jaws.

Fig. 2. In this figure, also, the outer alveolar plate of the jaws has been removed to show the succession of teeth. This is the state at six years of age. The *temporary* teeth are all shed between the ages of seven and fourteen, and are supplied by the *permanent teeth* already nearly perfectly formed, and situated at the roots of the former.

Li*   389

CHAPTER XIV.

PLATE XXIX.—FORAMEN OVALE, AND DUCTUS ARERIOSUS

FIG. 1. A view of the fœtal heart; *a*, the ascending, *b*, the descending vena cava; *c*, the right auricle; *d, e, f*, mark the elevated ring of the *foramen ovale*, or the opening between the two auricles.

FIG. 2. The fœtal heart; *a*, the pulmonary artery; *b, b*, its branches; *c*, the *ductus arteriosus*, or canal for transmitting the blood into, *d*, the aorta. As the lungs are useless in the fœtus, unless as a "prospective contrivance," the heart has to carry on a single circulation only: the free communication between the two auricles identifies them as one cavity; and the ventricles also force the blood into one vessel, the aorta.

390

PLATE XXIX.

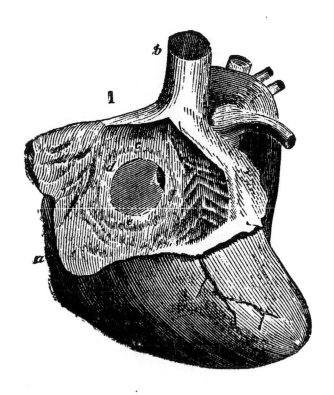

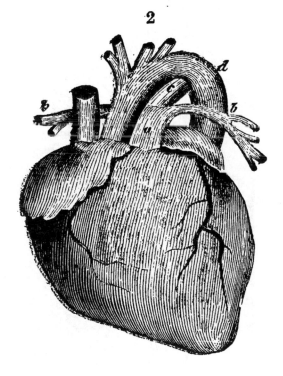

PLATE XXX.

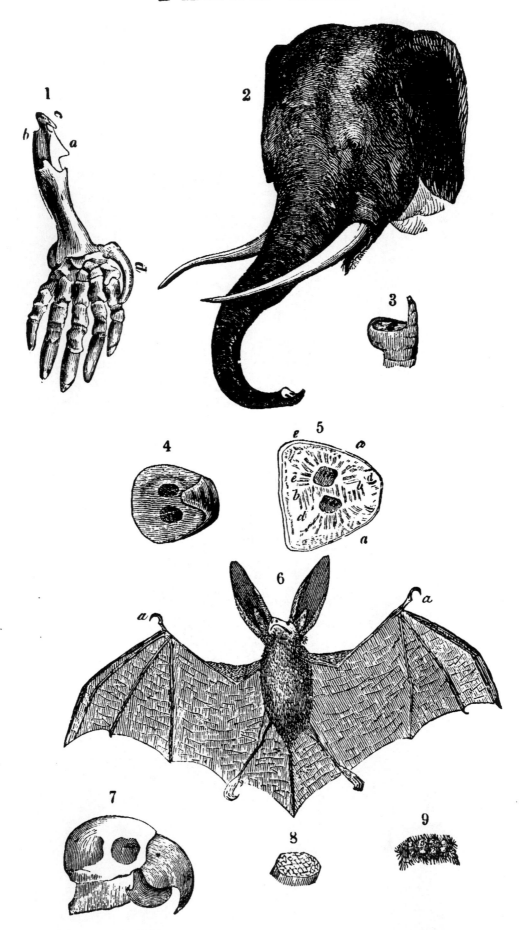

CHAPTERS XV. AND XVI.

PLATE XXX.—FORE EXTREMITY OF THE MOLE—HEAD OF THE ELEPHANT—FINGER-LIKE EXTREMITY OF THE PROBOSCIS—SECTION OF THE PROBOSCIS—BAT'S WING—BILL OF THE PARROT—EYES OF INSECTS—EYES OF A SPIDER.

FIG. 1. Is the fore extremity of the *mole* ; *a*, the *os humeri*, is peculiar, not only for its shortness, but in being articulated by *b*, one head to the scapula, and by *c*, another to the clavicle ; it is altogether of such a nature as to turn the palm outwards for working.

The foot, or we may name it the hand, has eleven bones in the *carpus* or wrist, which is two more than the carpus of man. One of which, *d*, is remarkable, and from its shape is called the *falciform bone;* it gives the shovel form to the hand.

FIG. 2. The head of the *Elephant*.

FIG. 3. and 4. The digitated extremity of the proboscis.

FIG. 5. A transverse section of the proboscis, showing, *a, a*, the two tubes or nostrils. Between the external integuments and the tubes are two sets of small muscles ; an inner one running in a transverse, and an outward one in a longitudinal direction : *b, b*, the *transverse* faciculi of muscles, some of which run across the proboscis, others in a radiated, and some in an oblique direction : *c, c*, the radiated, and *d, d*, the oblique fibres approximate the skin and the tubes, without contracting the cavity of the latter. The others, which pass across the proboscis, contract both the surface of the organ, and the canals it contains ; they can, at the same time, elongate the whole or a part of it : *e, e*, the *longitudinal* faciculi, forming four large muscles, which occupy all the exterior of the organ.

FIG. 6. The extended wings of the *bat*. Ostrologically considered, they are hands, the bony stretches of the membrane being the finger bones extremely elongated : *a, a*, the thumb, is short, and armed with a hooked nail, which those animals make use of to hang by, and to creep. The hind feet are weak, and have toes of equal length, armed also with hooked nails ; the membrane constituting the wing, is continued from the feet to the tail.

FIG. 7. The upper *mandible* of the *parrot*, which is articulated with the cranium by an elastic ligament, admitting of a considerable degree of motion.

FIG. 8. An eye compounded of a number of lenses. The eyes of insects differ widely from vertebrated animals, by being incapable of motion ; the compensation, therefore, is a greater number of eyes, or an eye compounded of a number of lenses. Hook computed the lenses in a horse-fly to amount to 7,000, and Leuwenhoek found the almost incredible number of 12,000 in the dragon-fly.

FIG. 9. The eyes of a *spider*, drawn from nature. The number of eyes in insects varies from two to sixteen. The spider here referred to answers the description of the garden spider, (*Epeira* Diadema,) the eyes of which are planted on three tubercles, four on the central one, and two on each side of the lateral ones.

CHAPTER XVI.

PLATE XXXI. —THE CHAMELEON, AND INTESTINE OF THE SEA-FOX.

FIG. 1. The *chameleon*, drawn from one of the species preserved n the Anatomy School, Christ Church, Oxford. The eyes of this creature are very peculiar: they are remarkably large, and project more than half their diameter. They are covered with a single eye-lid, with a small opening in it opposite the pupil. The eye-lid is granulated like every part of the surface of the body, with this difference, over the eye the granulations are disposed in concentric circles which form folds in that part to which the eye is turned: and as the lid is attached to the front of the eye, so it follows all its movements. The neck is not "inflexible," but its shortness, and the structure of the cervical vertebræ exceedingly limit the motion; this, however, is admirably compensated by the not less singular local position than motion of the eye, as the animal can see behind, before, or on either side, without turning the head.

FIG. 2. The spiral intestine of the *sea-fox* cut open; taken from a preparation in the museum of the Royal College of Surgeons, London. The sea-fox is not, as Paley supposes, a "quadruped;" but a species of shark, (squalus vulpes.) The convoluted intestinal tube is also found in some other genera of fish. In this specimen the internal membrane is converted into a spiral valve, having thirty-six coils; so that the alimentary substances, instead of passing speedily away, by proceeding round the turns of the valve, traverse a very considerable circuit: an extensive surface for the absorbents is thus provided.

FIG. 3. The *spiral valve* removed, showing the mode of its coiling.

396

PLATE XXXI.

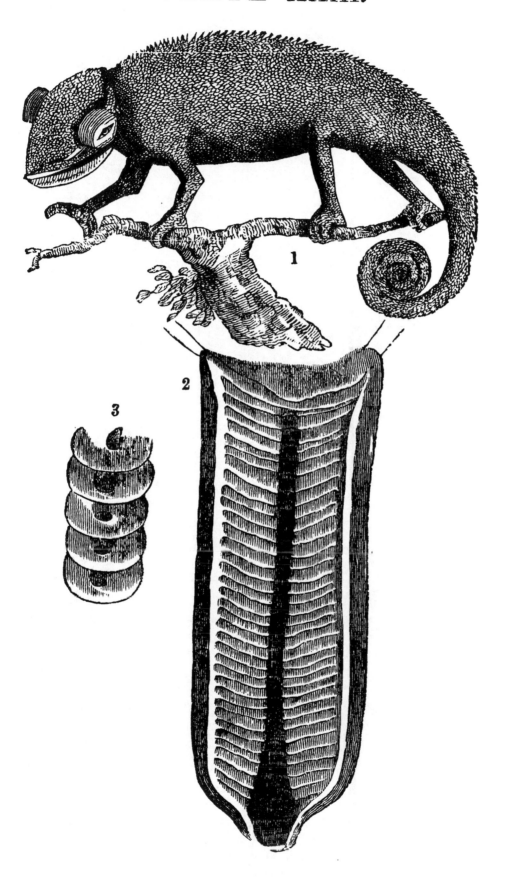

PLATE XXXII.

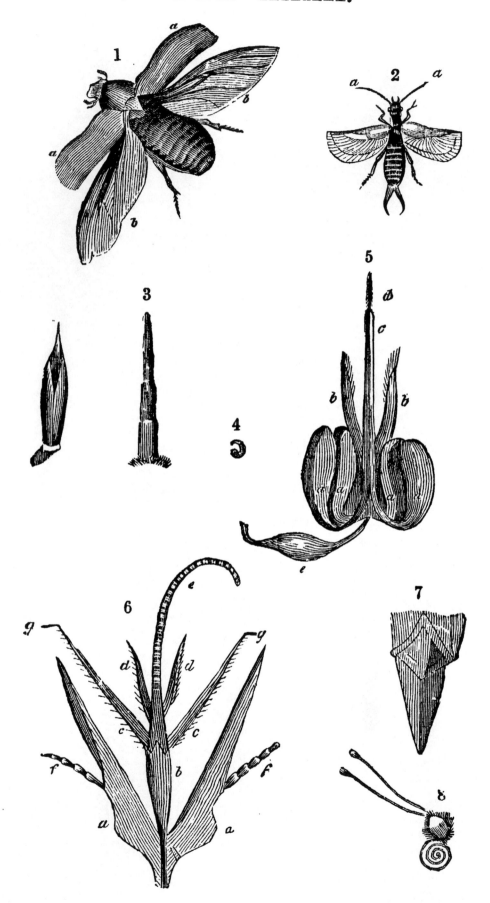

CHAPTER XIX.

PLATE XXXII.—THE WINGS OF THE BEETLE, AWL, STING OF THE BEE, PROBOSCIS, &c.

FIG. 1. Is an instance of the horny and gauze wings in one of the most beautiful of the beetle class of this country, the *cetonia aurata,* or rose chafer; showing the expanded *elytra, a, a :* the true wings, *b, b.*

Elytra are the wing covers of all the *coleoptera* order. They are frequently grooved, and curiously ornamented, in some species with scaly variegations of metallic lustre, as in the diamond beetle, and some species of Buprestis. One of the latter, of extraordinary brilliancy, forms an object in the "Cabinet of Beauty" in the Ashmolean Museum. The use of the elytra is to protect the wings and body; and they are of some assistance in flying.

FIG. 2. A specimen of the elytra covering half the body in the *ear-wig,* (forficula auricularia:) one of the elytra is extended, and the membranous wing unfolded; showing the numerous diverging *nervures,* or "muscular tendons," which run in horny tubes, to keep the wing extended. *a, a, antennæ* usually consist of a number of tubular joints, with a free motion in each, enabling the insect to give them every necessary flexure; they vary in number and in shape in the various orders, and are covered with hair, down, or bristles, frequently elegant and diversified, as every one may observe. Entomologists conceive, that the antennæ, by a peculiar structure, may collect notices from the atmosphere, receive vibrations, and communicate them to the sensorium, which, though not precisely to be called hearing, is something analogous to it, or may answer that purpose.

FIG. 3. The *awl* of the *œstrum bovis,* or *gad-fly,* highly magnified. It is formed of corneous substance, consisting of four joints, which slip into each other: the last of these terminate in five points, three of which are longer than the others, and are hooked: when united, they form an instrument like an auger or gimlet, with which the skin is pierced in a few seconds.

FIG. 4. One of the *hooks.*

FIG. 5. The *sting of a bee,* drawn from nature as it appears by means of a magnifier of very high powers: *a, a, a, a,* the apparatus for projecting the sting; *b,* the exterior, *c,* the interior sheath of, *a,* the *true sting,* which is divided into two parts barbed at the sides *e,* the bag which contains the *poison.*

FIG. 6. The *proboscis* of a bee extended, *a, a,* the case or sheath; *b,* the tube; *c,* the exterior; *d,* the interior fringes; *e,* the tongue; *f, f,* the exterior, *g, g,* the interior palpi.

FIG. 7. The appearance of the proboscis when contracted, and folded up.

FIG. 8. The head of a butterfly, showing the *coiled proboscis*

FIG. 9. *Ovipositor* of the *buprestis*

Kk*

CHAPTER XIX.

FIG. 1. The organs for forming the silk consist of two long vessels. They unite to form the *spinneret* (fusulus) through which the larva draw the silken thread employed in fabricating its cocoon. *a, a,* the *silk bags* *b,* the *spinneret.*

FIG. 2. The web of spiders is also a kind of silk, remarkable for its lightness and tenuity; it is spun from four or six anal spinnerets, the fluid matter forming the web being secreted in adjacent vessels. *a, b, c, d* the *spinnerets.*

FIG. 3. *Panorpa communis,* (Linn.) is an insect frequently seen in meadows during the early part of summer. It is a long-bodied fly, of moderate size, with four transparent wings, elegantly variegated with deep brown spots.

FIG. 4. The female glow-worm.

FIG. 5. The male of the same insect.

FIG. 6. The larva of some dragon-flies (*æshra* and *libellula, F.*) swim by strongly ejecting water from the anus. By first taking in the water, and then expelling it, they are enabled to swim. This may be seen by putting one of these larva into a plate with water. We find that while the animal moves forward, a currant of water is produced by this pumping in a contrary direction. Sometimes it will raise its tail out of the water, when a stream of water issues from it.

FIG. 7. The *spiracula*, or breathing pores of insects, are small ori fices in the trunk or abdomen, opening into a canal called the *tracheæ*, by which the air enters the body, or is expelled from it. In the larvæ or caterpillars, a trachea runs on each side of the body, under the skin, and generally opens externally by nine or ten apertures or spiraculæ; from these the same number of air-vessels of a silver color pass off to be dispersed through the body. *a, a, spiracula; b, b, trachea.*

FIG. 8. The pupæ of gnats suspend themselves on the surface of the water, by two auriform respiratory organs on the anterior part of the trunk, their abdomen being then folded under the breast; when disposed to descend, the animal unfolds it, and with sudden strokes which she gives with it and her anal swimmers to the water, she swims from right to left, as well as upwards and downwards, with the greatest ease.

FIG. 9. This is a well known fly, (*stratyonis chamæleon, F.*) chameleon fly. In its first state it inhabits the water, and often remains supported by its radiated tail, consisting of beautiful feathered hairs or plumes, on the surface, with its head downwards. But when it is disposed to seek the bottom or to descend, the radii of the tail is formed into a concavity including in it an air bubble; this is its swim bladder, and by the bending of its body from righ to left, contracting itself into the form of the letter S, and then extending itself again into a straight line, it moves itself in any direction.

PLATE XXXIII.

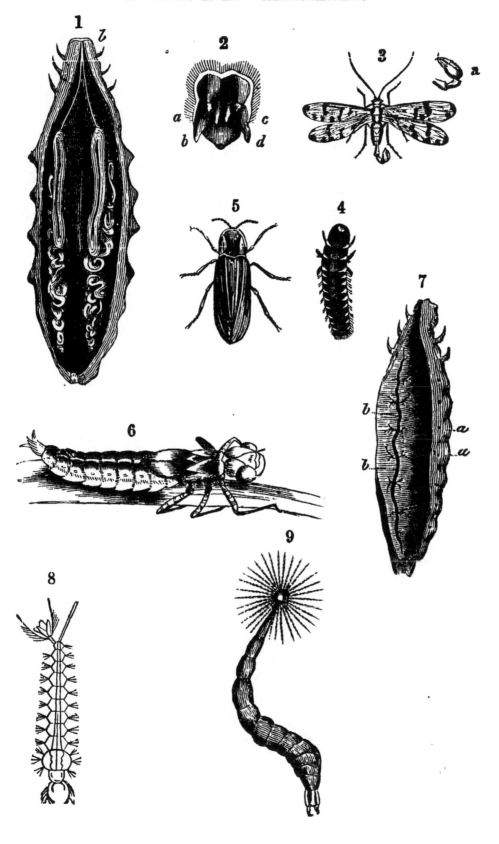

PLATE XXXIV.

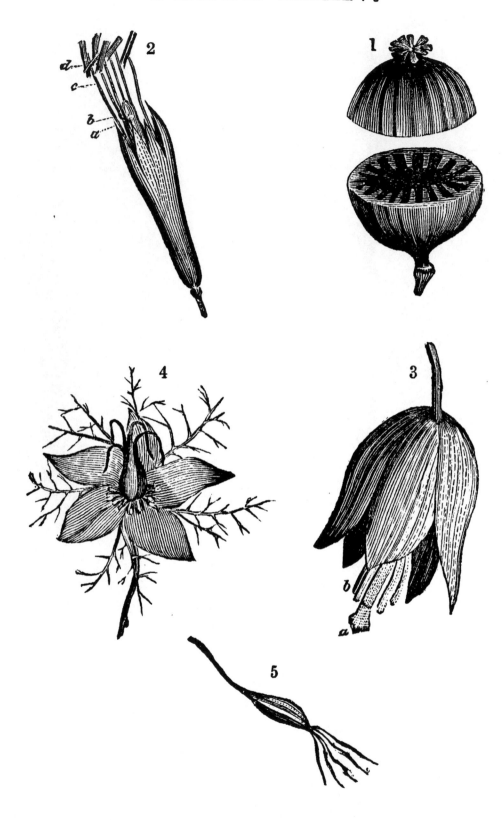

CHAPTER XX.

PLATE XXXIV. — THE CAPSULE, PISTIL, STAMINA, NIGELLA, PLUMULE, AND RADICLE.

FIG. 1. The *capsule* or seed-vessel of the poppy: (papaver somniferum:) it is divided to exhibit its internal structure.

FIG. 2. Is an instance of an erect flower, the agave Americana in which the pistil is shorter than the stamina. *a*, the pistil; *b*, the stigma; *c*, the stamina,; *d*, the antheræ.

FIG. 3. A flower of the *crown-imperial*. The relative length of the parts is now inverted. *a*, the pistil, *b*, the stamina.

FIG. 4. A blossom of the *nigella*.

FIG. 5. A grain of barley, showing the *plumule* and *radicle growing from it.*

407

CHAPTER XX.

PLATE XXV —VALLISNFRIA.

Fig. 1. *Valisneria spiralis*. The *female plant*, the flowers of which are purple. This is drawn from a specimen in the possession of Dr. Ogle.

Fig. 2. The *male plant*, producing white flowers; these when mature rise like air bubbles, and suddenly expanding when they reach the surface of the water, float about in such abundance as to cover it entirely. "Thus their pollen is scattered over the stigmas of the first mentioned blossoms, whose stalks soon afterwards resume their spiral figure, and the fruit comes to maturity at the bottom of the water."

Fig. 3. One of the separated *male* flowers magnified.

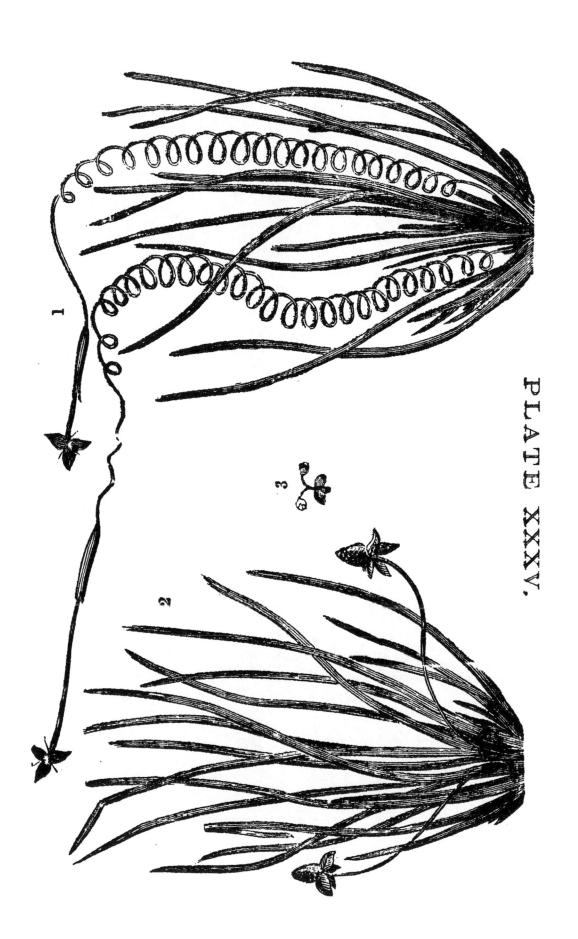

PLATE XXXV.

PLATE XXXVI.

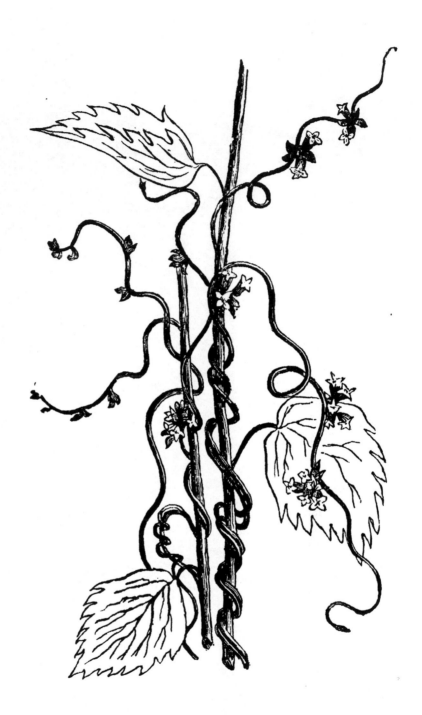

PLATE XXXVI. — CUSCUTA EUROPÆA.

This plant is a native of England, and is found in hedges, on clover, or on beans, where it proves exceedingly injurious to the crop. It flowers from June to August. The drawing was taken from a specimen which grew in the Physic Gardens, Oxford. It is represented twining about some nettles, on which it annually attaches itself.

"Of all the parasitical plants, the dodder (cuscuta) tribe are the most singular, trusting for their nourishment entirely to those vegetables about which they twine, and into whose tender bark they insert small villous tubercles serving as roots, the original root of the dodder withering away entirely, as soon as the young stem has fixed itself to any other plant; so that its connexion with the earth is cut off." English Botany, p. 55.

413

CHAPTER XX.

Plate XXXVII. — THE AUTUMNAL CROCUS

The *colchicum autumnale*. This plant before us exhibits a mode of fructification scarcely paralleled among British vegetables. The flowers appearing very late in autumn, the impregnated germen remains latent under ground close to the bulb till the following spring, when the capsule rises above the surface accompanied by several long upright leaves, and the seeds are ripened about June, after which the leaves decay. See British Botany, vol. i. p. 133. The plant is represented as it appears in *spring*; the root is divided to show the *seed vessel* near the bulb. The flower is remarkable for the length of its tube.

414

PLATE XXXVII.

PLATE XXXVIII.

CHAPTER XX.

PLATE XXXVIII. — THE DIONÆA MUSCIPULA.

The *dionæa muscipula*, or Venus's fly-trap. Some parts of this plant are so remarkable as to deserve a particular description. It is a native of North Carolina; the root perennial; leaves all radical, supported on long fleshy and strongly veined footstalks, leaving a small portion of this next the leaf naked: the leaf itself consists of two semi-oval lobes jointed at the back, so as to allow them to fold close together; they are fleshy, and when viewed through a lense glandular, sometimes of a reddish color on the upper surface; the sides of both lobes are furnished with a row of cartilaginous ciliæ which stand nearly at right angles with the surface of the leaf, and lock into each other when they close. Near the middle of each lobe are three small spines, which are supposed to assist in destroying the entrapped insect. In warm weather the lobes are fully expanded and highly irritable, and if a fly or other insect at this time light upon them they suddenly close, and the poor animal is imprisoned till it dies. See Curtis's Botanical Magazine, No. 785.

CHAPTER XXII.

PLATE XXXIX. — ASTRONOMY.

FIG. 1, 2. The remarkable ring which surrounds the planet Saturn.

FIG. 3 The earth an oblate spheroid. See note, p. 217.

FIG. 4 See note, p. 220

FIG. 5. See note, p. 221

FIG. 6. Centripetal forces illustrated. See notes, pp. 219 226.

420

PLATE XXXIX.

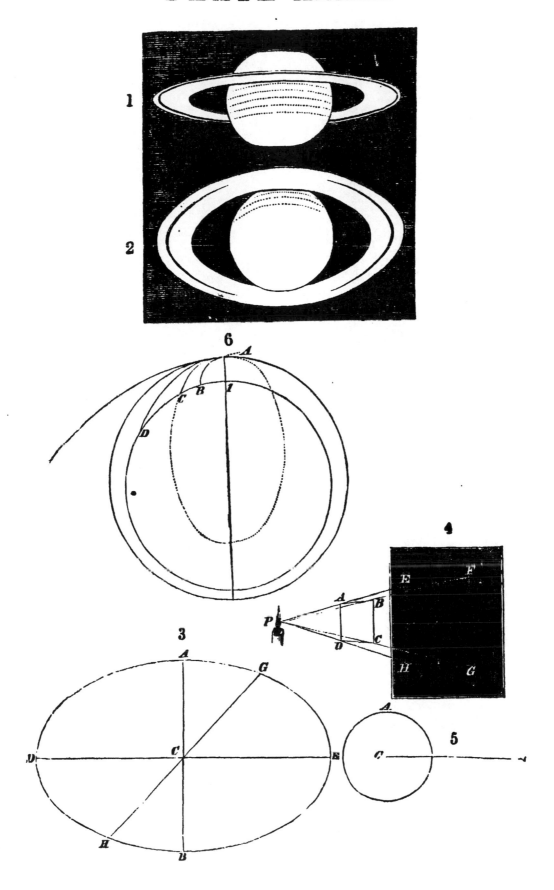